Passion! Betrayal! Outrage! Revenge!

AND WAIT 'LL YOU SEE PAGE TWO...

A LUANN BOOK

BY GREG EVANS

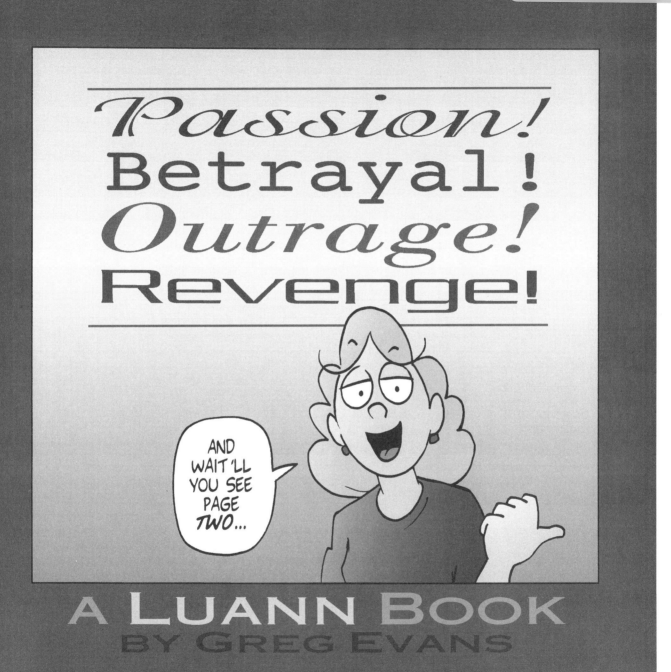

RUTLEDGE HILL PRESS®
Nashville, Tennessee

All of the cartoons that appear in this work have been previously published in various newspapers. *Luann* is distributed by United Feature Syndicate, Inc.

Published in Nashville, Tennessee, by Rutledge Hill Press®, Inc., 211 Seventh Avenue North, Nashville, Tennessee 37219.

Distributed in Canada by H. B. Fenn & Company, Ltd., 34 Nixon Road, Bolton, Ontario L7E 1W2. Distributed in Australia by The Five Mile Press Pty., Ltd., 22 Summit Road, Noble Park, Victoria 3174. Distributed in New Zealand by Southern Publishers Group, 22 Burleigh Street, Grafton, Auckland. Distributed in the United Kingdom by Verulam Publishing, Ltd., 152a Park Street Lane, Park Street, St. Albans, Hertfordshire AL2 2AU.

Library of Congress Cataloging-in-Publication Data
Evans, Greg.
    [Luann. Selections]
    Passion! betrayal! outrage! revenge! : a Luann book / by Greg Evans.
      p. cm.
    Selections from the author's comic strip: Luann.
    ISBN 1-55853-787-2 (pb)
    I. Title.
PN6728.L78E936   1999
741.5973—dc21   99-33246
                                   CIP

Printed in the United States of America
1 2 3 4 5 6 7 8 9—04 03 02 01 00 99

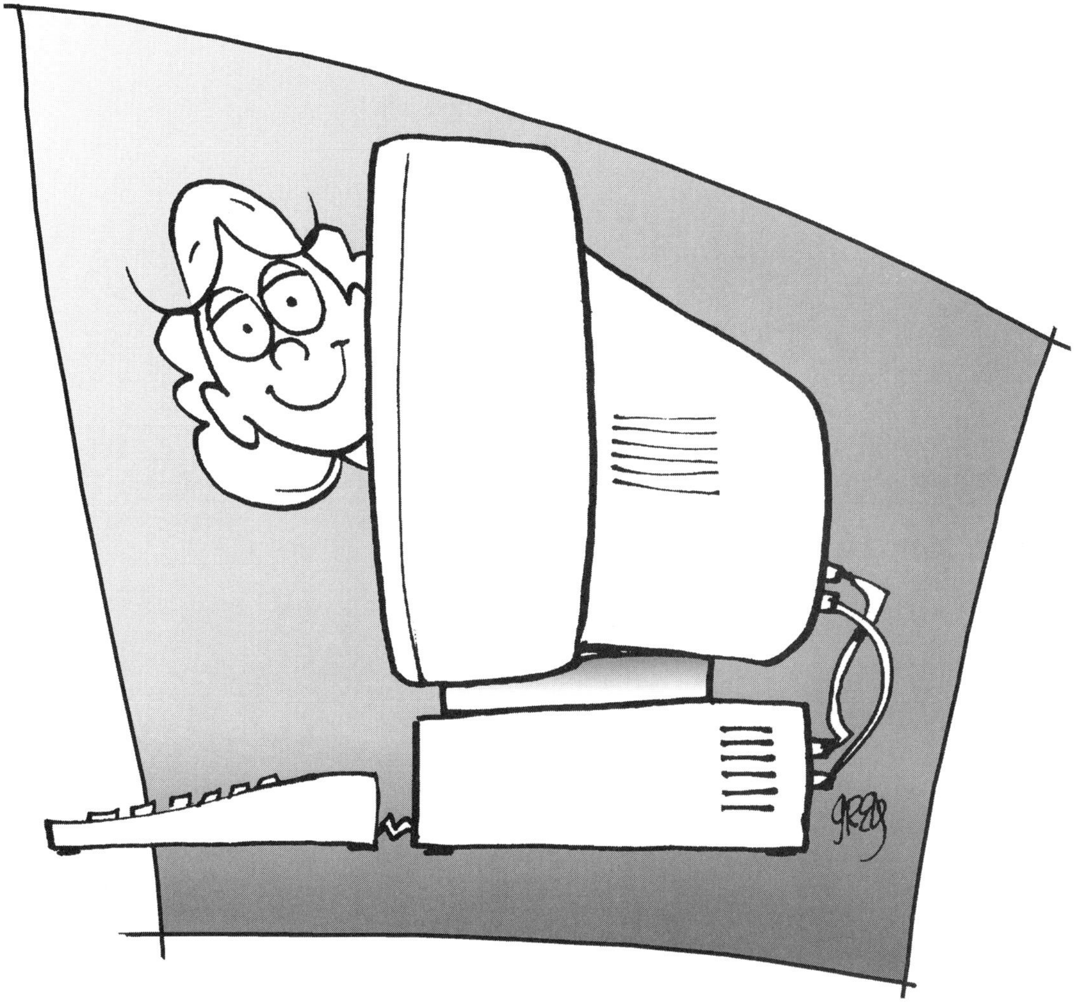
GREG

Find more cool *Luann* stuff and send e-mail to Greg Evans at: www.comics.com/comics/luann

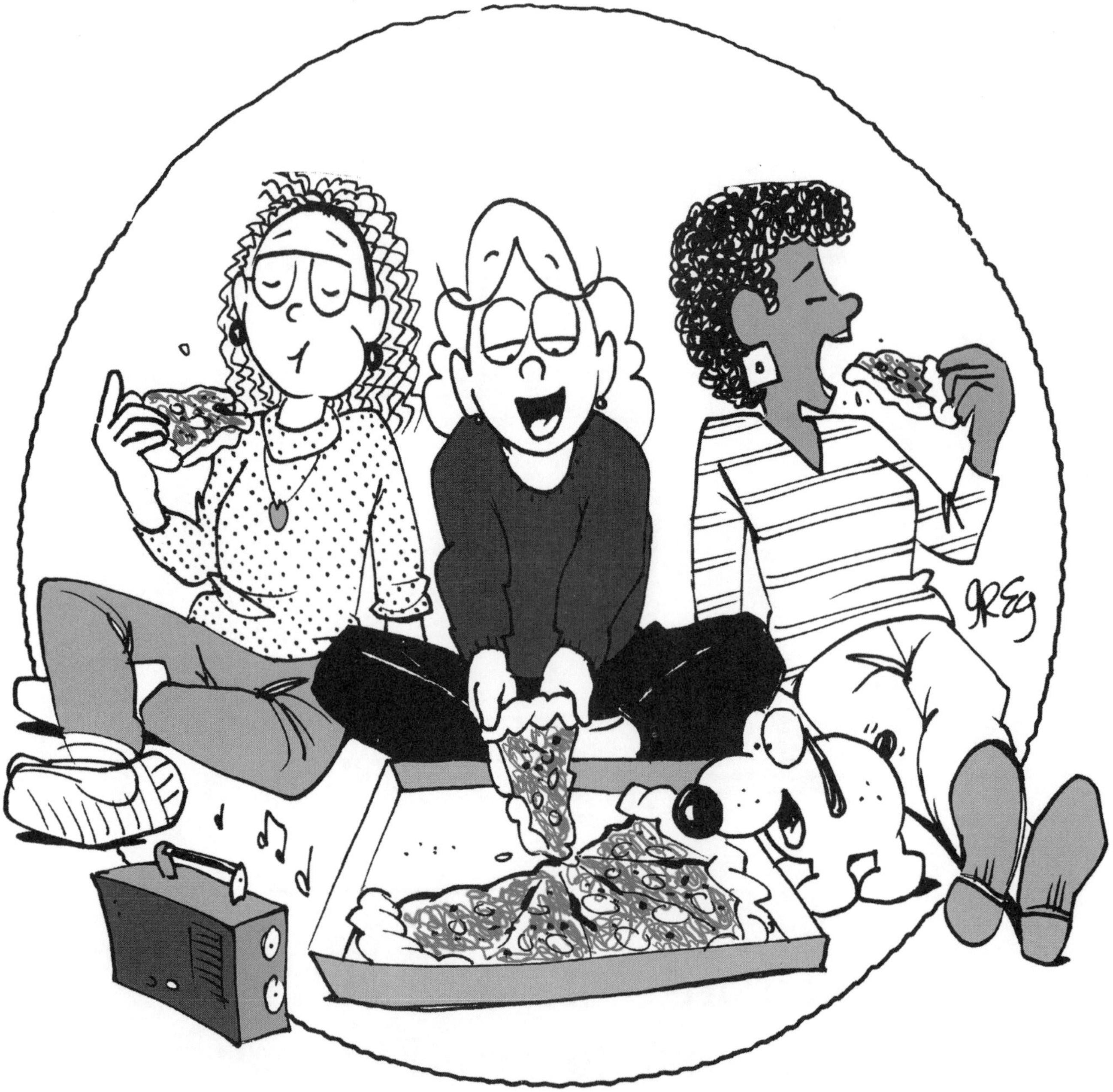

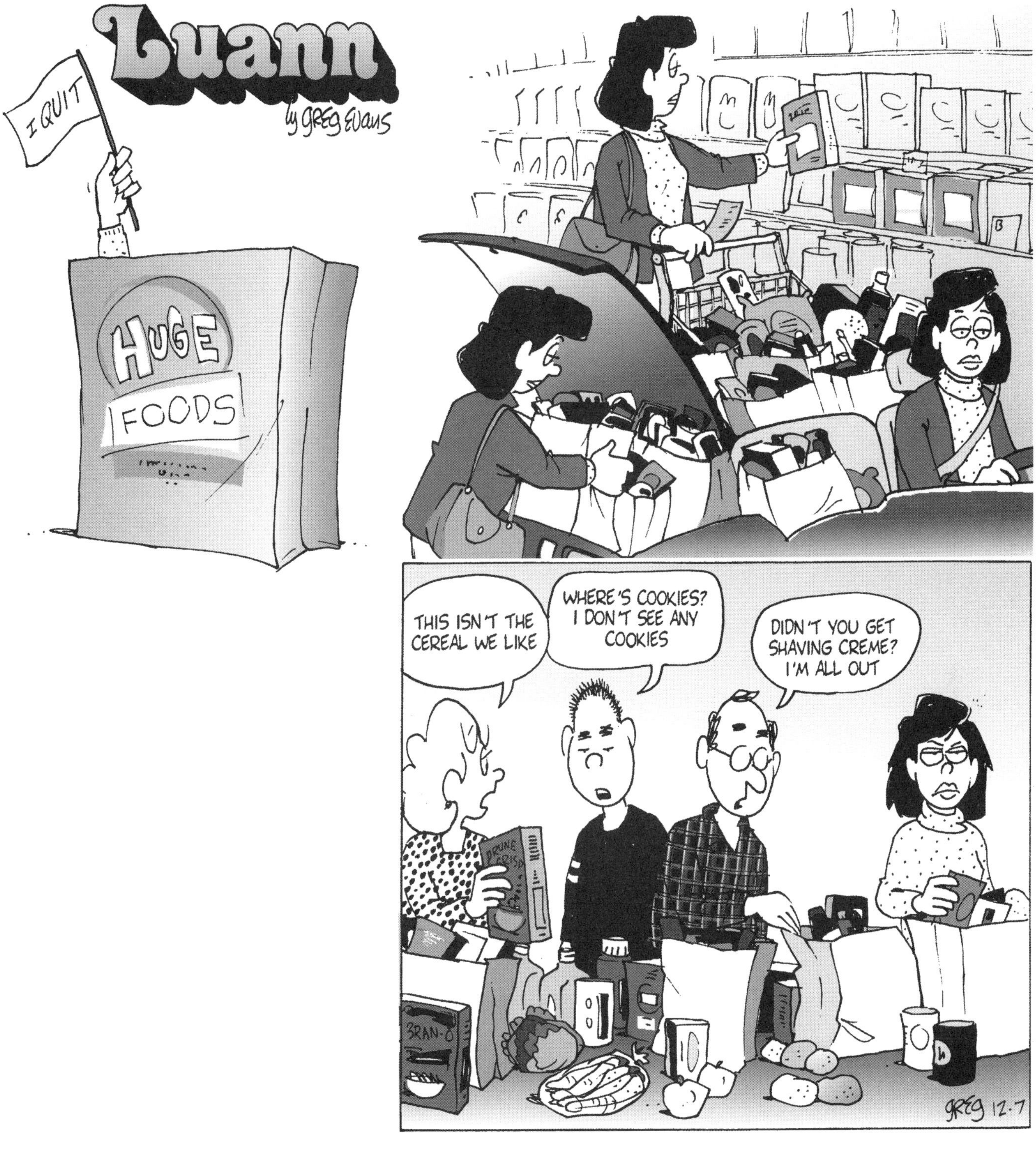
Luann
by GREG EVANS
I QUIT
HUGE
FOODS
THIS ISN'T THE CEREAL WE LIKE
WHERE'S COOKIES? I DON'T SEE ANY COOKIES
DIDN'T YOU GET SHAVING CREME? I'M ALL OUT
PRUNE CRISP
BRAN-O
GREG 12-7

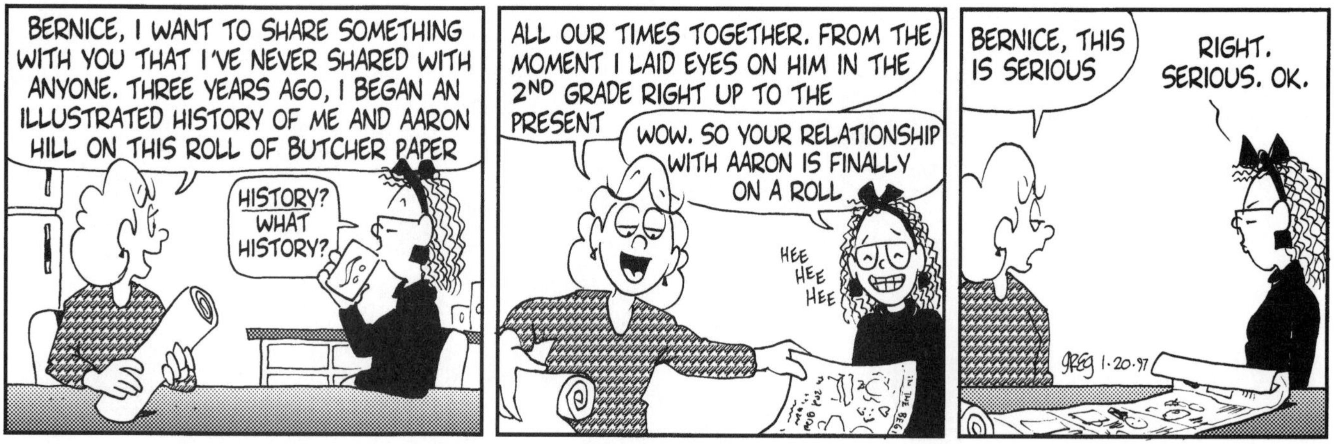
BERNICE, I WANT TO SHARE SOMETHING WITH YOU THAT I'VE NEVER SHARED WITH ANYONE. THREE YEARS AGO, I BEGAN AN ILLUSTRATED HISTORY OF ME AND AARON HILL ON THIS ROLL OF BUTCHER PAPER
HISTORY? WHAT HISTORY?
ALL OUR TIMES TOGETHER. FROM THE MOMENT I LAID EYES ON HIM IN THE 2ND GRADE RIGHT UP TO THE PRESENT
WOW. SO YOUR RELATIONSHIP WITH AARON IS FINALLY ON A ROLL
HEE HEE HEE
BERNICE, THIS IS SERIOUS
RIGHT. SERIOUS. OK.
GREG 1·20·97

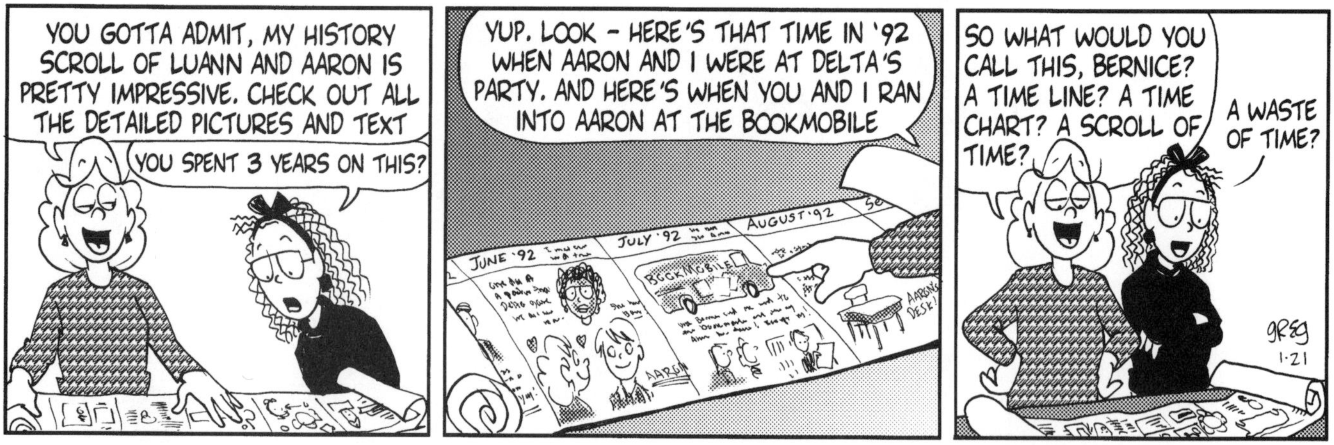
YOU GOTTA ADMIT, MY HISTORY SCROLL OF LUANN AND AARON IS PRETTY IMPRESSIVE. CHECK OUT ALL THE DETAILED PICTURES AND TEXT
YOU SPENT 3 YEARS ON THIS?
YUP. LOOK – HERE'S THAT TIME IN '92 WHEN AARON AND I WERE AT DELTA'S PARTY. AND HERE'S WHEN YOU AND I RAN INTO AARON AT THE BOOKMOBILE
JUNE '92
JULY '92
AUGUST '92
BOOKMOBILE
AARON'S DESK!
SO WHAT WOULD YOU CALL THIS, BERNICE? A TIME LINE? A TIME CHART? A SCROLL OF TIME?
A WASTE OF TIME?
GREG 1·21

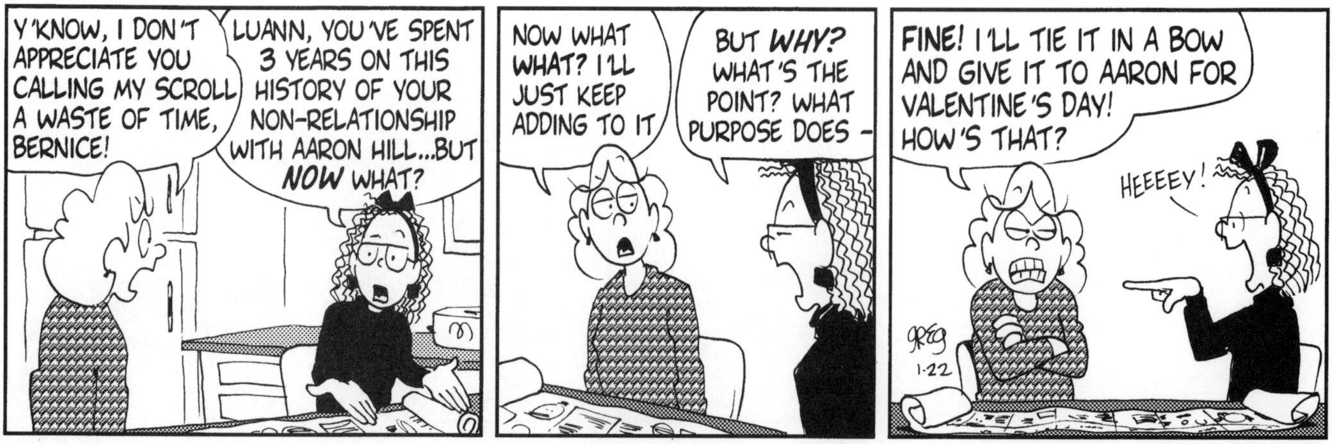
Y'KNOW, I DON'T APPRECIATE YOU CALLING MY SCROLL A WASTE OF TIME, BERNICE!
LUANN, YOU'VE SPENT 3 YEARS ON THIS HISTORY OF YOUR NON-RELATIONSHIP WITH AARON HILL...BUT NOW WHAT?
NOW WHAT WHAT? I'LL JUST KEEP ADDING TO IT
BUT WHY? WHAT'S THE POINT? WHAT PURPOSE DOES –
FINE! I'LL TIE IT IN A BOW AND GIVE IT TO AARON FOR VALENTINE'S DAY! HOW'S THAT?
HEEEEY!
GREG 1·22

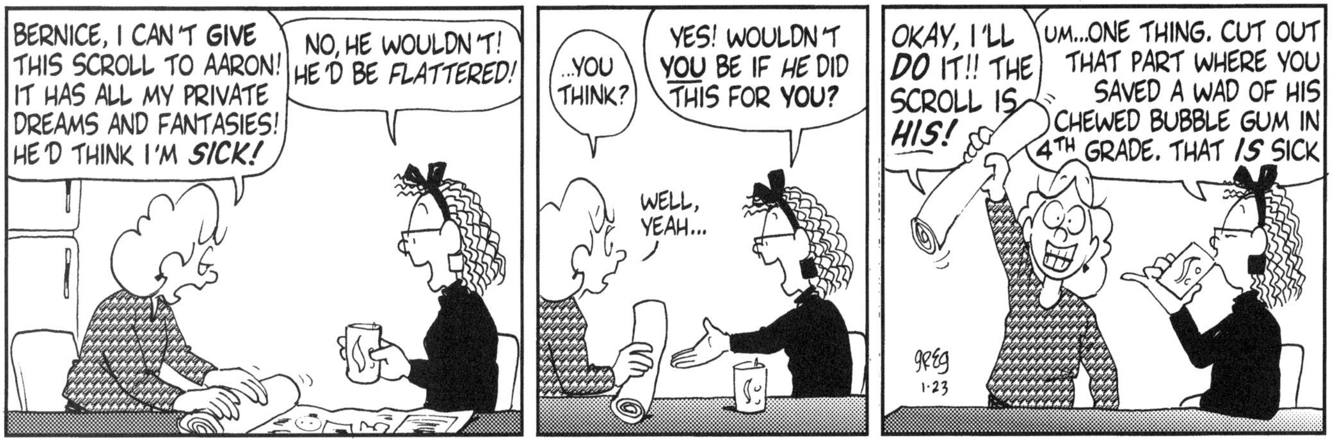
BERNICE, I CAN'T GIVE THIS SCROLL TO AARON! IT HAS ALL MY PRIVATE DREAMS AND FANTASIES! HE'D THINK I'M SICK!
NO, HE WOULDN'T! HE'D BE FLATTERED!
...YOU THINK?
YES! WOULDN'T YOU BE IF HE DID THIS FOR YOU?
WELL, YEAH...
OKAY, I'LL DO IT!! THE SCROLL IS HIS!
UM...ONE THING. CUT OUT THAT PART WHERE YOU SAVED A WAD OF HIS CHEWED BUBBLE GUM IN 4TH GRADE. THAT IS SICK
GREG 1·23

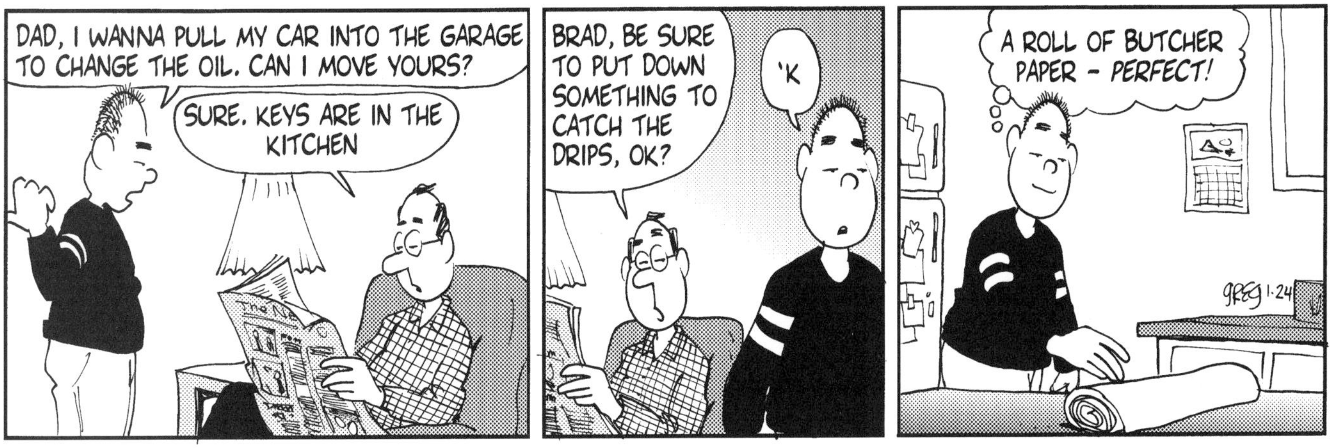
DAD, I WANNA PULL MY CAR INTO THE GARAGE TO CHANGE THE OIL. CAN I MOVE YOURS?
SURE. KEYS ARE IN THE KITCHEN
BRAD, BE SURE TO PUT DOWN SOMETHING TO CATCH THE DRIPS, OK?
'K
A ROLL OF BUTCHER PAPER – PERFECT!
GREG 1·24

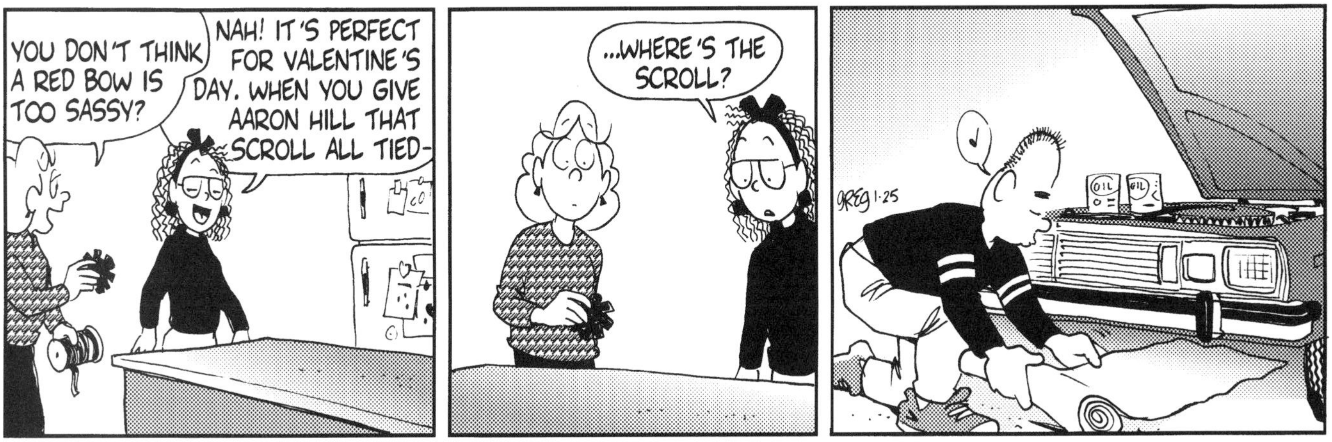
YOU DON'T THINK A RED BOW IS TOO SASSY?
NAH! IT'S PERFECT FOR VALENTINE'S DAY. WHEN YOU GIVE AARON HILL THAT SCROLL ALL TIED-
...WHERE'S THE SCROLL?
GREG 1·25
OIL
OIL

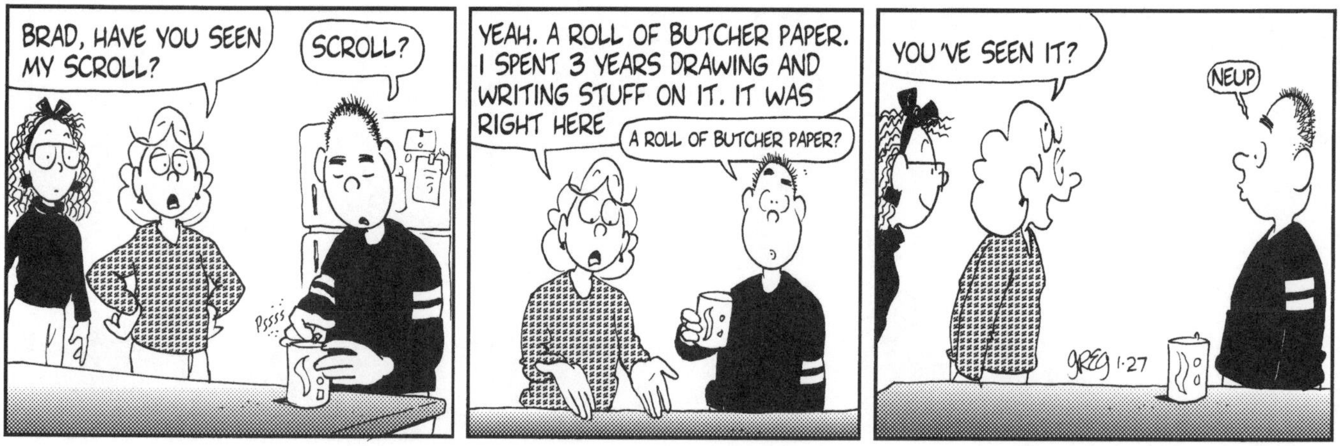
BRAD, HAVE YOU SEEN MY SCROLL?
SCROLL?
PSSSS
YEAH. A ROLL OF BUTCHER PAPER. I SPENT 3 YEARS DRAWING AND WRITING STUFF ON IT. IT WAS RIGHT HERE
A ROLL OF BUTCHER PAPER?
YOU'VE SEEN IT?
NEUP
GREG 1·27

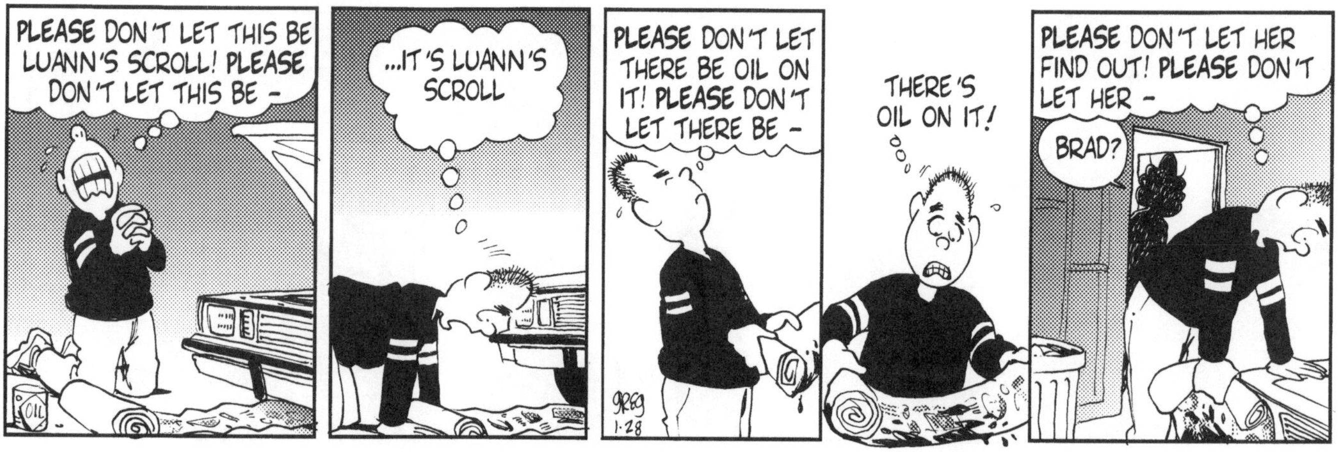
PLEASE DON'T LET THIS BE LUANN'S SCROLL! PLEASE DON'T LET THIS BE –
OIL
...IT'S LUANN'S SCROLL
PLEASE DON'T LET THERE BE OIL ON IT! PLEASE DON'T LET THERE BE –
GREG 1·28
THERE'S OIL ON IT!
PLEASE DON'T LET HER FIND OUT! PLEASE DON'T LET HER –
BRAD?

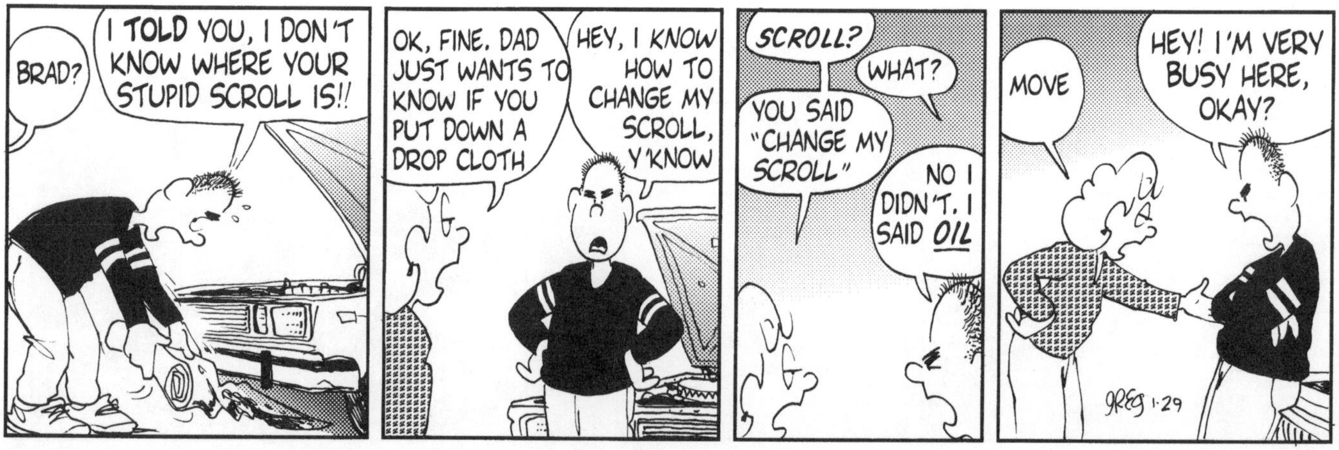
BRAD?
I TOLD YOU, I DON'T KNOW WHERE YOUR STUPID SCROLL IS!!
OK, FINE. DAD JUST WANTS TO KNOW IF YOU PUT DOWN A DROP CLOTH
HEY, I KNOW HOW TO CHANGE MY SCROLL, Y'KNOW
SCROLL?
WHAT?
YOU SAID "CHANGE MY SCROLL"
NO I DIDN'T. I SAID OIL
MOVE
HEY! I'M VERY BUSY HERE, OKAY?
GREG 1·29

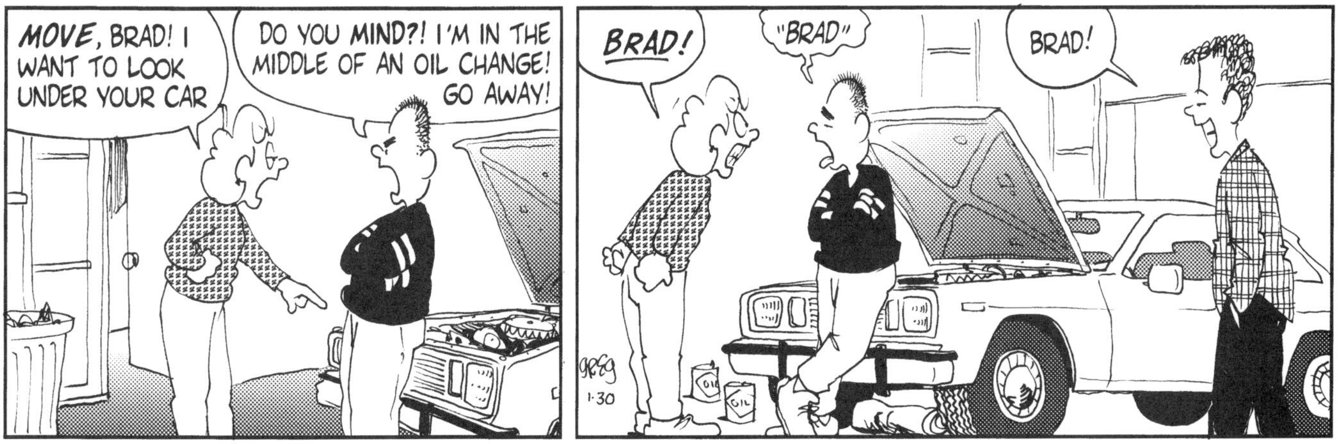
MOVE, BRAD! I WANT TO LOOK UNDER YOUR CAR
DO YOU MIND?! I'M IN THE MIDDLE OF AN OIL CHANGE! GO AWAY!
BRAD!
"BRAD"
BRAD!

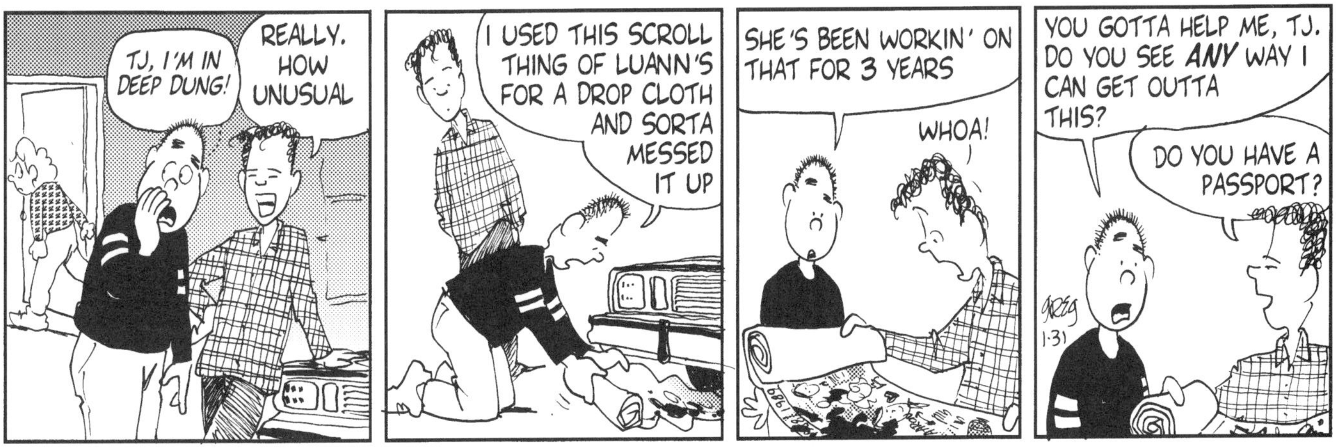
TJ, I'M IN DEEP DUNG!
REALLY. HOW UNUSUAL
I USED THIS SCROLL THING OF LUANN'S FOR A DROP CLOTH AND SORTA MESSED IT UP
SHE'S BEEN WORKIN' ON THAT FOR 3 YEARS
WHOA!
YOU GOTTA HELP ME, TJ. DO YOU SEE ANY WAY I CAN GET OUTTA THIS?
DO YOU HAVE A PASSPORT?

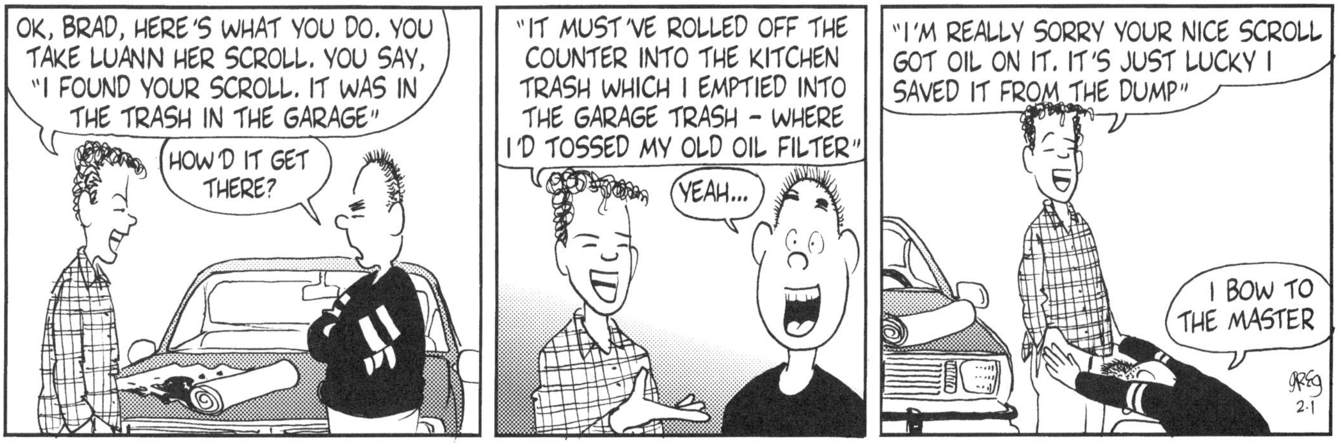
OK, BRAD, HERE'S WHAT YOU DO. YOU TAKE LUANN HER SCROLL. YOU SAY, "I FOUND YOUR SCROLL. IT WAS IN THE TRASH IN THE GARAGE"
HOW'D IT GET THERE?
"IT MUST'VE ROLLED OFF THE COUNTER INTO THE KITCHEN TRASH WHICH I EMPTIED INTO THE GARAGE TRASH – WHERE I'D TOSSED MY OLD OIL FILTER"
YEAH...
"I'M REALLY SORRY YOUR NICE SCROLL GOT OIL ON IT. IT'S JUST LUCKY I SAVED IT FROM THE DUMP"
I BOW TO THE MASTER

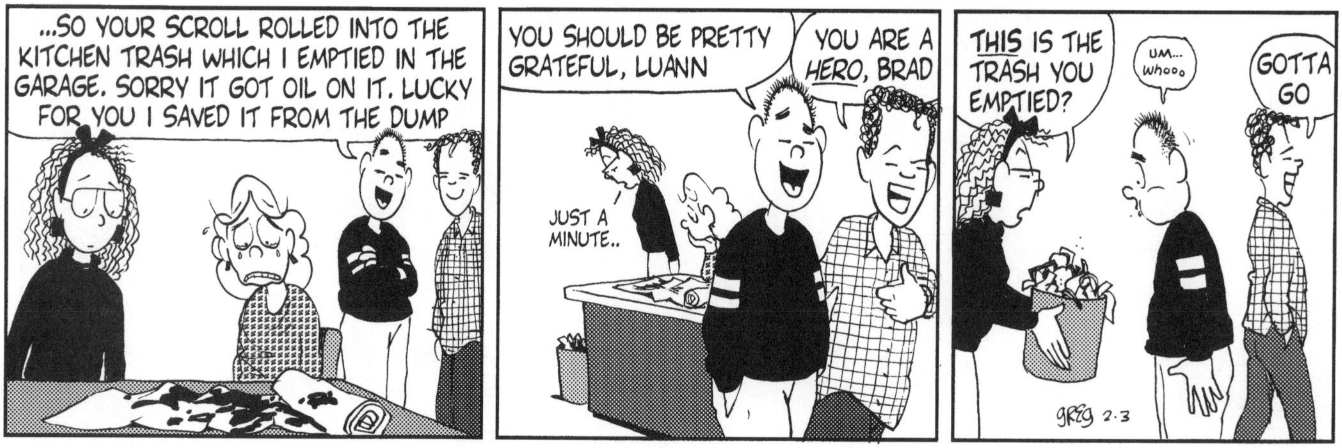
...SO YOUR SCROLL ROLLED INTO THE KITCHEN TRASH WHICH I EMPTIED IN THE GARAGE. SORRY IT GOT OIL ON IT. LUCKY FOR YOU I SAVED IT FROM THE DUMP
YOU SHOULD BE PRETTY GRATEFUL, LUANN
YOU ARE A HERO, BRAD
JUST A MINUTE..
THIS IS THE TRASH YOU EMPTIED?
UM... WHOOO
GOTTA GO
GREG 2.3

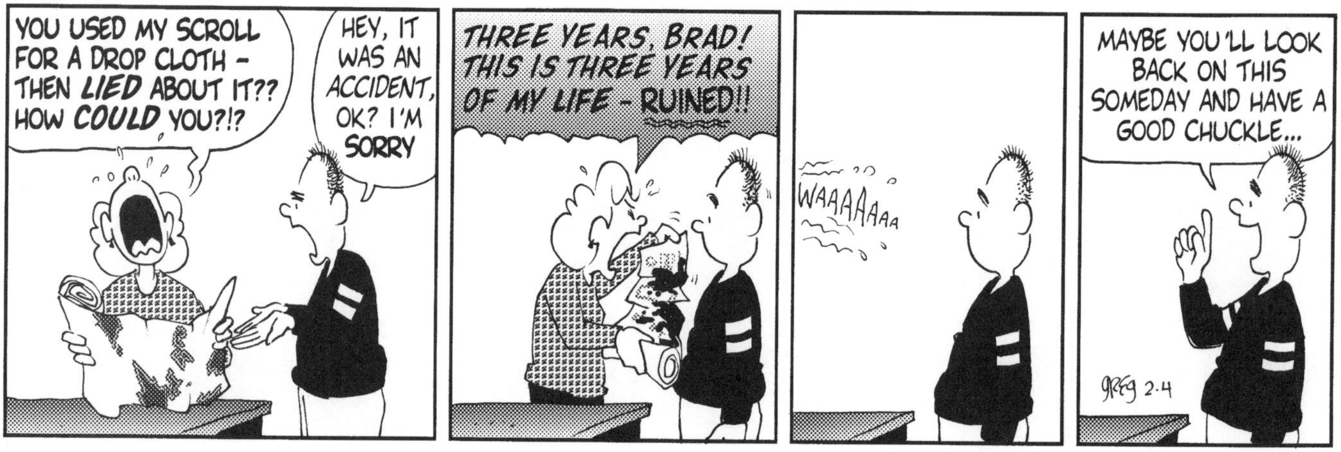
YOU USED MY SCROLL FOR A DROP CLOTH – THEN LIED ABOUT IT?? HOW COULD YOU?!?
HEY, IT WAS AN ACCIDENT, OK? I'M SORRY
THREE YEARS, BRAD! THIS IS THREE YEARS OF MY LIFE – RUINED!!
WAAAAAAAA
MAYBE YOU'LL LOOK BACK ON THIS SOMEDAY AND HAVE A GOOD CHUCKLE...
GREG 2.4

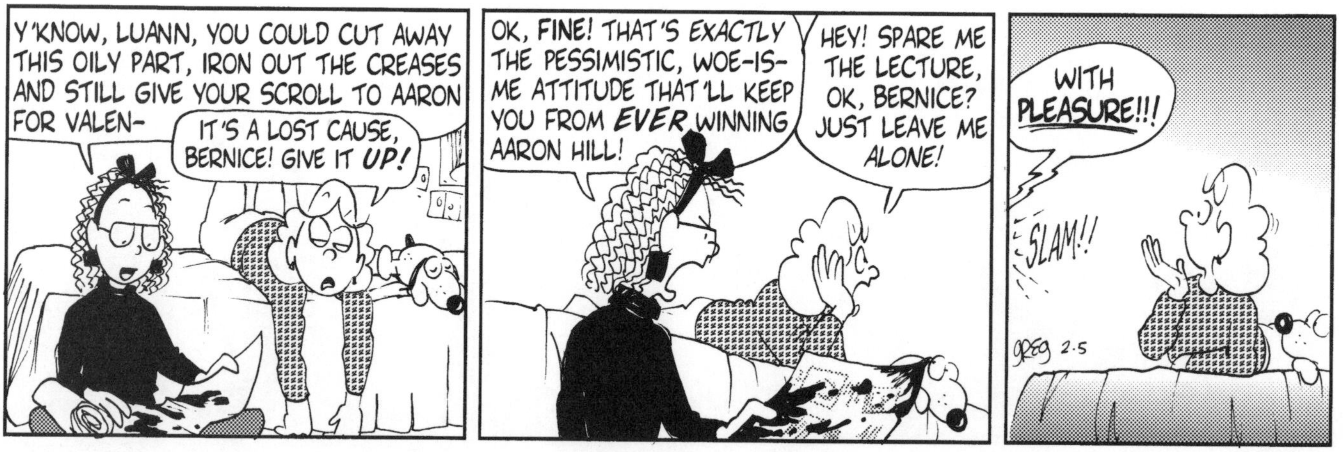
Y'KNOW, LUANN, YOU COULD CUT AWAY THIS OILY PART, IRON OUT THE CREASES AND STILL GIVE YOUR SCROLL TO AARON FOR VALEN–
IT'S A LOST CAUSE, BERNICE! GIVE IT UP!
OK, FINE! THAT'S EXACTLY THE PESSIMISTIC, WOE-IS-ME ATTITUDE THAT'LL KEEP YOU FROM EVER WINNING AARON HILL!
HEY! SPARE ME THE LECTURE, OK, BERNICE? JUST LEAVE ME ALONE!
WITH PLEASURE!!!
SLAM!!
GREG 2.5

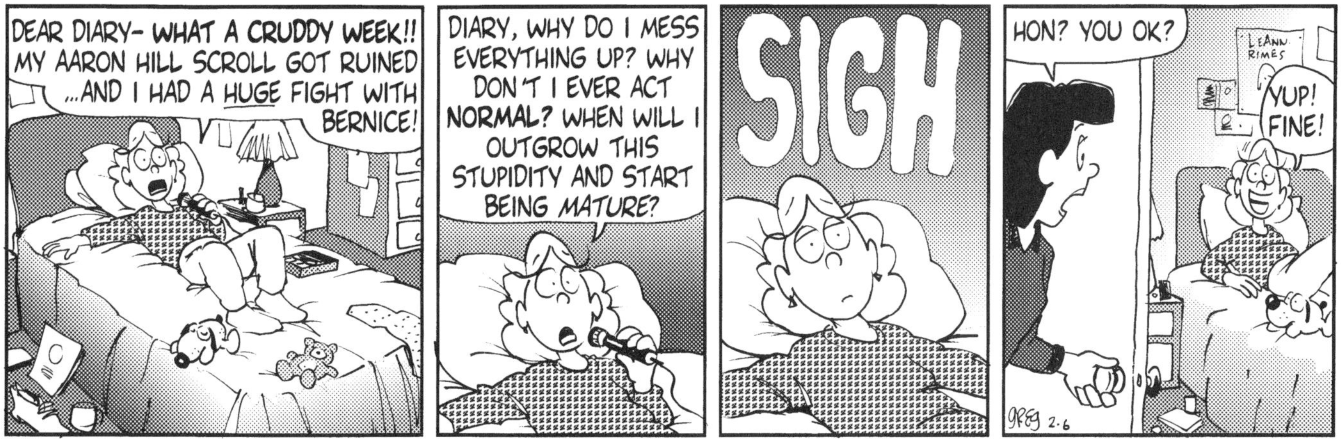
DEAR DIARY- WHAT A CRUDDY WEEK!! MY AARON HILL SCROLL GOT RUINED ...AND I HAD A HUGE FIGHT WITH BERNICE!
DIARY, WHY DO I MESS EVERYTHING UP? WHY DON'T I EVER ACT NORMAL? WHEN WILL I OUTGROW THIS STUPIDITY AND START BEING MATURE?
SIGH
HON? YOU OK?
LEANN RIMES
YUP! FINE!
GREG 2.6

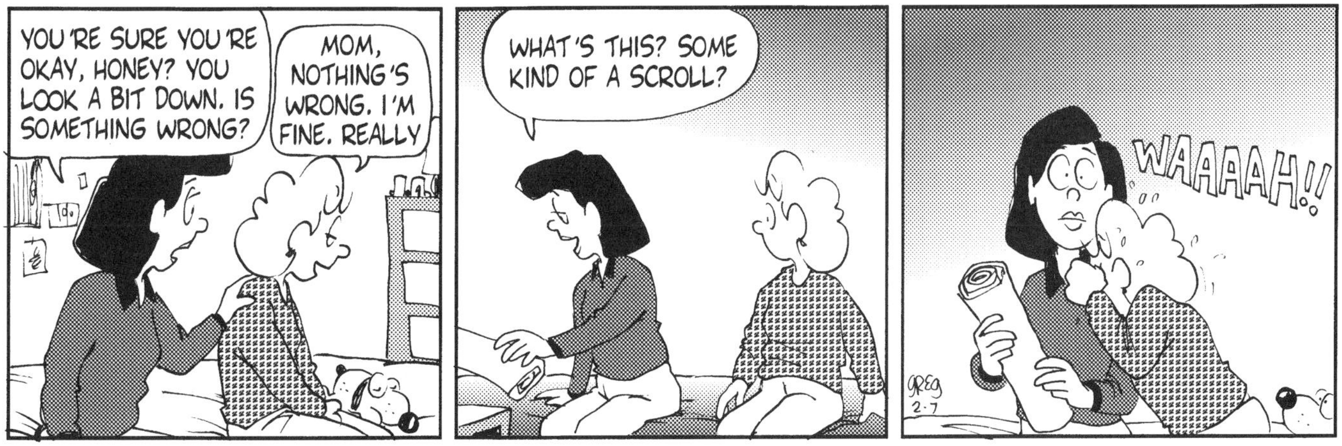
YOU'RE SURE YOU'RE OKAY, HONEY? YOU LOOK A BIT DOWN. IS SOMETHING WRONG?
MOM, NOTHING'S WRONG. I'M FINE. REALLY
WHAT'S THIS? SOME KIND OF A SCROLL?
WAAAAH!!
GREG 2.7

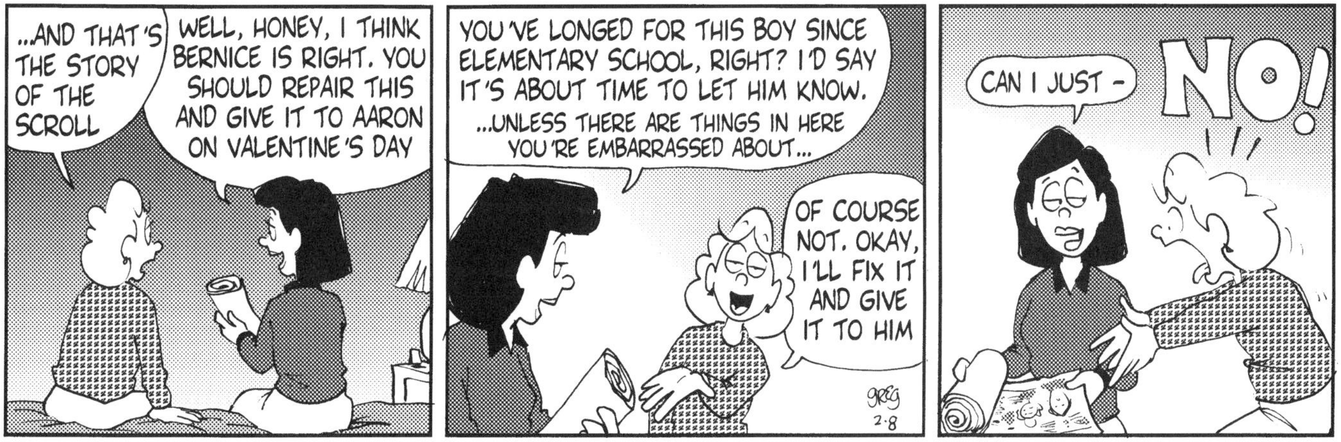
...AND THAT'S THE STORY OF THE SCROLL
WELL, HONEY, I THINK BERNICE IS RIGHT. YOU SHOULD REPAIR THIS AND GIVE IT TO AARON ON VALENTINE'S DAY
YOU'VE LONGED FOR THIS BOY SINCE ELEMENTARY SCHOOL, RIGHT? I'D SAY IT'S ABOUT TIME TO LET HIM KNOW. ...UNLESS THERE ARE THINGS IN HERE YOU'RE EMBARRASSED ABOUT...
OF COURSE NOT. OKAY, I'LL FIX IT AND GIVE IT TO HIM
GREG 2.8
CAN I JUST -
NO!

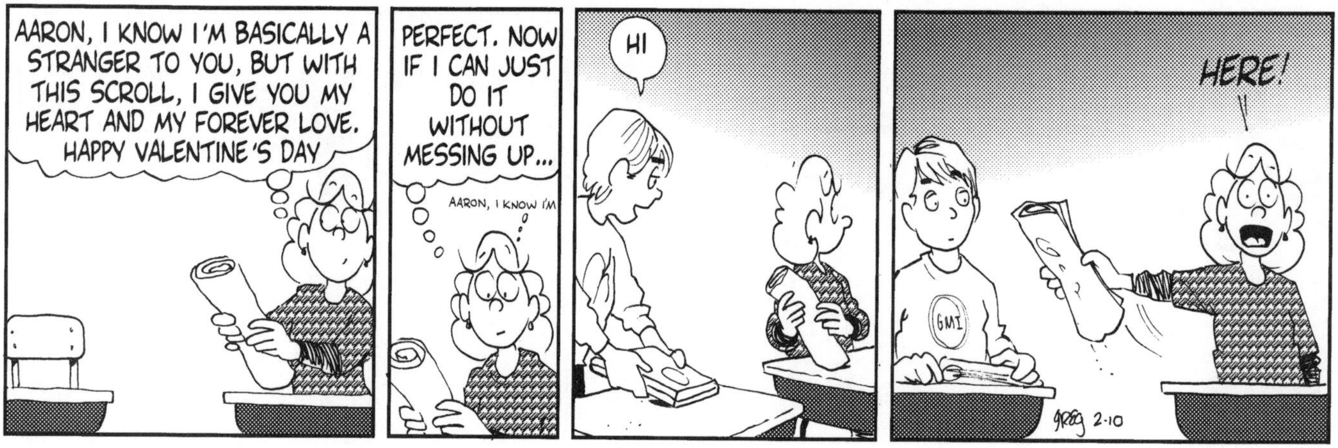
AARON, I KNOW I'M BASICALLY A STRANGER TO YOU, BUT WITH THIS SCROLL, I GIVE YOU MY HEART AND MY FOREVER LOVE. HAPPY VALENTINE'S DAY
PERFECT. NOW IF I CAN JUST DO IT WITHOUT MESSING UP...
AARON, I KNOW I'M
HI
HERE!
GMI
GREG 2-10

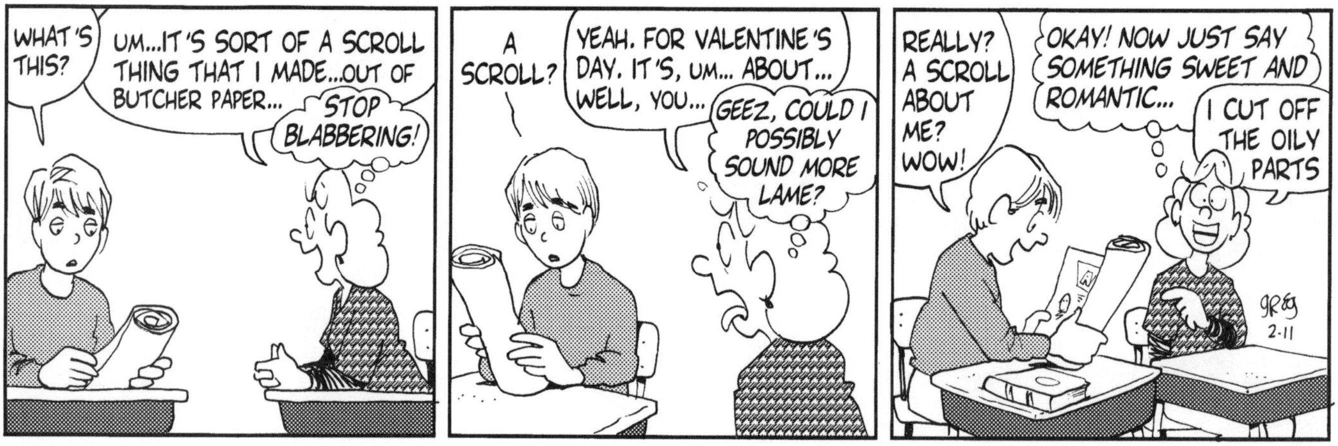
WHAT'S THIS?
UM...IT'S SORT OF A SCROLL THING THAT I MADE...OUT OF BUTCHER PAPER...
STOP BLABBERING!
A SCROLL?
YEAH. FOR VALENTINE'S DAY. IT'S, UM... ABOUT... WELL, YOU...
GEEZ, COULD I POSSIBLY SOUND MORE LAME?
REALLY? A SCROLL ABOUT ME? WOW!
OKAY! NOW JUST SAY SOMETHING SWEET AND ROMANTIC...
I CUT OFF THE OILY PARTS
GREG 2-11

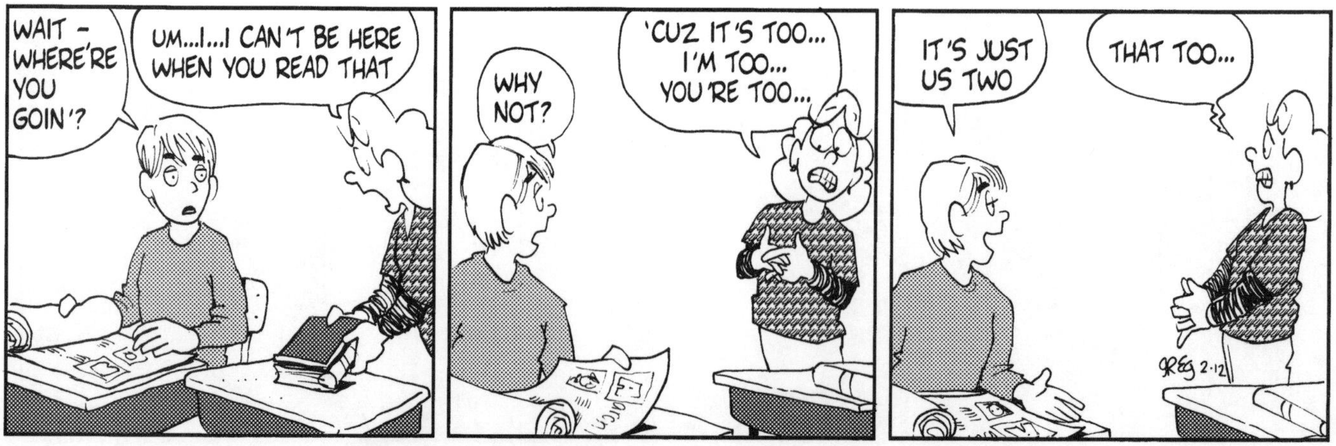
WAIT – WHERE'RE YOU GOIN'?
UM...I...I CAN'T BE HERE WHEN YOU READ THAT
WHY NOT?
'CUZ IT'S TOO... I'M TOO... YOU'RE TOO...
IT'S JUST US TWO
THAT TOO...
GREG 2-12

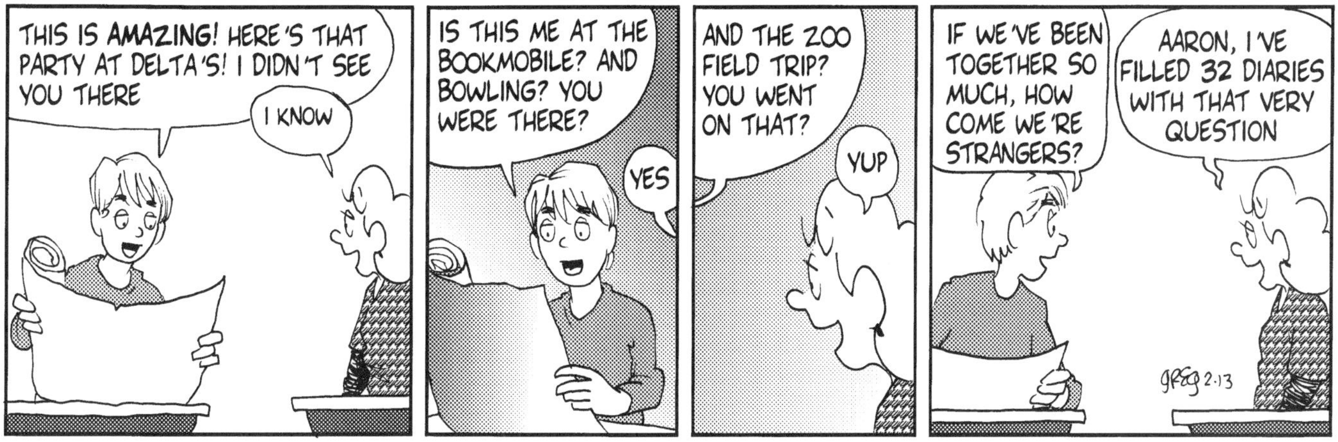
THIS IS AMAZING! HERE'S THAT PARTY AT DELTA'S! I DIDN'T SEE YOU THERE
I KNOW
IS THIS ME AT THE BOOKMOBILE? AND BOWLING? YOU WERE THERE?
YES
AND THE ZOO FIELD TRIP? YOU WENT ON THAT?
YUP
IF WE'VE BEEN TOGETHER SO MUCH, HOW COME WE'RE STRANGERS?
AARON, I'VE FILLED 32 DIARIES WITH THAT VERY QUESTION
GREG 2.13

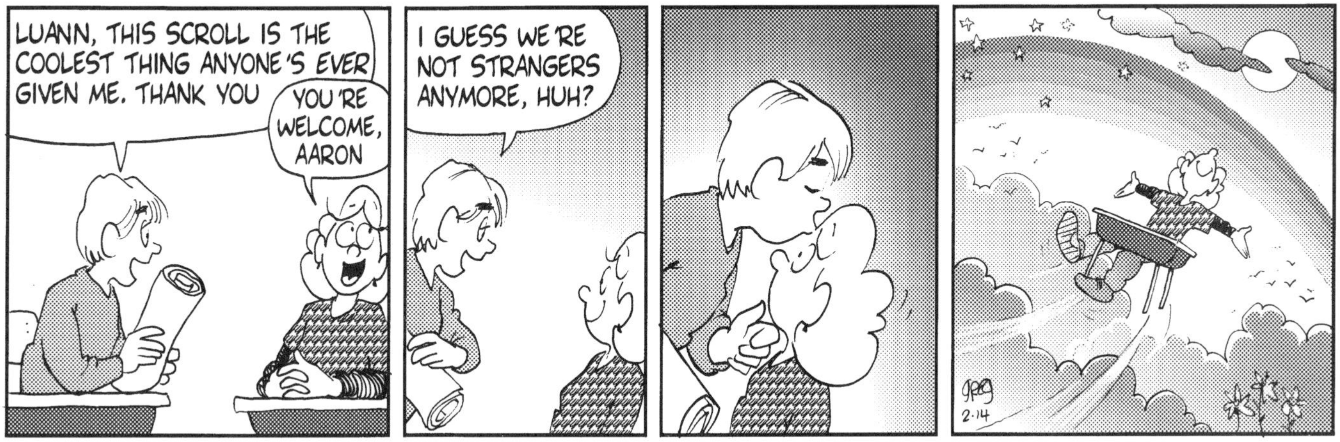
LUANN, THIS SCROLL IS THE COOLEST THING ANYONE'S EVER GIVEN ME. THANK YOU
YOU'RE WELCOME, AARON
I GUESS WE'RE NOT STRANGERS ANYMORE, HUH?
GREG 2.14

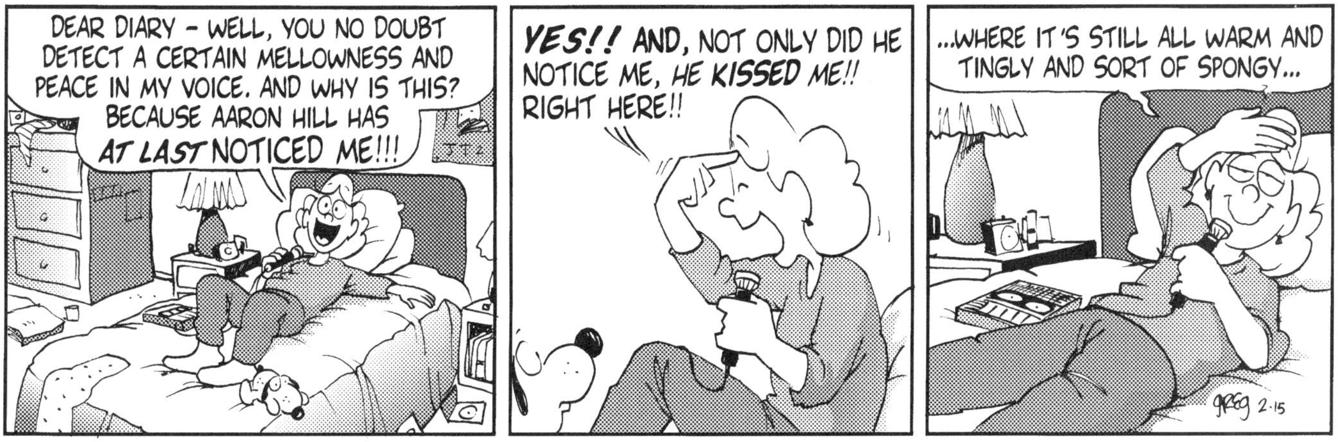
DEAR DIARY - WELL, YOU NO DOUBT DETECT A CERTAIN MELLOWNESS AND PEACE IN MY VOICE. AND WHY IS THIS? BECAUSE AARON HILL HAS AT LAST NOTICED ME!!!
YES!! AND, NOT ONLY DID HE NOTICE ME, HE KISSED ME!! RIGHT HERE!!
...WHERE IT'S STILL ALL WARM AND TINGLY AND SORT OF SPONGY...
GREG 2.15

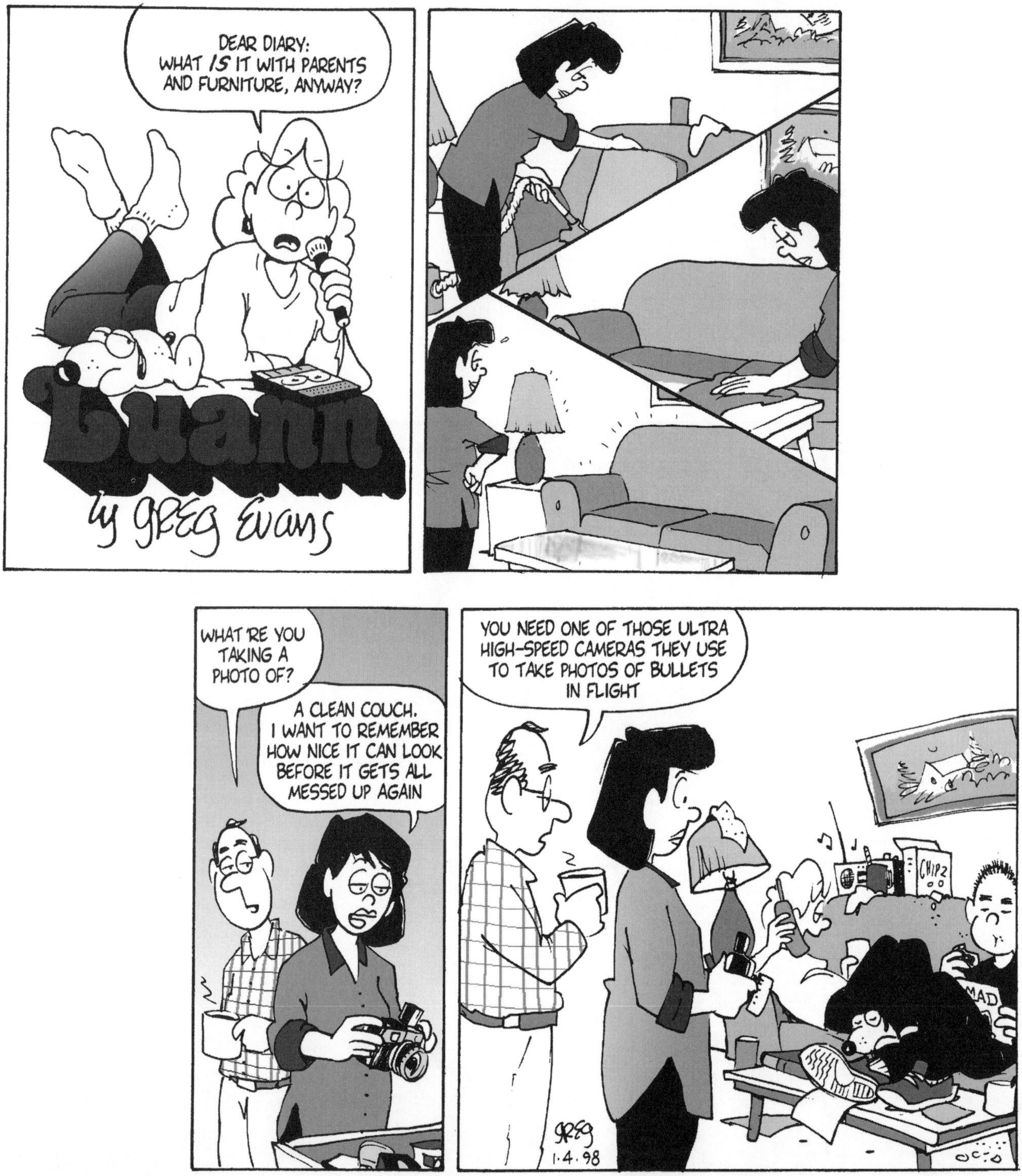
DEAR DIARY:
WHAT IS IT WITH PARENTS AND FURNITURE, ANYWAY?
Luann
by GREG Evans
WHAT'RE YOU TAKING A PHOTO OF?
A CLEAN COUCH. I WANT TO REMEMBER HOW NICE IT CAN LOOK BEFORE IT GETS ALL MESSED UP AGAIN
YOU NEED ONE OF THOSE ULTRA HIGH-SPEED CAMERAS THEY USE TO TAKE PHOTOS OF BULLETS IN FLIGHT
CHIPZ
MAD
GREG
1·4·98

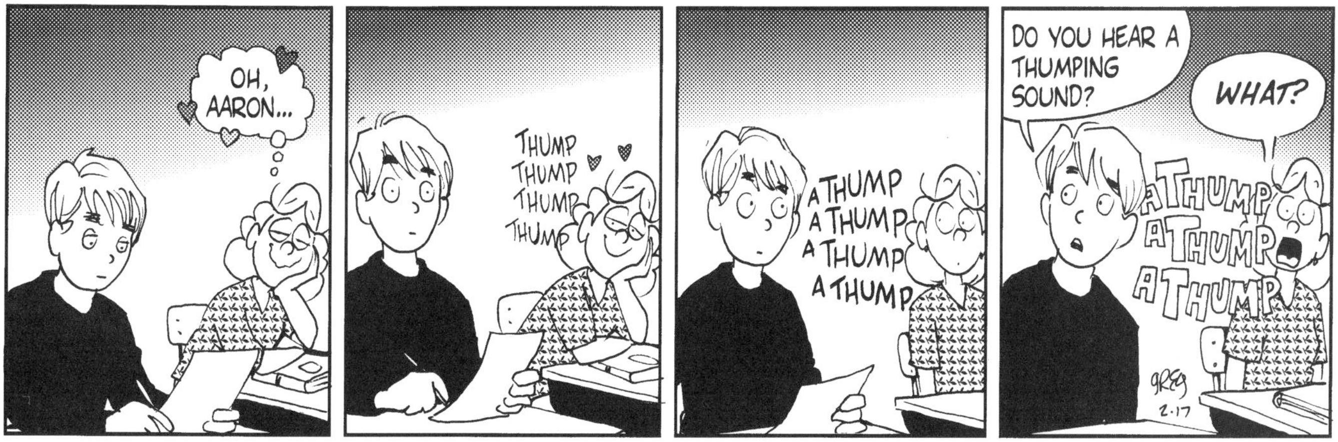
OH, AARON...
THUMP THUMP THUMP THUMP
A THUMP A THUMP A THUMP A THUMP
DO YOU HEAR A THUMPING SOUND?
WHAT?
A THUMP A THUMP A THUMP
GREG 2·17

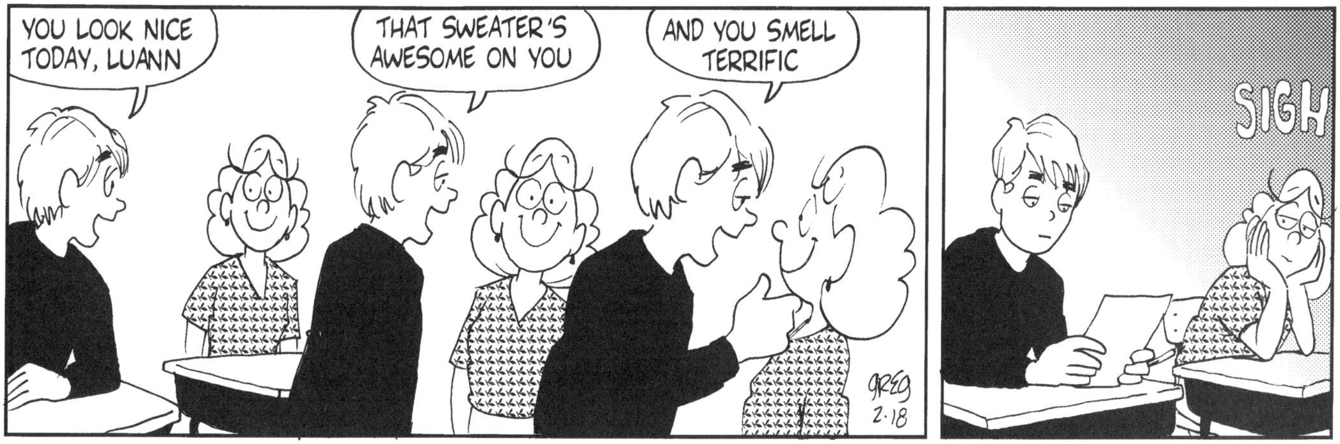
YOU LOOK NICE TODAY, LUANN
THAT SWEATER'S AWESOME ON YOU
AND YOU SMELL TERRIFIC
GREG 2·18
SIGH

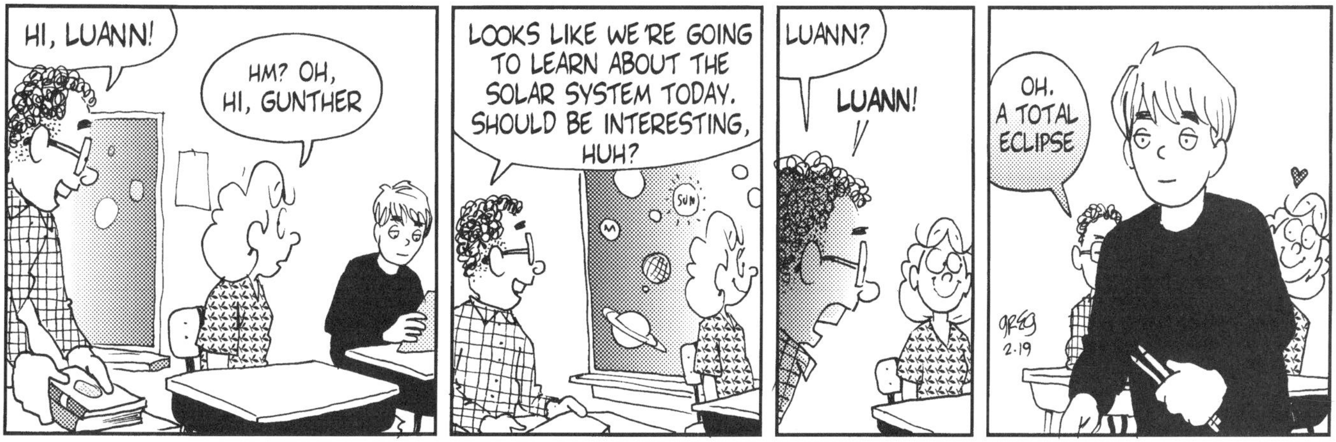
HI, LUANN!
HM? OH, HI, GUNTHER
LOOKS LIKE WE'RE GOING TO LEARN ABOUT THE SOLAR SYSTEM TODAY. SHOULD BE INTERESTING, HUH?
SUN
LUANN?
LUANN!
GREG 2·19
OH. A TOTAL ECLIPSE

LUANN...?

M?

UM... I WAS WONDERING... THE SWEETHEART DANCE IS COMING UP AND, UM... I WAS THINKING MAYBE... WELL, WOULD YOU GO WITH ME?

UH... NO

OH. AARON HILL ALREADY ASKED YOU?

YES. WELL, NOT, Y'KNOW, TECHNICALLY ASKED AS OF, Y'KNOW, THIS EXACT MOMENT...

greg 2·20

LUANN, WHAT AM I TO YOU?

HUH?

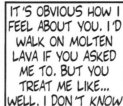

IT'S OBVIOUS HOW I FEEL ABOUT YOU. I'D WALK ON MOLTEN LAVA IF YOU ASKED ME TO. BUT YOU TREAT ME LIKE... WELL, I DON'T KNOW

AM I A CASUAL PAL? A GOOD FRIEND? A POSSIBLE BOYFRIEND?? OR AM I JUST A SECOND BANANA TO AARON HILL? I NEVER KNOW WHERE I STAND WITH YOU

AND YOU KNOW WHAT? I'M TIRED OF WONDERING. SO MAKE A CHOICE, LUANN. WHO'S IT GOING TO BE: ME OR AARON HILL?

greg 2·21

DEAR DIARY: WELL, HERE'S A MESS FOR YOU: NOW THAT AARON HAS FINALLY NOTICED ME, I THOUGHT MAYBE HE'D ASK ME TO THE SWEETHEART DANCE. INSTEAD, GUNTHER DID!

...SIGH... AARON'S MY DREAM GUY – HE EVEN KISSED ME WHEN I GAVE HIM THE SCROLL – BUT WILL HE EVER REALLY CARE FOR ME? I HAVE NO IDEA. GUNTHER SURE CARES – AND HE'S A SWEETIE – BUT HE'S NOT MY DREAM GUY...

SO HERE'S THE QUESTION: DO I REJECT GUNTHER AND KEEP WAITING FOR AARON OR DO I FORGET MY DREAM AND ACCEPT WHAT GUNTHER HAS TO OFFER?

greg 2·22

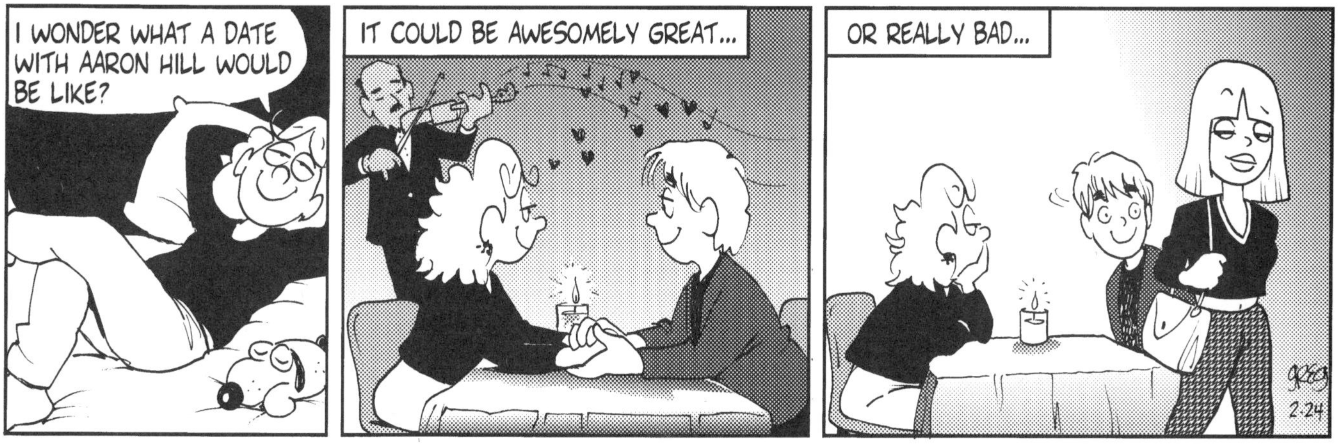
I WONDER WHAT A DATE WITH AARON HILL WOULD BE LIKE?
IT COULD BE AWESOMELY GREAT...
OR REALLY BAD...

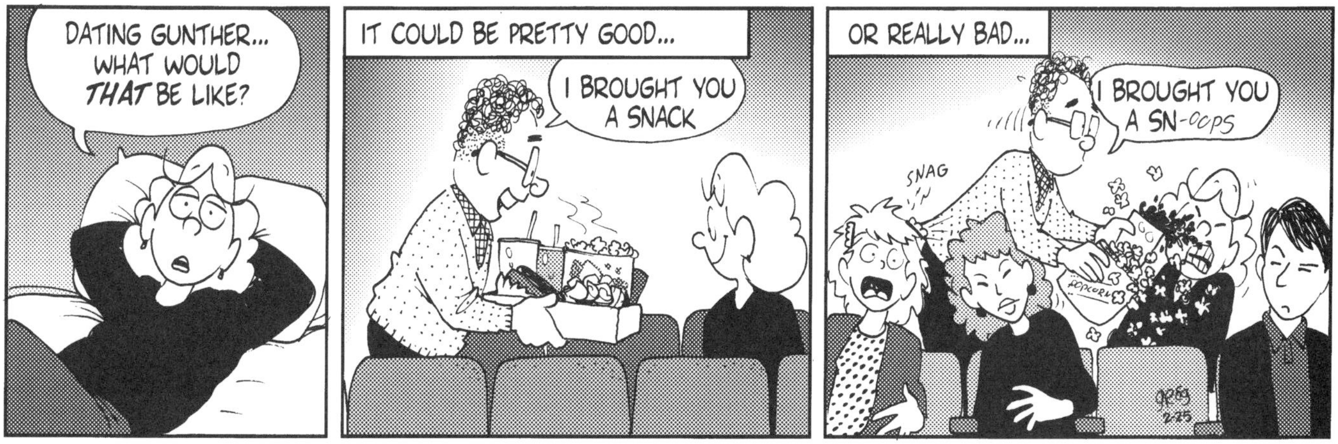
DATING GUNTHER... WHAT WOULD *THAT* BE LIKE?
IT COULD BE PRETTY GOOD...
I BROUGHT YOU A SNACK
OR REALLY BAD...
I BROUGHT YOU A SN-OOPS
SNAG

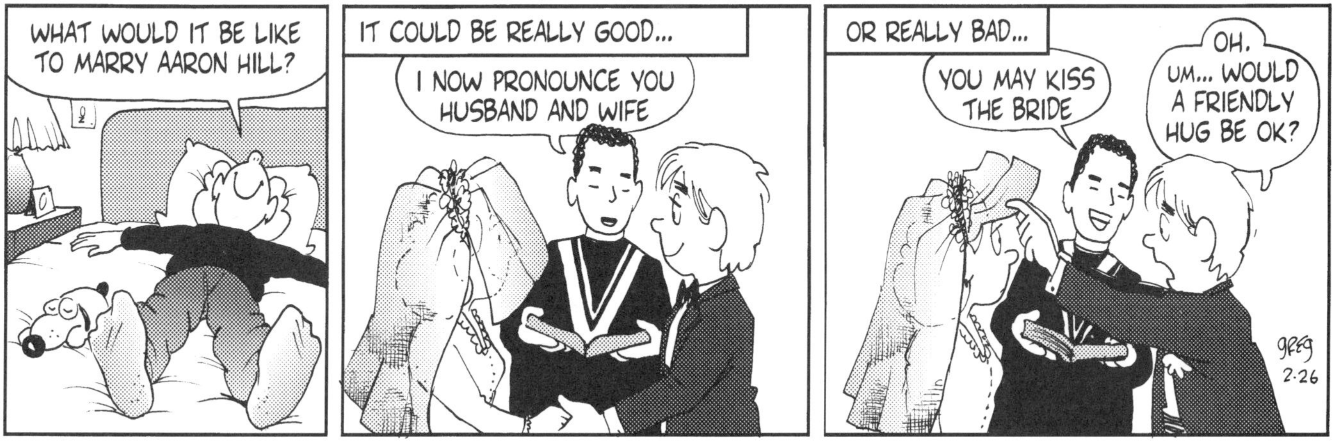
WHAT WOULD IT BE LIKE TO MARRY AARON HILL?
IT COULD BE REALLY GOOD...
I NOW PRONOUNCE YOU HUSBAND AND WIFE
OR REALLY BAD...
YOU MAY KISS THE BRIDE
OH. UM... WOULD A FRIENDLY HUG BE OK?

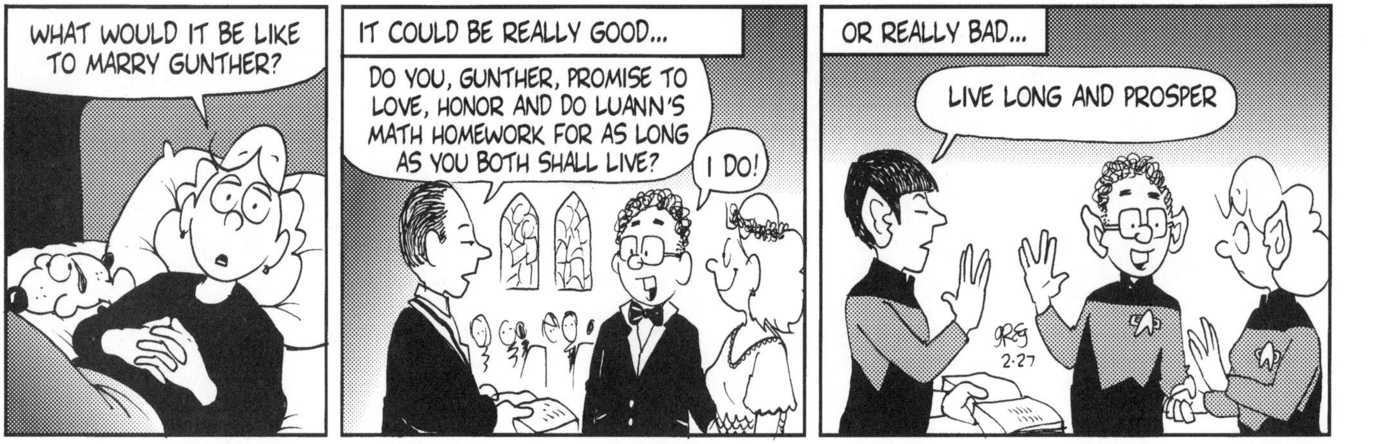
WHAT WOULD IT BE LIKE TO MARRY GUNTHER?
IT COULD BE REALLY GOOD...
DO YOU, GUNTHER, PROMISE TO LOVE, HONOR AND DO LUANN'S MATH HOMEWORK FOR AS LONG AS YOU BOTH SHALL LIVE?
I DO!
OR REALLY BAD...
LIVE LONG AND PROSPER

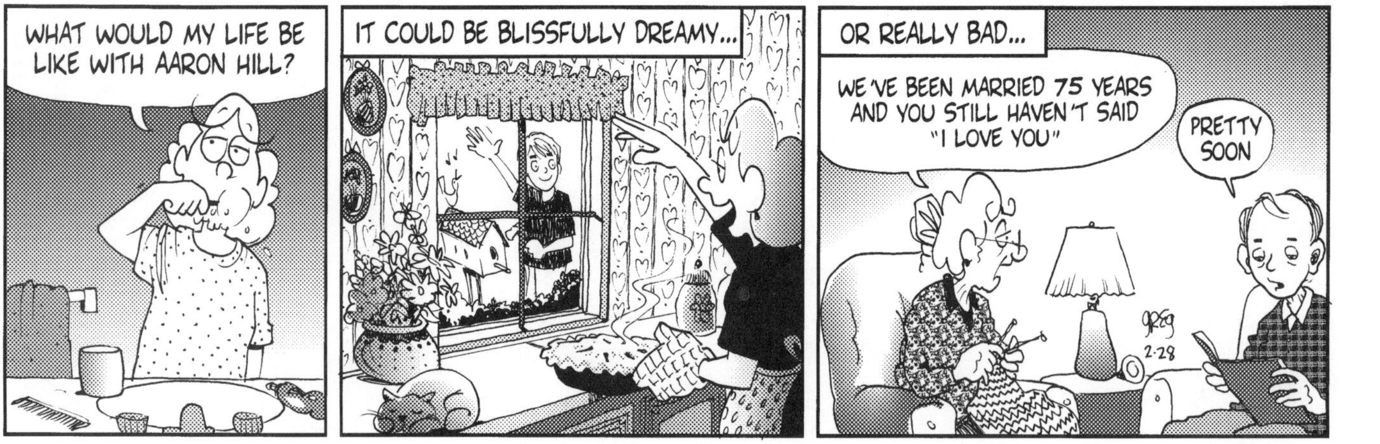
WHAT WOULD MY LIFE BE LIKE WITH AARON HILL?
IT COULD BE BLISSFULLY DREAMY...
OR REALLY BAD...
WE'VE BEEN MARRIED 75 YEARS AND YOU STILL HAVEN'T SAID "I LOVE YOU"
PRETTY SOON

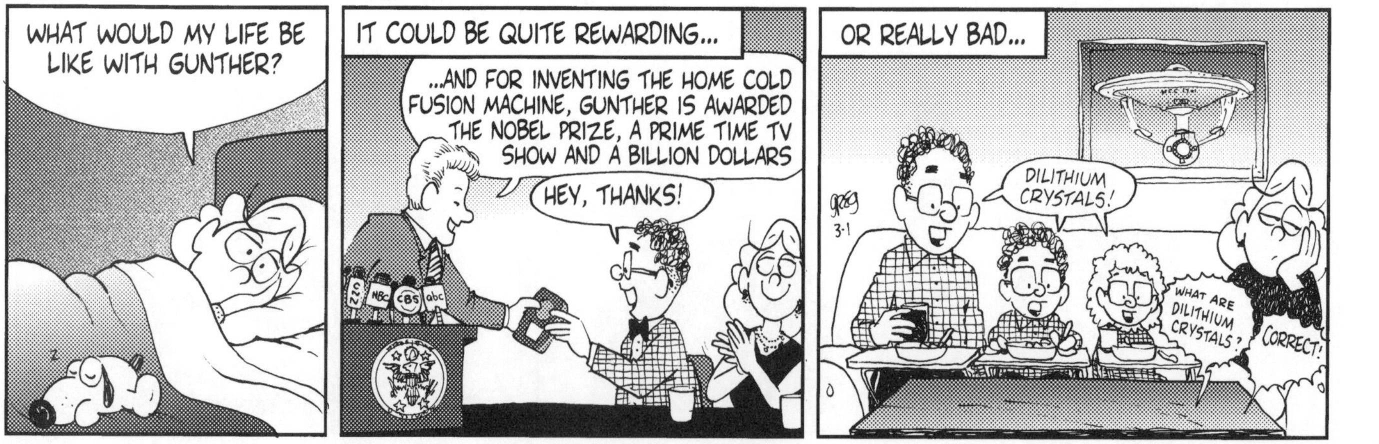
WHAT WOULD MY LIFE BE LIKE WITH GUNTHER?
IT COULD BE QUITE REWARDING...
...AND FOR INVENTING THE HOME COLD FUSION MACHINE, GUNTHER IS AWARDED THE NOBEL PRIZE, A PRIME TIME TV SHOW AND A BILLION DOLLARS
HEY, THANKS!
OR REALLY BAD...
DILITHIUM CRYSTALS!
WHAT ARE DILITHIUM CRYSTALS?
CORRECT!

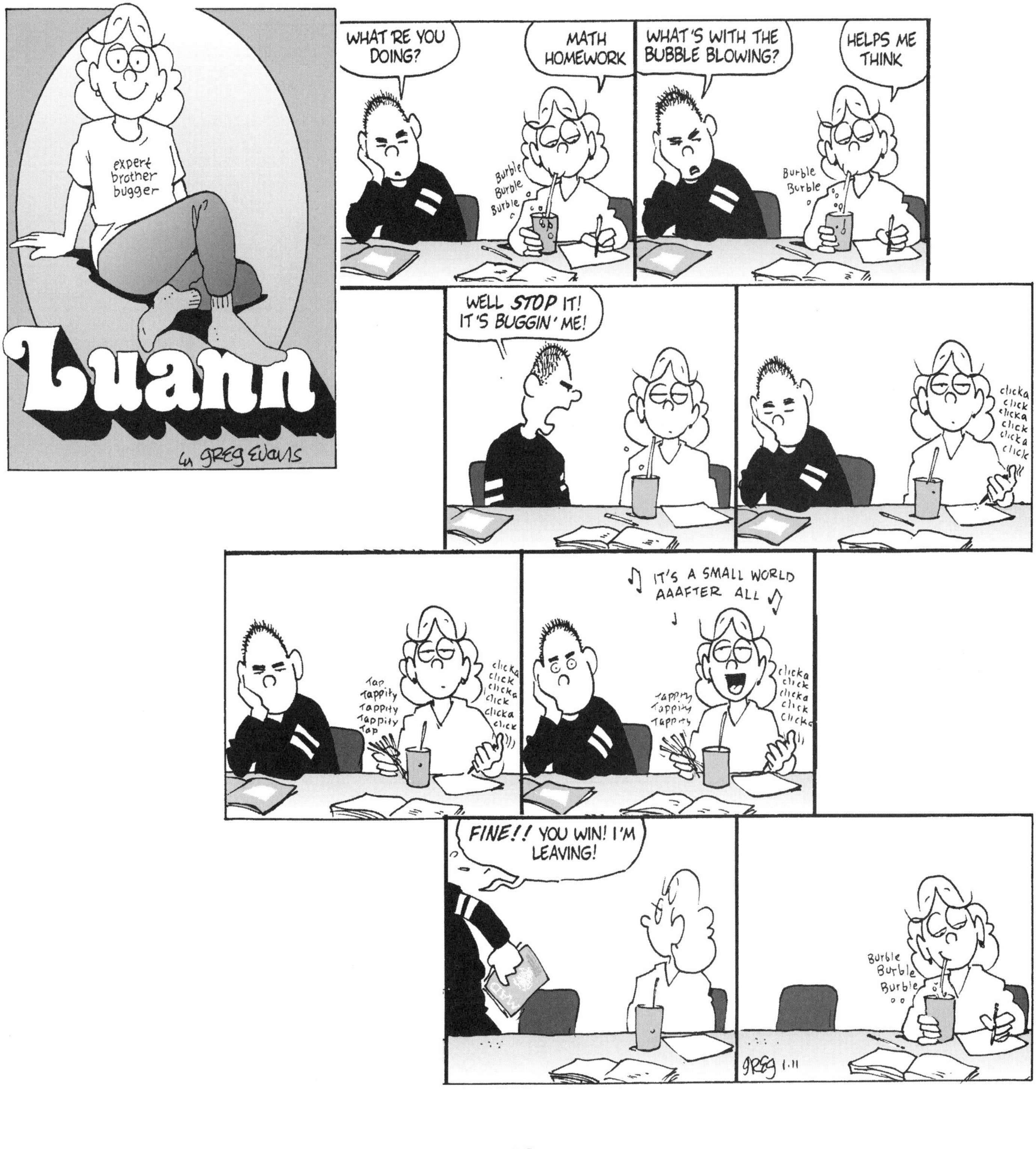
expert brother bugger
Luann
by GREG EVANS
WHAT'RE YOU DOING?
MATH HOMEWORK
Burble Burble Burble
WHAT'S WITH THE BUBBLE BLOWING?
HELPS ME THINK
Burble Burble
WELL STOP IT! IT'S BUGGIN' ME!
clicka click clicka click clicka click
Tap Tappity Tappity Tappity Tap
clicka click clicka click clicka click
IT'S A SMALL WORLD AAAFTER ALL
Tappity Tappity Tappity
clicka click clicka click clicka
FINE!! YOU WIN! I'M LEAVING!
Burble Burble Burble
GREG 1-11

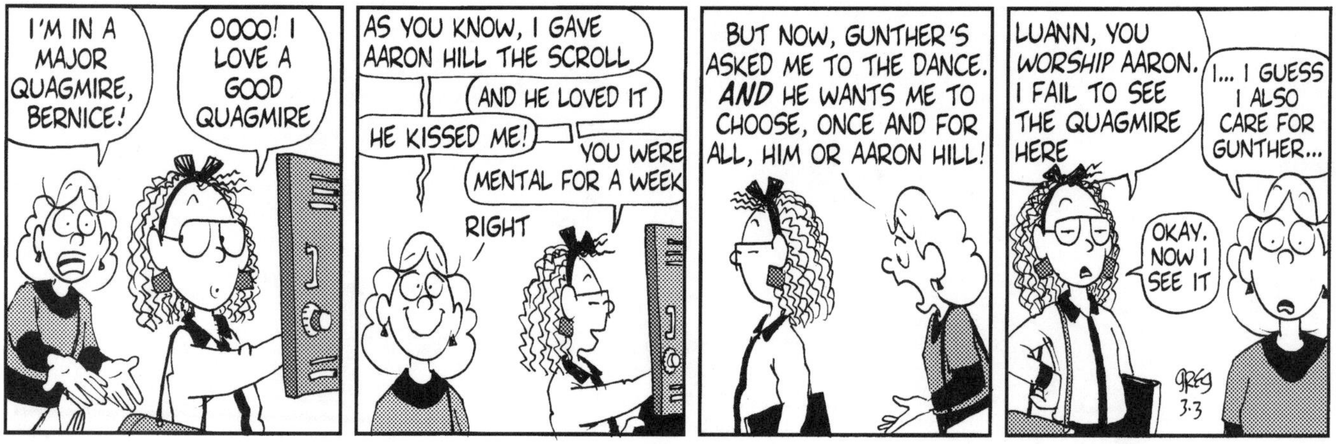
I'M IN A MAJOR QUAGMIRE, BERNICE!
OOOO! I LOVE A GOOD QUAGMIRE
AS YOU KNOW, I GAVE AARON HILL THE SCROLL
AND HE LOVED IT
HE KISSED ME!
YOU WERE MENTAL FOR A WEEK
RIGHT
BUT NOW, GUNTHER'S ASKED ME TO THE DANCE. AND HE WANTS ME TO CHOOSE, ONCE AND FOR ALL, HIM OR AARON HILL!
LUANN, YOU WORSHIP AARON. I FAIL TO SEE THE QUAGMIRE HERE
I... I GUESS I ALSO CARE FOR GUNTHER...
OKAY, NOW I SEE IT
GREG 3-3

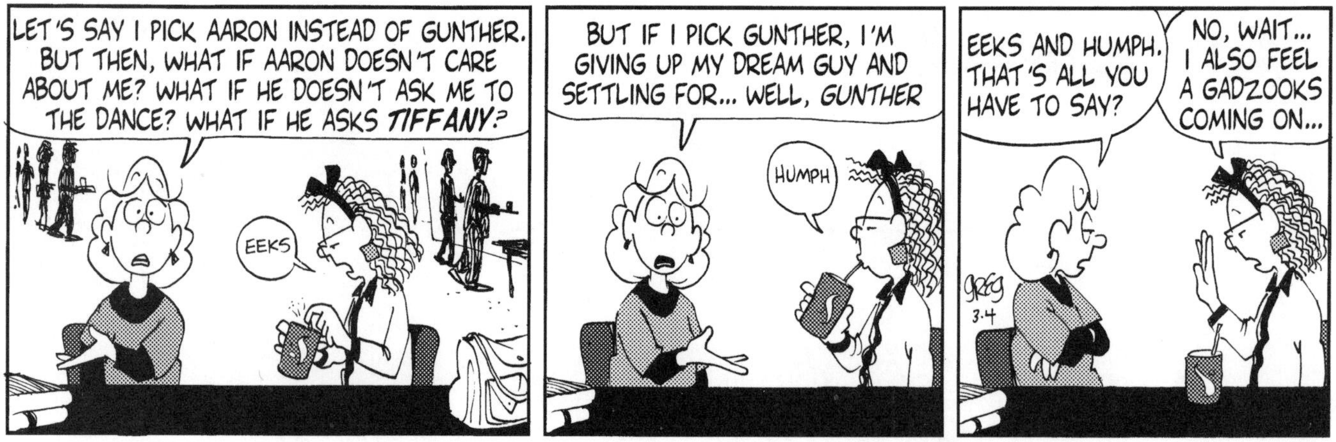
LET'S SAY I PICK AARON INSTEAD OF GUNTHER. BUT THEN, WHAT IF AARON DOESN'T CARE ABOUT ME? WHAT IF HE DOESN'T ASK ME TO THE DANCE? WHAT IF HE ASKS TIFFANY?
EEKS
BUT IF I PICK GUNTHER, I'M GIVING UP MY DREAM GUY AND SETTLING FOR... WELL, GUNTHER
HUMPH
EEKS AND HUMPH. THAT'S ALL YOU HAVE TO SAY?
NO, WAIT... I ALSO FEEL A GADZOOKS COMING ON...
GREG 3-4

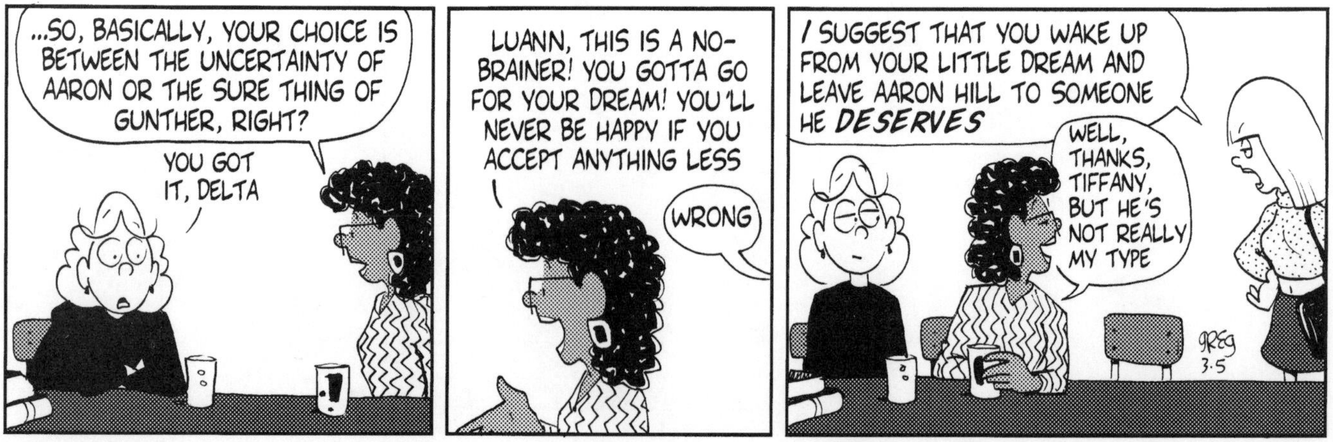
...SO, BASICALLY, YOUR CHOICE IS BETWEEN THE UNCERTAINTY OF AARON OR THE SURE THING OF GUNTHER, RIGHT?
YOU GOT IT, DELTA
LUANN, THIS IS A NO-BRAINER! YOU GOTTA GO FOR YOUR DREAM! YOU'LL NEVER BE HAPPY IF YOU ACCEPT ANYTHING LESS
WRONG
I SUGGEST THAT YOU WAKE UP FROM YOUR LITTLE DREAM AND LEAVE AARON HILL TO SOMEONE HE DESERVES
WELL, THANKS, TIFFANY, BUT HE'S NOT REALLY MY TYPE
GREG 3-5

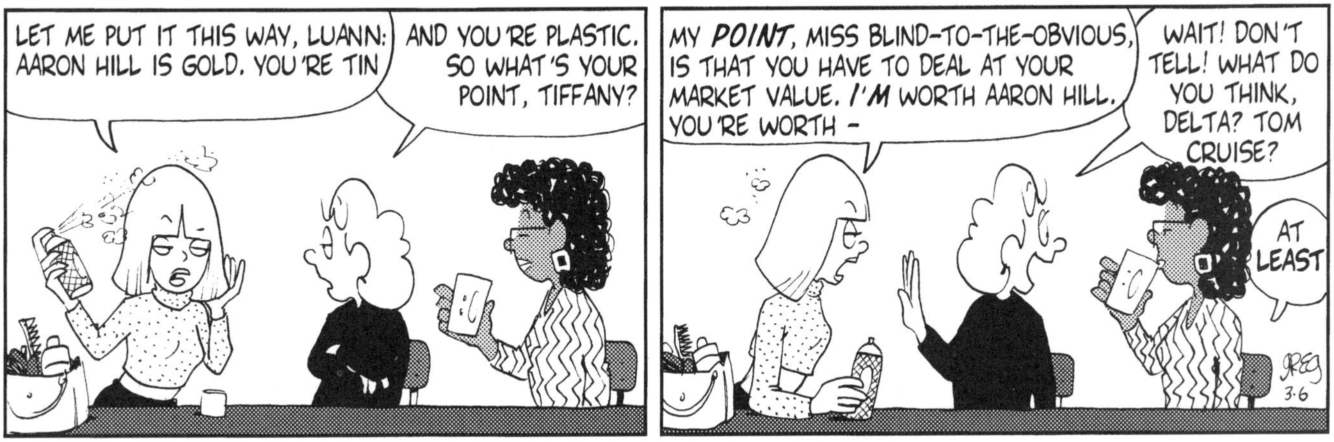
LET ME PUT IT THIS WAY, LUANN: AARON HILL IS GOLD. YOU'RE TIN
AND YOU'RE PLASTIC. SO WHAT'S YOUR POINT, TIFFANY?
MY POINT, MISS BLIND-TO-THE-OBVIOUS, IS THAT YOU HAVE TO DEAL AT YOUR MARKET VALUE. I'M WORTH AARON HILL. YOU'RE WORTH –
WAIT! DON'T TELL! WHAT DO YOU THINK, DELTA? TOM CRUISE?
AT LEAST
GREG 3·6

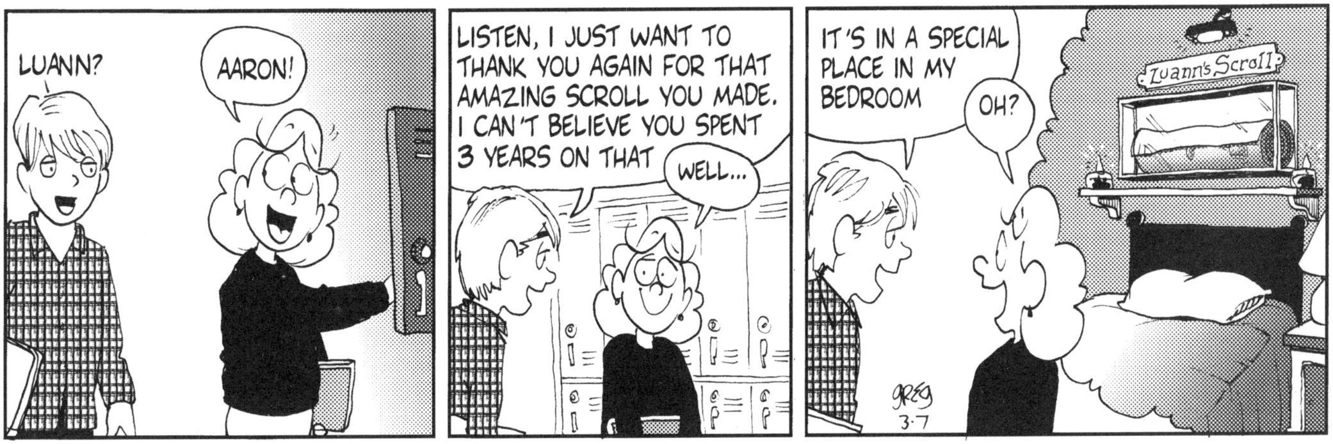
LUANN?
AARON!
LISTEN, I JUST WANT TO THANK YOU AGAIN FOR THAT AMAZING SCROLL YOU MADE. I CAN'T BELIEVE YOU SPENT 3 YEARS ON THAT
WELL...
IT'S IN A SPECIAL PLACE IN MY BEDROOM
OH?
Luann's Scroll
GREG 3·7

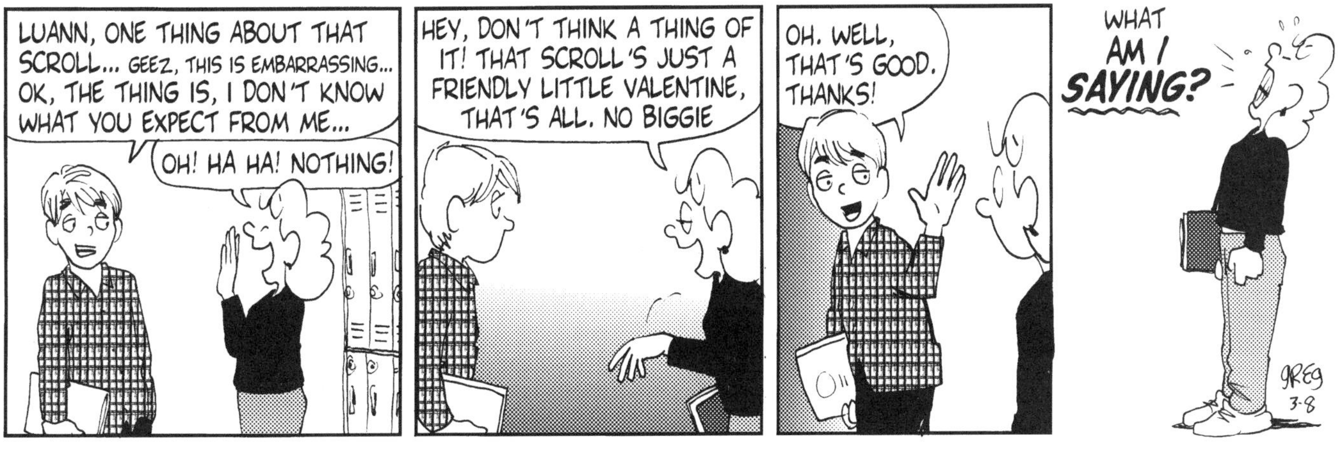
LUANN, ONE THING ABOUT THAT SCROLL... GEEZ, THIS IS EMBARRASSING... OK, THE THING IS, I DON'T KNOW WHAT YOU EXPECT FROM ME...
OH! HA HA! NOTHING!
HEY, DON'T THINK A THING OF IT! THAT SCROLL'S JUST A FRIENDLY LITTLE VALENTINE, THAT'S ALL. NO BIGGIE
OH. WELL, THAT'S GOOD. THANKS!
WHAT AM I SAYING?
GREG 3·8

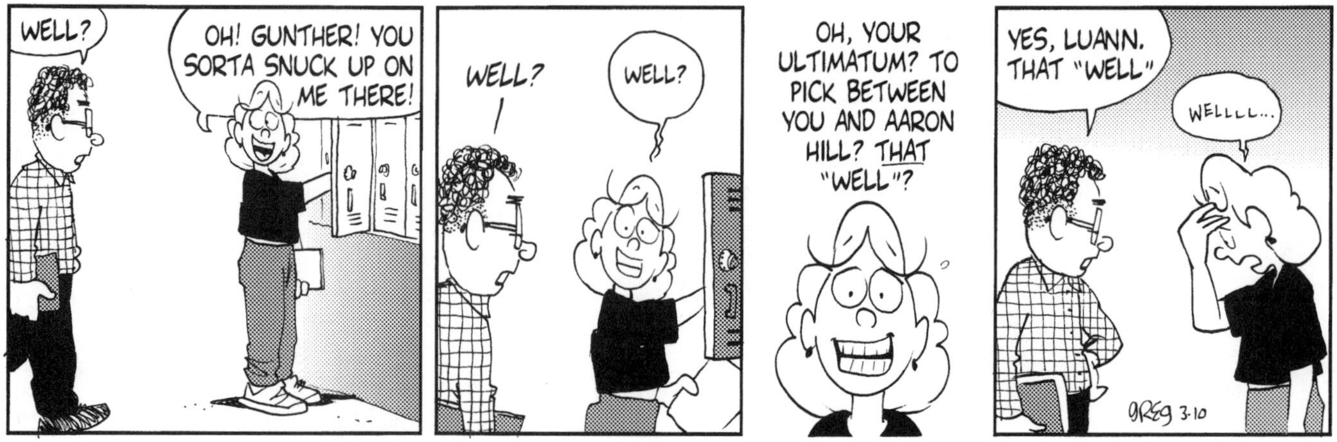
WELL?
OH! GUNTHER! YOU SORTA SNUCK UP ON ME THERE!
WELL?
WELL?
OH, YOUR ULTIMATUM? TO PICK BETWEEN YOU AND AARON HILL? THAT "WELL"?
YES, LUANN. THAT "WELL"
WELLLL...
GREG 3·10

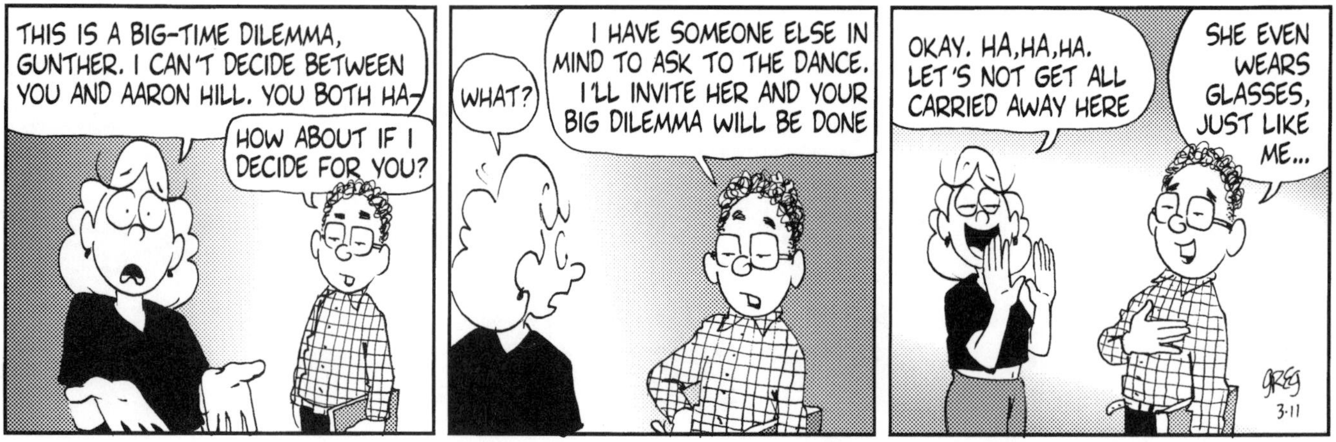
THIS IS A BIG-TIME DILEMMA, GUNTHER. I CAN'T DECIDE BETWEEN YOU AND AARON HILL. YOU BOTH HA-
HOW ABOUT IF I DECIDE FOR YOU?
WHAT?
I HAVE SOMEONE ELSE IN MIND TO ASK TO THE DANCE. I'LL INVITE HER AND YOUR BIG DILEMMA WILL BE DONE
OKAY. HA,HA,HA. LET'S NOT GET ALL CARRIED AWAY HERE
SHE EVEN WEARS GLASSES, JUST LIKE ME...
GREG 3·11

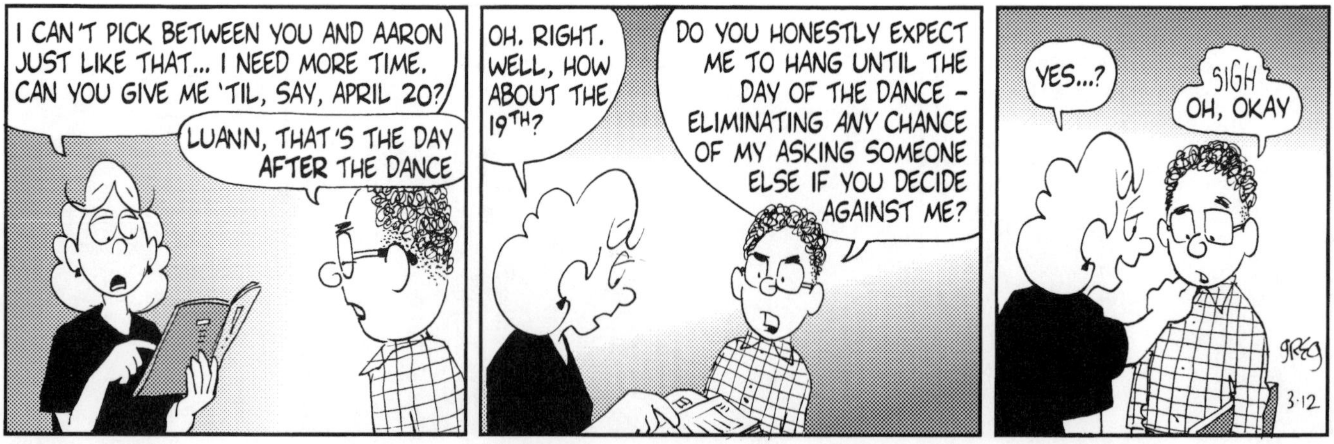
I CAN'T PICK BETWEEN YOU AND AARON JUST LIKE THAT... I NEED MORE TIME. CAN YOU GIVE ME 'TIL, SAY, APRIL 20?
LUANN, THAT'S THE DAY AFTER THE DANCE
OH. RIGHT. WELL, HOW ABOUT THE 19TH?
DO YOU HONESTLY EXPECT ME TO HANG UNTIL THE DAY OF THE DANCE – ELIMINATING ANY CHANCE OF MY ASKING SOMEONE ELSE IF YOU DECIDE AGAINST ME?
YES...?
SIGH
OH, OKAY
GREG 3·12

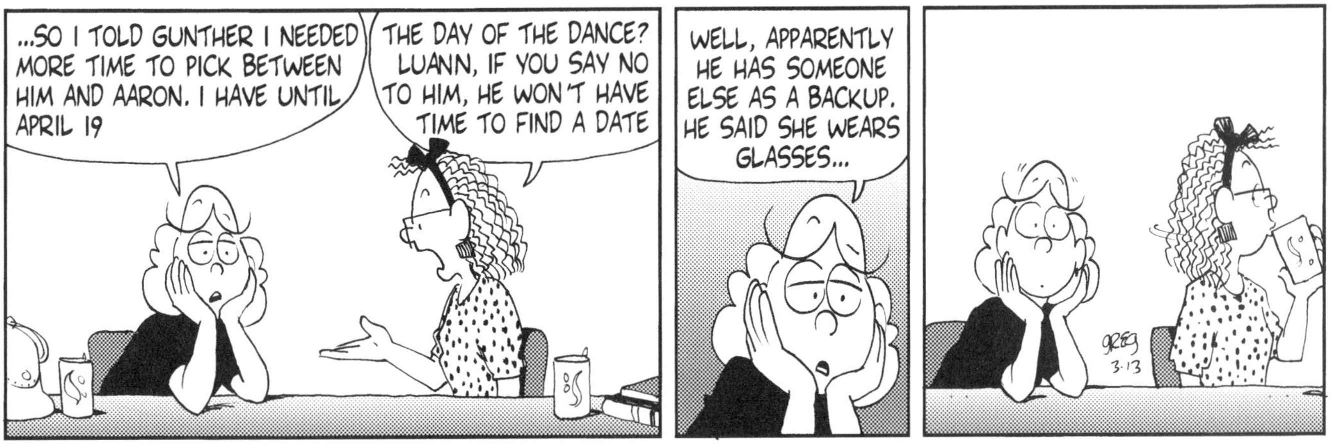
...SO I TOLD GUNTHER I NEEDED MORE TIME TO PICK BETWEEN HIM AND AARON. I HAVE UNTIL APRIL 19
THE DAY OF THE DANCE? LUANN, IF YOU SAY NO TO HIM, HE WON'T HAVE TIME TO FIND A DATE
WELL, APPARENTLY HE HAS SOMEONE ELSE AS A BACKUP. HE SAID SHE WEARS GLASSES...

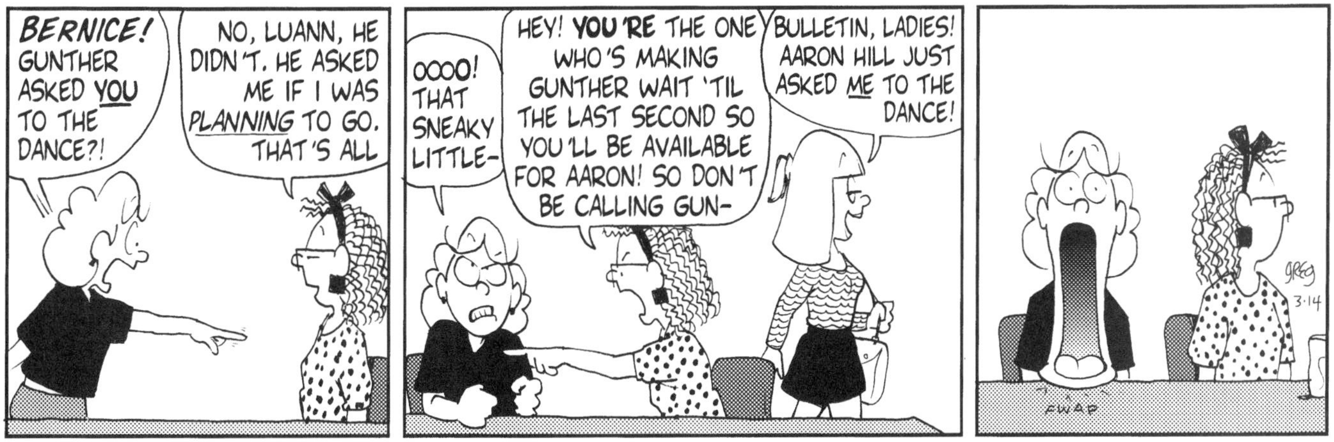
BERNICE! GUNTHER ASKED YOU TO THE DANCE?!
NO, LUANN, HE DIDN'T. HE ASKED ME IF I WAS PLANNING TO GO. THAT'S ALL
OOOO! THAT SNEAKY LITTLE-
HEY! YOU'RE THE ONE WHO'S MAKING GUNTHER WAIT 'TIL THE LAST SECOND SO YOU'LL BE AVAILABLE FOR AARON! SO DON'T BE CALLING GUN-
BULLETIN, LADIES! AARON HILL JUST ASKED ME TO THE DANCE!
FWAP

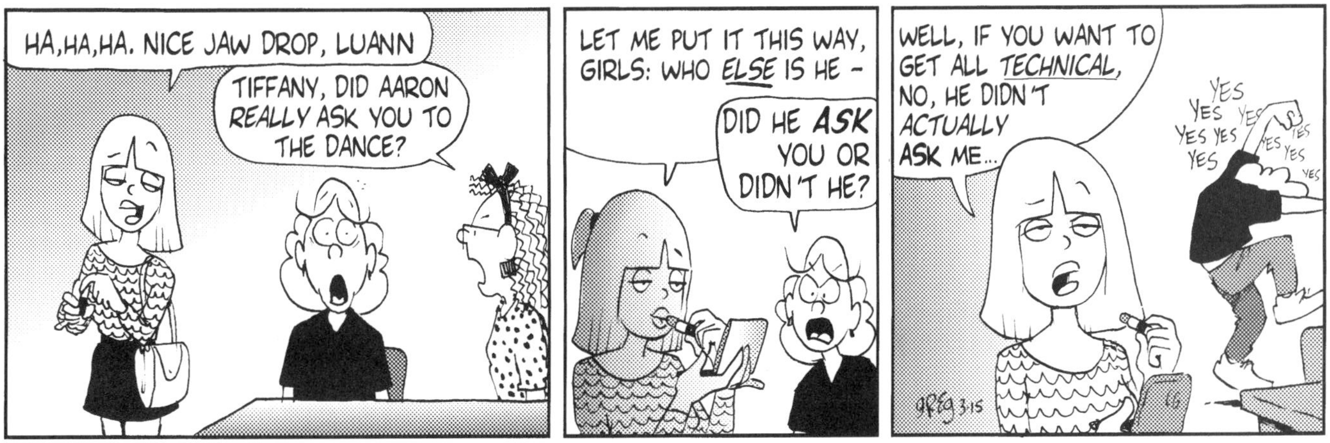
HA,HA,HA. NICE JAW DROP, LUANN
TIFFANY, DID AARON REALLY ASK YOU TO THE DANCE?
LET ME PUT IT THIS WAY, GIRLS: WHO ELSE IS HE -
DID HE ASK YOU OR DIDN'T HE?
WELL, IF YOU WANT TO GET ALL TECHNICAL, NO, HE DIDN'T ACTUALLY ASK ME...
YES YES YES YES YES YES YES YES YES YES

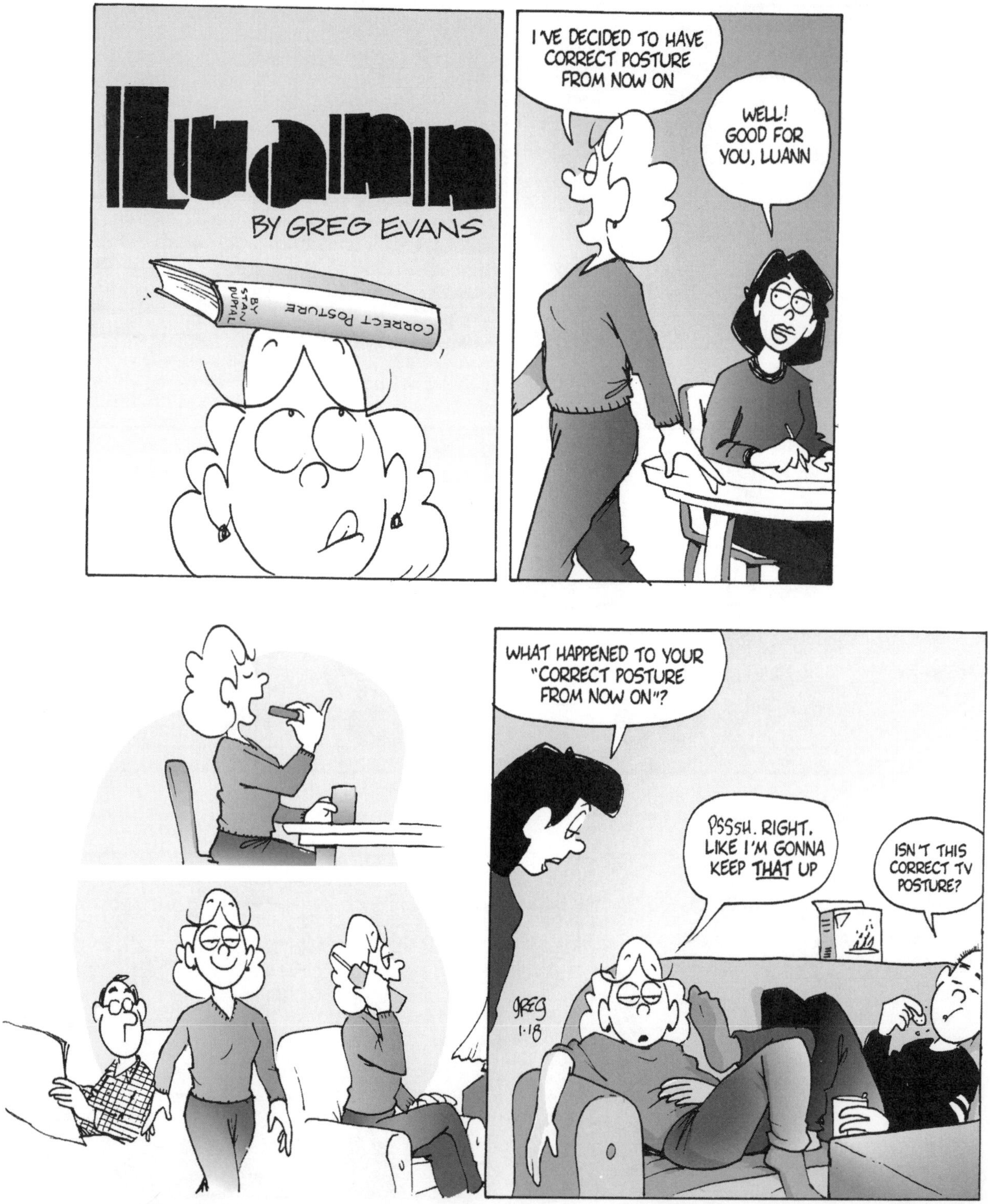
Luann
BY GREG EVANS
CORRECT POSTURE BY STAN DUPTAL
I'VE DECIDED TO HAVE CORRECT POSTURE FROM NOW ON
WELL! GOOD FOR YOU, LUANN
WHAT HAPPENED TO YOUR "CORRECT POSTURE FROM NOW ON"?
PSSSH. RIGHT. LIKE I'M GONNA KEEP THAT UP
ISN'T THIS CORRECT TV POSTURE?
GREG 1·18

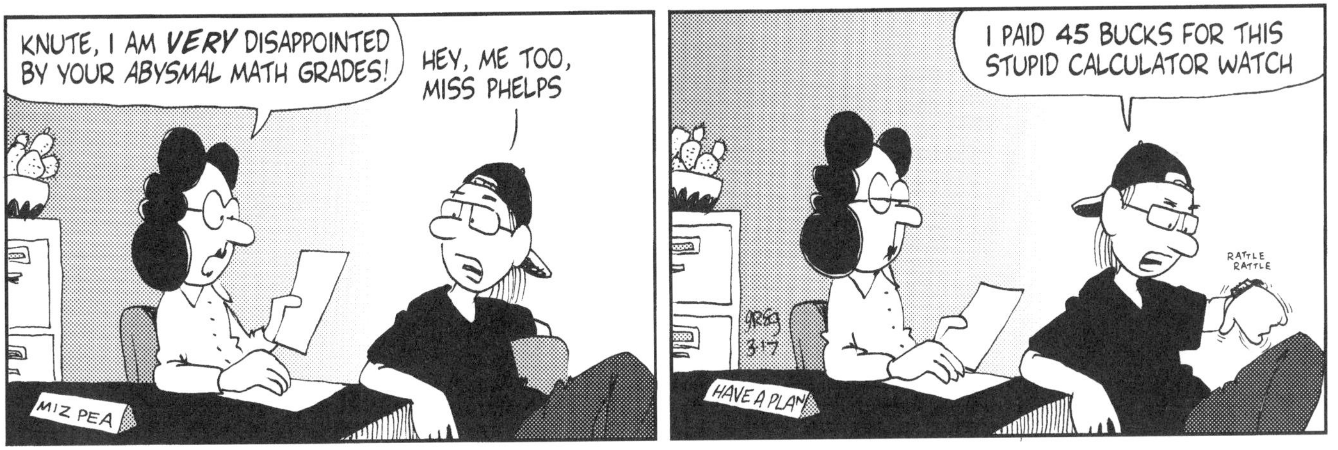
KNUTE, I AM VERY DISAPPOINTED BY YOUR ABYSMAL MATH GRADES!
HEY, ME TOO, MISS PHELPS
MIZ PEA
I PAID 45 BUCKS FOR THIS STUPID CALCULATOR WATCH
RATTLE RATTLE
HAVE A PLAN

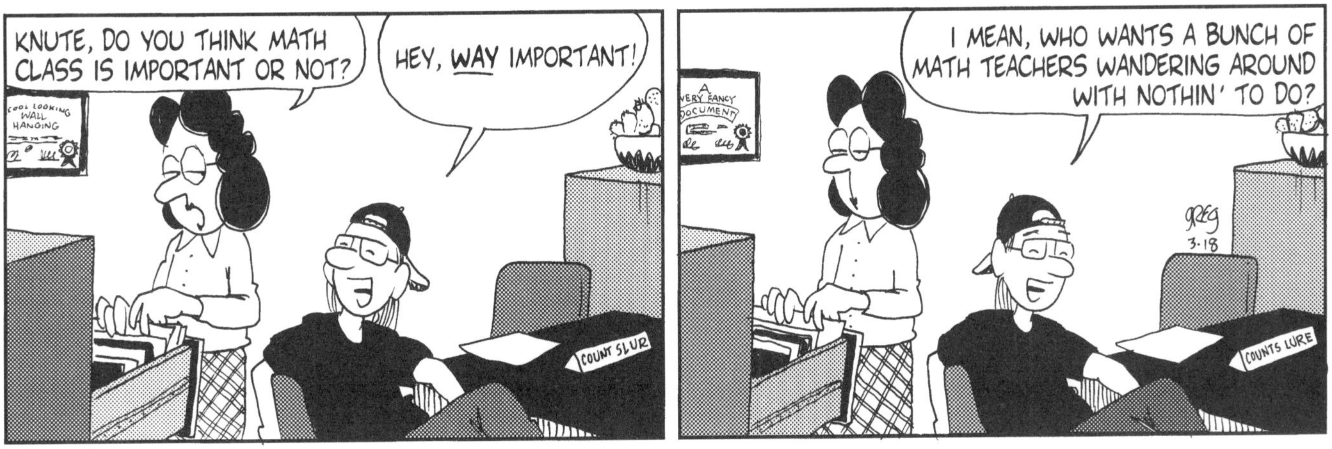
KNUTE, DO YOU THINK MATH CLASS IS IMPORTANT OR NOT?
HEY, WAY IMPORTANT!
COOL LOOKING WALL HANGING
COUNT SLUR
I MEAN, WHO WANTS A BUNCH OF MATH TEACHERS WANDERING AROUND WITH NOTHIN' TO DO?
A VERY FANCY DOCUMENT
COUNTS LURE

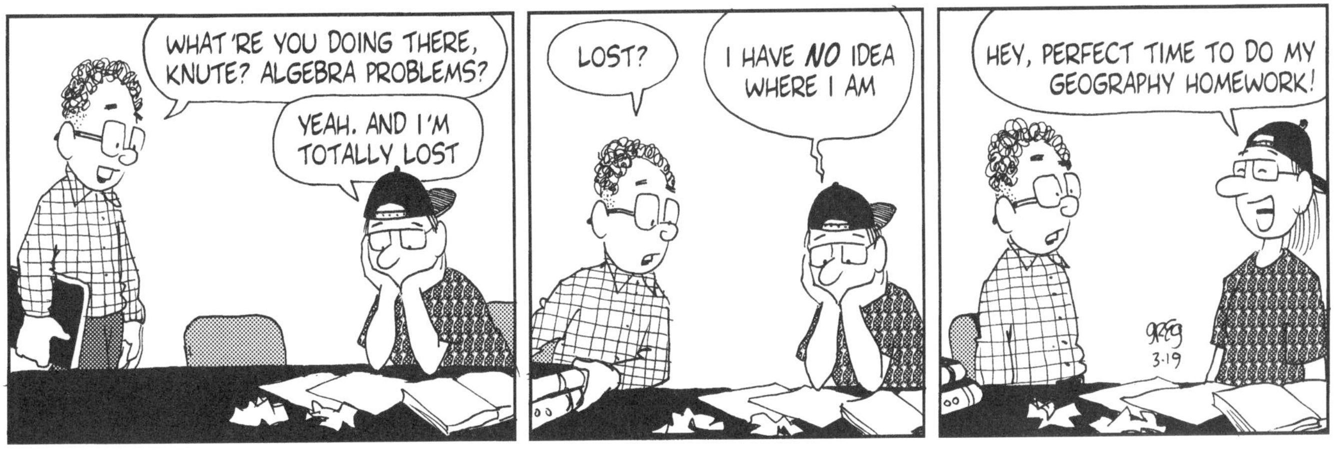
WHAT'RE YOU DOING THERE, KNUTE? ALGEBRA PROBLEMS?
YEAH. AND I'M TOTALLY LOST
LOST?
I HAVE NO IDEA WHERE I AM
HEY, PERFECT TIME TO DO MY GEOGRAPHY HOMEWORK!

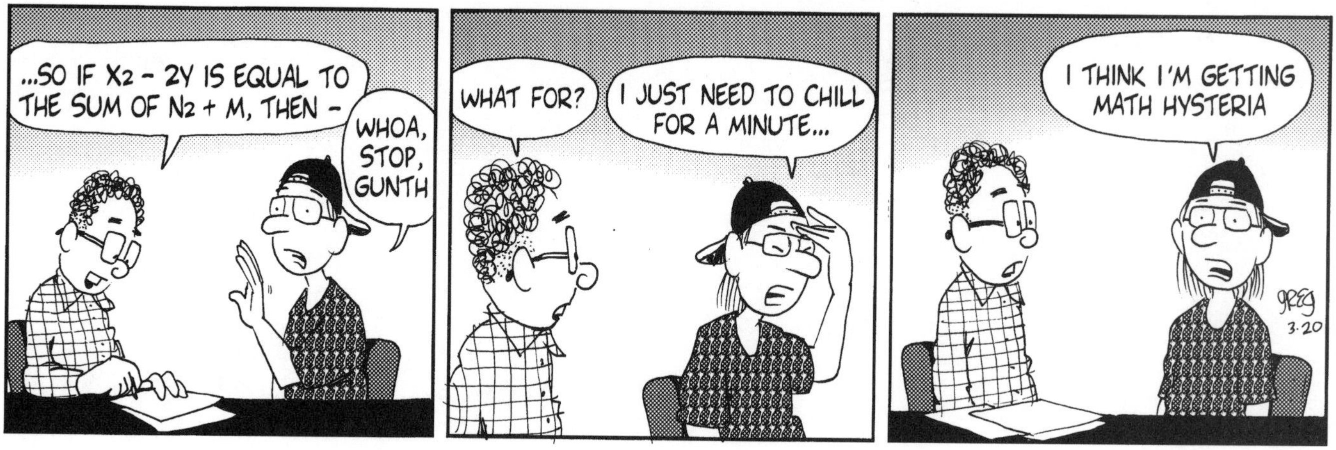
...SO IF $X_2 - 2Y$ IS EQUAL TO THE SUM OF $N_2 + M$, THEN -
WHOA, STOP, GUNTH
WHAT FOR?
I JUST NEED TO CHILL FOR A MINUTE...
I THINK I'M GETTING MATH HYSTERIA
3·20

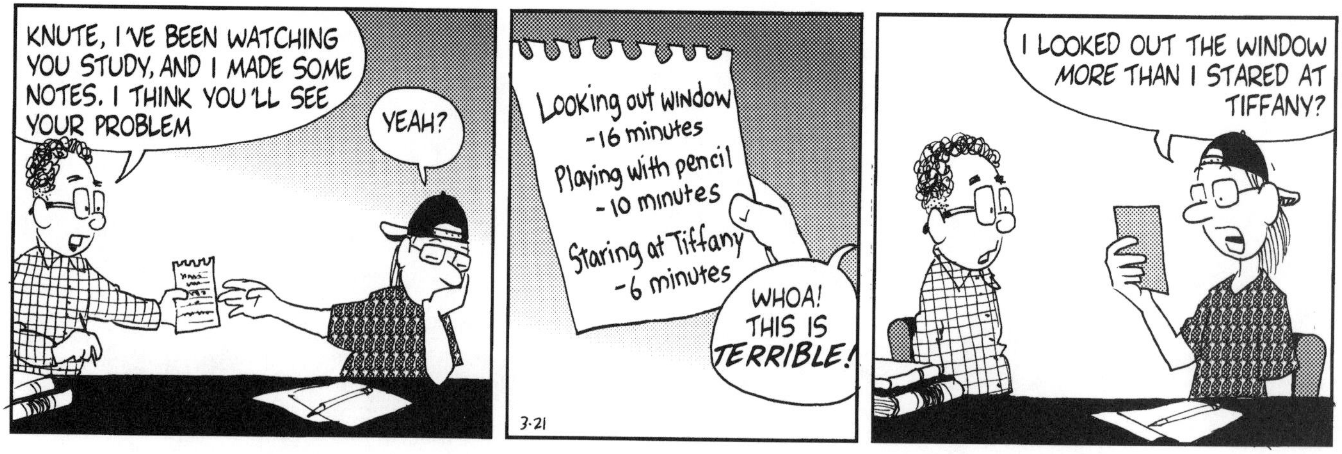
KNUTE, I'VE BEEN WATCHING YOU STUDY, AND I MADE SOME NOTES. I THINK YOU'LL SEE YOUR PROBLEM
YEAH?
Looking out window -16 minutes
Playing with pencil -10 minutes
Staring at Tiffany -6 minutes
WHOA! THIS IS TERRIBLE!
3·21
I LOOKED OUT THE WINDOW MORE THAN I STARED AT TIFFANY?

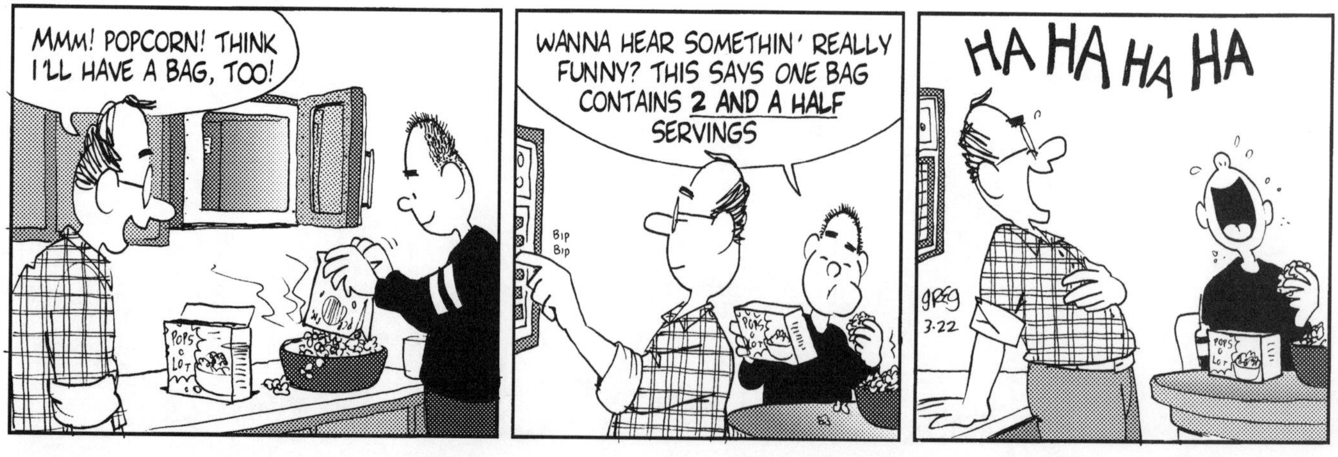
MMM! POPCORN! THINK I'LL HAVE A BAG, TOO!
POPS O LOT
WANNA HEAR SOMETHIN' REALLY FUNNY? THIS SAYS ONE BAG CONTAINS 2 AND A HALF SERVINGS
BIP BIP
HA HA HA HA
3·22

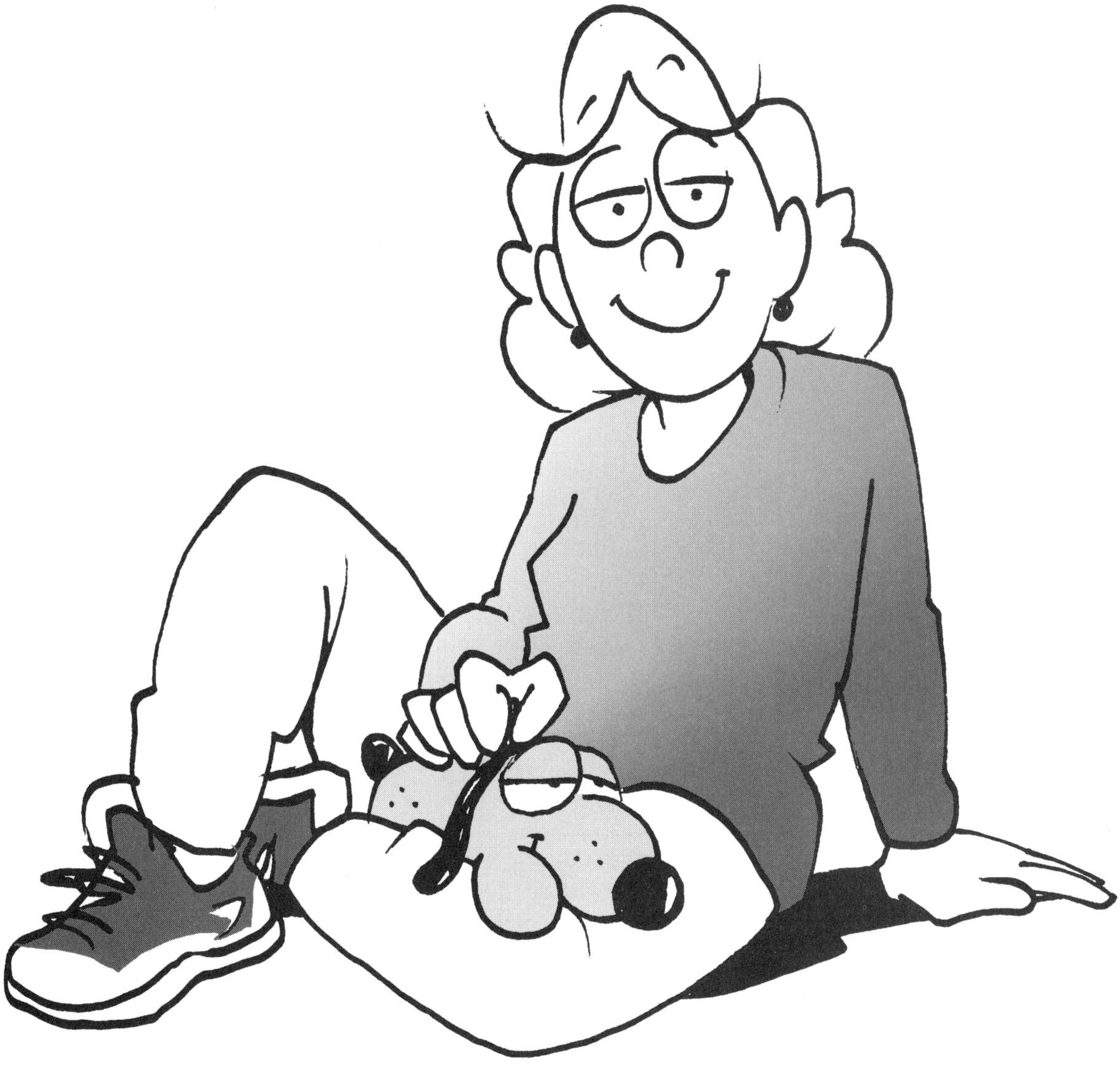

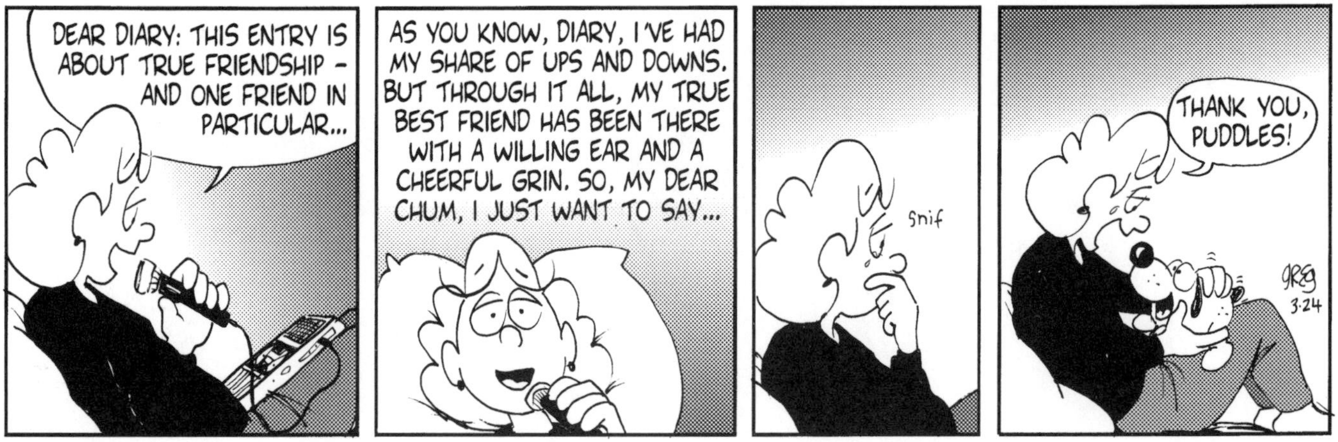
DEAR DIARY: THIS ENTRY IS ABOUT TRUE FRIENDSHIP - AND ONE FRIEND IN PARTICULAR...
AS YOU KNOW, DIARY, I'VE HAD MY SHARE OF UPS AND DOWNS. BUT THROUGH IT ALL, MY TRUE BEST FRIEND HAS BEEN THERE WITH A WILLING EAR AND A CHEERFUL GRIN. SO, MY DEAR CHUM, I JUST WANT TO SAY...
snif
THANK YOU, PUDDLES!
GREG 3·24

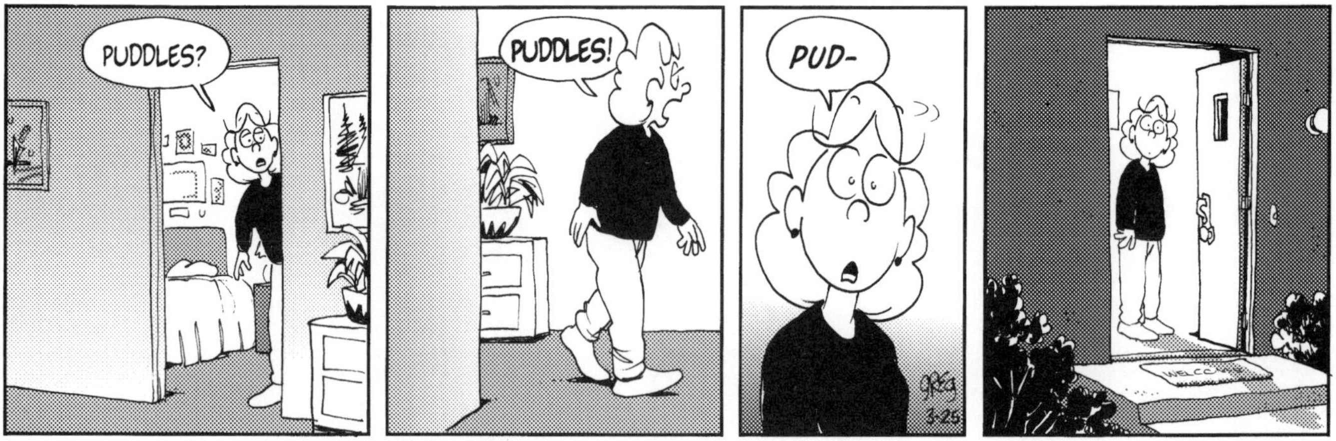
PUDDLES?
PUDDLES!
PUD-
GREG 3·25

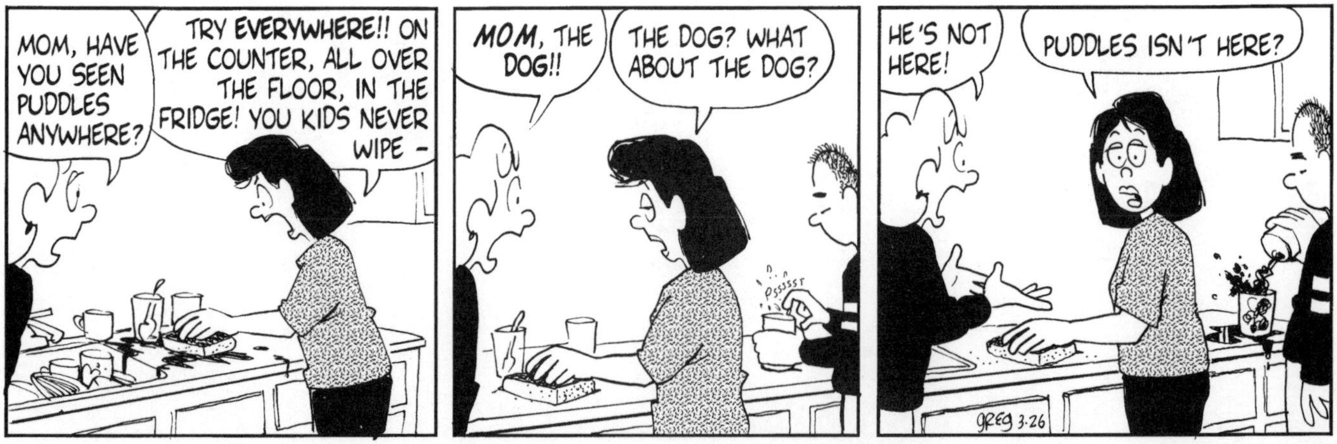
MOM, HAVE YOU SEEN PUDDLES ANYWHERE?
TRY EVERYWHERE!! ON THE COUNTER, ALL OVER THE FLOOR, IN THE FRIDGE! YOU KIDS NEVER WIPE -
MOM, THE DOG!!
THE DOG? WHAT ABOUT THE DOG?
HE'S NOT HERE!
PUDDLES ISN'T HERE?
GREG 3·26

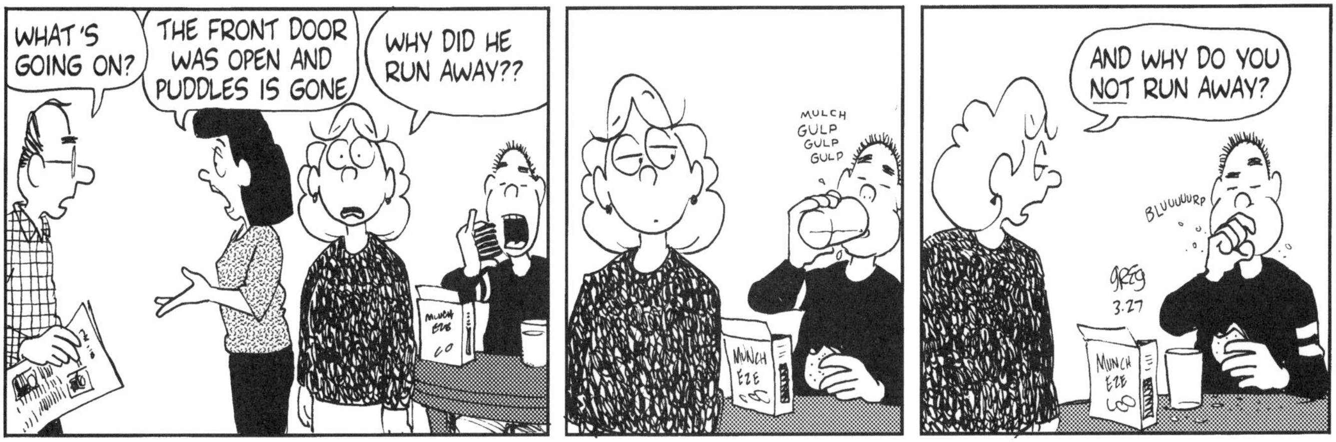
WHAT'S GOING ON?
THE FRONT DOOR WAS OPEN AND PUDDLES IS GONE
WHY DID HE RUN AWAY??
MUNCH EZE
MULCH GULP GULP GULP
MUNCH EZE
AND WHY DO YOU NOT RUN AWAY?
BLUUUUURP
GREG 3·27
MUNCH EZE

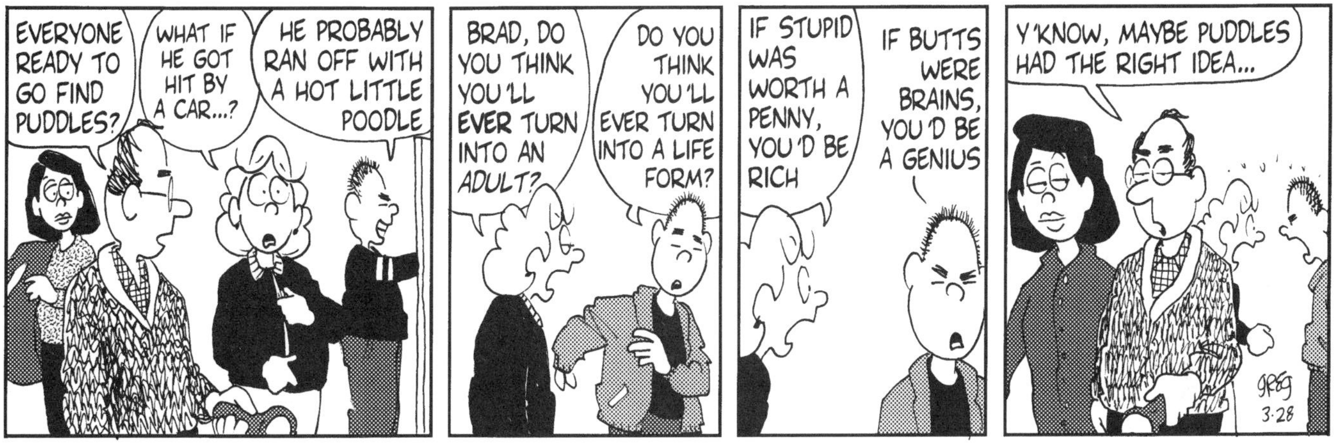
EVERYONE READY TO GO FIND PUDDLES?
WHAT IF HE GOT HIT BY A CAR...?
HE PROBABLY RAN OFF WITH A HOT LITTLE POODLE
BRAD, DO YOU THINK YOU'LL EVER TURN INTO AN ADULT?
DO YOU THINK YOU'LL EVER TURN INTO A LIFE FORM?
IF STUPID WAS WORTH A PENNY, YOU'D BE RICH
IF BUTTS WERE BRAINS, YOU'D BE A GENIUS
Y'KNOW, MAYBE PUDDLES HAD THE RIGHT IDEA...
GREG 3·28

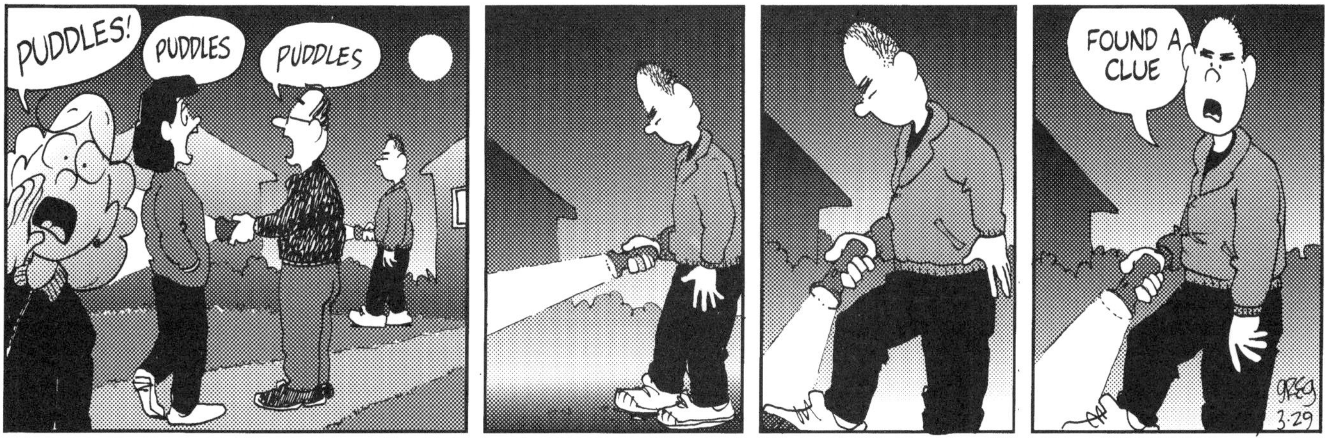
PUDDLES!
PUDDLES
PUDDLES
FOUND A CLUE
GREG 3·29

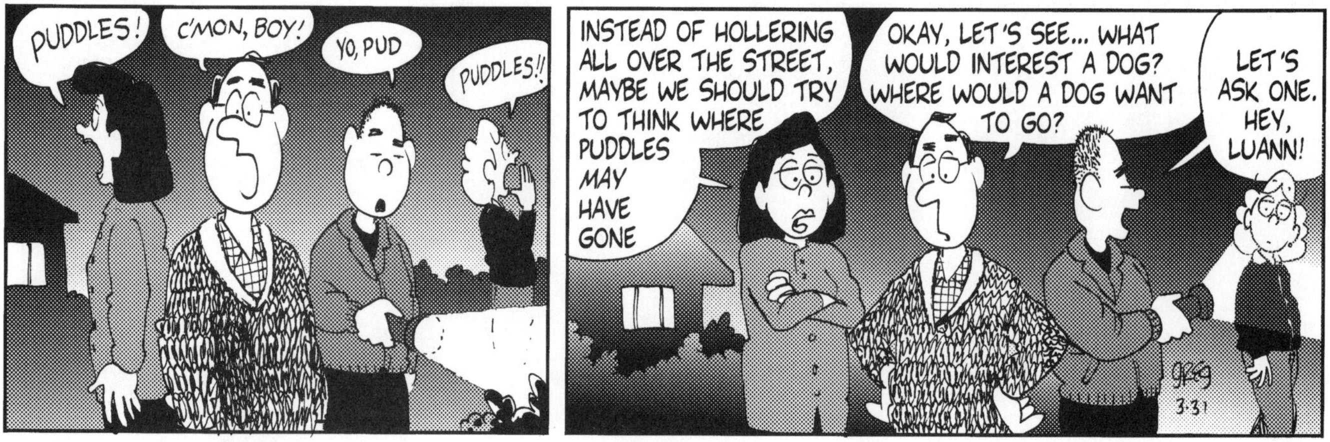
PUDDLES!
C'MON, BOY!
YO, PUD
PUDDLES!!
INSTEAD OF HOLLERING ALL OVER THE STREET, MAYBE WE SHOULD TRY TO THINK WHERE PUDDLES *MAY* HAVE GONE
OKAY, LET'S SEE... WHAT WOULD INTEREST A DOG? WHERE WOULD A DOG WANT TO GO?
LET'S ASK ONE. HEY, LUANN!
GREG 3·31

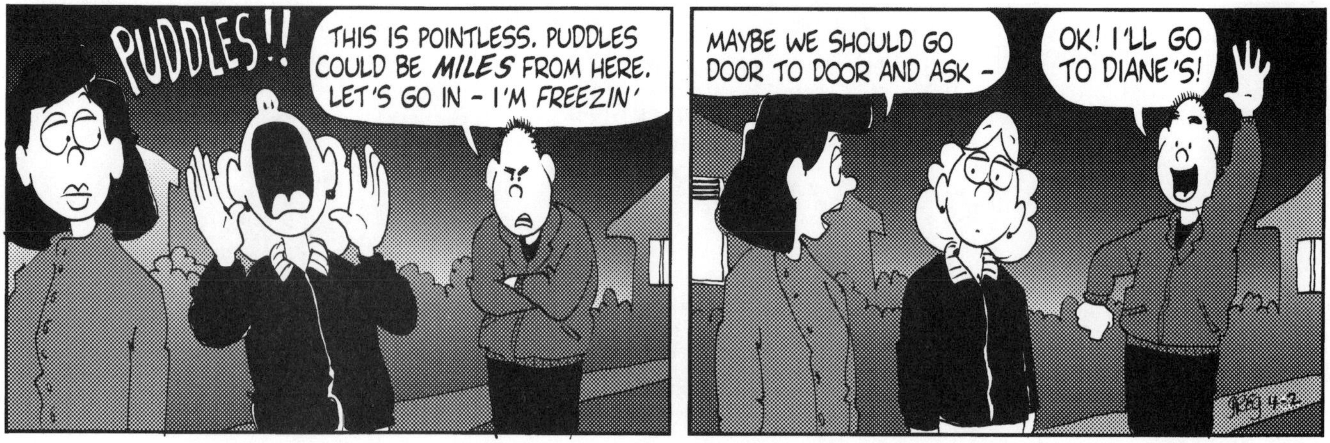
PUDDLES!!
THIS IS POINTLESS. PUDDLES COULD BE ***MILES*** FROM HERE. LET'S GO IN – I'M *FREEZIN'*
MAYBE WE SHOULD GO DOOR TO DOOR AND ASK –
OK! I'LL GO TO DIANE'S!
GREG 4-2

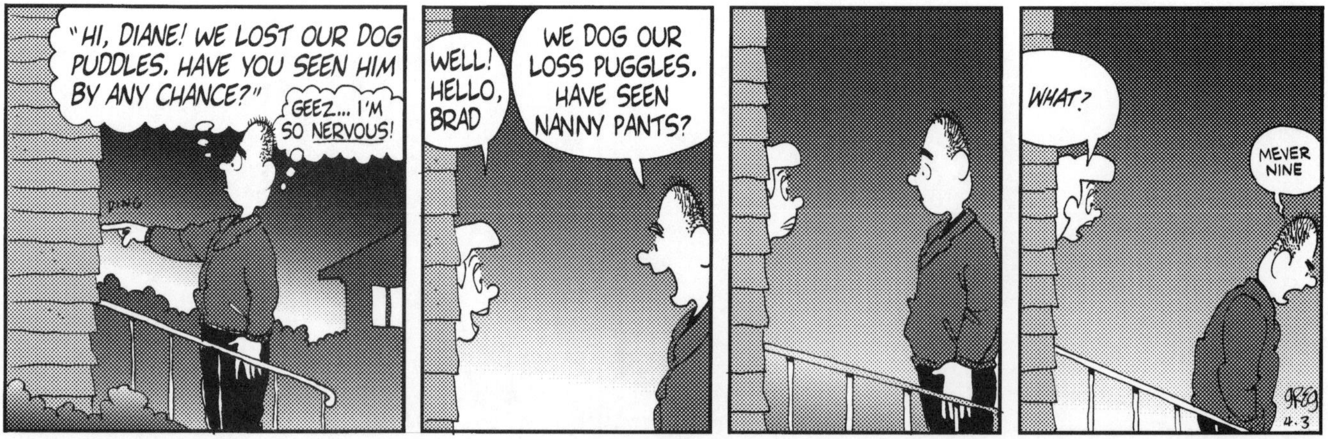
"HI, DIANE! WE LOST OUR DOG PUDDLES. HAVE YOU SEEN HIM BY ANY CHANCE?"
GEEZ... I'M SO NERVOUS!
WELL! HELLO, BRAD
WE DOG OUR LOSS PUGGLES. HAVE SEEN NANNY PANTS?
WHAT?
MEVER NINE
GREG 4·3

HI, SHANNON. HI, LINDY. LISTEN, I LOST MY LITTLE DOG PUDDLES. IF YOU SEE HIM, WOULD YOU CALL M-
OKAY
SLAM
Puzzle hafta go home now?
NO, LINDY. "FINDERS KEEPERS, LOSERS WIENERS"

...SO SHANNON AND LINDY SAW PUDDLES IN OUR YARD AND DECIDED TO CLAIM HIM
THANK YOU FOR RETURNING HIM, MRS LEWIS. WE'VE BEEN *SO* UPSET
MY PLEASURE. I'M JUST SORRY HE LOOKS SO AWFUL...
OHMYGAW!! IS PUDDLES **HURT?** WHAT HA-

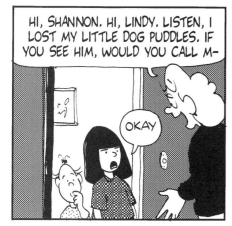

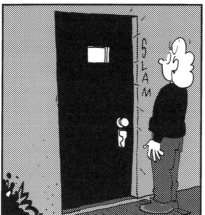

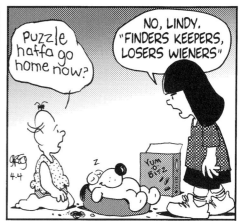

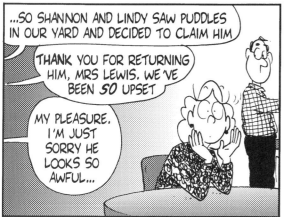

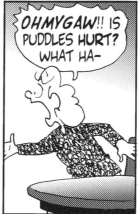

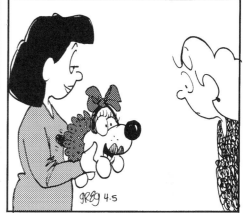

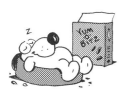

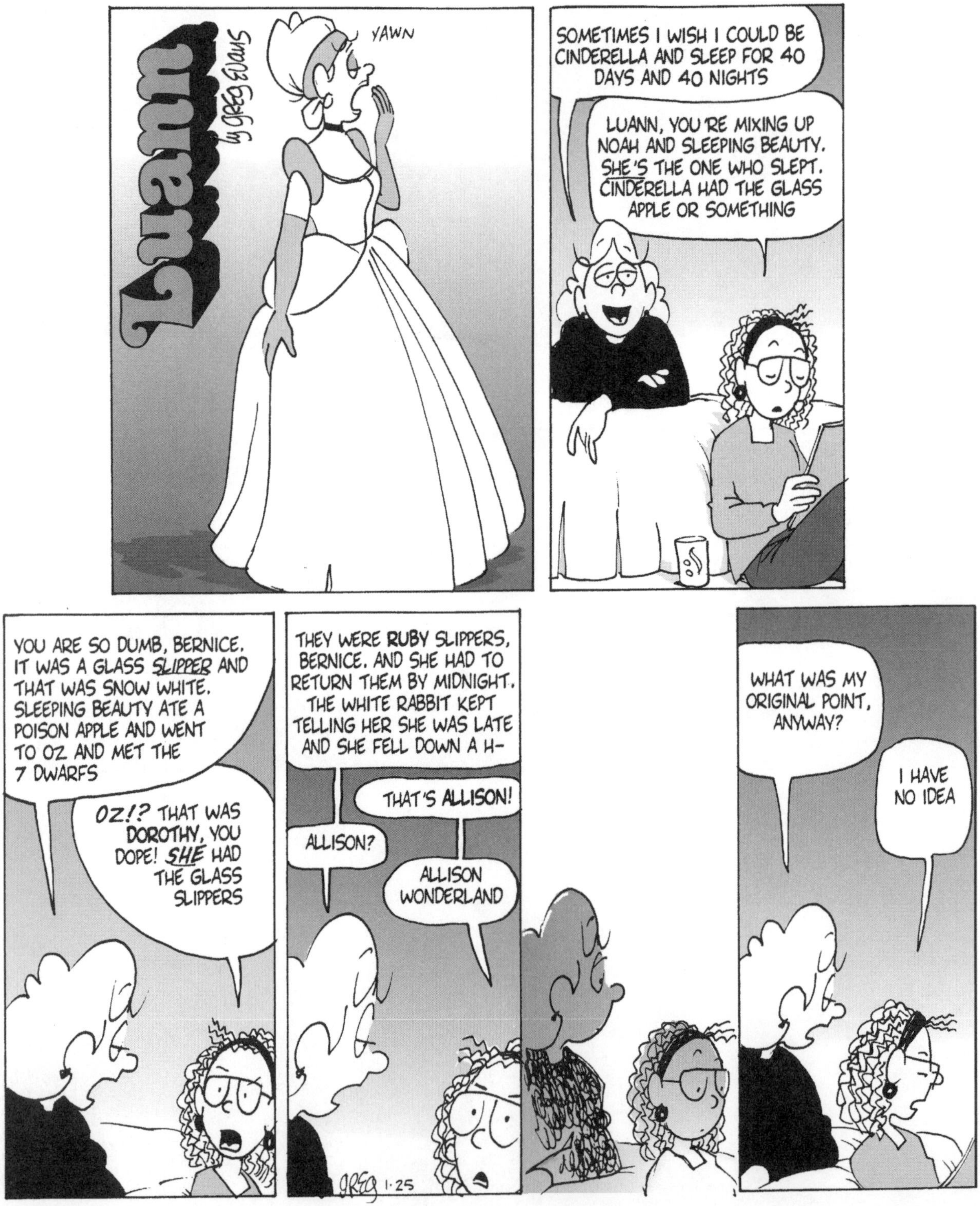
Luann
by Greg Evans
YAWN
SOMETIMES I WISH I COULD BE CINDERELLA AND SLEEP FOR 40 DAYS AND 40 NIGHTS
LUANN, YOU'RE MIXING UP NOAH AND SLEEPING BEAUTY. SHE'S THE ONE WHO SLEPT. CINDERELLA HAD THE GLASS APPLE OR SOMETHING
YOU ARE SO DUMB, BERNICE. IT WAS A GLASS SLIPPER AND THAT WAS SNOW WHITE. SLEEPING BEAUTY ATE A POISON APPLE AND WENT TO OZ AND MET THE 7 DWARFS
OZ!? THAT WAS DOROTHY, YOU DOPE! SHE HAD THE GLASS SLIPPERS
THEY WERE RUBY SLIPPERS, BERNICE. AND SHE HAD TO RETURN THEM BY MIDNIGHT. THE WHITE RABBIT KEPT TELLING HER SHE WAS LATE AND SHE FELL DOWN A H–
THAT'S ALLISON!
ALLISON?
ALLISON WONDERLAND
WHAT WAS MY ORIGINAL POINT, ANYWAY?
I HAVE NO IDEA
GREG 1·25

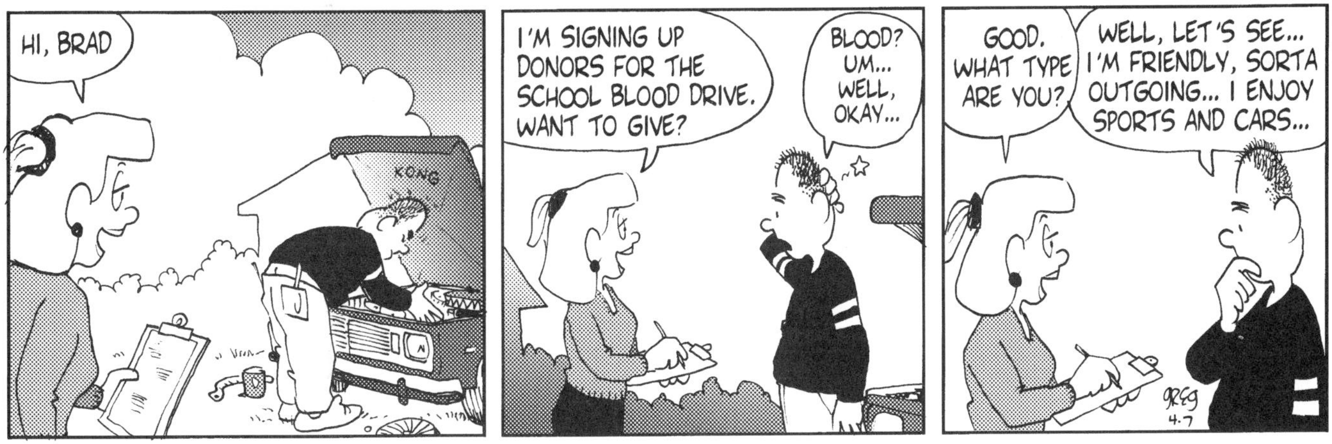
HI, BRAD
KONG
I'M SIGNING UP DONORS FOR THE SCHOOL BLOOD DRIVE. WANT TO GIVE?
BLOOD? UM... WELL, OKAY...
GOOD. WHAT TYPE ARE YOU?
WELL, LET'S SEE... I'M FRIENDLY, SORTA OUTGOING... I ENJOY SPORTS AND CARS...

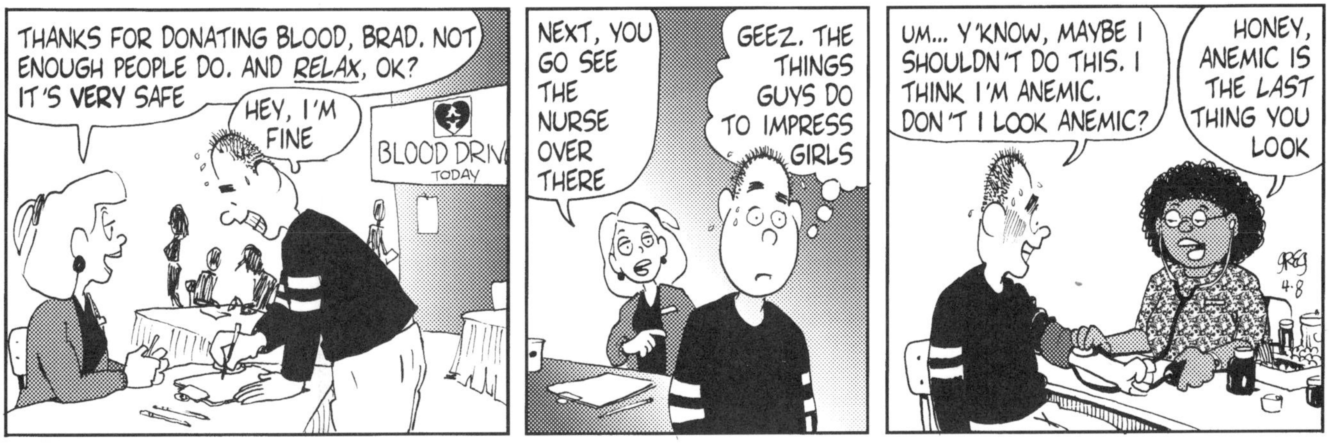
THANKS FOR DONATING BLOOD, BRAD. NOT ENOUGH PEOPLE DO. AND RELAX, OK? IT'S VERY SAFE
HEY, I'M FINE
BLOOD DRIVE TODAY
NEXT, YOU GO SEE THE NURSE OVER THERE
GEEZ. THE THINGS GUYS DO TO IMPRESS GIRLS
UM... Y'KNOW, MAYBE I SHOULDN'T DO THIS. I THINK I'M ANEMIC. DON'T I LOOK ANEMIC?
HONEY, ANEMIC IS THE LAST THING YOU LOOK

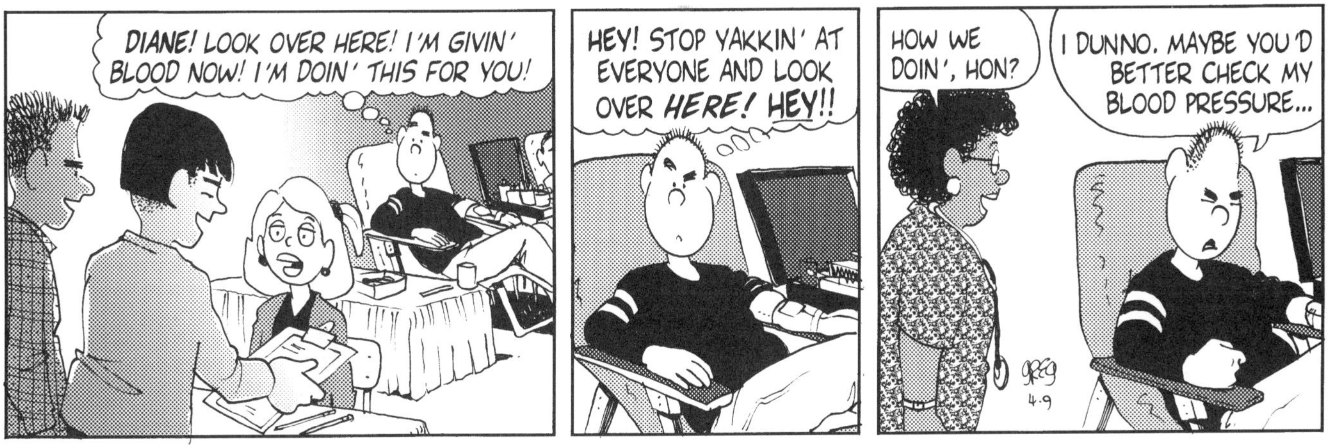
DIANE! LOOK OVER HERE! I'M GIVIN' BLOOD NOW! I'M DOIN' THIS FOR YOU!
HEY! STOP YAKKIN' AT EVERYONE AND LOOK OVER HERE! HEY!!
HOW WE DOIN', HON?
I DUNNO. MAYBE YOU'D BETTER CHECK MY BLOOD PRESSURE...

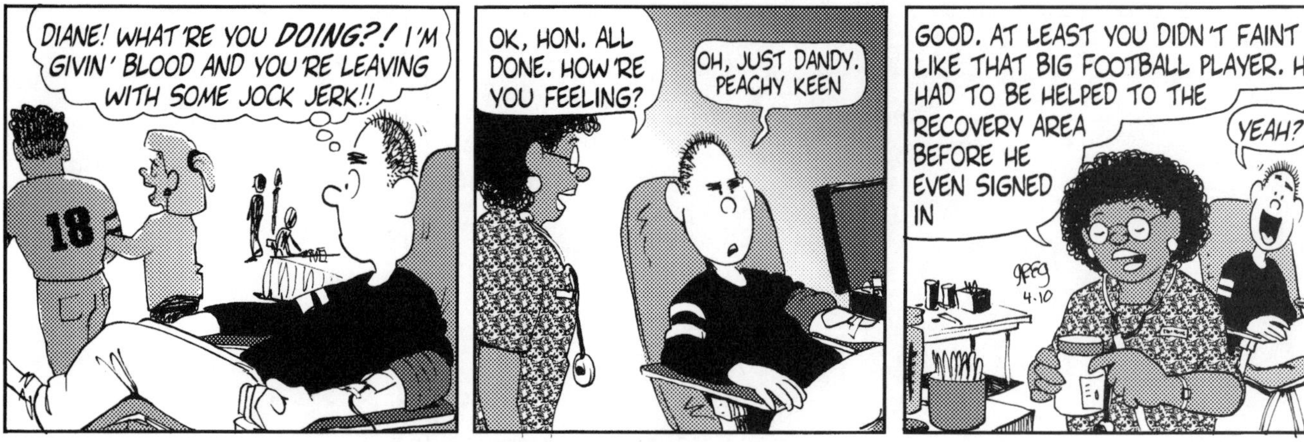
DIANE! WHAT'RE YOU *DOING?!* I'M GIVIN' BLOOD AND YOU'RE LEAVING WITH SOME JOCK JERK!!
OK, HON. ALL DONE. HOW'RE YOU FEELING?
OH, JUST DANDY. PEACHY KEEN
GOOD. AT LEAST YOU DIDN'T FAINT LIKE THAT BIG FOOTBALL PLAYER. HE HAD TO BE HELPED TO THE RECOVERY AREA BEFORE HE EVEN SIGNED IN
YEAH?
GREG 4·10

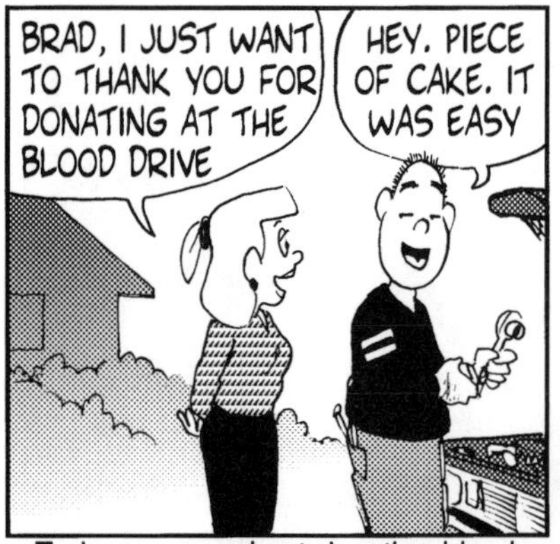
BRAD, I JUST WANT TO THANK YOU FOR DONATING AT THE BLOOD DRIVE
HEY. PIECE OF CAKE. IT WAS EASY

To learn more about donating blood, call 1-888-BLOOD88

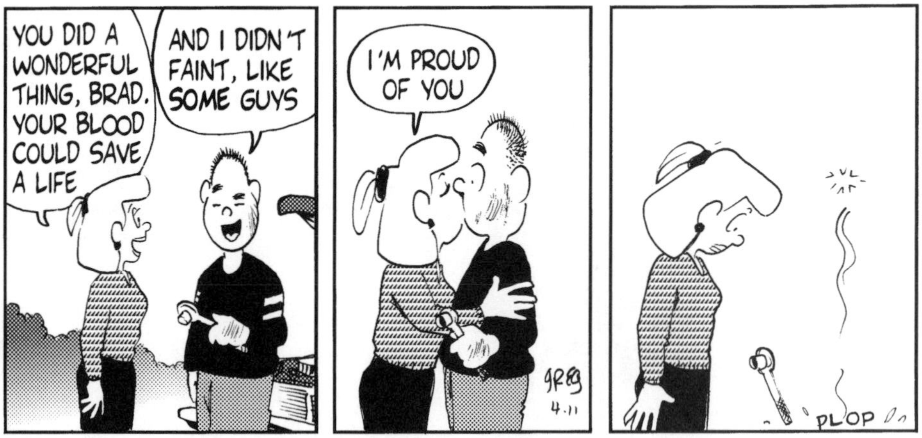
YOU DID A WONDERFUL THING, BRAD. YOUR BLOOD COULD SAVE A LIFE
AND I DIDN'T FAINT, LIKE SOME GUYS
I'M PROUD OF YOU
GREG 4·11
PLOP

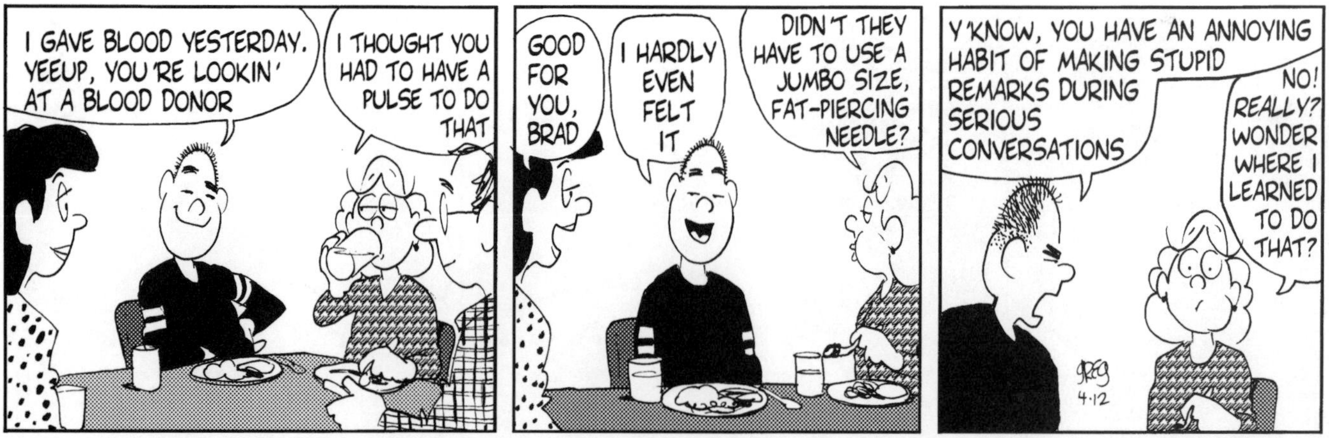
I GAVE BLOOD YESTERDAY. YEEUP, YOU'RE LOOKIN' AT A BLOOD DONOR
I THOUGHT YOU HAD TO HAVE A PULSE TO DO THAT
GOOD FOR YOU, BRAD
I HARDLY EVEN FELT IT
DIDN'T THEY HAVE TO USE A JUMBO SIZE, FAT-PIERCING NEEDLE?
Y'KNOW, YOU HAVE AN ANNOYING HABIT OF MAKING STUPID REMARKS DURING SERIOUS CONVERSATIONS
NO! *REALLY?* WONDER WHERE I LEARNED TO DO THAT?
GREG 4·12

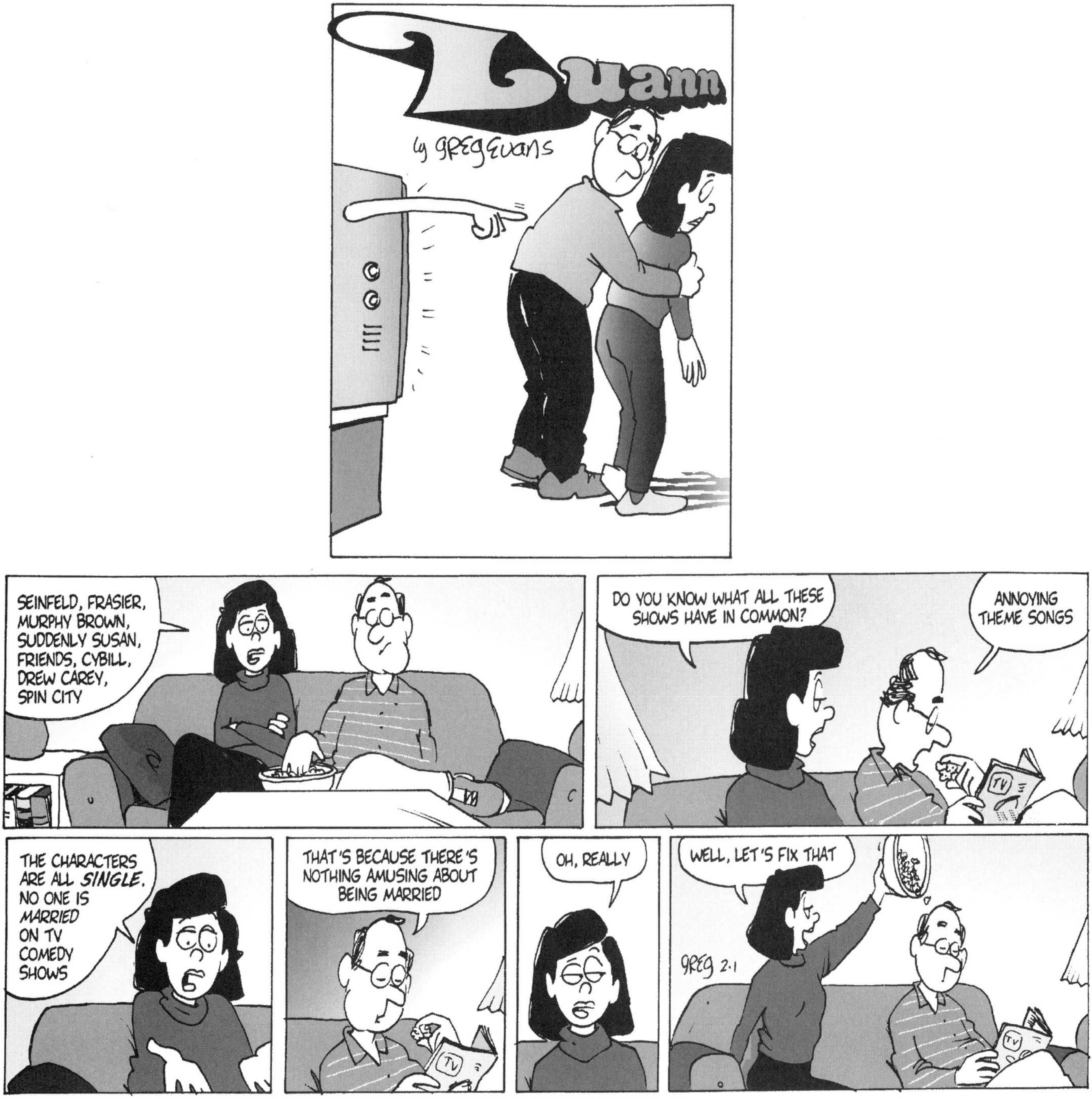
Luann
by GREG EVANS
SEINFELD, FRASIER, MURPHY BROWN, SUDDENLY SUSAN, FRIENDS, CYBILL, DREW CAREY, SPIN CITY
DO YOU KNOW WHAT ALL THESE SHOWS HAVE IN COMMON?
ANNOYING THEME SONGS
THE CHARACTERS ARE ALL SINGLE. NO ONE IS MARRIED ON TV COMEDY SHOWS
THAT'S BECAUSE THERE'S NOTHING AMUSING ABOUT BEING MARRIED
OH, REALLY
WELL, LET'S FIX THAT
GREG 2.1

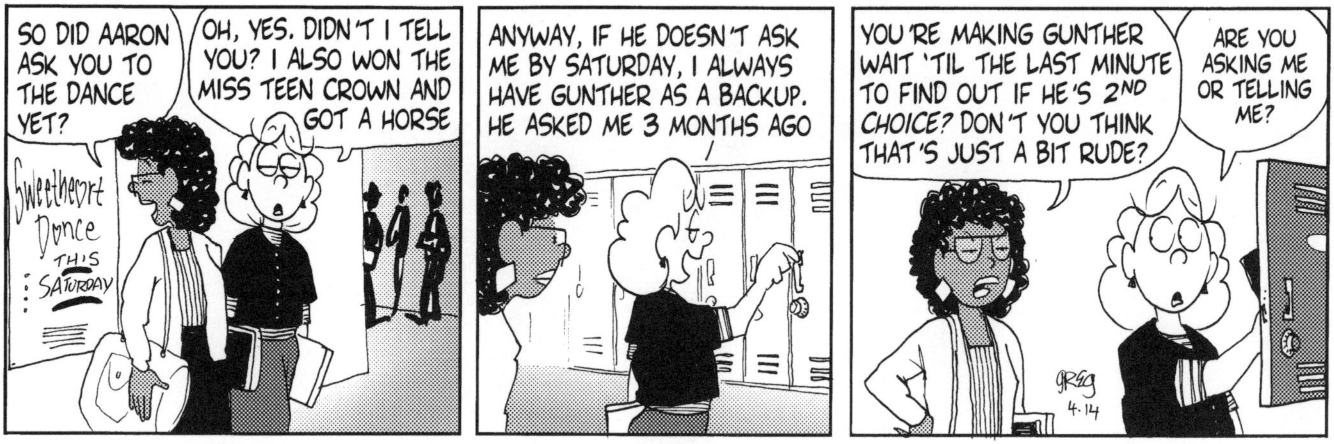
SO DID AARON ASK YOU TO THE DANCE YET?
OH, YES. DIDN'T I TELL YOU? I ALSO WON THE MISS TEEN CROWN AND GOT A HORSE
Sweetheart Dance THIS SATURDAY
ANYWAY, IF HE DOESN'T ASK ME BY SATURDAY, I ALWAYS HAVE GUNTHER AS A BACKUP. HE ASKED ME 3 MONTHS AGO
YOU'RE MAKING GUNTHER WAIT 'TIL THE LAST MINUTE TO FIND OUT IF HE'S 2ND *CHOICE?* DON'T YOU THINK THAT'S JUST A BIT RUDE?
ARE YOU ASKING ME OR TELLING ME?
GREG 4-14

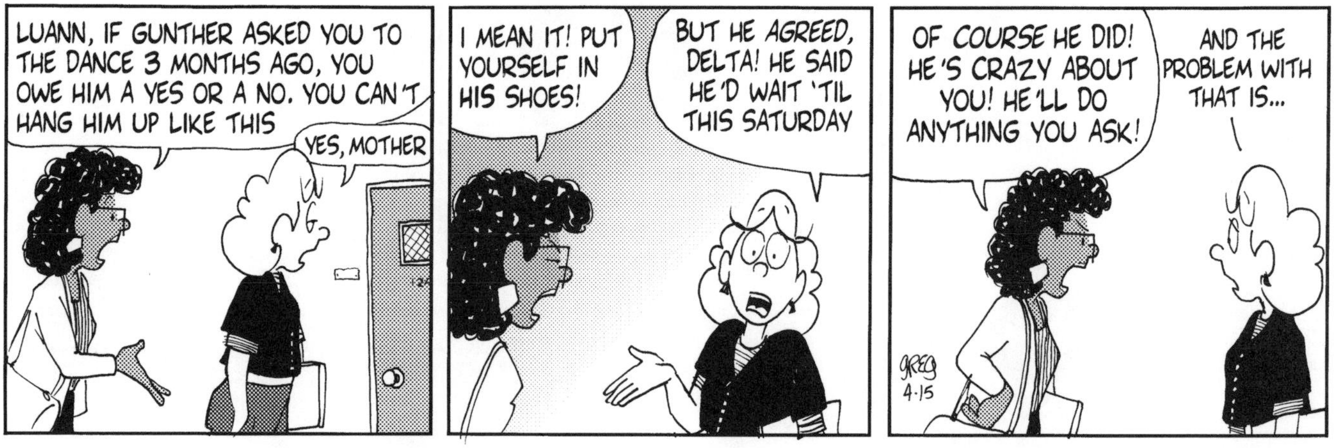
LUANN, IF GUNTHER ASKED YOU TO THE DANCE 3 MONTHS AGO, YOU OWE HIM A YES OR A NO. YOU CAN'T HANG HIM UP LIKE THIS
YES, MOTHER
I MEAN IT! PUT YOURSELF IN HIS SHOES!
BUT HE *AGREED,* DELTA! HE SAID HE'D WAIT 'TIL THIS SATURDAY
OF *COURSE* HE DID! HE'S CRAZY ABOUT YOU! HE'LL DO ANYTHING YOU ASK!
AND THE PROBLEM WITH THAT IS...
GREG 4-15

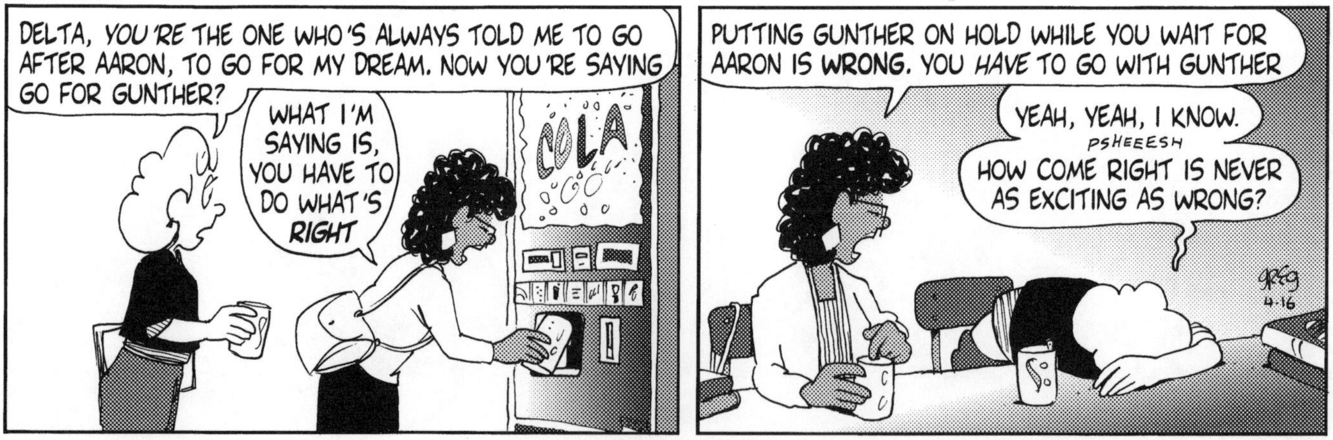
DELTA, *YOU'RE* THE ONE WHO'S ALWAYS TOLD ME TO GO AFTER AARON, TO GO FOR MY DREAM. NOW YOU'RE SAYING GO FOR GUNTHER?
WHAT I'M SAYING IS, YOU HAVE TO DO WHAT'S **RIGHT**
COLA
PUTTING GUNTHER ON HOLD WHILE YOU WAIT FOR AARON IS **WRONG**. YOU *HAVE* TO GO WITH GUNTHER
YEAH, YEAH, I KNOW.
PSHEEESH
HOW COME RIGHT IS NEVER AS EXCITING AS WRONG?
GREG 4-16

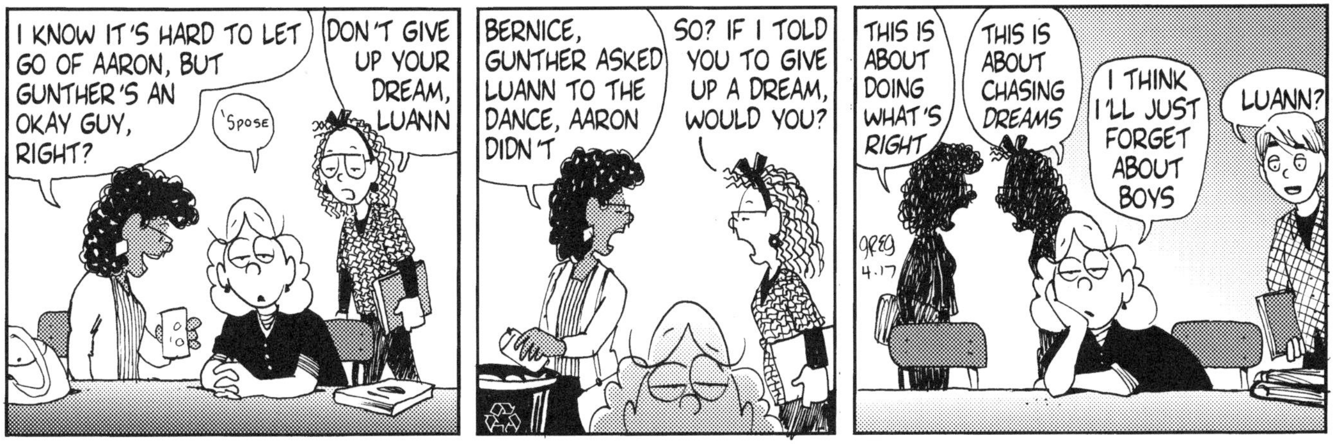
I KNOW IT'S HARD TO LET GO OF AARON, BUT GUNTHER'S AN OKAY GUY, RIGHT?
'SPOSE
DON'T GIVE UP YOUR DREAM, LUANN
BERNICE, GUNTHER ASKED LUANN TO THE DANCE, AARON DIDN'T
SO? IF I TOLD YOU TO GIVE UP A DREAM, WOULD YOU?
THIS IS ABOUT DOING WHAT'S RIGHT
THIS IS ABOUT CHASING *DREAMS*
I THINK I'LL JUST FORGET ABOUT BOYS
LUANN?
GREG 4.17

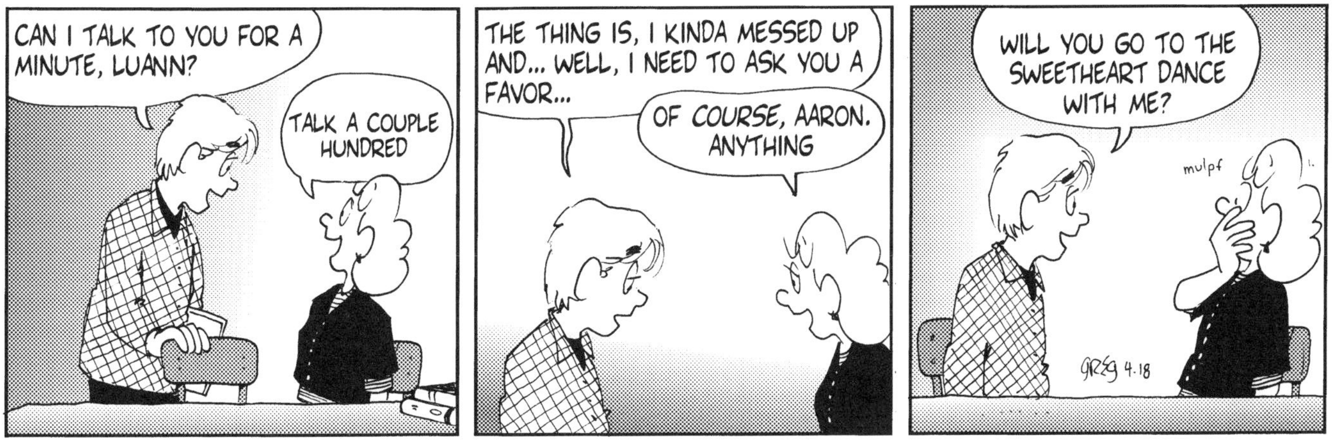
CAN I TALK TO YOU FOR A MINUTE, LUANN?
TALK A COUPLE HUNDRED
THE THING IS, I KINDA MESSED UP AND... WELL, I NEED TO ASK YOU A FAVOR...
OF *COURSE*, AARON. ANYTHING
WILL YOU GO TO THE SWEETHEART DANCE WITH ME?
mulpf
GREG 4.18

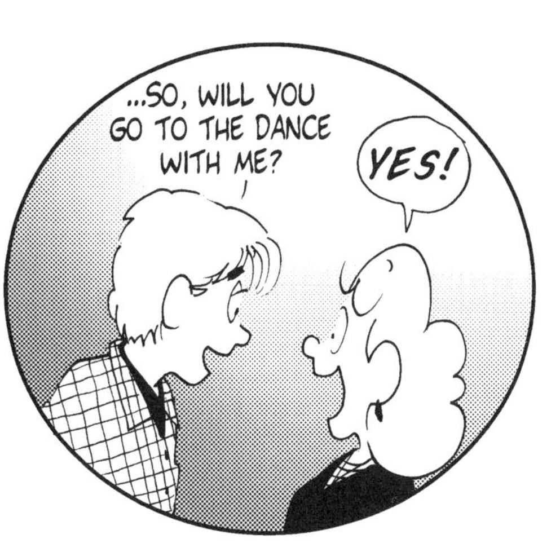
...SO, WILL YOU GO TO THE DANCE WITH ME?
YES!

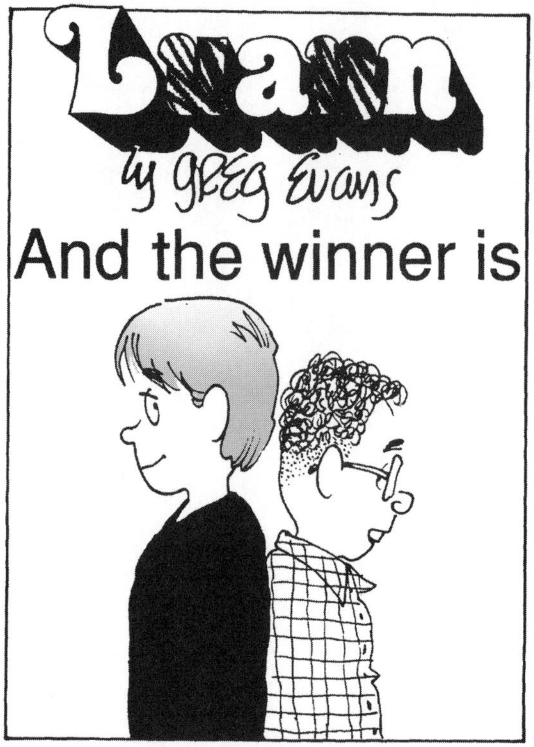

Luann
by Greg Evans
And the winner is

IT'S AARON HILL!

In February, readers were asked to help Luann choose between Aaron Hill and Gunther Berger. Thanks to all of you who voted by computer and mail. Here are the final results:

TOTAL VOTES
43,537

AARON: 23,836

GUNTHER: 19,701

Plus, there were nearly 5,000 write-in votes for "neither."

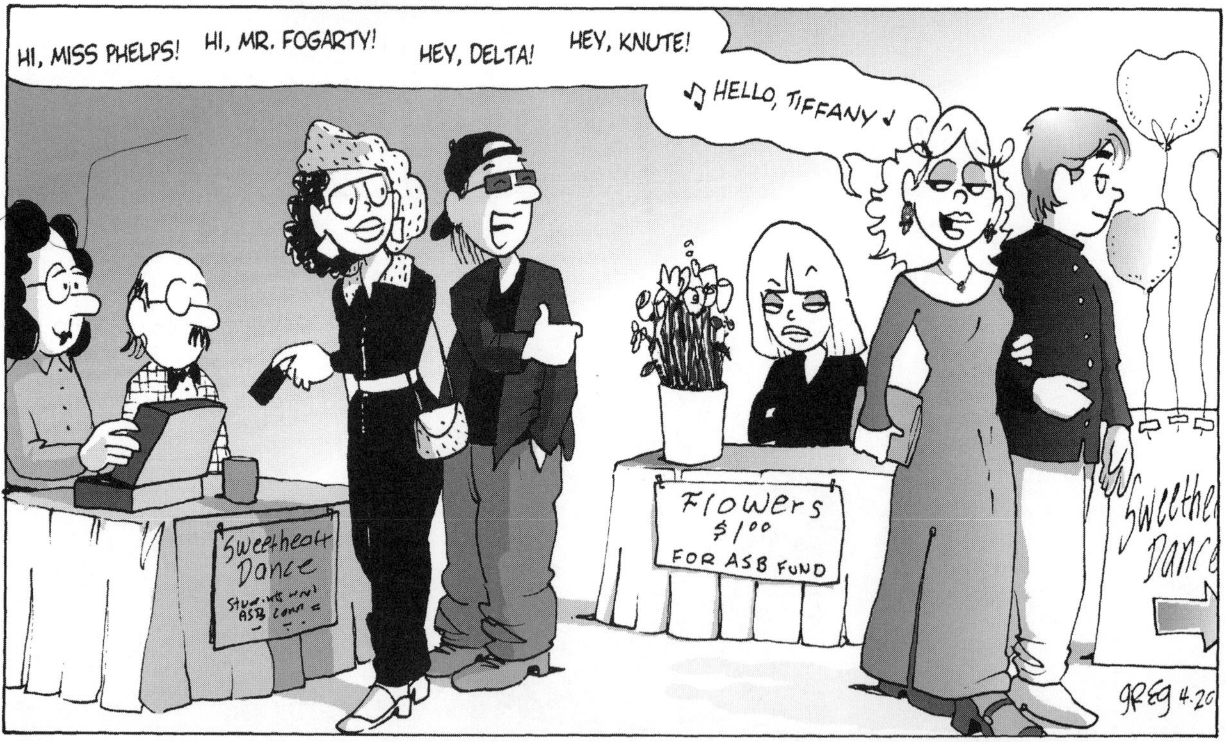

HI, MISS PHELPS!
HI, MR. FOGARTY!
HEY, DELTA!
HEY, KNUTE!
♫ HELLO, TIFFANY ♩
Sweetheart Dance
Flowers $1.00 FOR ASB FUND
GREG 4-20

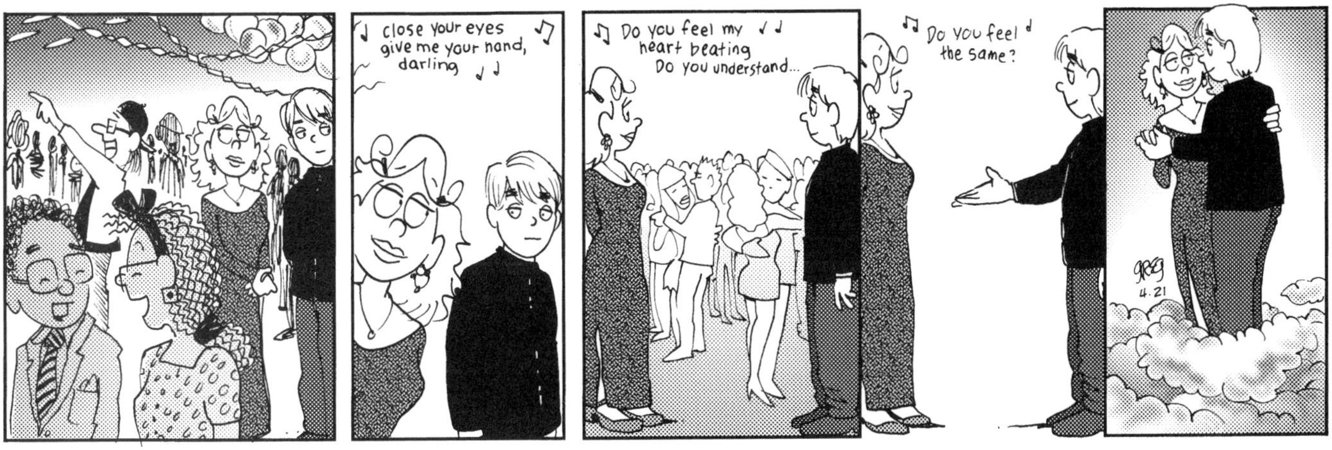
close your eyes give me your hand, darling
Do you feel my heart beating Do you understand...
Do you feel the same?

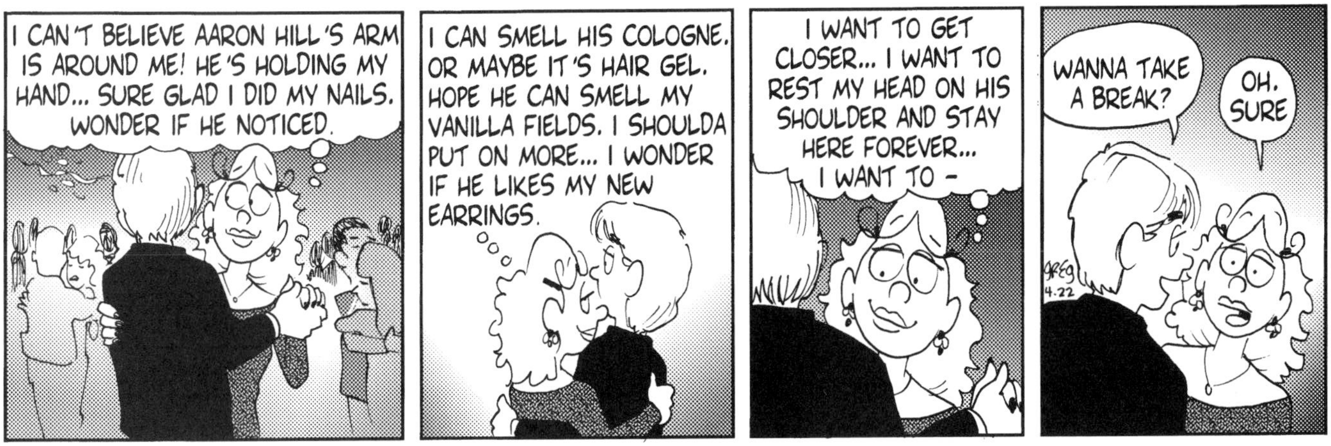
I CAN'T BELIEVE AARON HILL'S ARM IS AROUND ME! HE'S HOLDING MY HAND... SURE GLAD I DID MY NAILS. WONDER IF HE NOTICED.
I CAN SMELL HIS COLOGNE. OR MAYBE IT'S HAIR GEL. HOPE HE CAN SMELL MY VANILLA FIELDS. I SHOULDA PUT ON MORE... I WONDER IF HE LIKES MY NEW EARRINGS.
I WANT TO GET CLOSER... I WANT TO REST MY HEAD ON HIS SHOULDER AND STAY HERE FOREVER... I WANT TO –
WANNA TAKE A BREAK?
OH. SURE

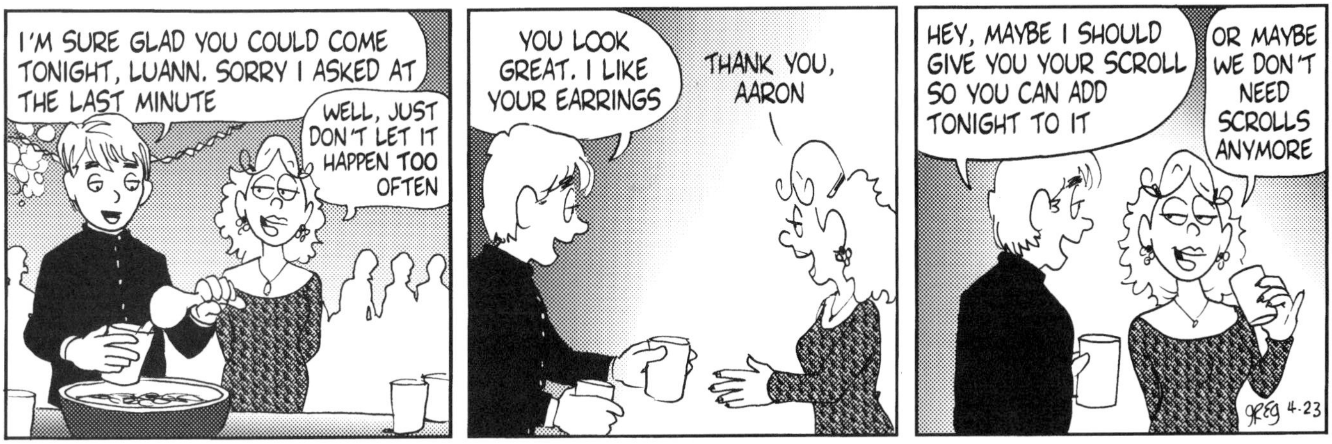
I'M SURE GLAD YOU COULD COME TONIGHT, LUANN. SORRY I ASKED AT THE LAST MINUTE
WELL, JUST DON'T LET IT HAPPEN TOO OFTEN
YOU LOOK GREAT. I LIKE YOUR EARRINGS
THANK YOU, AARON
HEY, MAYBE I SHOULD GIVE YOU YOUR SCROLL SO YOU CAN ADD TONIGHT TO IT
OR MAYBE WE DON'T NEED SCROLLS ANYMORE

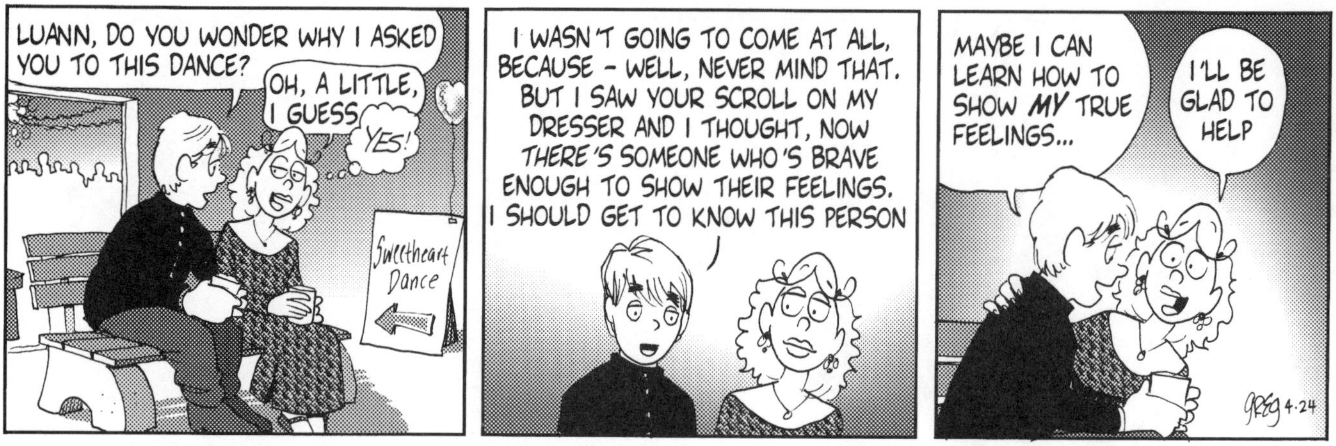
LUANN, DO YOU WONDER WHY I ASKED YOU TO THIS DANCE?
OH, A LITTLE, I GUESS
YES!
Sweetheart Dance
I WASN'T GOING TO COME AT ALL, BECAUSE - WELL, NEVER MIND THAT. BUT I SAW YOUR SCROLL ON MY DRESSER AND I THOUGHT, NOW THERE'S SOMEONE WHO'S BRAVE ENOUGH TO SHOW THEIR FEELINGS. I SHOULD GET TO KNOW THIS PERSON
MAYBE I CAN LEARN HOW TO SHOW MY TRUE FEELINGS...
I'LL BE GLAD TO HELP
4·24

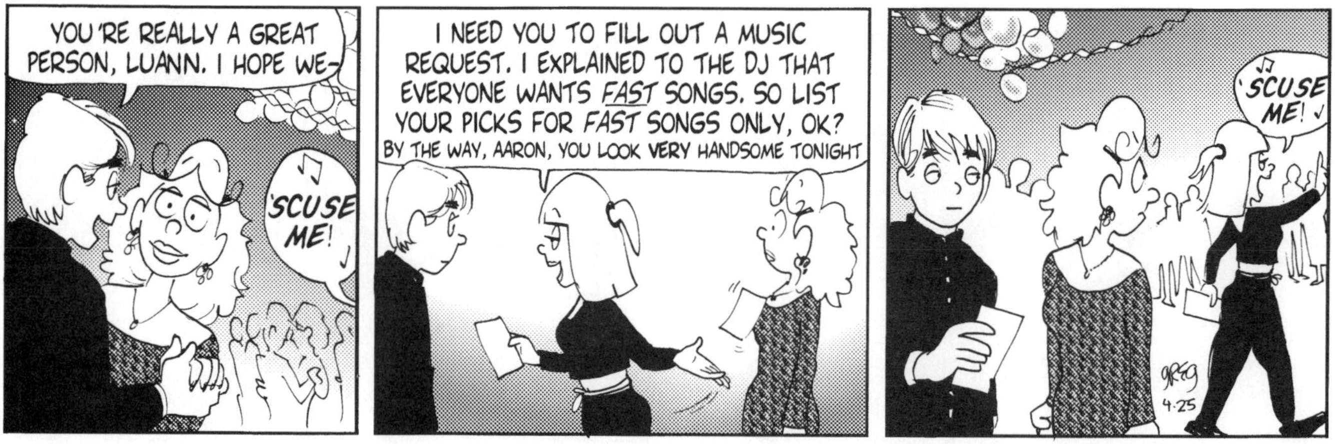
YOU'RE REALLY A GREAT PERSON, LUANN. I HOPE WE-
'SCUSE ME!
I NEED YOU TO FILL OUT A MUSIC REQUEST. I EXPLAINED TO THE DJ THAT EVERYONE WANTS FAST SONGS. SO LIST YOUR PICKS FOR FAST SONGS ONLY, OK?
BY THE WAY, AARON, YOU LOOK VERY HANDSOME TONIGHT
'SCUSE ME!
4·25

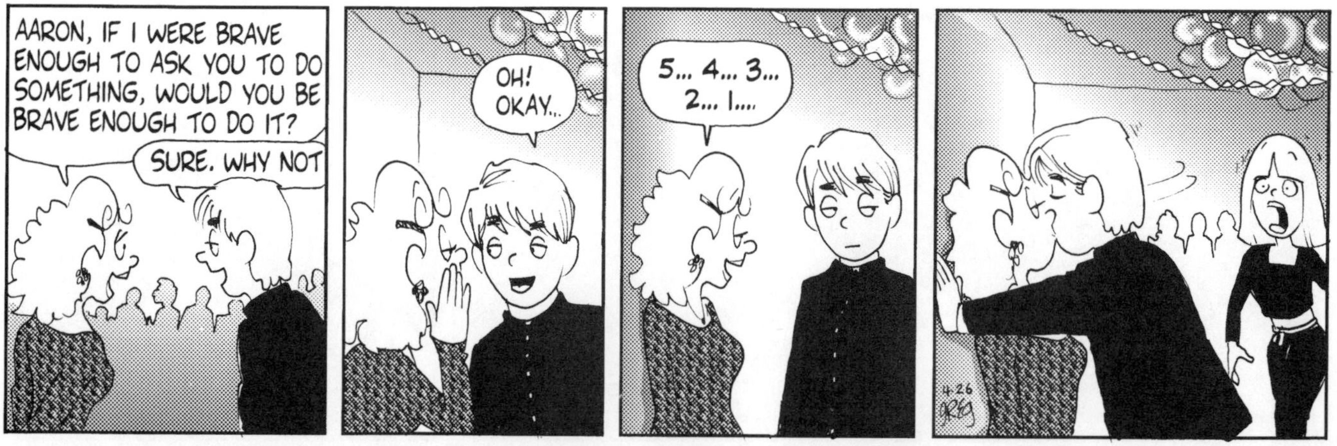
AARON, IF I WERE BRAVE ENOUGH TO ASK YOU TO DO SOMETHING, WOULD YOU BE BRAVE ENOUGH TO DO IT?
SURE. WHY NOT
OH! OKAY...
5... 4... 3... 2... 1....
4·26

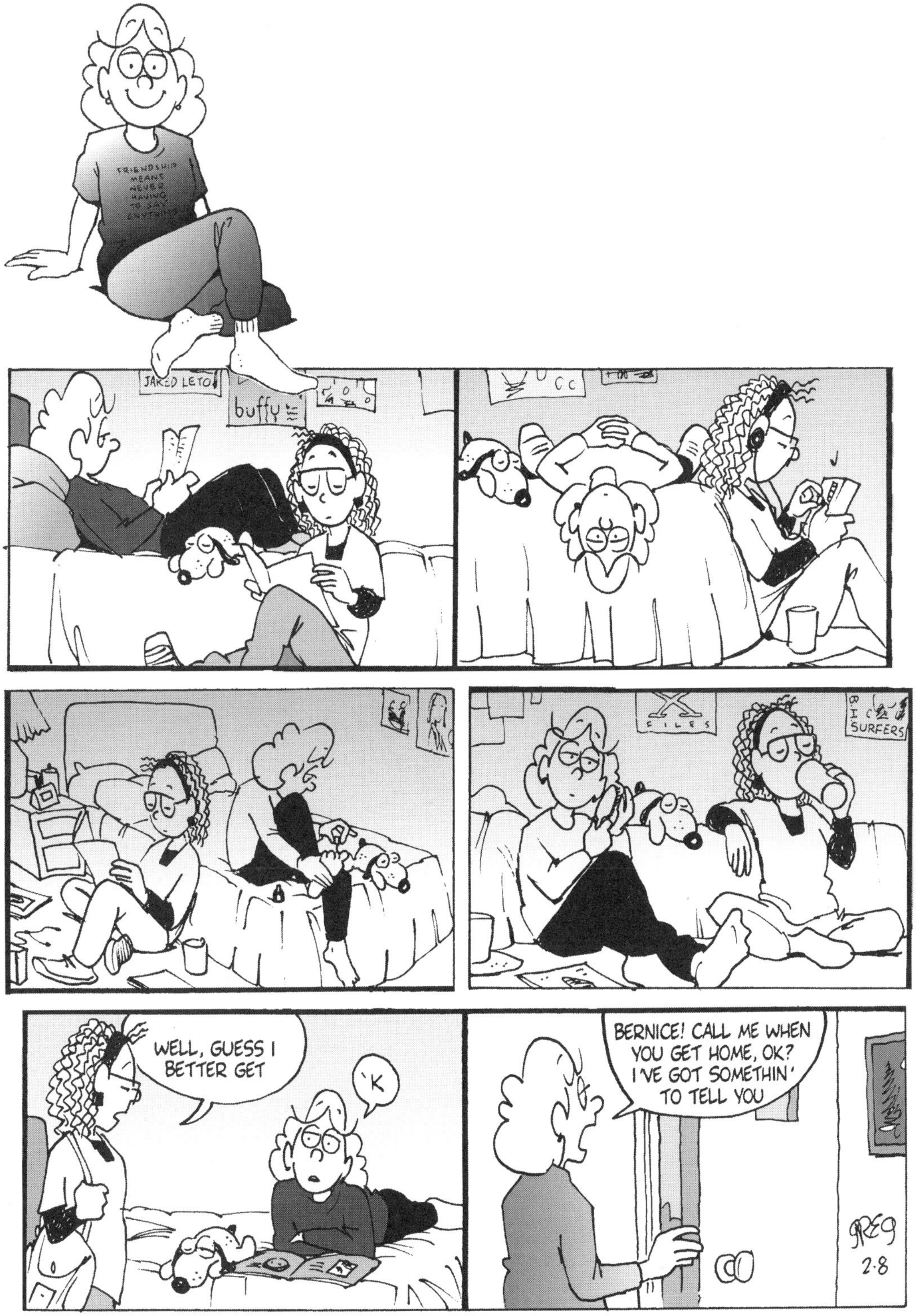
FRIENDSHIP MEANS NEVER HAVING TO SAY ANYTHING
JARED LETO
buffy
X FILES
SURFERS
WELL, GUESS I BETTER GET
'K
BERNICE! CALL ME WHEN YOU GET HOME, OK? I'VE GOT SOMETHIN' TO TELL YOU
GREG 2·8

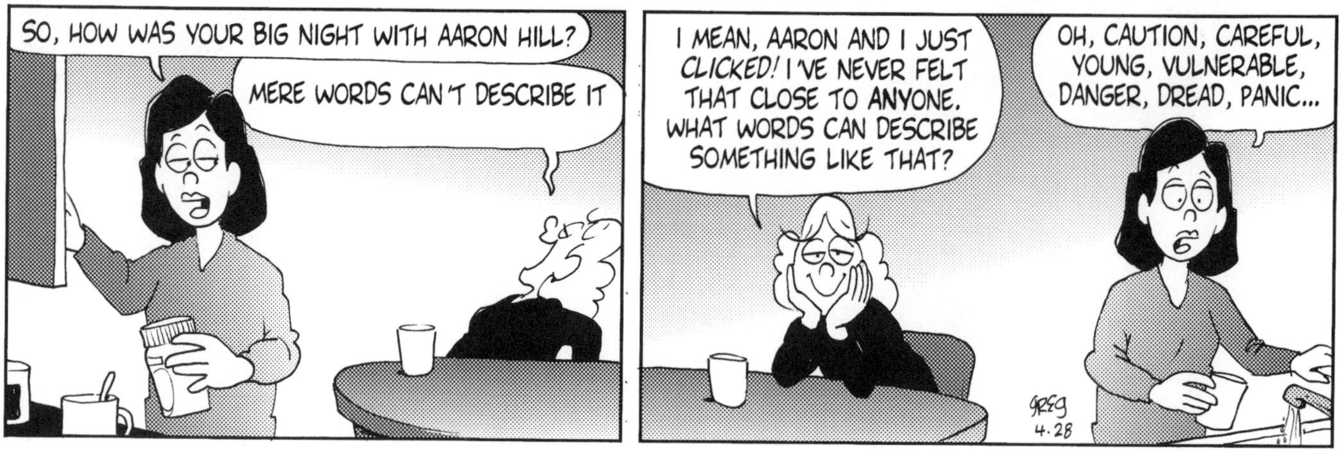
SO, HOW WAS YOUR BIG NIGHT WITH AARON HILL?
MERE WORDS CAN'T DESCRIBE IT
I MEAN, AARON AND I JUST CLICKED! I'VE NEVER FELT THAT CLOSE TO ANYONE. WHAT WORDS CAN DESCRIBE SOMETHING LIKE THAT?
OH, CAUTION, CAREFUL, YOUNG, VULNERABLE, DANGER, DREAD, PANIC...
GREG 4-28

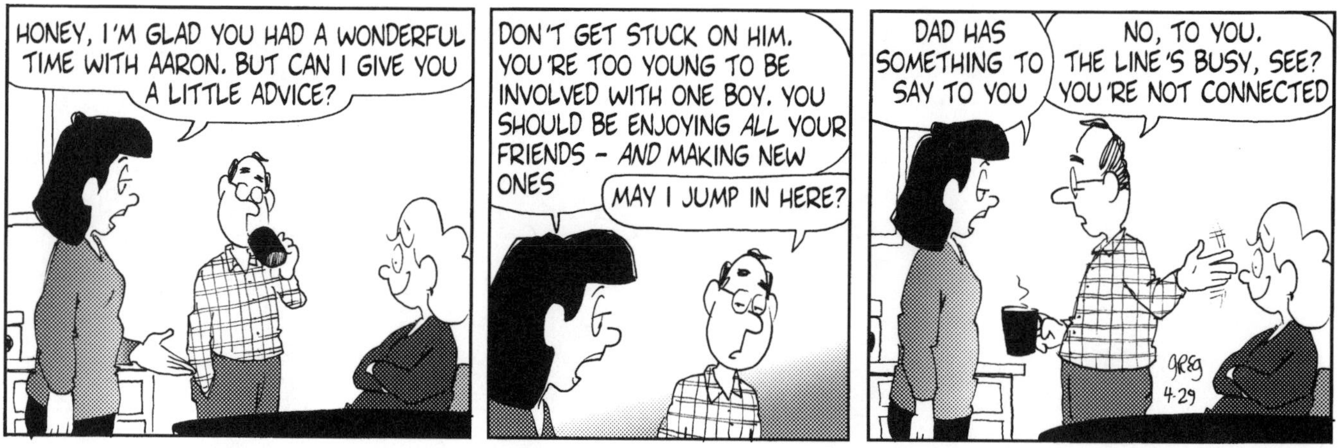
HONEY, I'M GLAD YOU HAD A WONDERFUL TIME WITH AARON. BUT CAN I GIVE YOU A LITTLE ADVICE?
DON'T GET STUCK ON HIM. YOU'RE TOO YOUNG TO BE INVOLVED WITH ONE BOY. YOU SHOULD BE ENJOYING ALL YOUR FRIENDS - AND MAKING NEW ONES
MAY I JUMP IN HERE?
DAD HAS SOMETHING TO SAY TO YOU
NO, TO YOU. THE LINE'S BUSY, SEE? YOU'RE NOT CONNECTED
GREG 4-29

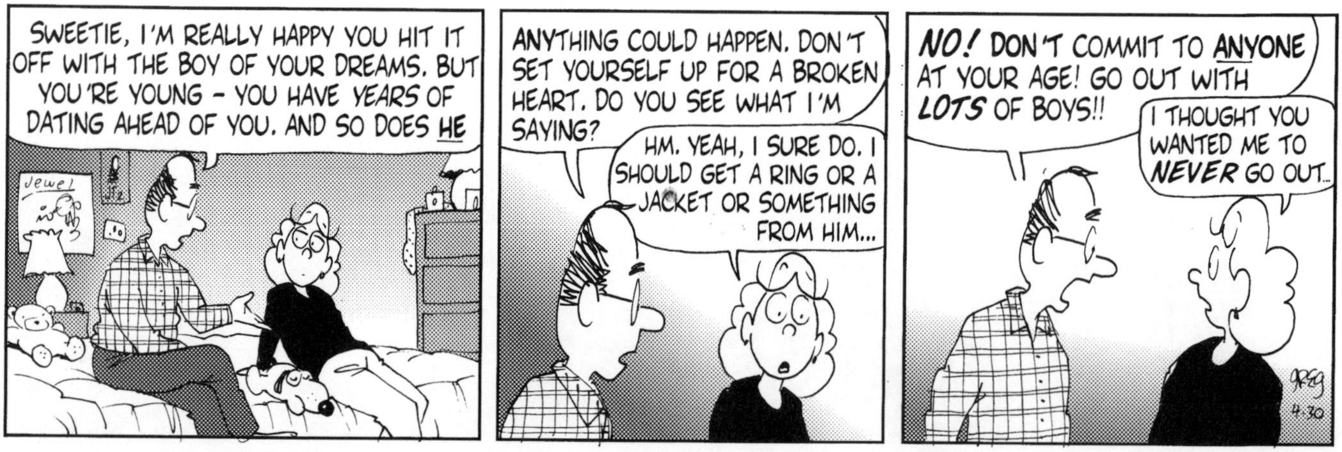
SWEETIE, I'M REALLY HAPPY YOU HIT IT OFF WITH THE BOY OF YOUR DREAMS. BUT YOU'RE YOUNG - YOU HAVE YEARS OF DATING AHEAD OF YOU. AND SO DOES HE
ANYTHING COULD HAPPEN. DON'T SET YOURSELF UP FOR A BROKEN HEART. DO YOU SEE WHAT I'M SAYING?
HM. YEAH, I SURE DO. I SHOULD GET A RING OR A JACKET OR SOMETHING FROM HIM...
NO! DON'T COMMIT TO ANYONE AT YOUR AGE! GO OUT WITH LOTS OF BOYS!!
I THOUGHT YOU WANTED ME TO NEVER GO OUT...
GREG 4-30

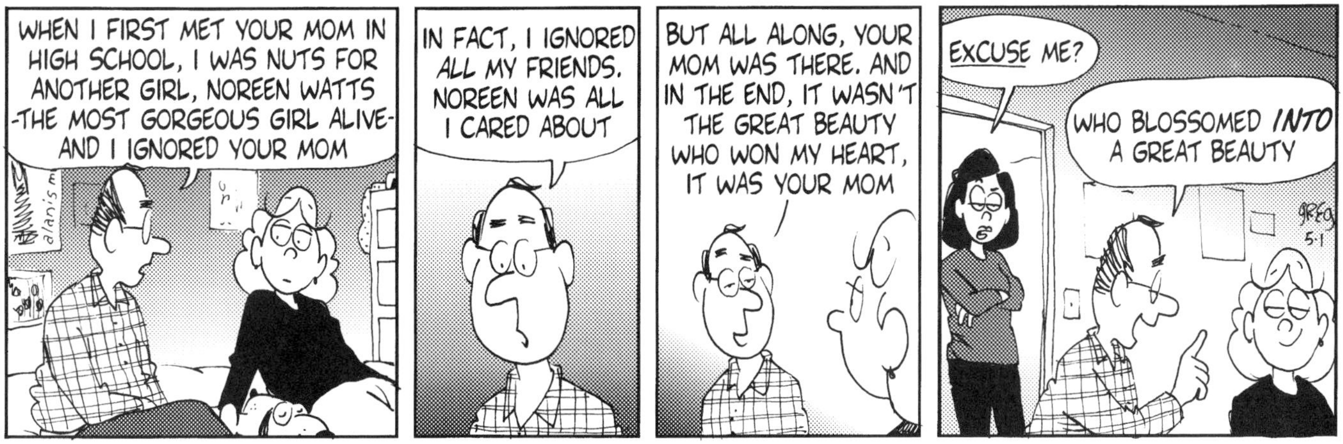
WHEN I FIRST MET YOUR MOM IN HIGH SCHOOL, I WAS NUTS FOR ANOTHER GIRL, NOREEN WATTS -THE MOST GORGEOUS GIRL ALIVE- AND I IGNORED YOUR MOM
IN FACT, I IGNORED ALL MY FRIENDS. NOREEN WAS ALL I CARED ABOUT
BUT ALL ALONG, YOUR MOM WAS THERE. AND IN THE END, IT WASN'T THE GREAT BEAUTY WHO WON MY HEART, IT WAS YOUR MOM
EXCUSE ME?
WHO BLOSSOMED INTO A GREAT BEAUTY

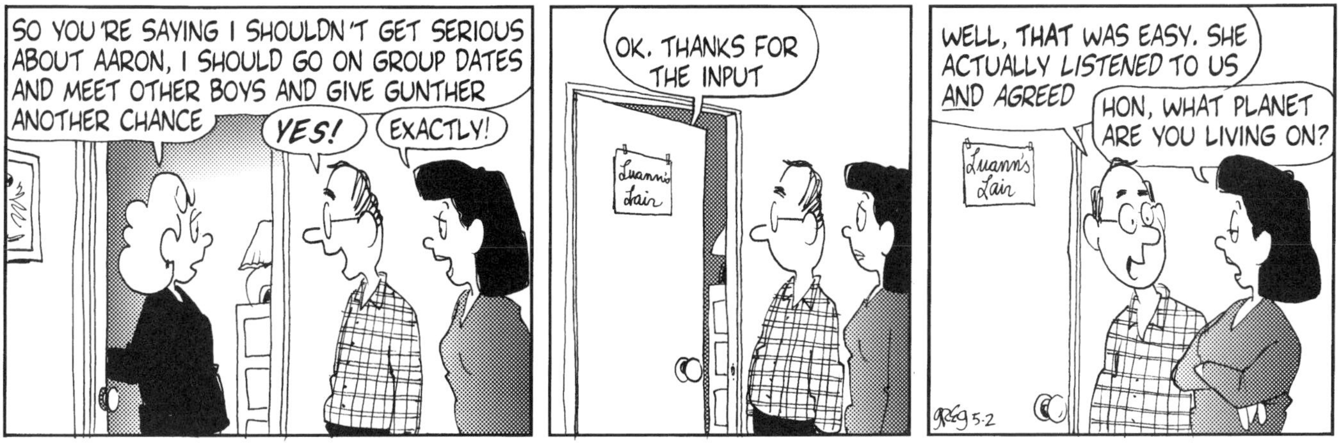
SO YOU'RE SAYING I SHOULDN'T GET SERIOUS ABOUT AARON, I SHOULD GO ON GROUP DATES AND MEET OTHER BOYS AND GIVE GUNTHER ANOTHER CHANCE
YES!
EXACTLY!
OK. THANKS FOR THE INPUT
Luann's Lair
WELL, THAT WAS EASY. SHE ACTUALLY LISTENED TO US AND AGREED
HON, WHAT PLANET ARE YOU LIVING ON?
Luann's Lair

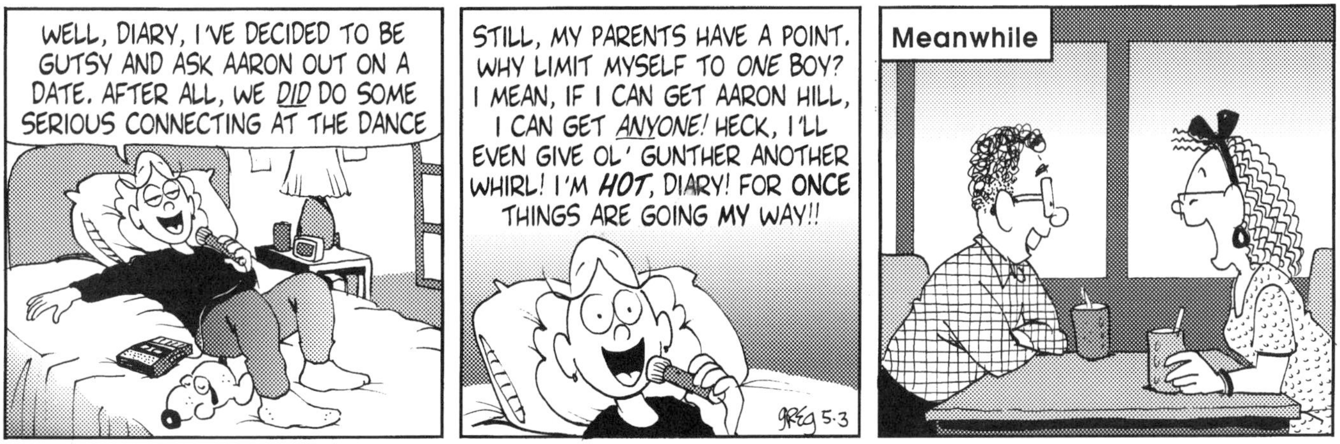
WELL, DIARY, I'VE DECIDED TO BE GUTSY AND ASK AARON OUT ON A DATE. AFTER ALL, WE DID DO SOME SERIOUS CONNECTING AT THE DANCE
STILL, MY PARENTS HAVE A POINT. WHY LIMIT MYSELF TO ONE BOY? I MEAN, IF I CAN GET AARON HILL, I CAN GET ANYONE! HECK, I'LL EVEN GIVE OL' GUNTHER ANOTHER WHIRL! I'M HOT, DIARY! FOR ONCE THINGS ARE GOING MY WAY!!
Meanwhile

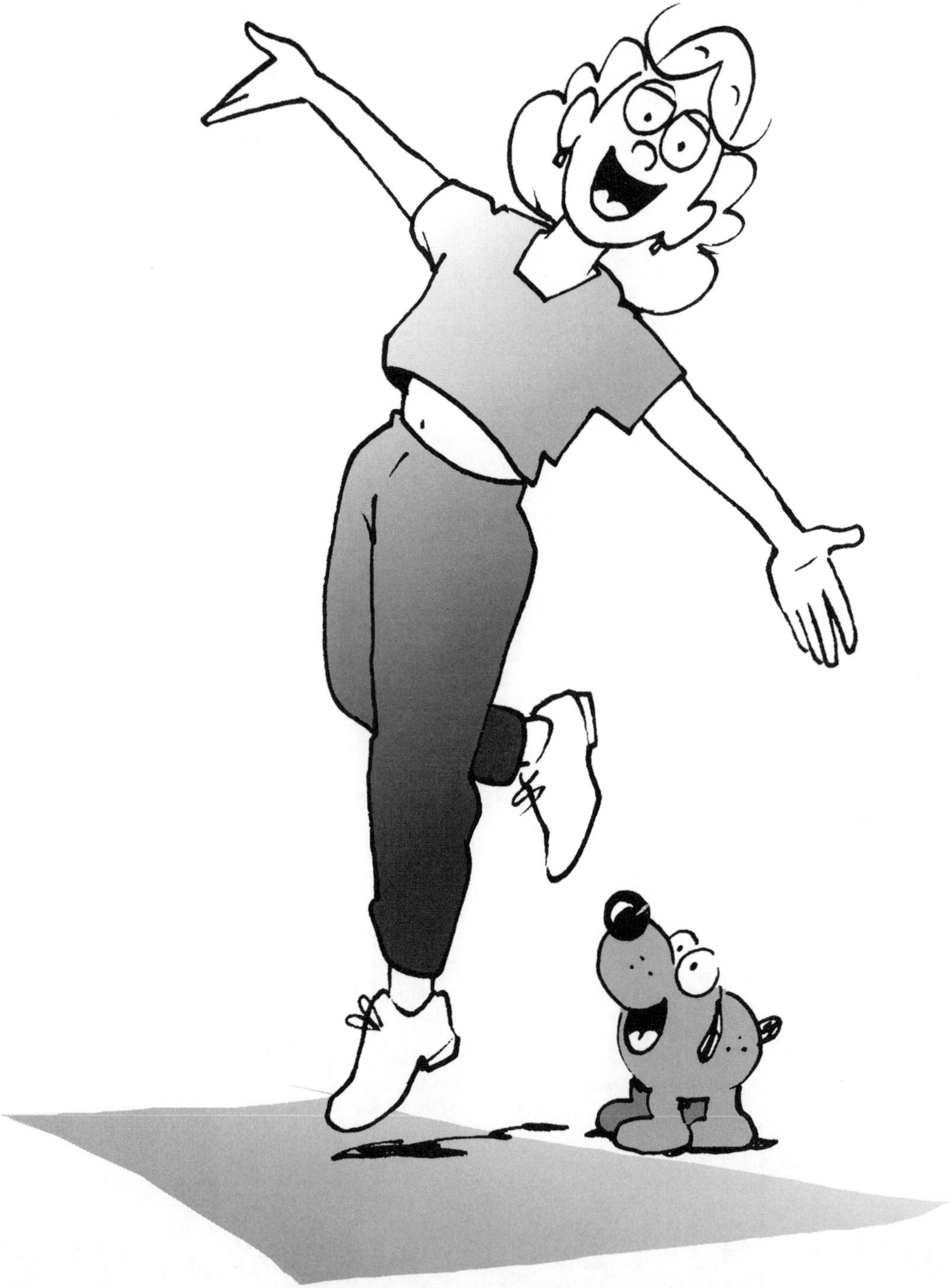

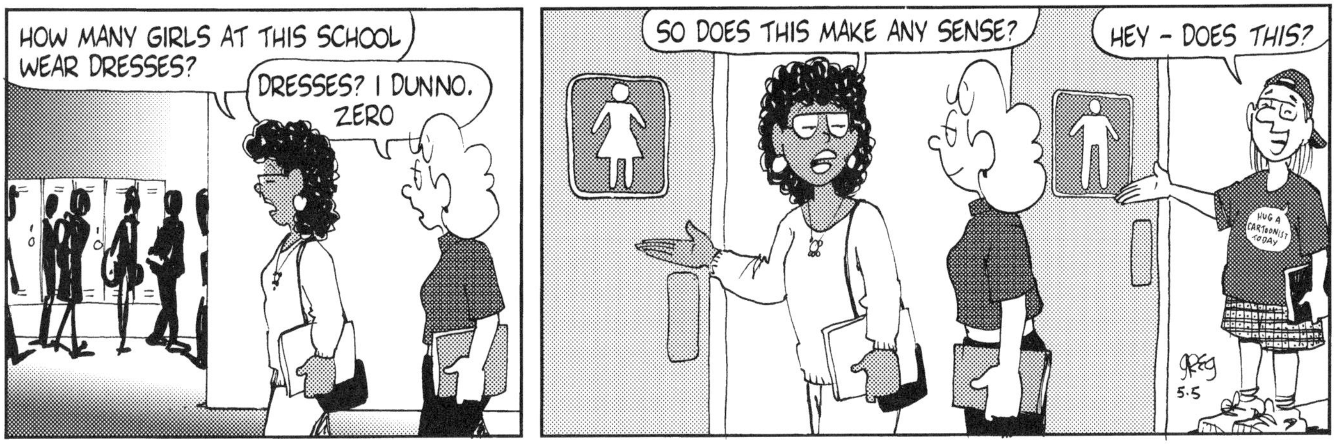
HOW MANY GIRLS AT THIS SCHOOL WEAR DRESSES?
DRESSES? I DUNNO. ZERO
SO DOES THIS MAKE ANY SENSE?
HEY – DOES THIS?
HUG A CARTOONIST TODAY
GREG 5·5

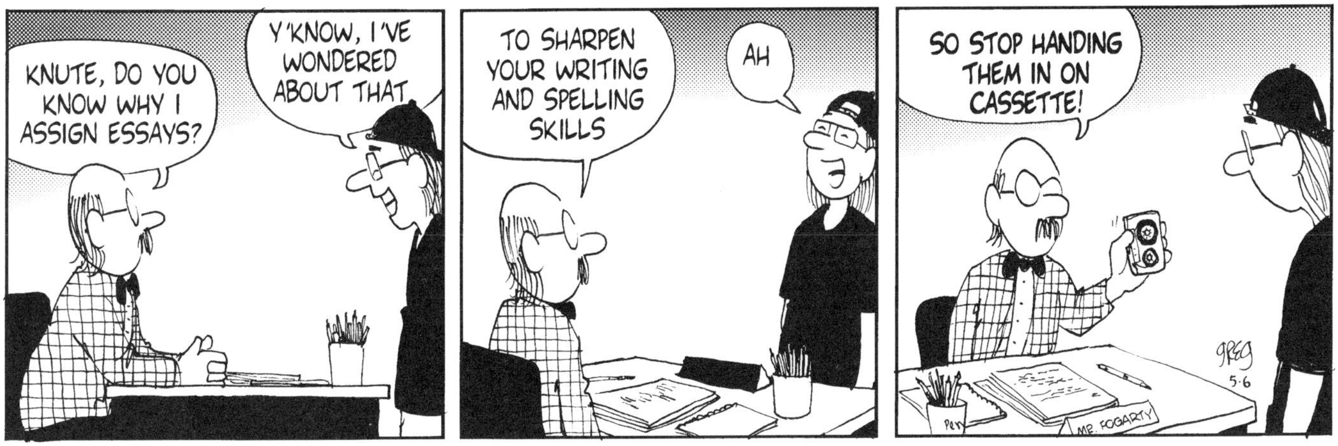
KNUTE, DO YOU KNOW WHY I ASSIGN ESSAYS?
Y'KNOW, I'VE WONDERED ABOUT THAT
TO SHARPEN YOUR WRITING AND SPELLING SKILLS
AH
SO STOP HANDING THEM IN ON CASSETTE!
MR. FOGARTY
GREG 5·6

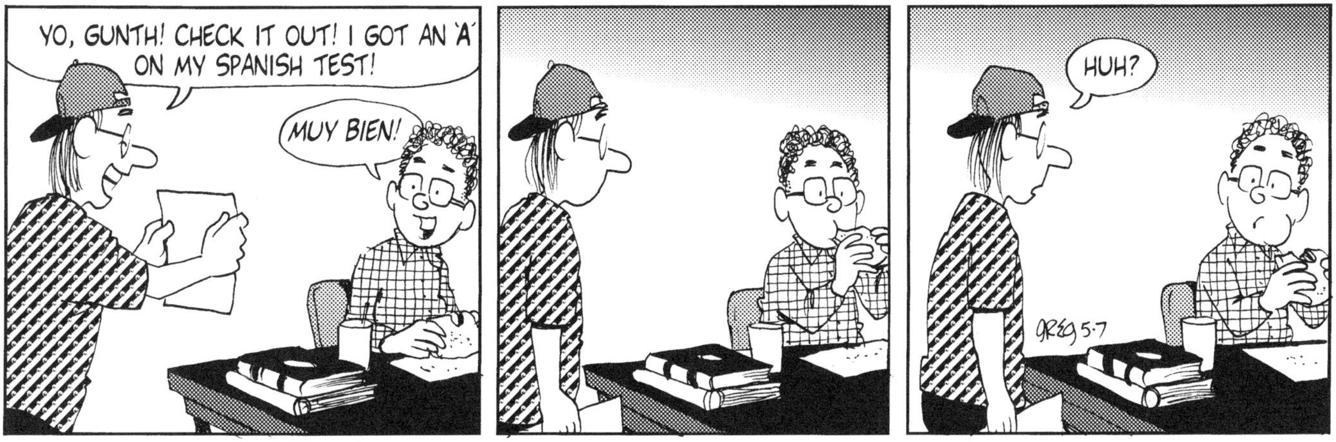
YO, GUNTH! CHECK IT OUT! I GOT AN 'A' ON MY SPANISH TEST!
MUY BIEN!
HUH?
GREG 5·7

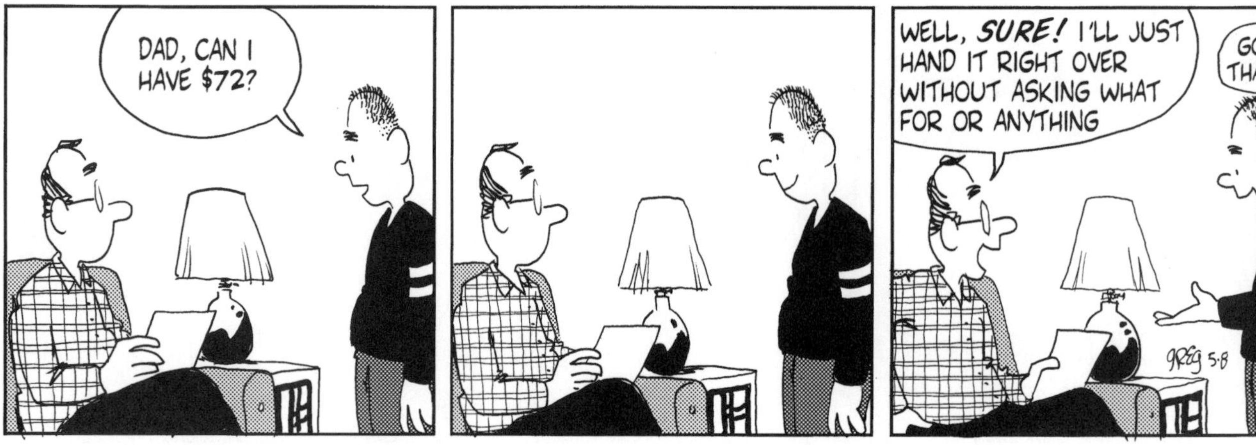
DAD, CAN I HAVE $72?
WELL, SURE! I'LL JUST HAND IT RIGHT OVER WITHOUT ASKING WHAT FOR OR ANYTHING
GOOD. THANKS

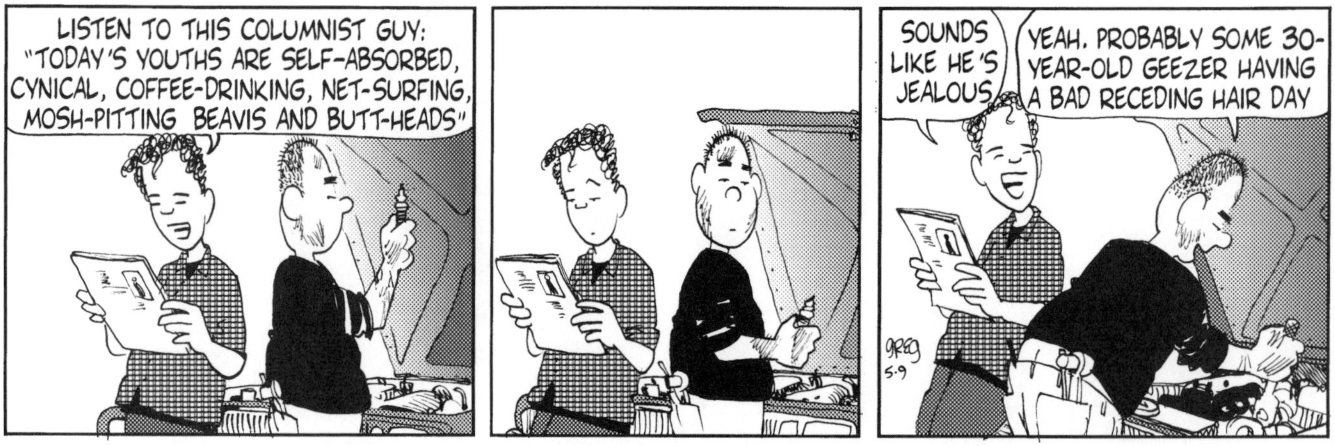
LISTEN TO THIS COLUMNIST GUY: "TODAY'S YOUTHS ARE SELF-ABSORBED, CYNICAL, COFFEE-DRINKING, NET-SURFING, MOSH-PITTING BEAVIS AND BUTT-HEADS"
SOUNDS LIKE HE'S JEALOUS
YEAH. PROBABLY SOME 30-YEAR-OLD GEEZER HAVING A BAD RECEDING HAIR DAY

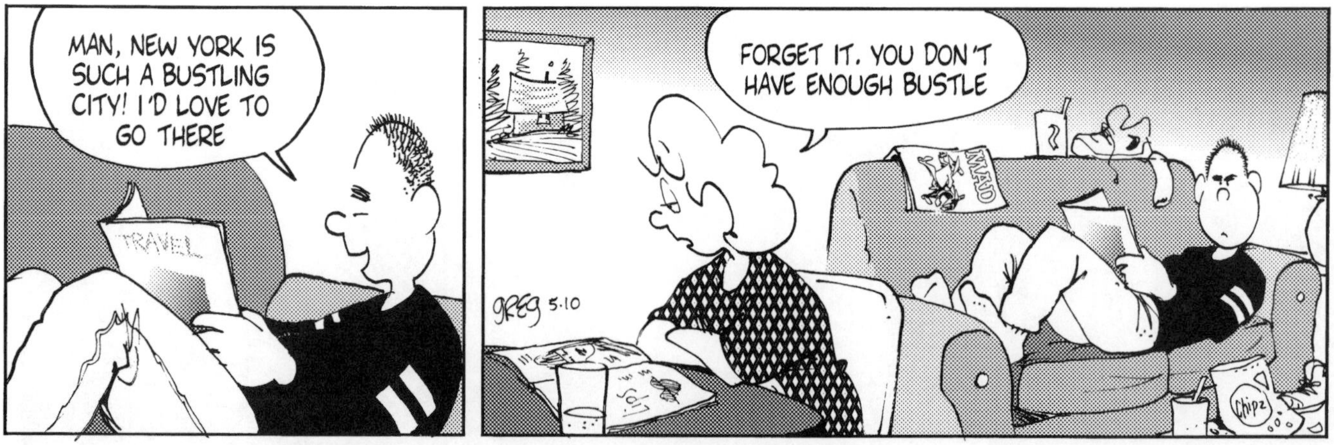
MAN, NEW YORK IS SUCH A BUSTLING CITY! I'D LOVE TO GO THERE
TRAVEL
FORGET IT. YOU DON'T HAVE ENOUGH BUSTLE
MAD

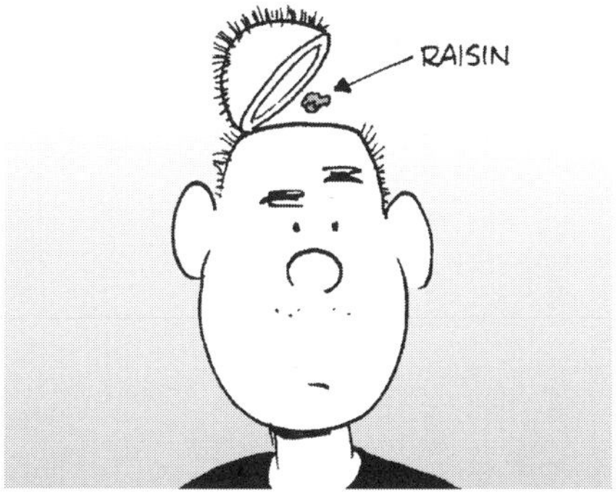
RAISIN

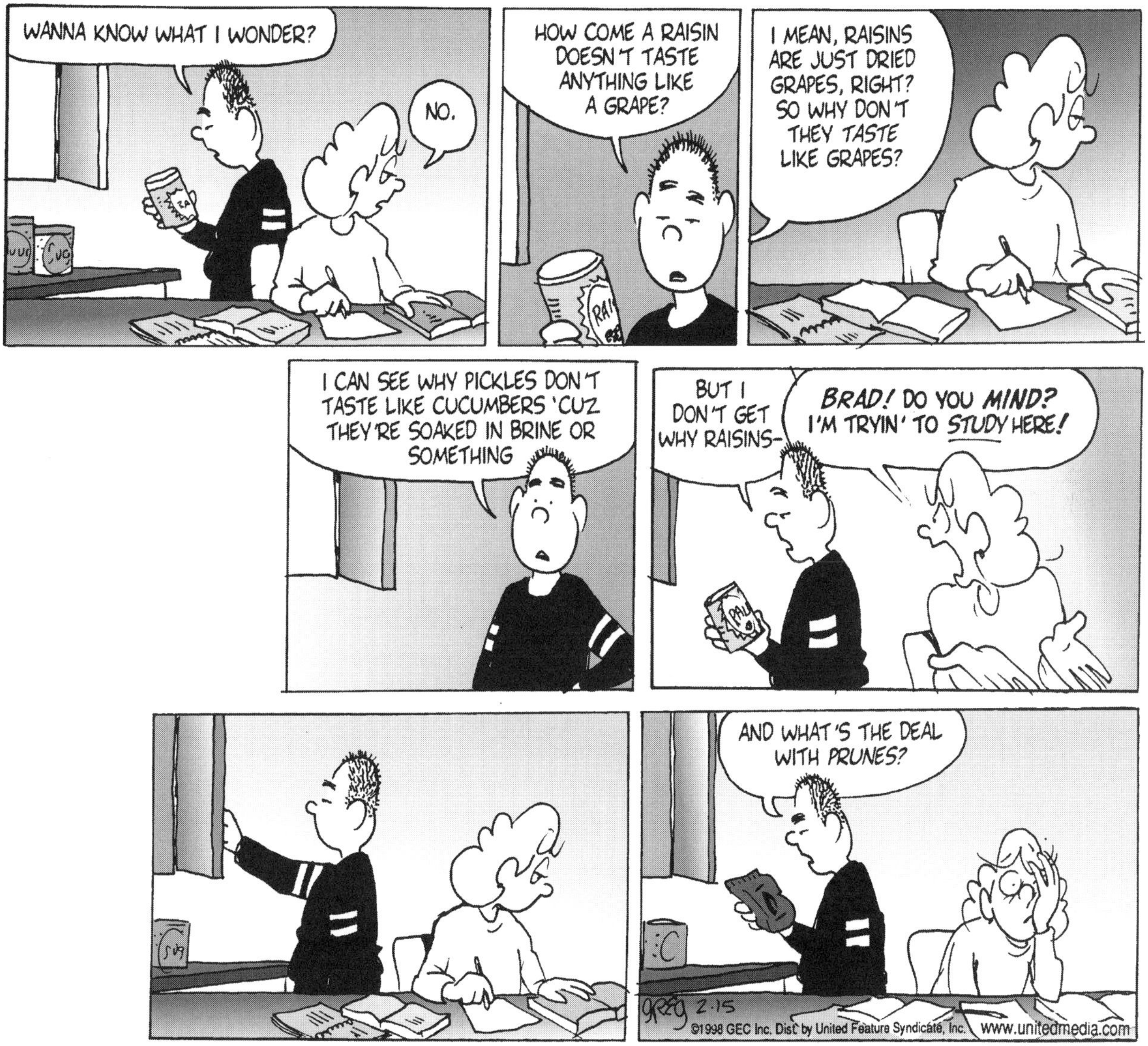
WANNA KNOW WHAT I WONDER?
NO.
HOW COME A RAISIN DOESN'T TASTE ANYTHING LIKE A GRAPE?
I MEAN, RAISINS ARE JUST DRIED GRAPES, RIGHT? SO WHY DON'T THEY *TASTE* LIKE GRAPES?
I CAN SEE WHY PICKLES DON'T TASTE LIKE CUCUMBERS 'CUZ THEY'RE SOAKED IN BRINE OR SOMETHING
BUT I DON'T GET WHY RAISINS-
BRAD! DO YOU *MIND?* I'M TRYIN' TO STUDY HERE!
AND WHAT'S THE DEAL WITH *PRUNES?*
GREG 2·15
©1998 GEC Inc. Dist. by United Feature Syndicate, Inc.
www.unitedmedia.com

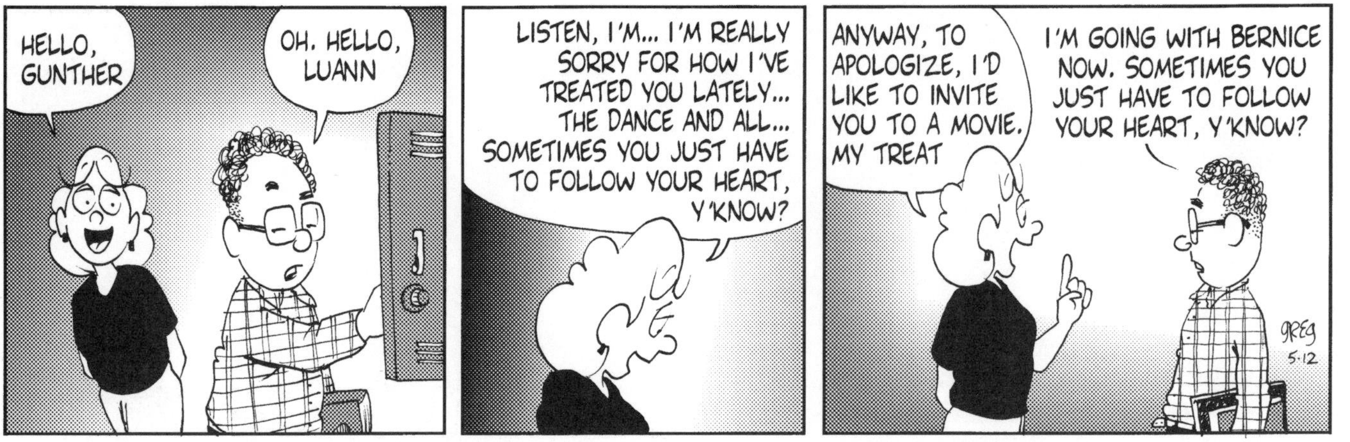
HELLO, GUNTHER
OH. HELLO, LUANN
LISTEN, I'M... I'M REALLY SORRY FOR HOW I'VE TREATED YOU LATELY... THE DANCE AND ALL... SOMETIMES YOU JUST HAVE TO FOLLOW YOUR HEART, Y'KNOW?
ANYWAY, TO APOLOGIZE, I'D LIKE TO INVITE YOU TO A MOVIE. MY TREAT
I'M GOING WITH BERNICE NOW. SOMETIMES YOU JUST HAVE TO FOLLOW YOUR HEART, Y'KNOW?
GREG 5-12

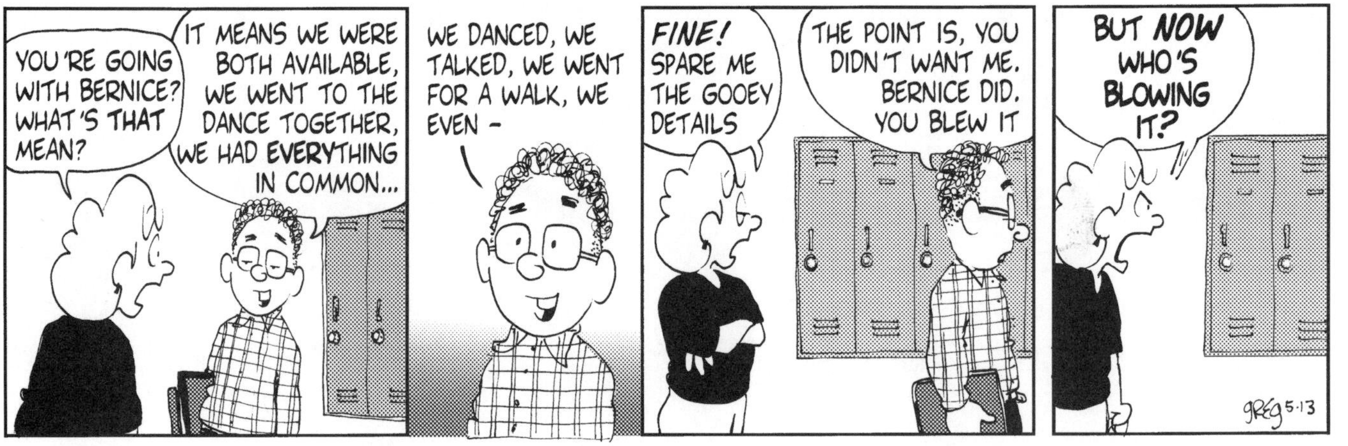
YOU'RE GOING WITH BERNICE? WHAT'S THAT MEAN?
IT MEANS WE WERE BOTH AVAILABLE, WE WENT TO THE DANCE TOGETHER, WE HAD EVERYTHING IN COMMON...
WE DANCED, WE TALKED, WE WENT FOR A WALK, WE EVEN –
FINE! SPARE ME THE GOOEY DETAILS
THE POINT IS, YOU DIDN'T WANT ME. BERNICE DID. YOU BLEW IT
BUT NOW WHO'S BLOWING IT?
GREG 5-13

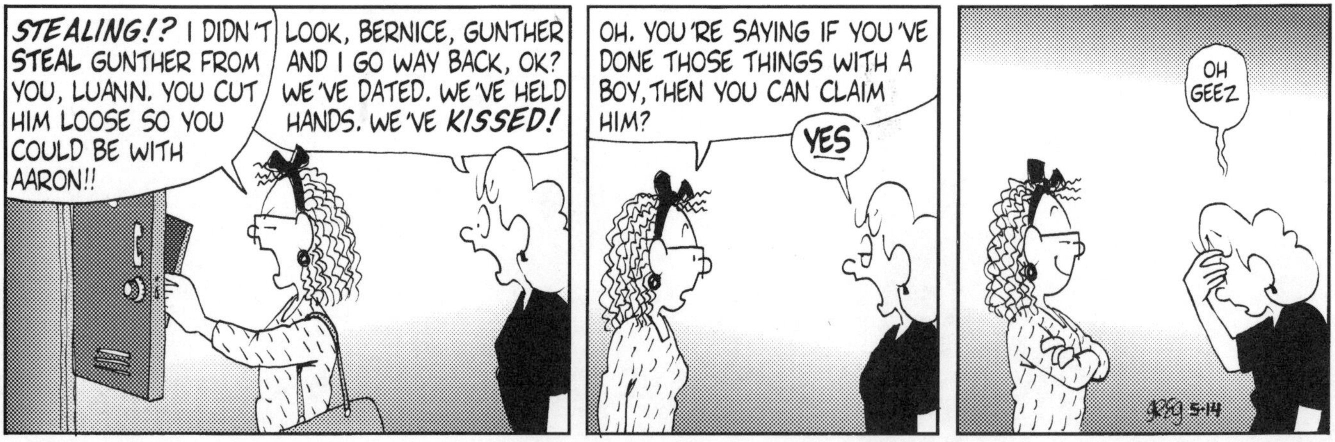
STEALING!? I DIDN'T STEAL GUNTHER FROM YOU, LUANN. YOU CUT HIM LOOSE SO YOU COULD BE WITH AARON!!
LOOK, BERNICE, GUNTHER AND I GO WAY BACK, OK? WE'VE DATED. WE'VE HELD HANDS. WE'VE KISSED!
OH. YOU'RE SAYING IF YOU'VE DONE THOSE THINGS WITH A BOY, THEN YOU CAN CLAIM HIM?
YES
OH GEEZ
GREG 5-14

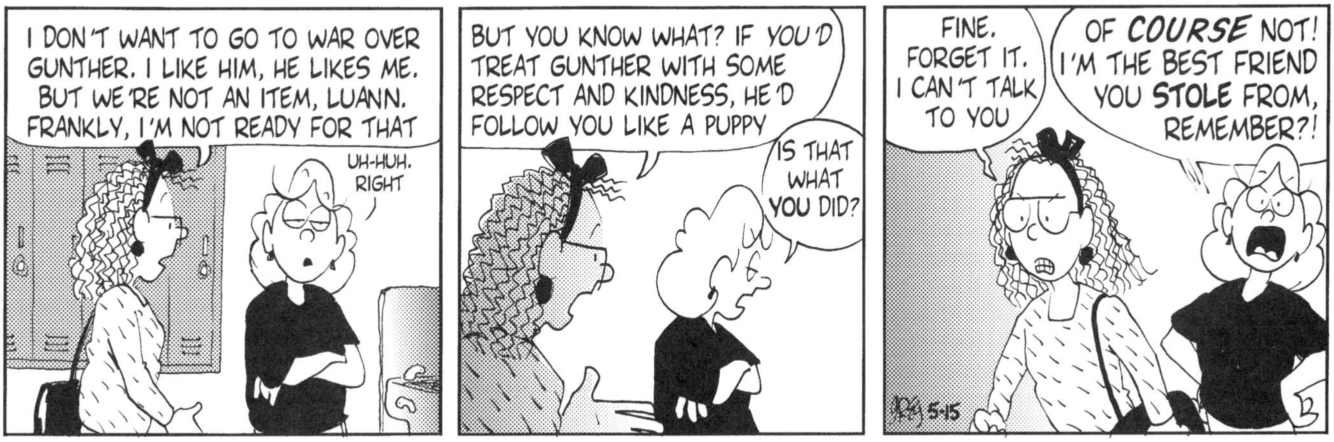
I DON'T WANT TO GO TO WAR OVER GUNTHER. I LIKE HIM, HE LIKES ME. BUT WE'RE NOT AN ITEM, LUANN. FRANKLY, I'M NOT READY FOR THAT
UH-HUH. RIGHT
BUT YOU KNOW WHAT? IF *YOU'D* TREAT GUNTHER WITH SOME RESPECT AND KINDNESS, HE'D FOLLOW YOU LIKE A PUPPY
IS THAT WHAT **YOU** DID?
FINE. FORGET IT. I CAN'T TALK TO YOU
OF ***COURSE*** NOT! I'M THE BEST FRIEND YOU **STOLE** FROM, REMEMBER?!

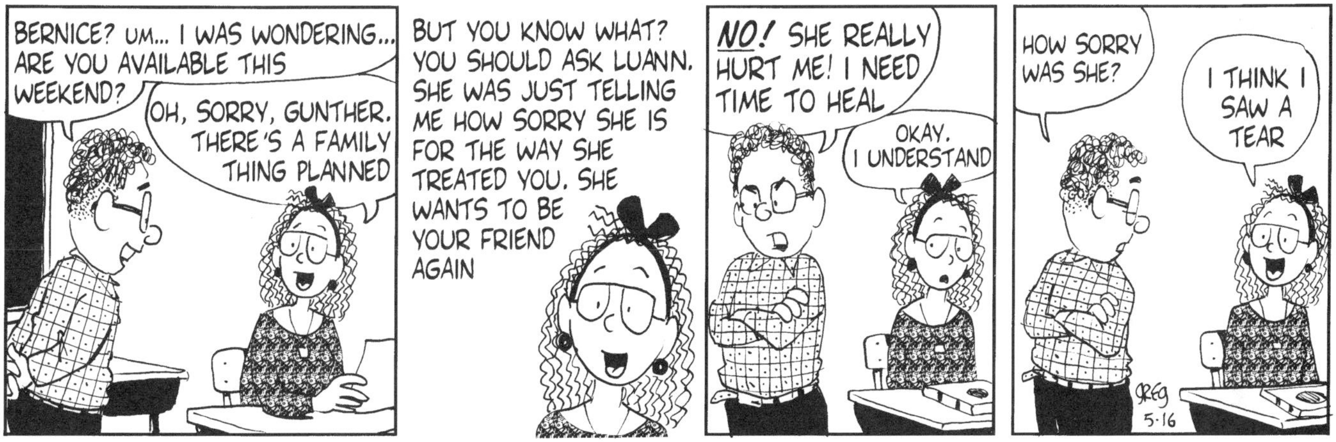
BERNICE? UM... I WAS WONDERING... ARE YOU AVAILABLE THIS WEEKEND?
OH, SORRY, GUNTHER. THERE'S A FAMILY THING PLANNED
BUT YOU KNOW WHAT? YOU SHOULD ASK LUANN. SHE WAS JUST TELLING ME HOW SORRY SHE IS FOR THE WAY SHE TREATED YOU. SHE WANTS TO BE YOUR FRIEND AGAIN
NO! SHE REALLY HURT ME! I NEED TIME TO HEAL
OKAY. I UNDERSTAND
HOW SORRY WAS SHE?
I THINK I SAW A TEAR

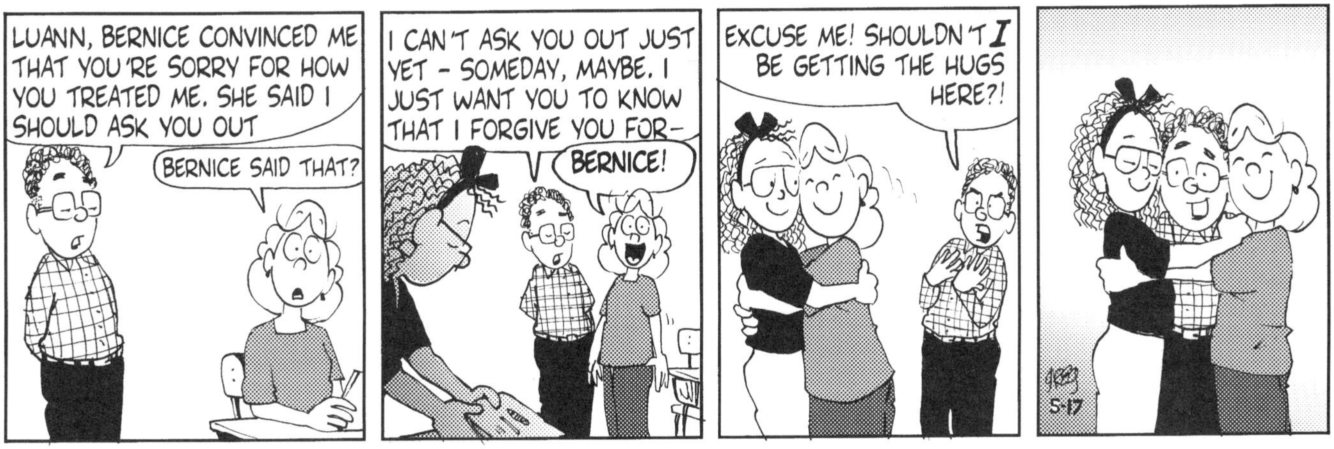
LUANN, BERNICE CONVINCED ME THAT YOU'RE SORRY FOR HOW YOU TREATED ME. SHE SAID I SHOULD ASK YOU OUT
BERNICE SAID THAT?
I CAN'T ASK YOU OUT JUST YET - SOMEDAY, MAYBE. I JUST WANT YOU TO KNOW THAT I FORGIVE YOU FOR-
BERNICE!
EXCUSE ME! SHOULDN'T ***I*** BE GETTING THE HUGS HERE?!

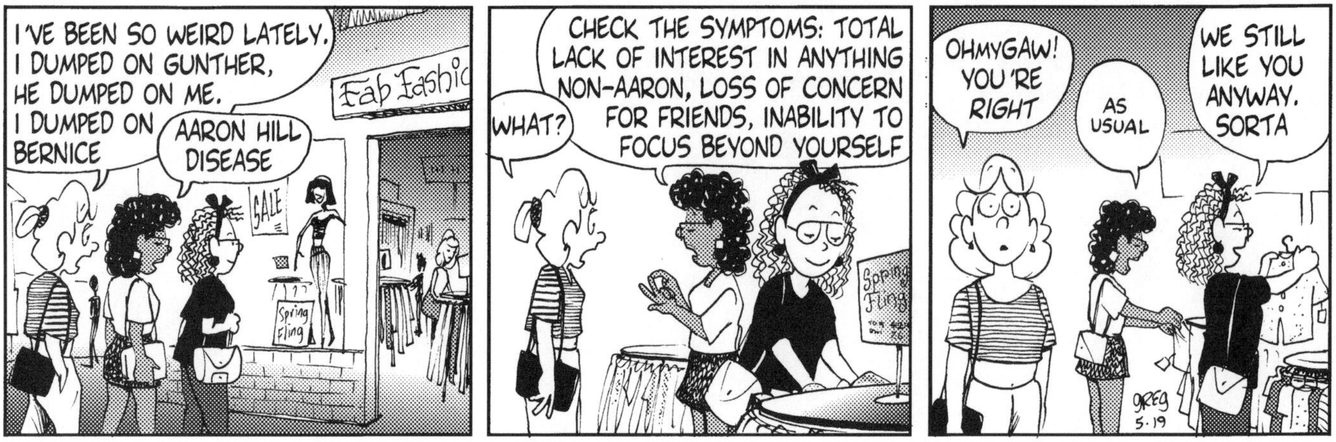
I'VE BEEN SO WEIRD LATELY. I DUMPED ON GUNTHER, HE DUMPED ON ME. I DUMPED ON BERNICE
AARON HILL DISEASE
SALE
Spring Fling
WHAT?
CHECK THE SYMPTOMS: TOTAL LACK OF INTEREST IN ANYTHING NON-AARON, LOSS OF CONCERN FOR FRIENDS, INABILITY TO FOCUS BEYOND YOURSELF
Spring Fling
OHMYGAW! YOU'RE *RIGHT*
AS USUAL
WE STILL LIKE YOU ANYWAY. SORTA
GREG 5.19

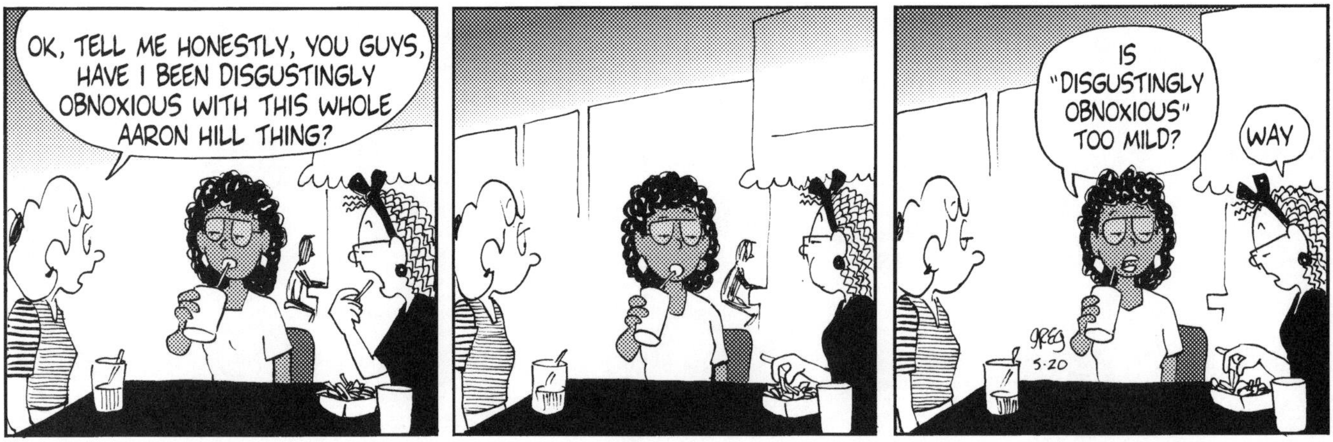
OK, TELL ME HONESTLY, YOU GUYS, HAVE I BEEN DISGUSTINGLY OBNOXIOUS WITH THIS WHOLE AARON HILL THING?
IS "DISGUSTINGLY OBNOXIOUS" TOO MILD?
WAY
GREG 5.20

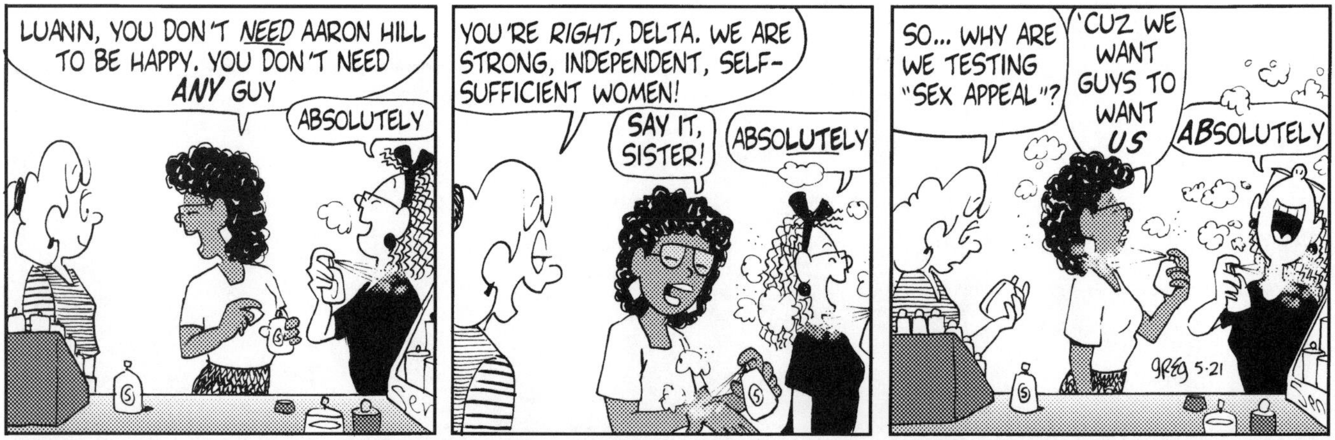
LUANN, YOU DON'T NEED AARON HILL TO BE HAPPY. YOU DON'T NEED ***ANY*** GUY
ABSOLUTELY
YOU'RE *RIGHT*, DELTA. WE ARE STRONG, INDEPENDENT, SELF-SUFFICIENT WOMEN!
SAY IT, SISTER!
ABSOLUTELY
SO... WHY ARE WE TESTING "SEX APPEAL"?
'CUZ WE WANT GUYS TO WANT ***US***
ABSOLUTELY
GREG 5.21

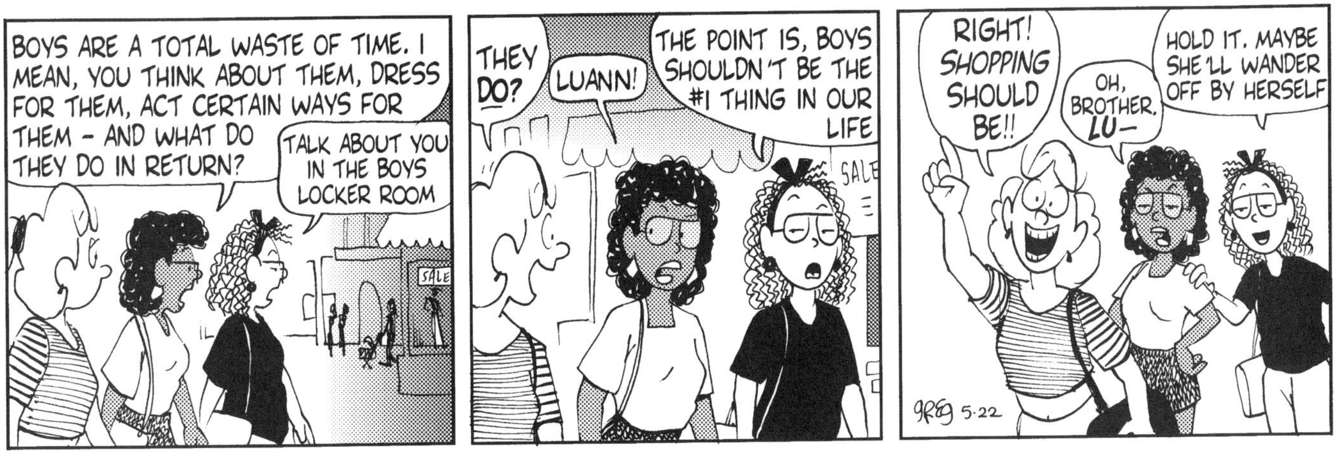
BOYS ARE A TOTAL WASTE OF TIME. I MEAN, YOU THINK ABOUT THEM, DRESS FOR THEM, ACT CERTAIN WAYS FOR THEM - AND WHAT DO THEY DO IN RETURN?
TALK ABOUT YOU IN THE BOYS LOCKER ROOM
SALE
THEY DO?
LUANN!
THE POINT IS, BOYS SHOULDN'T BE THE #1 THING IN OUR LIFE
SALE
RIGHT! SHOPPING SHOULD BE!!
OH, BROTHER. LU—
HOLD IT. MAYBE SHE'LL WANDER OFF BY HERSELF

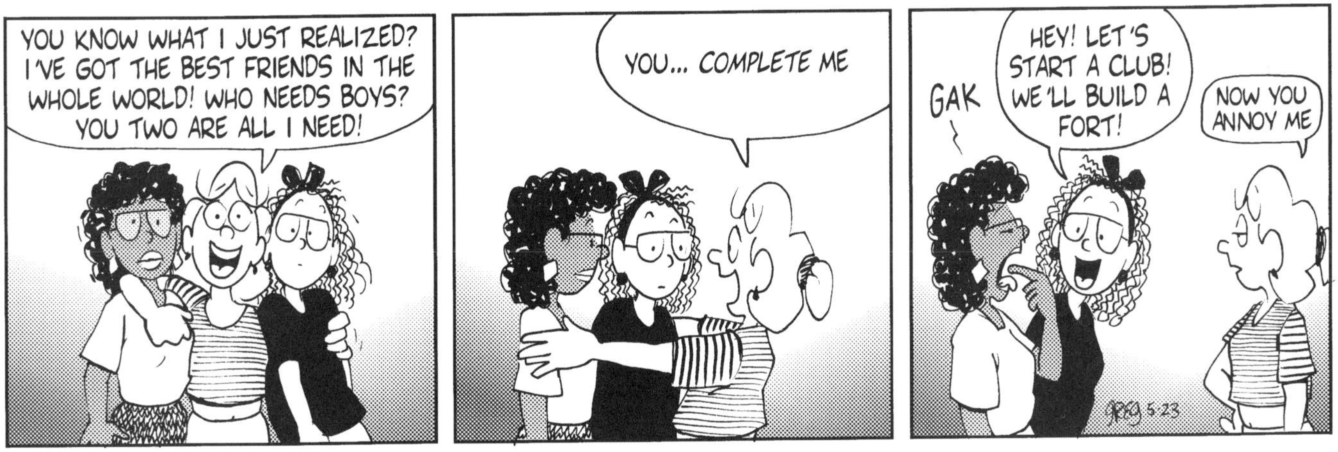
YOU KNOW WHAT I JUST REALIZED? I'VE GOT THE BEST FRIENDS IN THE WHOLE WORLD! WHO NEEDS BOYS? YOU TWO ARE ALL I NEED!
YOU... COMPLETE ME
GAK
HEY! LET'S START A CLUB! WE'LL BUILD A FORT!
NOW YOU ANNOY ME

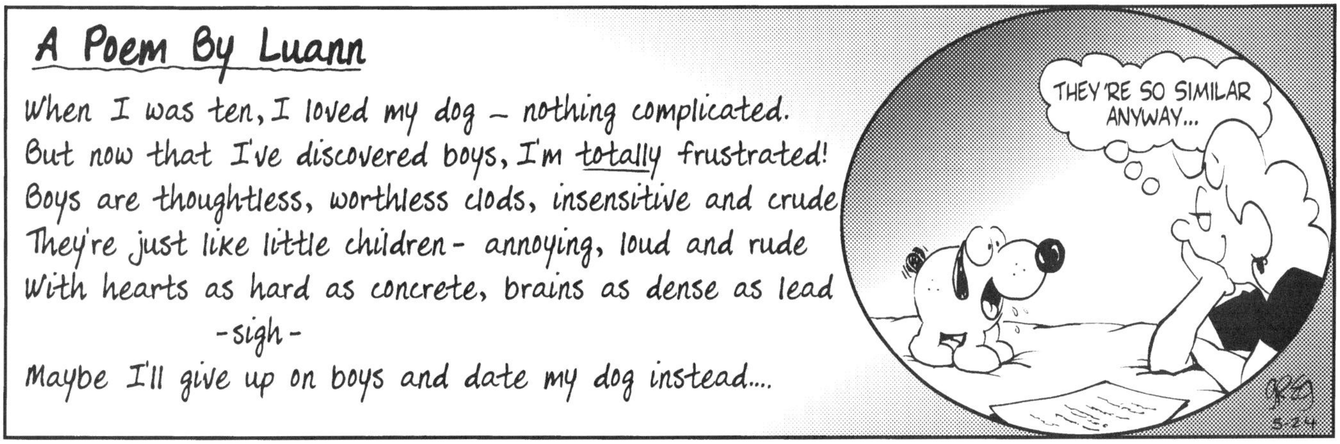
A Poem By Luann
When I was ten, I loved my dog – nothing complicated.
But now that I've discovered boys, I'm totally frustrated!
Boys are thoughtless, worthless clods, insensitive and crude
They're just like little children - annoying, loud and rude
With hearts as hard as concrete, brains as dense as lead
-sigh-
Maybe I'll give up on boys and date my dog instead....
THEY'RE SO SIMILAR ANYWAY...

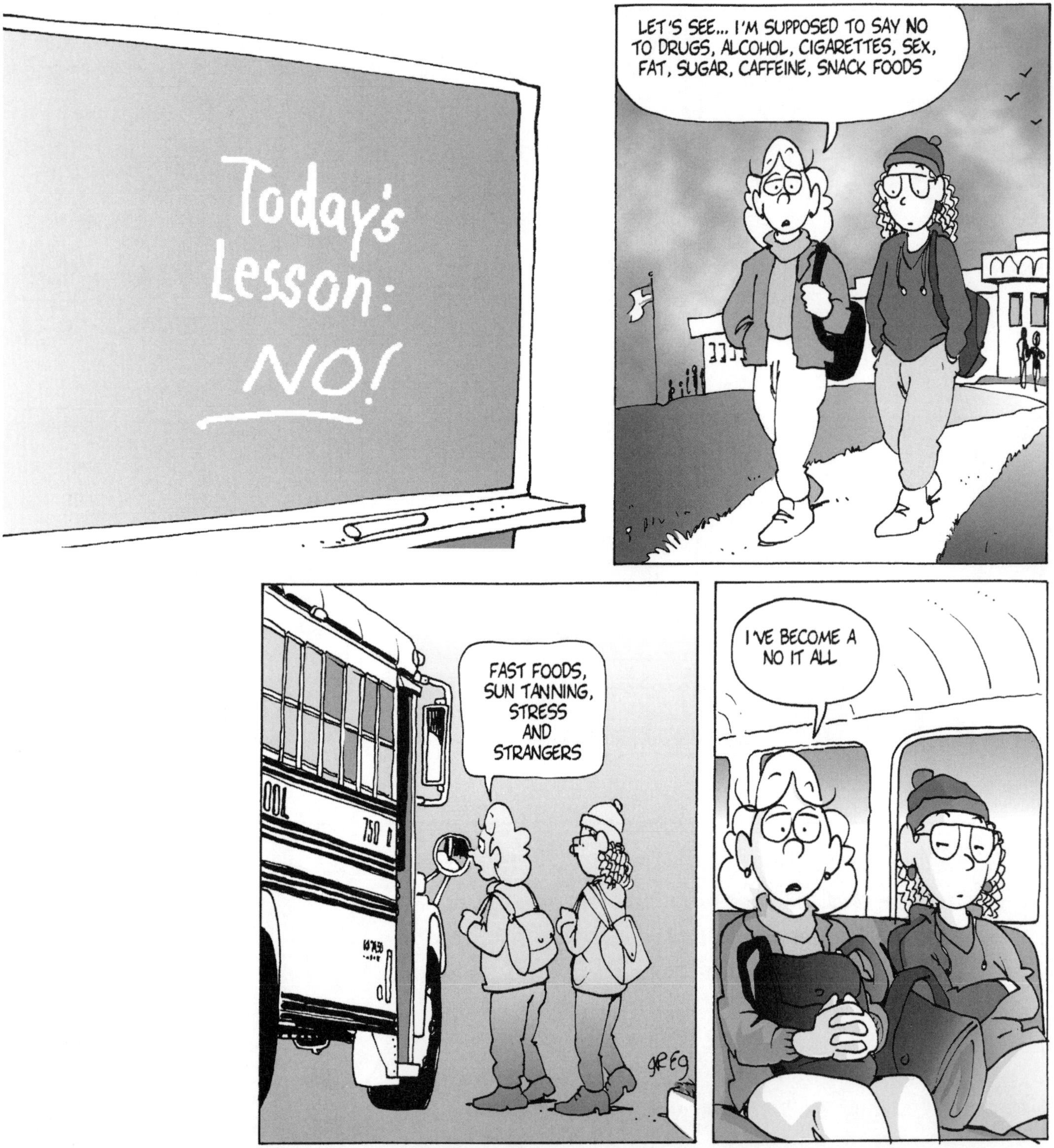
Today's Lesson: NO!
LET'S SEE... I'M SUPPOSED TO SAY NO TO DRUGS, ALCOHOL, CIGARETTES, SEX, FAT, SUGAR, CAFFEINE, SNACK FOODS
FAST FOODS, SUN TANNING, STRESS AND STRANGERS
I'VE BECOME A NO IT ALL

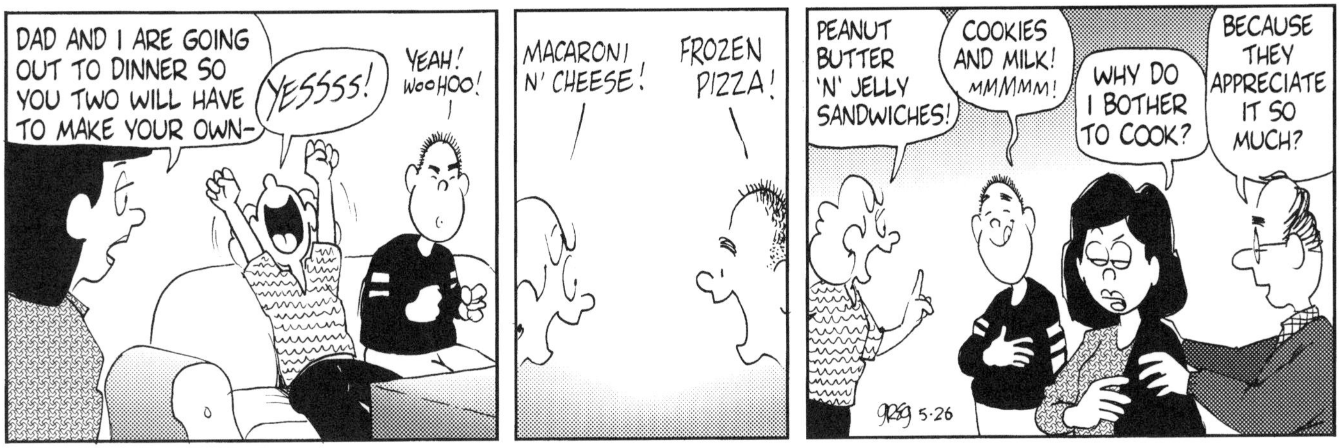
DAD AND I ARE GOING OUT TO DINNER SO YOU TWO WILL HAVE TO MAKE YOUR OWN-
YESSSS!
YEAH! WOOHOO!
MACARONI N' CHEESE!
FROZEN PIZZA!
PEANUT BUTTER 'N' JELLY SANDWICHES!
COOKIES AND MILK! MMMMM!
WHY DO I BOTHER TO COOK?
BECAUSE THEY APPRECIATE IT SO MUCH?
GREG 5·26

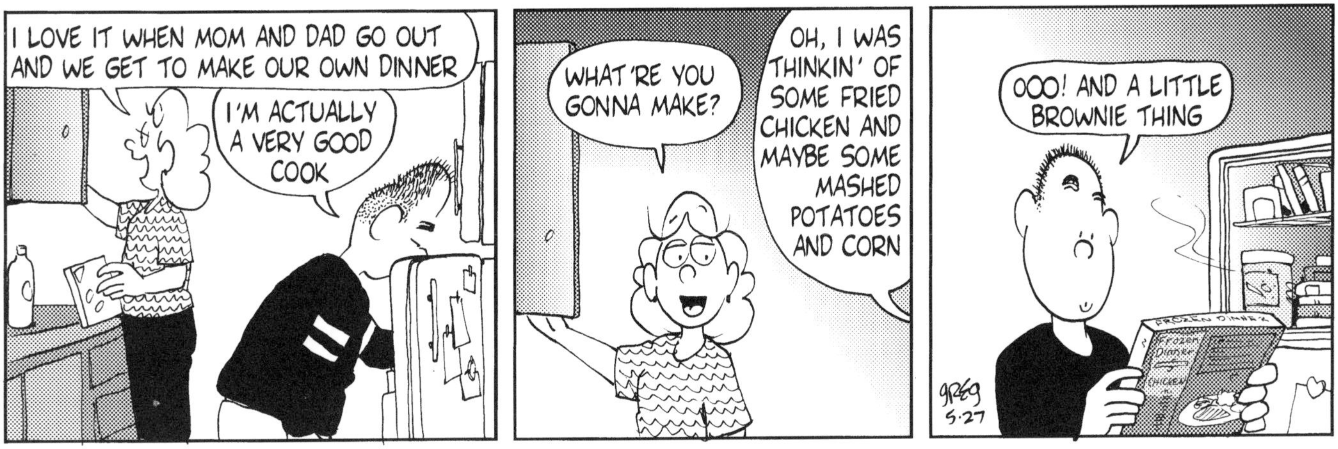
I LOVE IT WHEN MOM AND DAD GO OUT AND WE GET TO MAKE OUR OWN DINNER
I'M ACTUALLY A VERY GOOD COOK
WHAT'RE YOU GONNA MAKE?
OH, I WAS THINKIN' OF SOME FRIED CHICKEN AND MAYBE SOME MASHED POTATOES AND CORN
OOO! AND A LITTLE BROWNIE THING
GREG 5·27

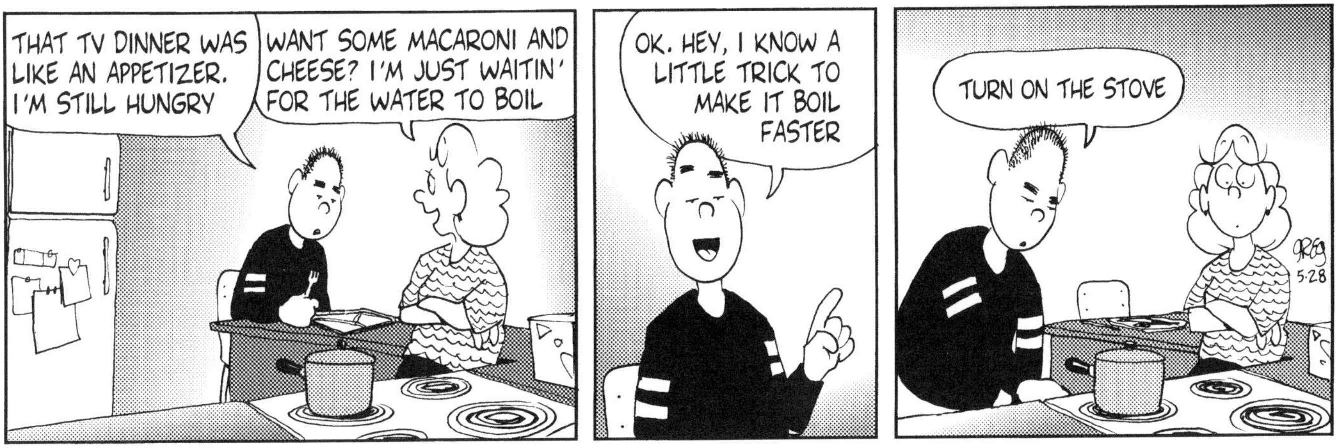
THAT TV DINNER WAS LIKE AN APPETIZER. I'M STILL HUNGRY
WANT SOME MACARONI AND CHEESE? I'M JUST WAITIN' FOR THE WATER TO BOIL
OK. HEY, I KNOW A LITTLE TRICK TO MAKE IT BOIL FASTER
TURN ON THE STOVE
GREG 5·28

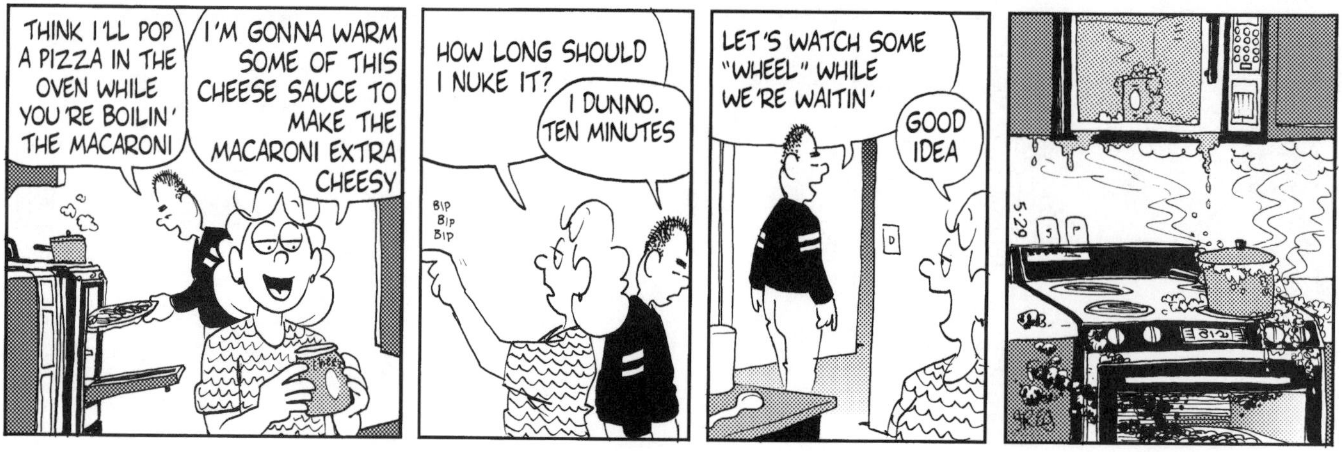
THINK I'LL POP A PIZZA IN THE OVEN WHILE YOU'RE BOILIN' THE MACARONI
I'M GONNA WARM SOME OF THIS CHEESE SAUCE TO MAKE THE MACARONI EXTRA CHEESY
HOW LONG SHOULD I NUKE IT?
I DUNNO. TEN MINUTES
BIP BIP BIP
LET'S WATCH SOME "WHEEL" WHILE WE'RE WAITIN'
GOOD IDEA
5-29

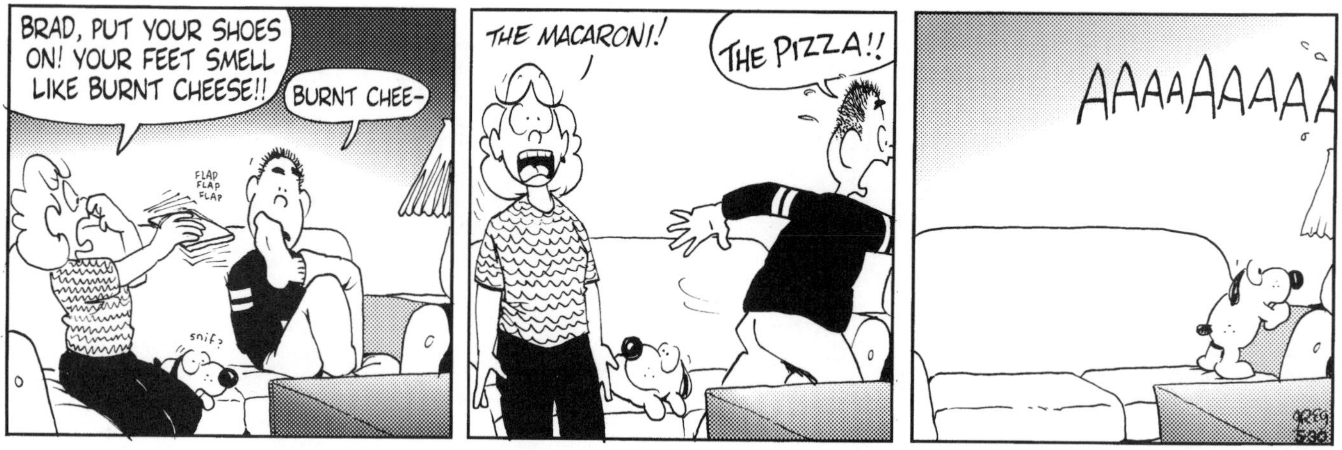
BRAD, PUT YOUR SHOES ON! YOUR FEET SMELL LIKE BURNT CHEESE!!
BURNT CHEE-
FLAP FLAP FLAP
snif?
THE MACARONI!
THE PIZZA!!
AAAAAAAAA
5-30

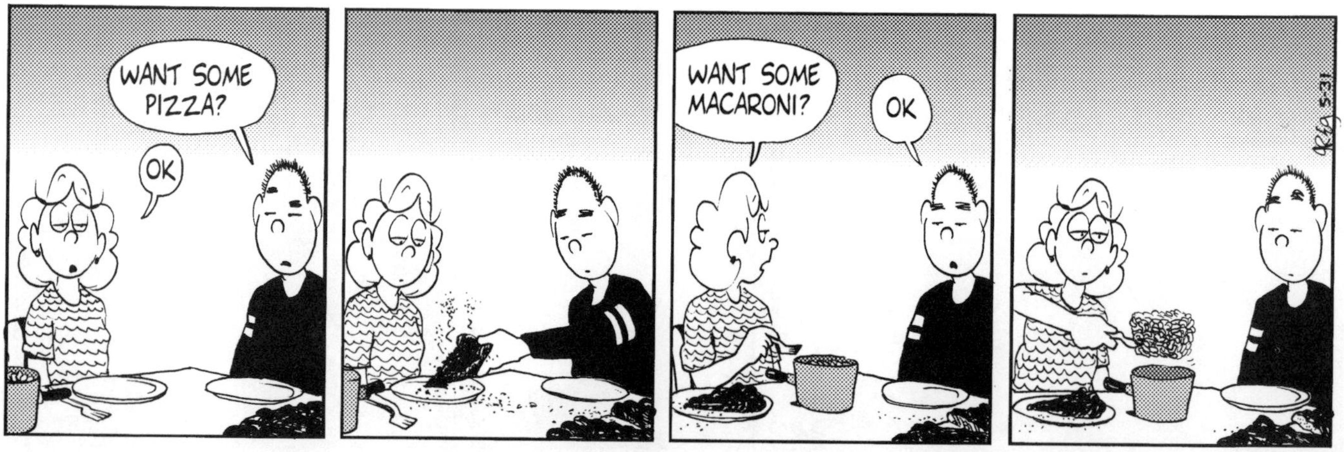
WANT SOME PIZZA?
OK
WANT SOME MACARONI?
OK
5-31

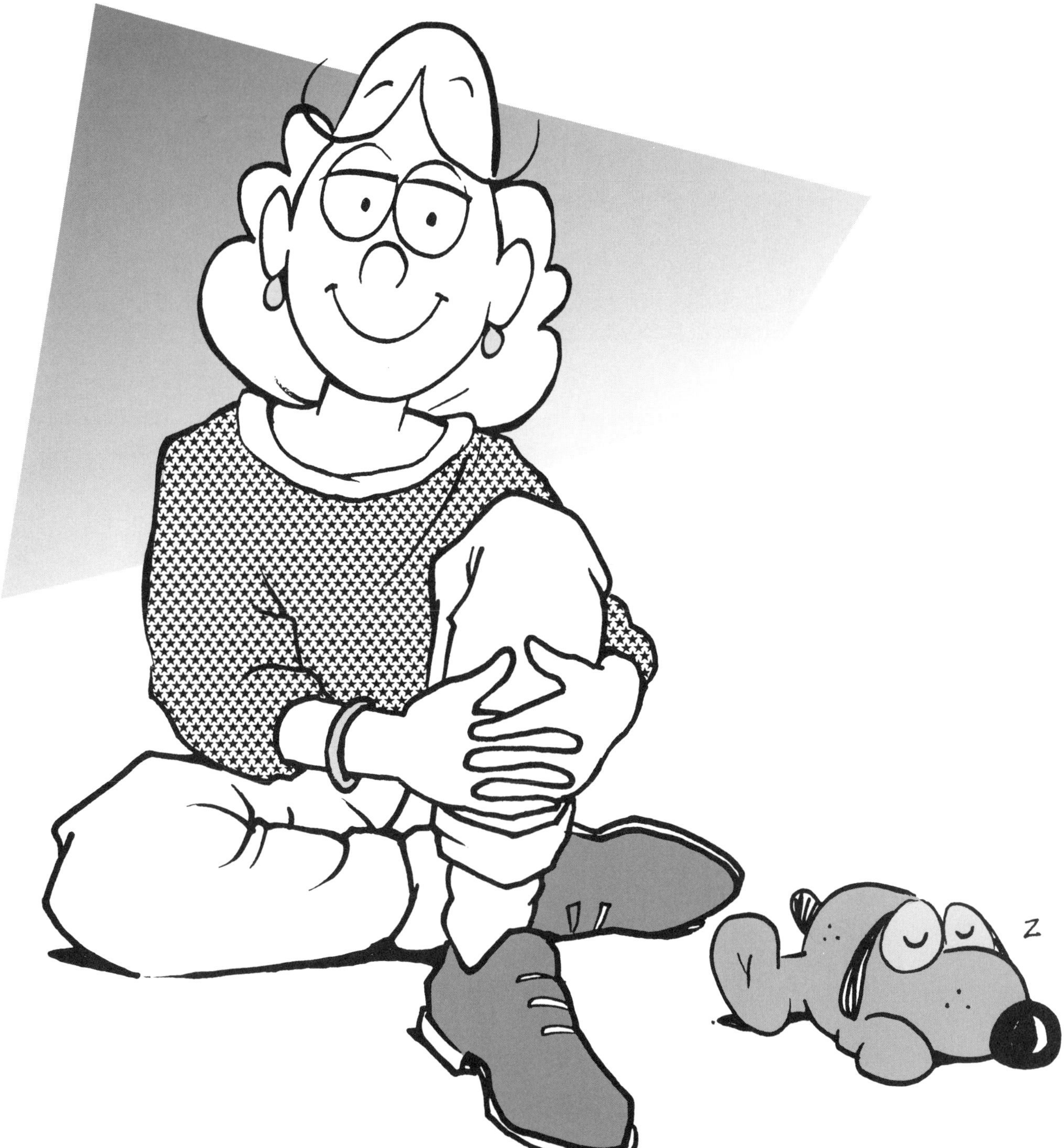
Z

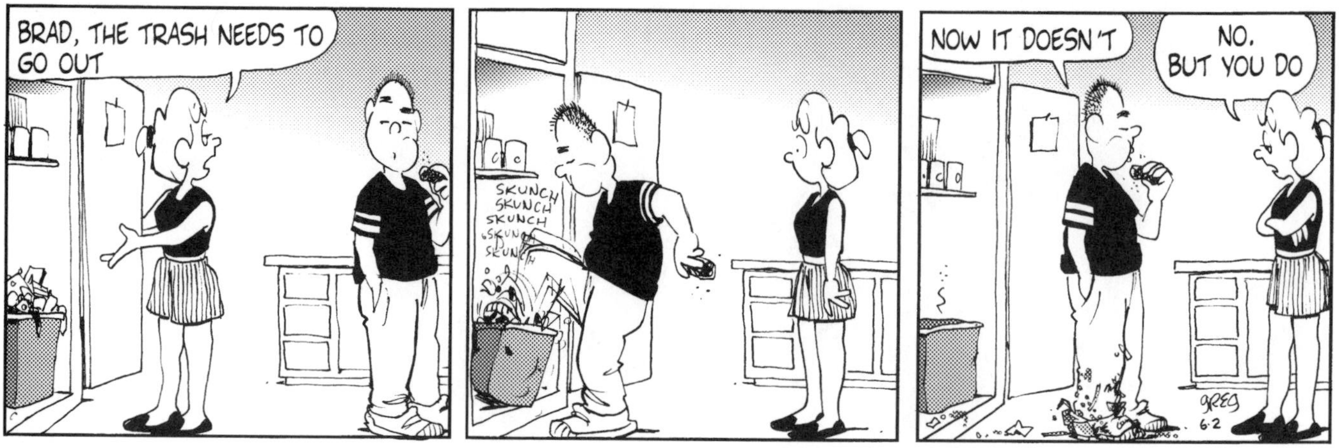
BRAD, THE TRASH NEEDS TO GO OUT
SKUNCH
SKUNCH
SKUNCH
NOW IT DOESN'T
NO. BUT YOU DO
GREG 6·2

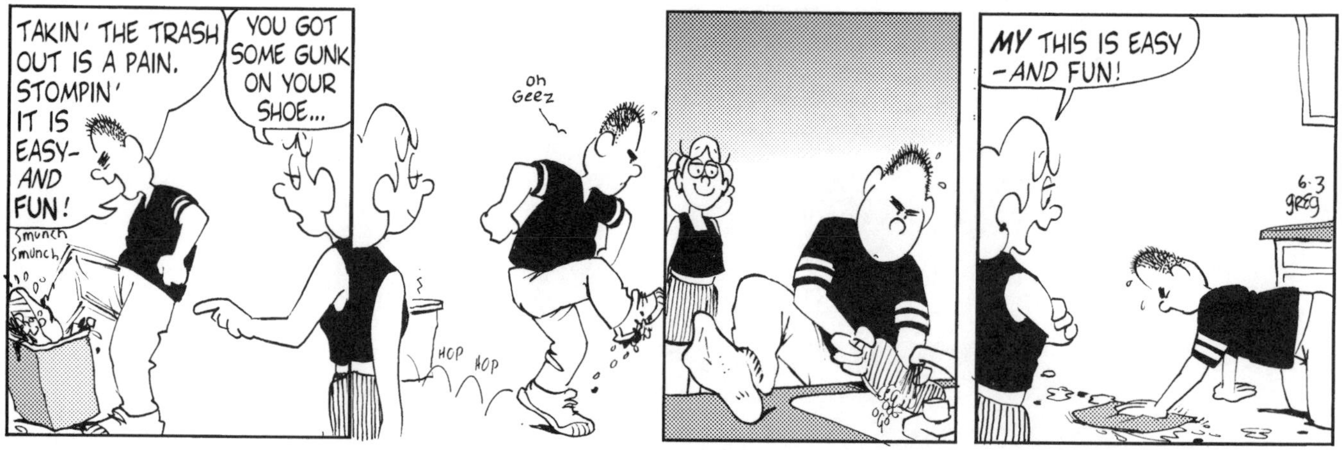
TAKIN' THE TRASH OUT IS A PAIN. STOMPIN' IT IS EASY- AND FUN!
smunch
smunch
YOU GOT SOME GUNK ON YOUR SHOE...
oh Geez
HOP
HOP
MY THIS IS EASY -AND FUN!
6·3 GREG

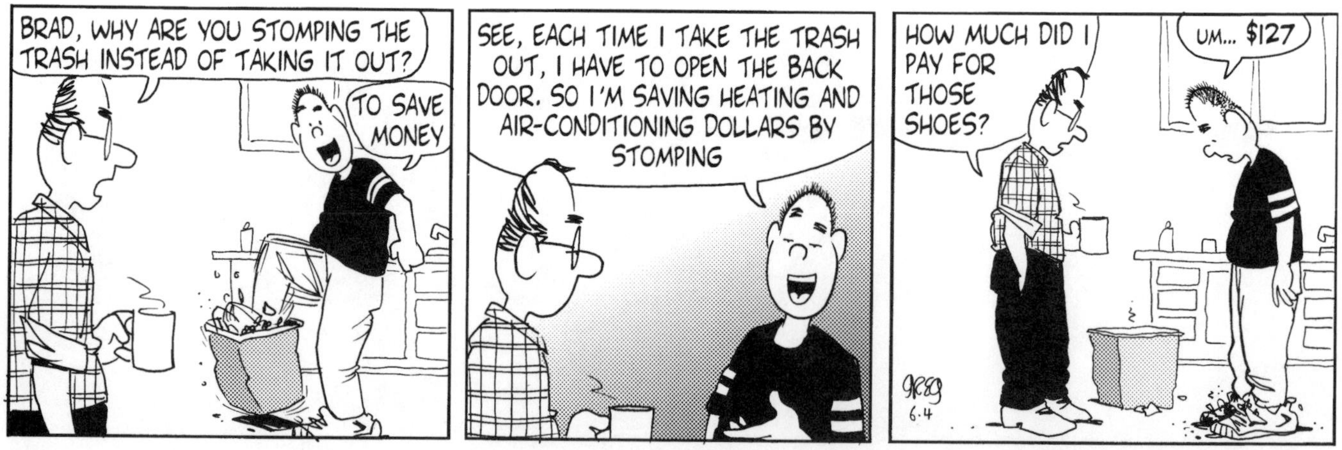
BRAD, WHY ARE YOU STOMPING THE TRASH INSTEAD OF TAKING IT OUT?
TO SAVE MONEY
SEE, EACH TIME I TAKE THE TRASH OUT, I HAVE TO OPEN THE BACK DOOR. SO I'M SAVING HEATING AND AIR-CONDITIONING DOLLARS BY STOMPING
HOW MUCH DID I PAY FOR THOSE SHOES?
UM... $127
GREG 6·4

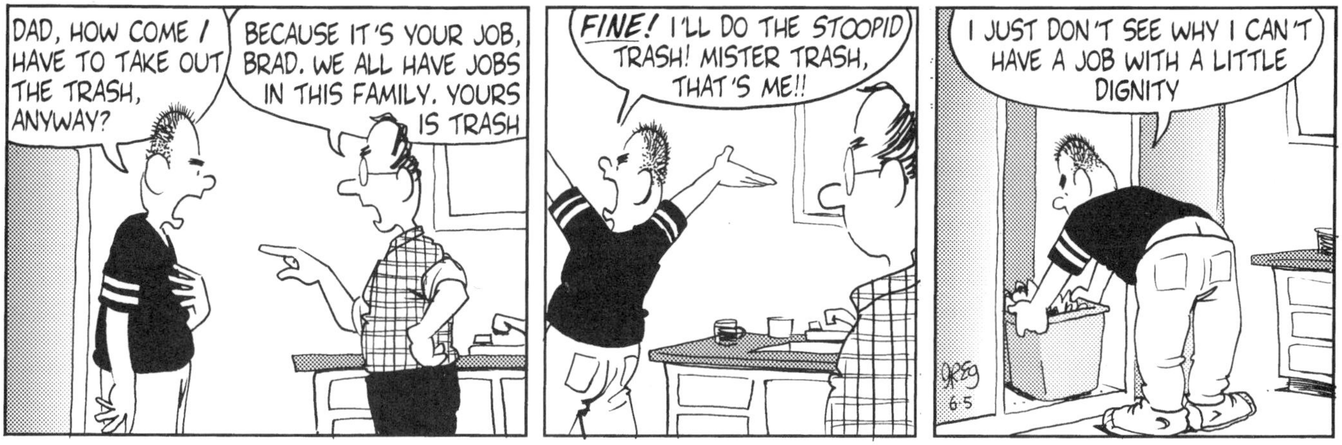
DAD, HOW COME I HAVE TO TAKE OUT THE TRASH, ANYWAY?
BECAUSE IT'S YOUR JOB, BRAD. WE ALL HAVE JOBS IN THIS FAMILY. YOURS IS TRASH
FINE! I'LL DO THE STOOPID TRASH! MISTER TRASH, THAT'S ME!!
I JUST DON'T SEE WHY I CAN'T HAVE A JOB WITH A LITTLE DIGNITY

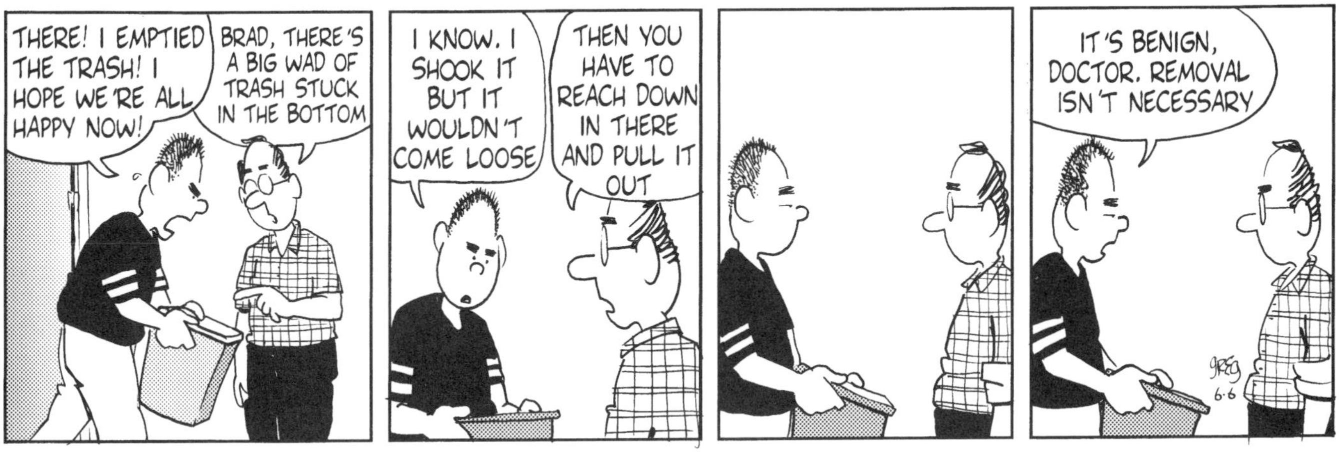
THERE! I EMPTIED THE TRASH! I HOPE WE'RE ALL HAPPY NOW!
BRAD, THERE'S A BIG WAD OF TRASH STUCK IN THE BOTTOM
I KNOW. I SHOOK IT BUT IT WOULDN'T COME LOOSE
THEN YOU HAVE TO REACH DOWN IN THERE AND PULL IT OUT
IT'S BENIGN, DOCTOR. REMOVAL ISN'T NECESSARY

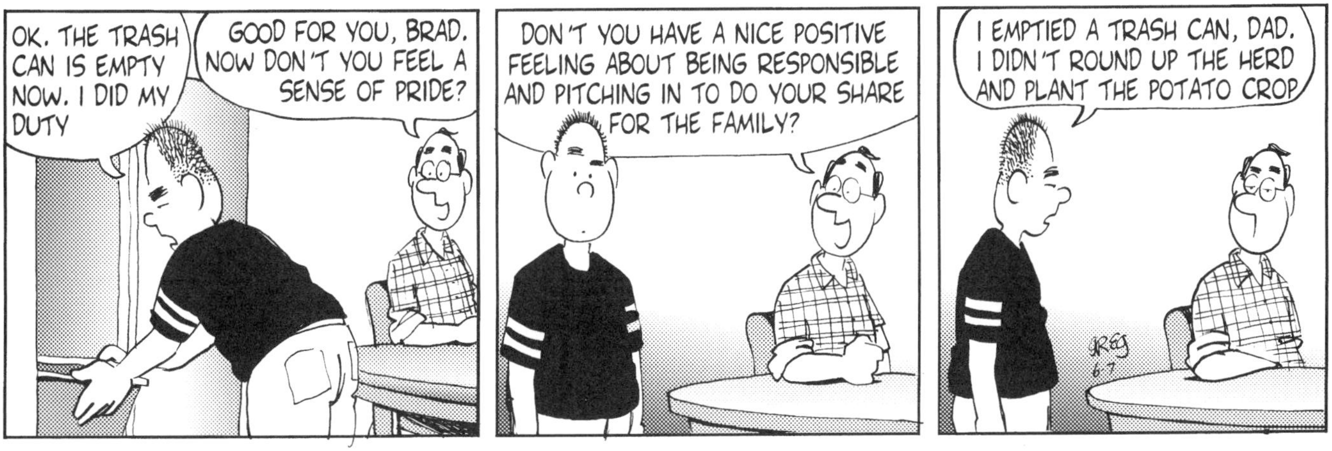
OK. THE TRASH CAN IS EMPTY NOW. I DID MY DUTY
GOOD FOR YOU, BRAD. NOW DON'T YOU FEEL A SENSE OF PRIDE?
DON'T YOU HAVE A NICE POSITIVE FEELING ABOUT BEING RESPONSIBLE AND PITCHING IN TO DO YOUR SHARE FOR THE FAMILY?
I EMPTIED A TRASH CAN, DAD. I DIDN'T ROUND UP THE HERD AND PLANT THE POTATO CROP

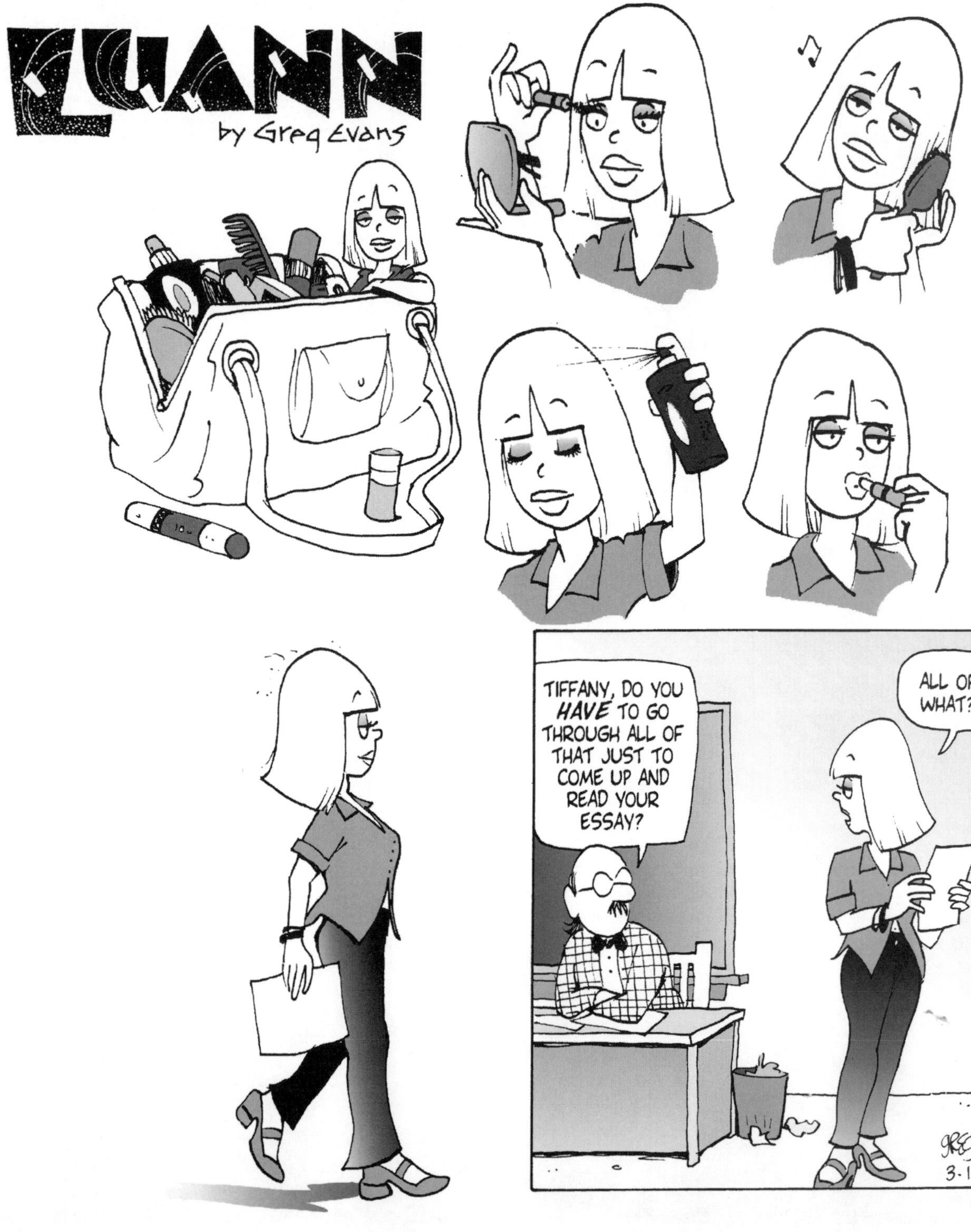

LUANN
by Greg Evans
TIFFANY, DO YOU *HAVE* TO GO THROUGH ALL OF THAT JUST TO COME UP AND READ YOUR ESSAY?
ALL OF WHAT?
GREG
3-1

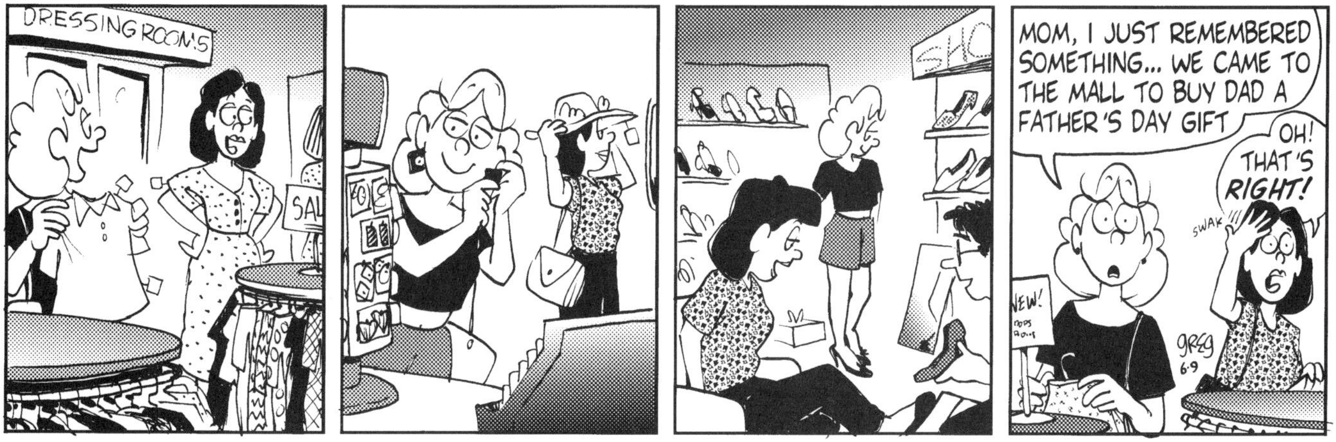
DRESSING ROOMS
MOM, I JUST REMEMBERED SOMETHING... WE CAME TO THE MALL TO BUY DAD A FATHER'S DAY GIFT
OH! THAT'S *RIGHT!*
SWAK
GREG 6·9

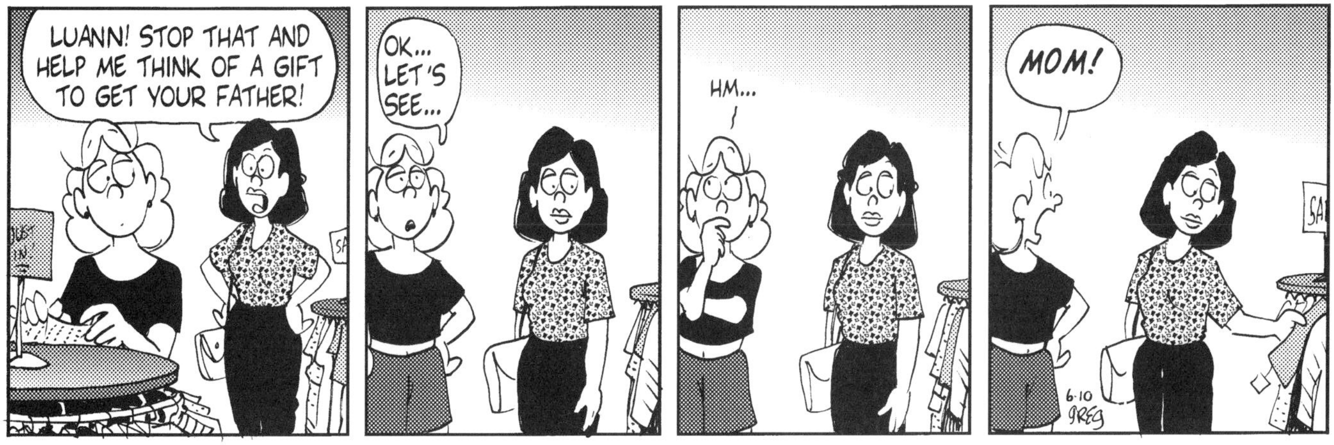
LUANN! STOP THAT AND HELP ME THINK OF A GIFT TO GET YOUR FATHER!
OK... LET'S SEE...
HM...
MOM!
6·10 GREG

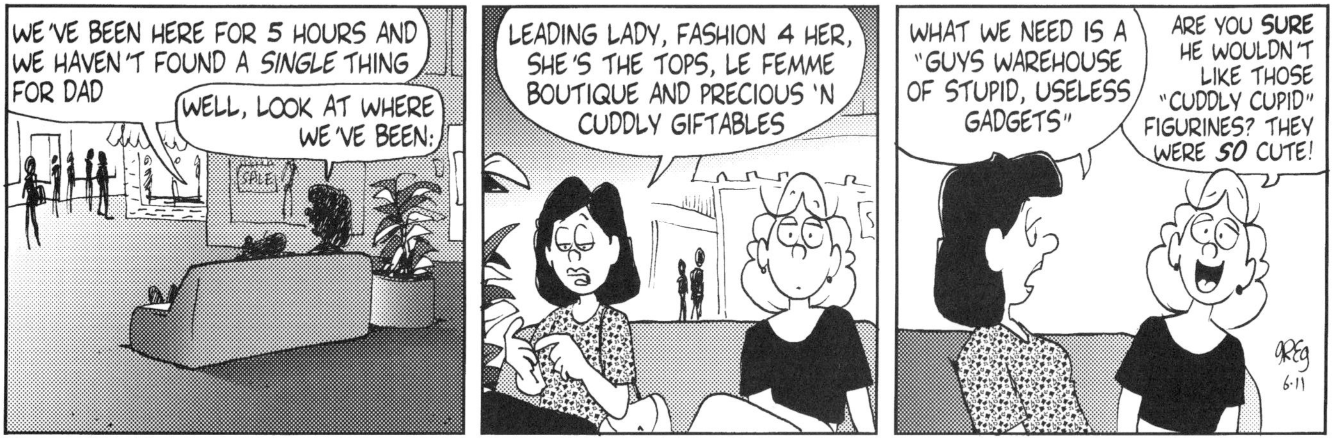
WE'VE BEEN HERE FOR 5 HOURS AND WE HAVEN'T FOUND A *SINGLE* THING FOR DAD
WELL, LOOK AT WHERE WE'VE BEEN:
SALE
LEADING LADY, FASHION 4 HER, SHE'S THE TOPS, LE FEMME BOUTIQUE AND PRECIOUS 'N CUDDLY GIFTABLES
WHAT WE NEED IS A "GUYS WAREHOUSE OF STUPID, USELESS GADGETS"
ARE YOU **SURE** HE WOULDN'T LIKE THOSE "CUDDLY CUPID" FIGURINES? THEY WERE ***SO*** CUTE!
GREG 6·11

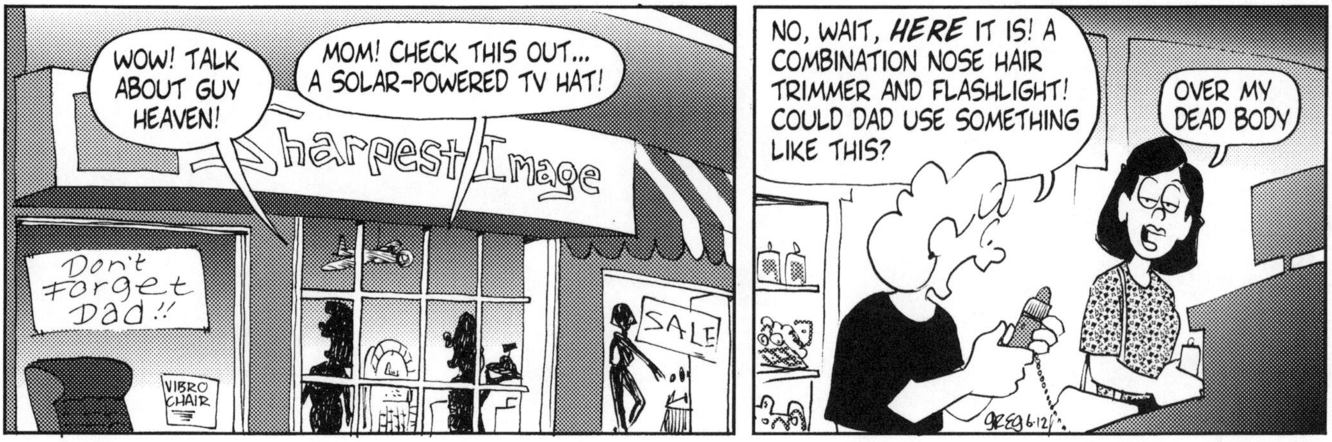
WOW! TALK ABOUT GUY HEAVEN!
MOM! CHECK THIS OUT... A SOLAR-POWERED TV HAT!
Sharpest Image
Don't Forget Dad!!
VIBRO CHAIR
SALE
NO, WAIT, HERE IT IS! A COMBINATION NOSE HAIR TRIMMER AND FLASHLIGHT! COULD DAD USE SOMETHING LIKE THIS?
OVER MY DEAD BODY

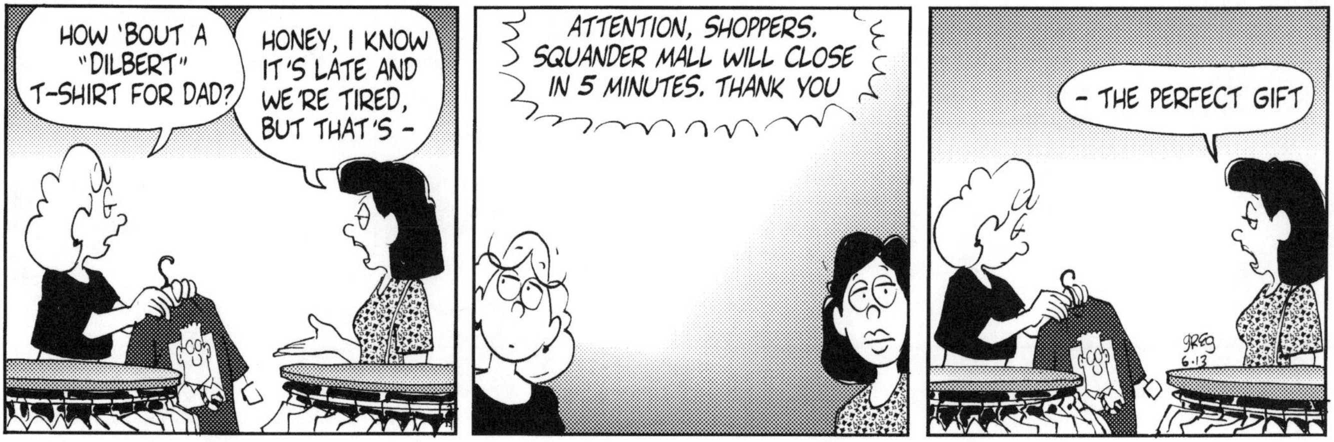
HOW 'BOUT A "DILBERT" T-SHIRT FOR DAD?
HONEY, I KNOW IT'S LATE AND WE'RE TIRED, BUT THAT'S –
ATTENTION, SHOPPERS. SQUANDER MALL WILL CLOSE IN 5 MINUTES. THANK YOU
– THE PERFECT GIFT

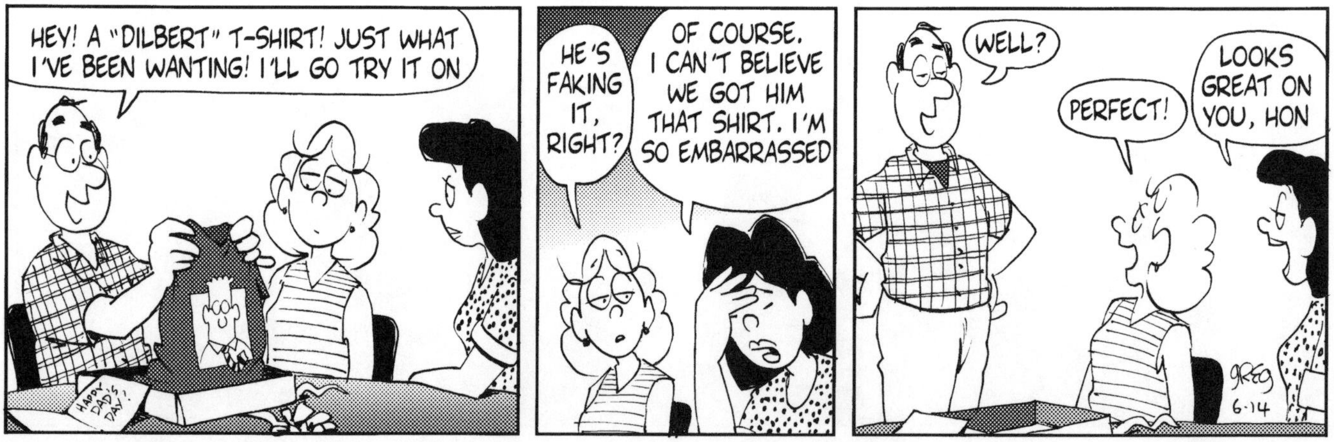
HEY! A "DILBERT" T-SHIRT! JUST WHAT I'VE BEEN WANTING! I'LL GO TRY IT ON
HAPPY DAD'S DAY!
HE'S FAKING IT, RIGHT?
OF COURSE. I CAN'T BELIEVE WE GOT HIM THAT SHIRT. I'M SO EMBARRASSED
WELL?
PERFECT!
LOOKS GREAT ON YOU, HON

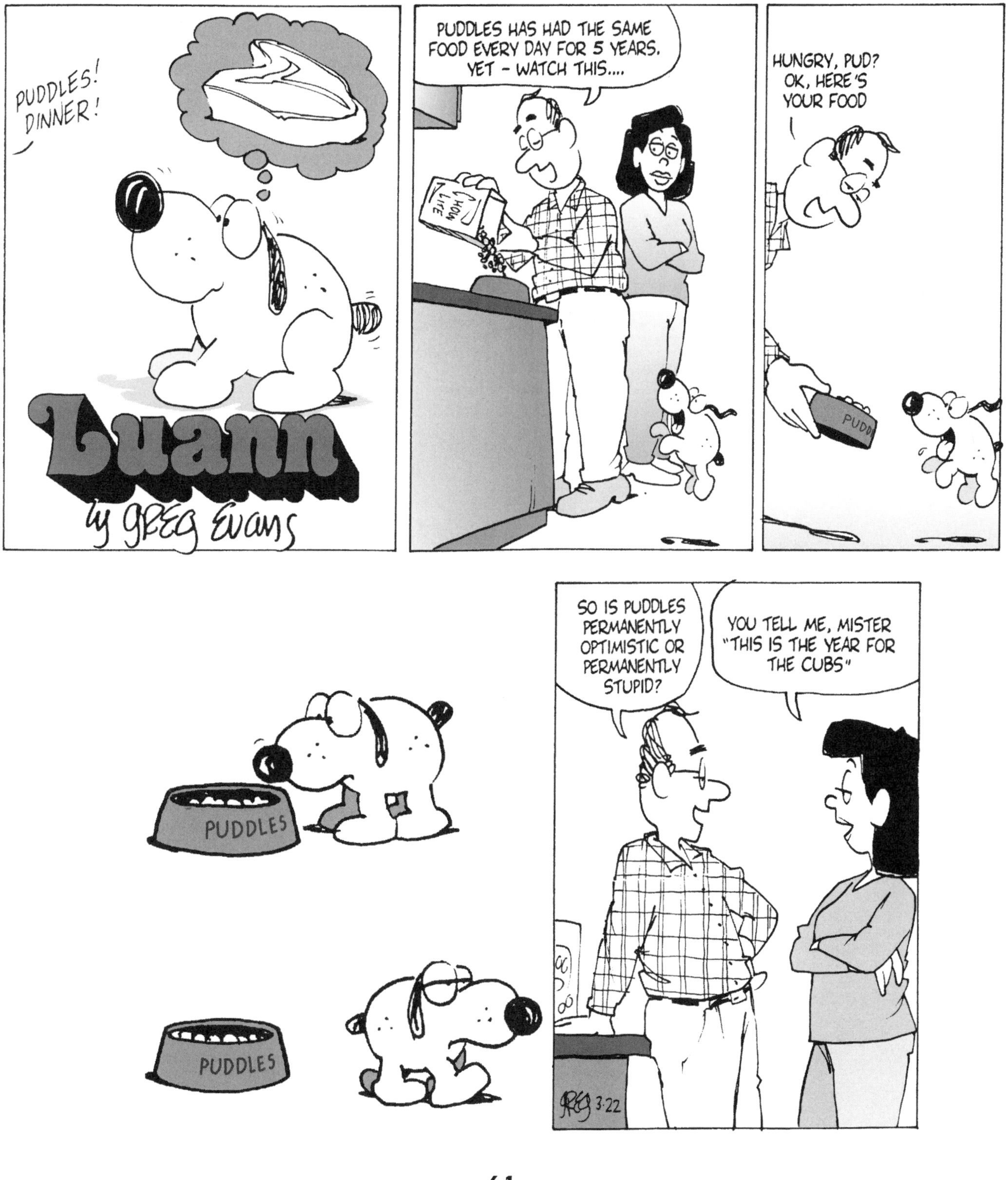
PUDDLES! DINNER!
Luann
by GREG EVANS
PUDDLES HAS HAD THE SAME FOOD EVERY DAY FOR 5 YEARS. YET - WATCH THIS....
CHOW LIFE
HUNGRY, PUD? OK, HERE'S YOUR FOOD
PUDDLES
PUDDLES
SO IS PUDDLES PERMANENTLY OPTIMISTIC OR PERMANENTLY STUPID?
YOU TELL ME, MISTER "THIS IS THE YEAR FOR THE CUBS"
GREG 3·22

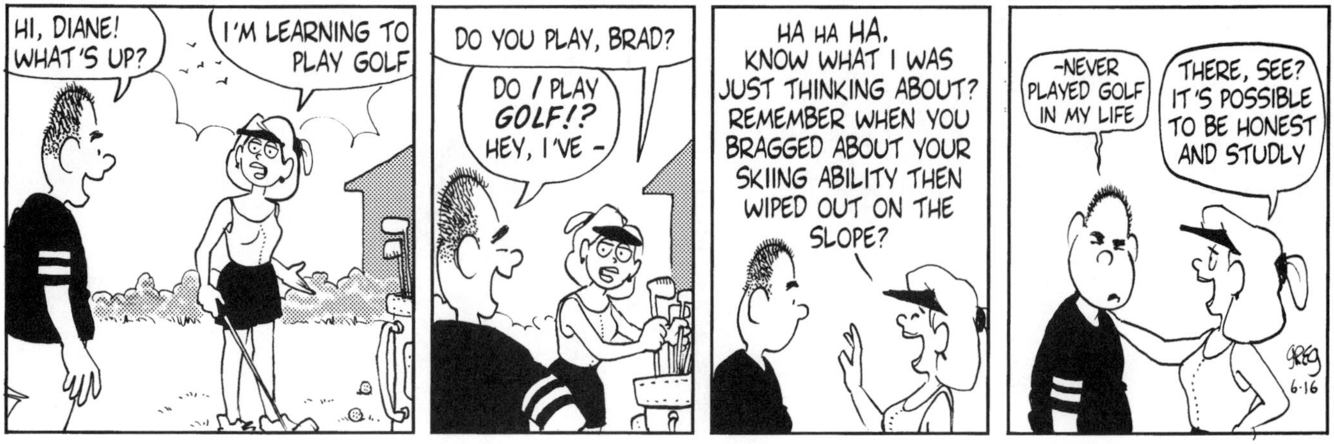
HI, DIANE! WHAT'S UP?
I'M LEARNING TO PLAY GOLF
DO YOU PLAY, BRAD?
DO *I* PLAY ***GOLF!?*** HEY, I'VE –
HA HA HA. KNOW WHAT I WAS JUST THINKING ABOUT? REMEMBER WHEN YOU BRAGGED ABOUT YOUR SKIING ABILITY THEN WIPED OUT ON THE SLOPE?
–NEVER PLAYED GOLF IN MY LIFE
THERE, SEE? IT'S POSSIBLE TO BE HONEST AND STUDLY
GREG 6·16

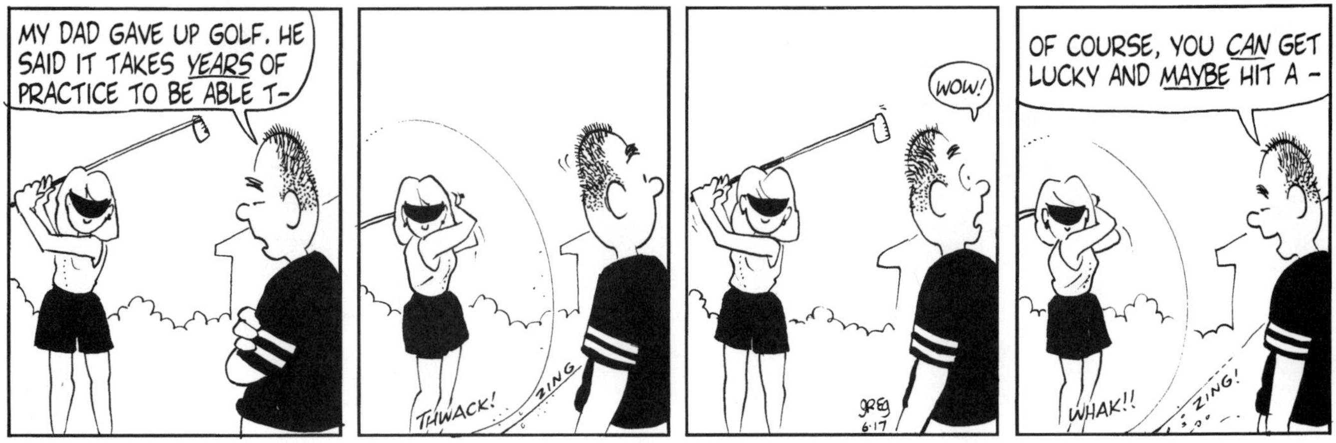
MY DAD GAVE UP GOLF. HE SAID IT TAKES YEARS OF PRACTICE TO BE ABLE T–
THWACK!
ZING
WOW!
GREG 6·17
OF COURSE, YOU CAN GET LUCKY AND MAYBE HIT A –
WHAK!!
ZING!

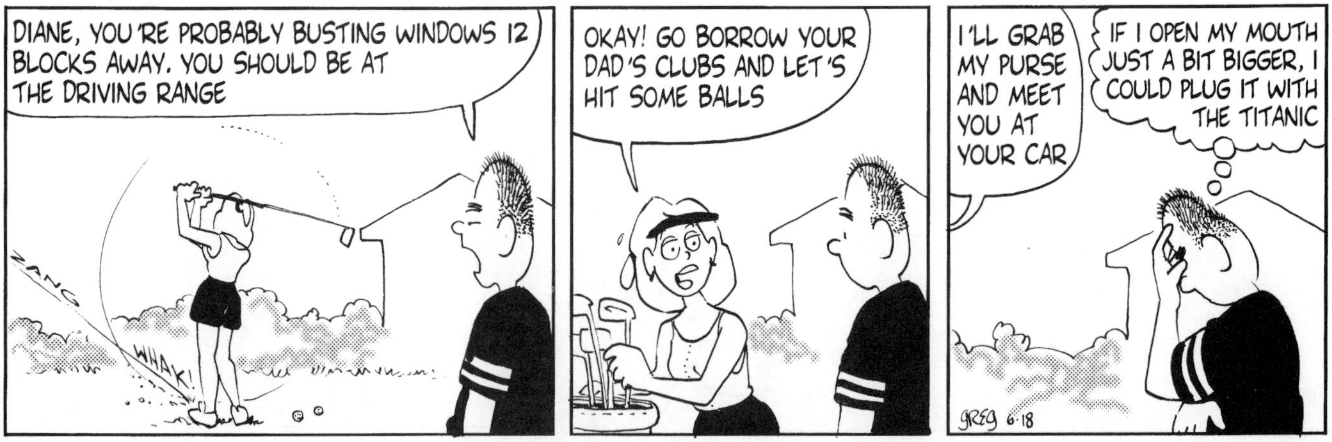
DIANE, YOU'RE PROBABLY BUSTING WINDOWS 12 BLOCKS AWAY. YOU SHOULD BE AT THE DRIVING RANGE
ZANG
WHAK!
OKAY! GO BORROW YOUR DAD'S CLUBS AND LET'S HIT SOME BALLS
I'LL GRAB MY PURSE AND MEET YOU AT YOUR CAR
IF I OPEN MY MOUTH JUST A BIT BIGGER, I COULD PLUG IT WITH THE TITANIC
GREG 6·18

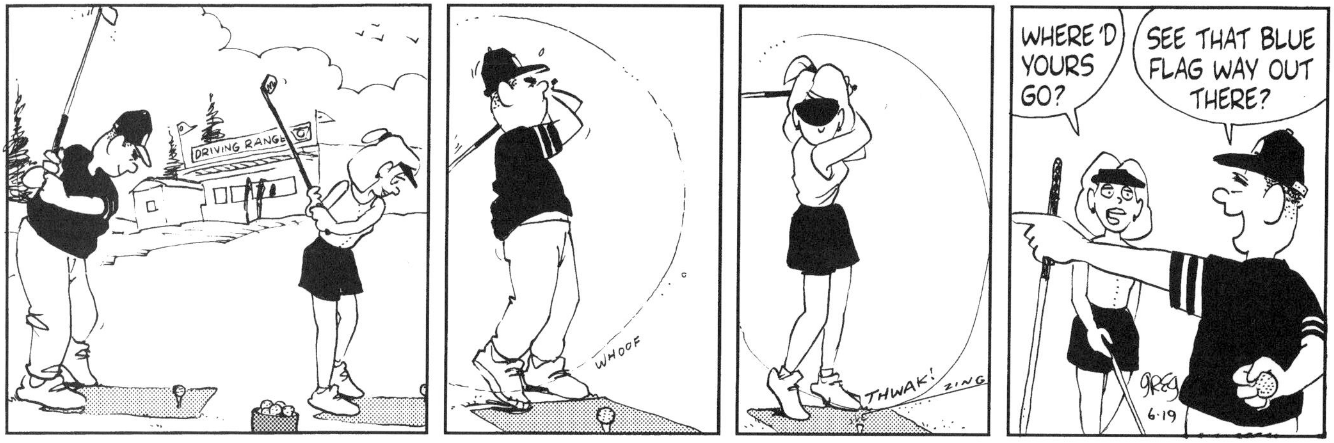
DRIVING RANGE
WHOOF
THWAK!
ZING
WHERE'D YOURS GO?
SEE THAT BLUE FLAG WAY OUT THERE?
GREG 6·19

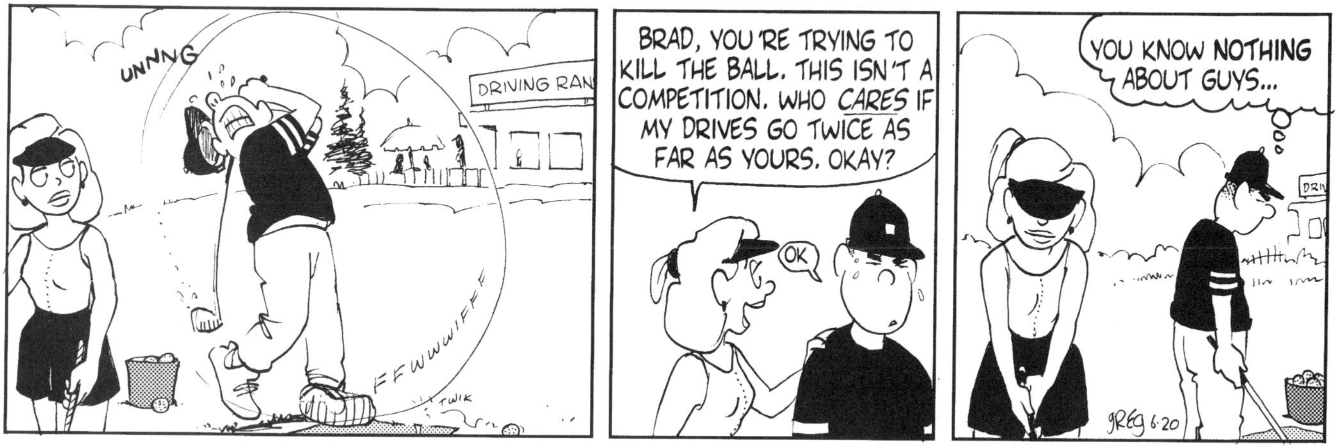
UNNNG
FFWWWIFFF
TWIK
BRAD, YOU'RE TRYING TO KILL THE BALL. THIS ISN'T A COMPETITION. WHO CARES IF MY DRIVES GO TWICE AS FAR AS YOURS. OKAY?
OK
YOU KNOW **NOTHING** ABOUT GUYS...
GREG 6·20

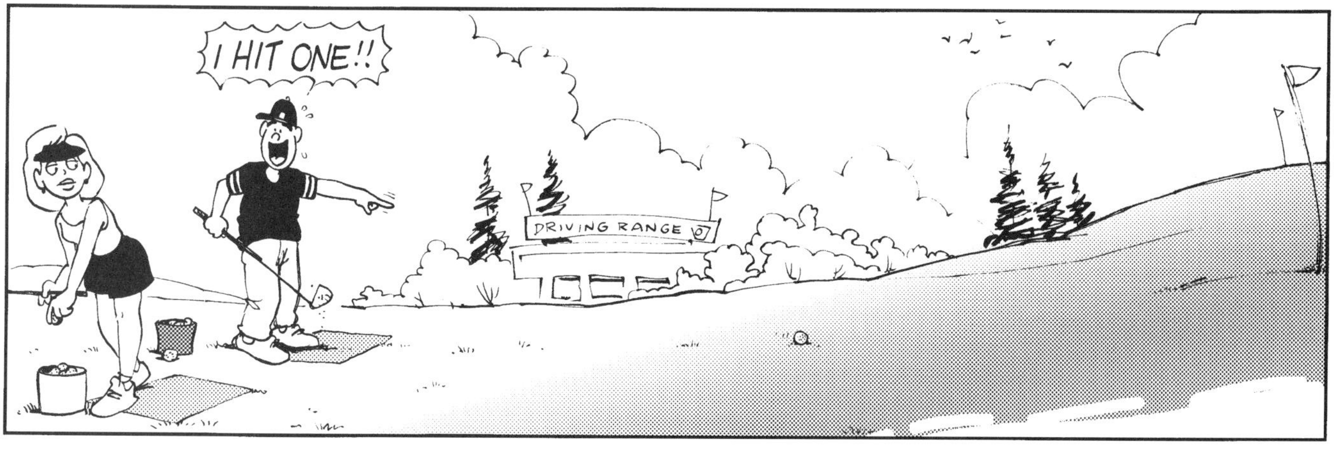
I HIT ONE!!
DRIVING RANGE

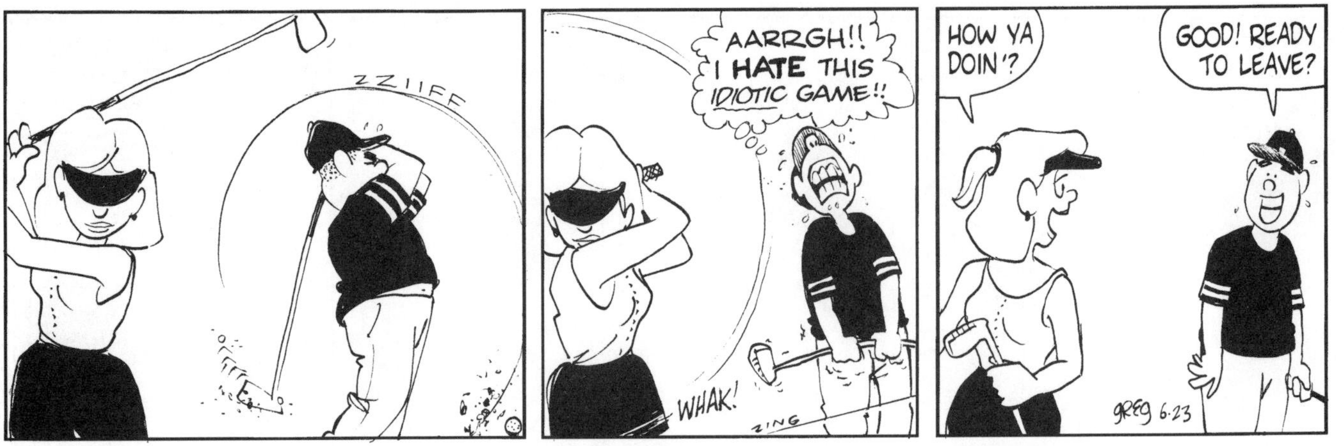
ZZIIFF
AARRGH!! I **HATE** THIS *IDIOTIC* GAME!!
WHAK!
ZING
HOW YA DOIN'?
GOOD! READY TO LEAVE?
GREG 6·23

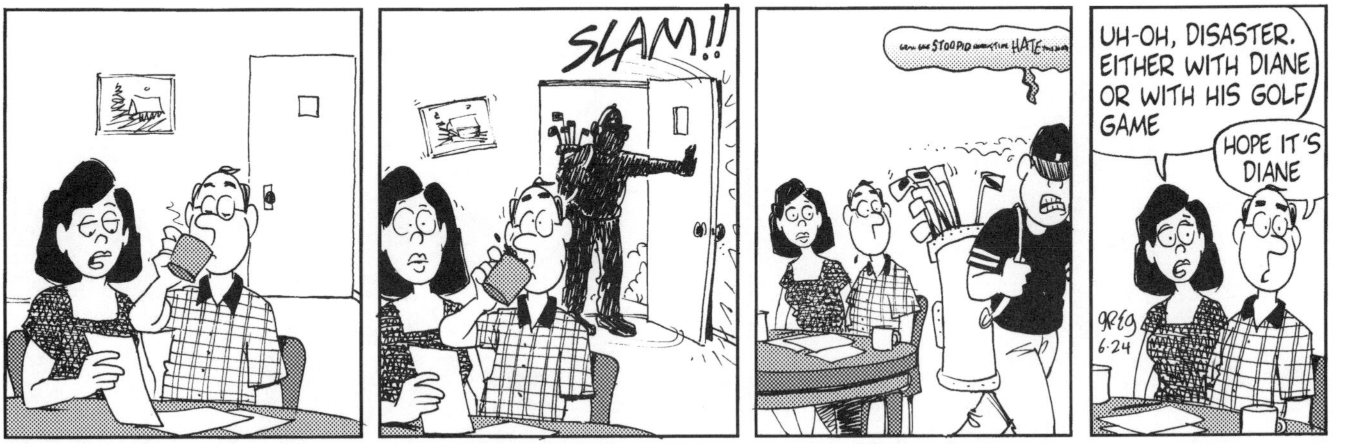
SLAM!!
UH-OH, DISASTER. EITHER WITH DIANE OR WITH HIS GOLF GAME
HOPE IT'S DIANE
GREG 6·24

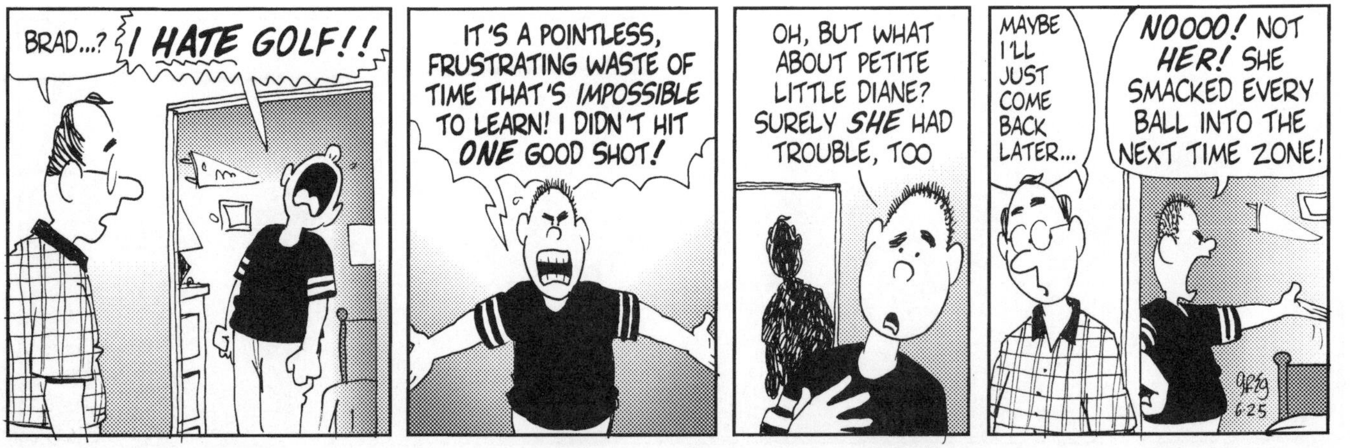
BRAD...?
*I **HATE** GOLF!!*
IT'S A POINTLESS, FRUSTRATING WASTE OF TIME THAT'S *IMPOSSIBLE* TO LEARN! I DIDN'T HIT ***ONE*** GOOD SHOT!
OH, BUT WHAT ABOUT PETITE LITTLE DIANE? SURELY ***SHE*** HAD TROUBLE, TOO
MAYBE I'LL JUST COME BACK LATER...
NOOOO! NOT ***HER!*** SHE SMACKED EVERY BALL INTO THE NEXT TIME ZONE!
GREG 6·25

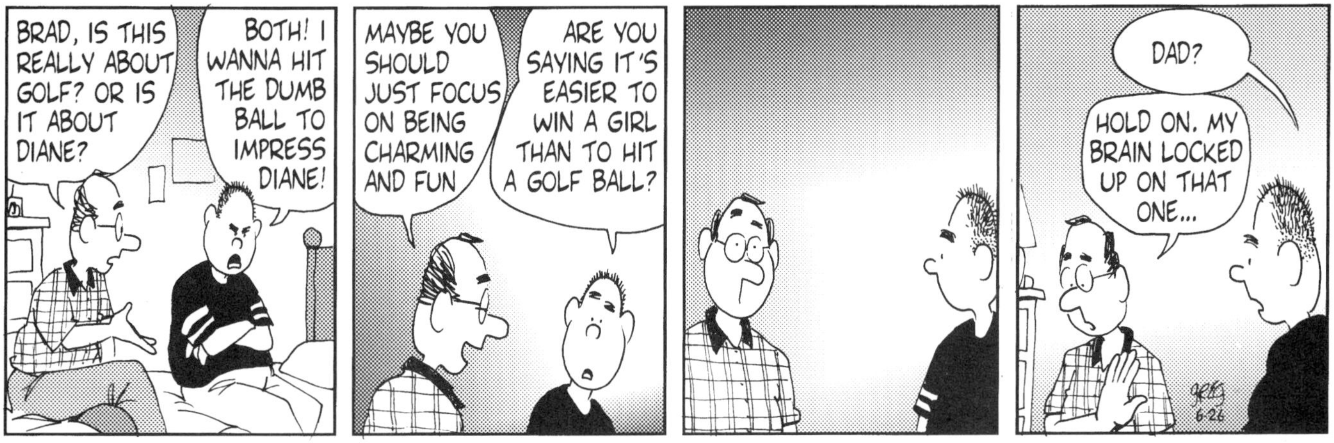
BRAD, IS THIS REALLY ABOUT GOLF? OR IS IT ABOUT DIANE?
BOTH! I WANNA HIT THE DUMB BALL TO IMPRESS DIANE!
MAYBE YOU SHOULD JUST FOCUS ON BEING CHARMING AND FUN
ARE YOU SAYING IT'S EASIER TO WIN A GIRL THAN TO HIT A GOLF BALL?
DAD?
HOLD ON. MY BRAIN LOCKED UP ON THAT ONE...
6-26

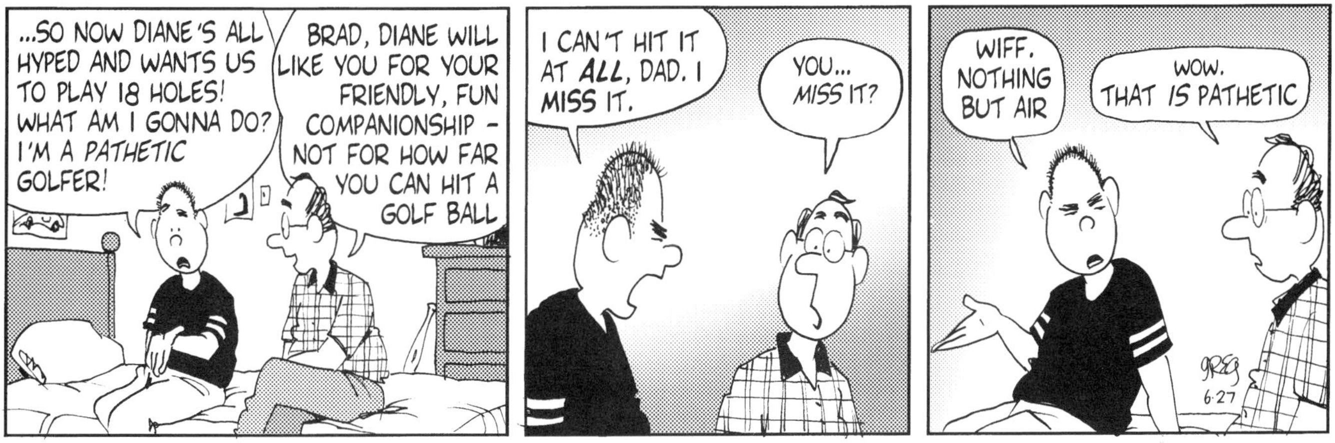
...SO NOW DIANE'S ALL HYPED AND WANTS US TO PLAY 18 HOLES! WHAT AM I GONNA DO? I'M A *PATHETIC* GOLFER!
BRAD, DIANE WILL LIKE YOU FOR YOUR FRIENDLY, FUN COMPANIONSHIP – NOT FOR HOW FAR YOU CAN HIT A GOLF BALL
I CAN'T HIT IT AT **ALL**, DAD. I **MISS** IT.
YOU... *MISS* IT?
WIFF. NOTHING BUT AIR
WOW. THAT *IS* PATHETIC
6-27

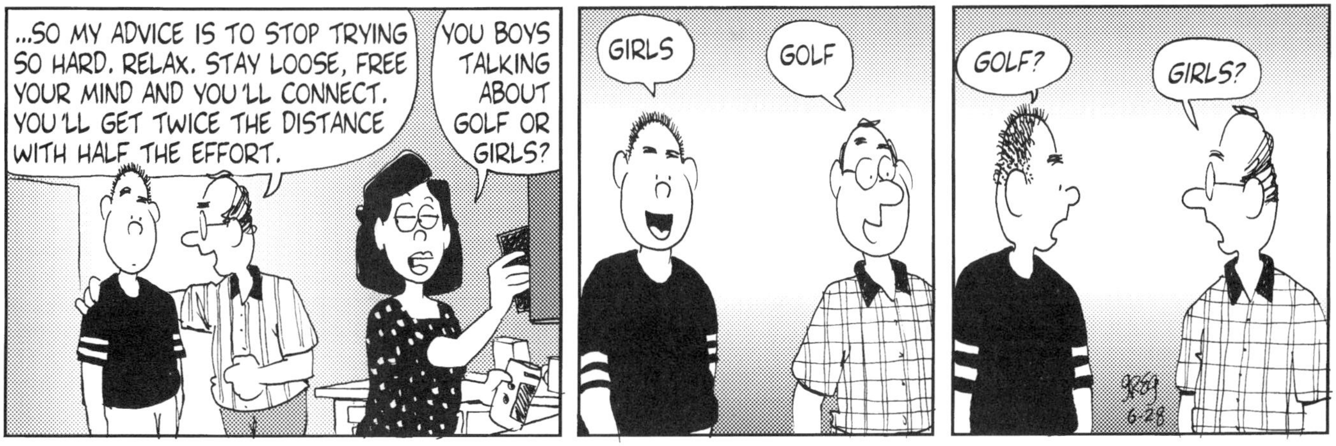
...SO MY ADVICE IS TO STOP TRYING SO HARD. RELAX. STAY LOOSE, FREE YOUR MIND AND YOU'LL CONNECT. YOU'LL GET TWICE THE DISTANCE WITH HALF THE EFFORT.
YOU BOYS TALKING ABOUT GOLF OR GIRLS?
GIRLS
GOLF
GOLF?
GIRLS?
6-28

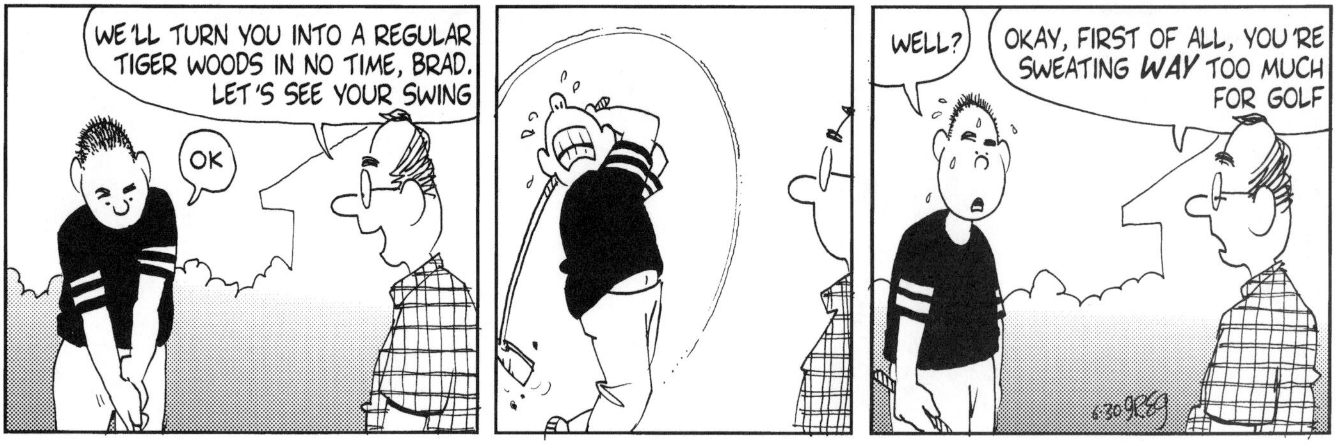
WE'LL TURN YOU INTO A REGULAR TIGER WOODS IN NO TIME, BRAD. LET'S SEE YOUR SWING
OK
WELL?
OKAY, FIRST OF ALL, YOU'RE SWEATING *WAY* TOO MUCH FOR GOLF

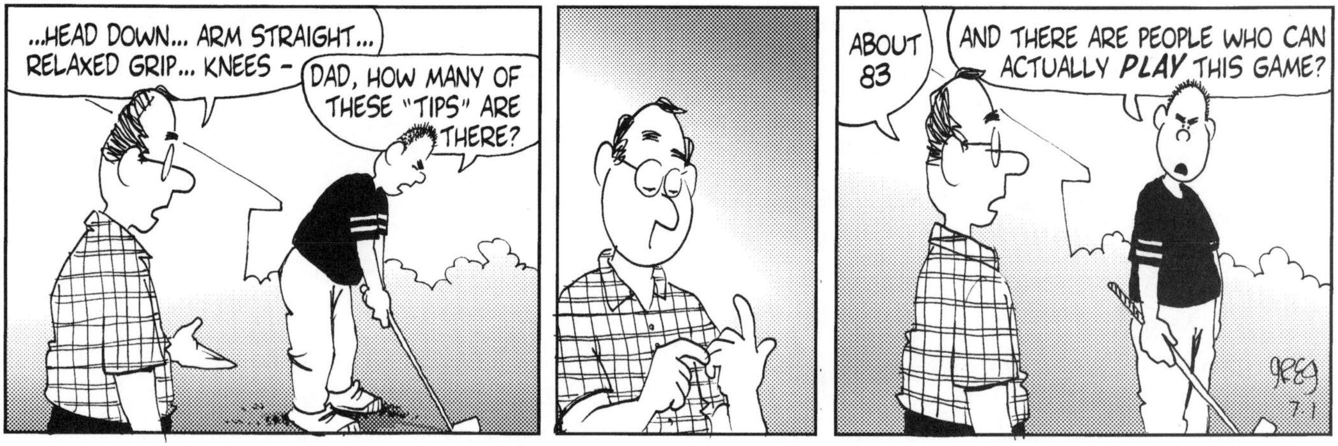
...HEAD DOWN... ARM STRAIGHT... RELAXED GRIP... KNEES –
DAD, HOW MANY OF THESE "TIPS" ARE THERE?
ABOUT 83
AND THERE ARE PEOPLE WHO CAN ACTUALLY *PLAY* THIS GAME?

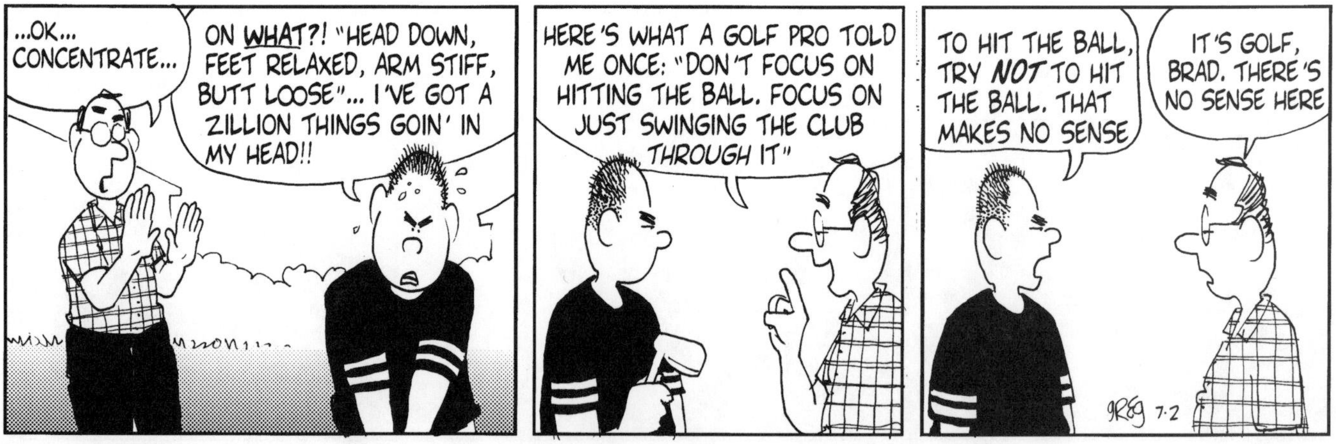
...OK... CONCENTRATE...
ON WHAT?! "HEAD DOWN, FEET RELAXED, ARM STIFF, BUTT LOOSE"... I'VE GOT A ZILLION THINGS GOIN' IN MY HEAD!!
HERE'S WHAT A GOLF PRO TOLD ME ONCE: "DON'T FOCUS ON HITTING THE BALL. FOCUS ON JUST SWINGING THE CLUB *THROUGH* IT"
TO HIT THE BALL, TRY *NOT* TO HIT THE BALL. THAT MAKES NO SENSE
IT'S GOLF, BRAD. THERE'S NO SENSE HERE

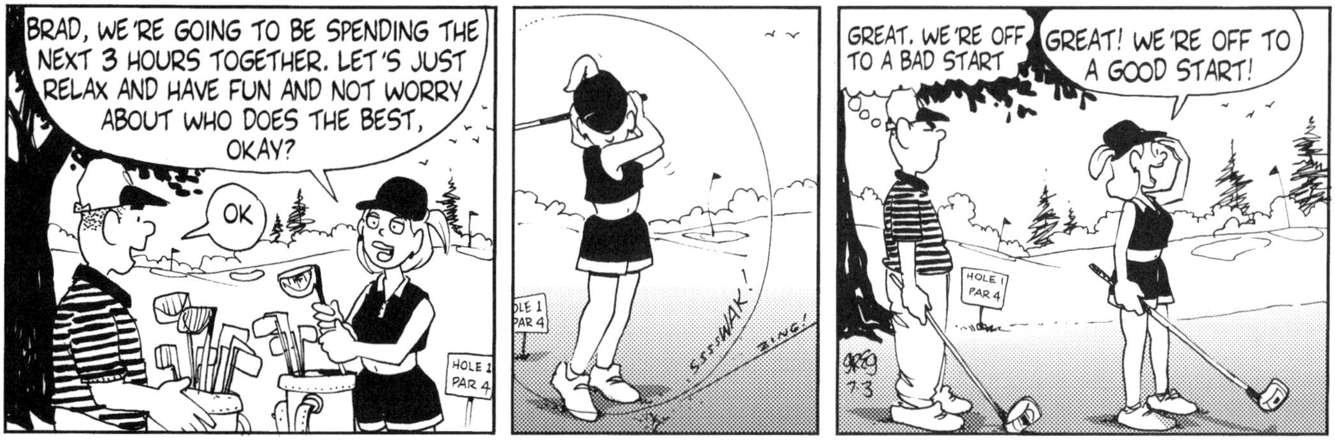
BRAD, WE'RE GOING TO BE SPENDING THE NEXT 3 HOURS TOGETHER. LET'S JUST RELAX AND HAVE FUN AND NOT WORRY ABOUT WHO DOES THE BEST, OKAY?
OK
HOLE 1 PAR 4
SSSWAK!
ZING!
GREAT. WE'RE OFF TO A BAD START
GREAT! WE'RE OFF TO A GOOD START!
HOLE 1 PAR 4
GREG 7-3

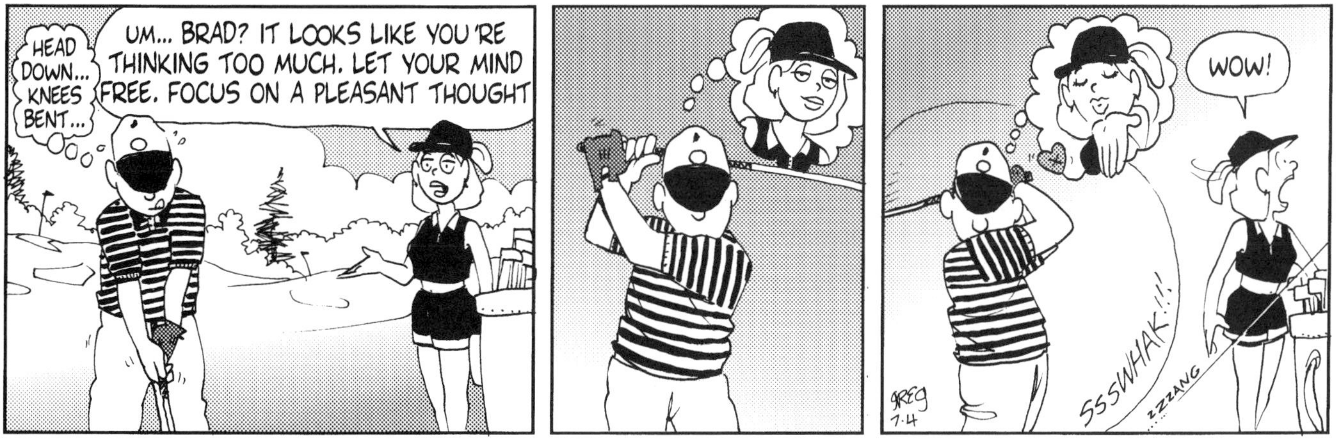
HEAD DOWN... KNEES BENT...
UM... BRAD? IT LOOKS LIKE YOU'RE THINKING TOO MUCH. LET YOUR MIND FREE. FOCUS ON A PLEASANT THOUGHT
WOW!
SSSWHAK!!
ZZZANG
GREG 7-4

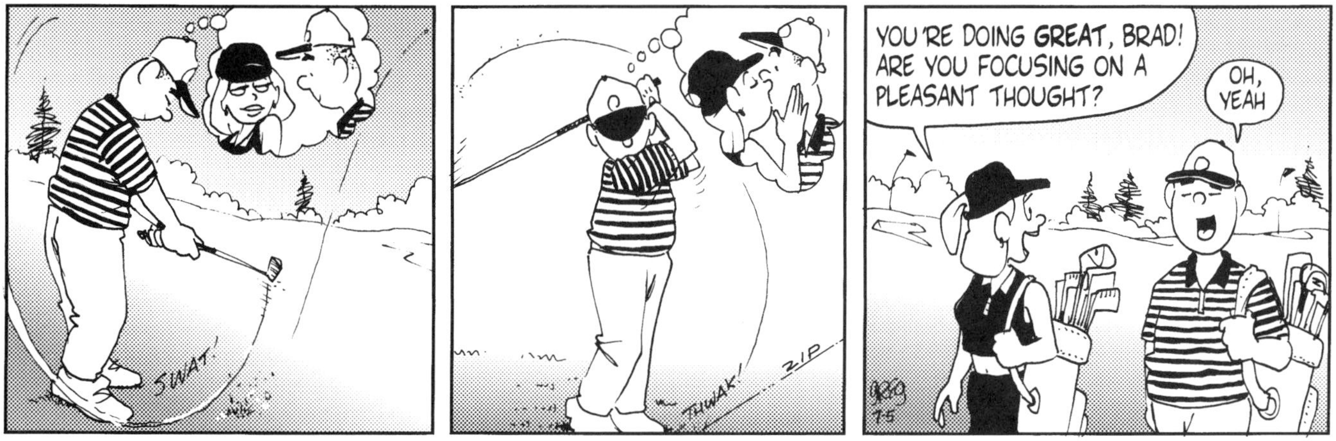
SWAT!
THWAK!
ZIP
YOU'RE DOING **GREAT**, BRAD! ARE YOU FOCUSING ON A PLEASANT THOUGHT?
OH, YEAH
GREG 7-5

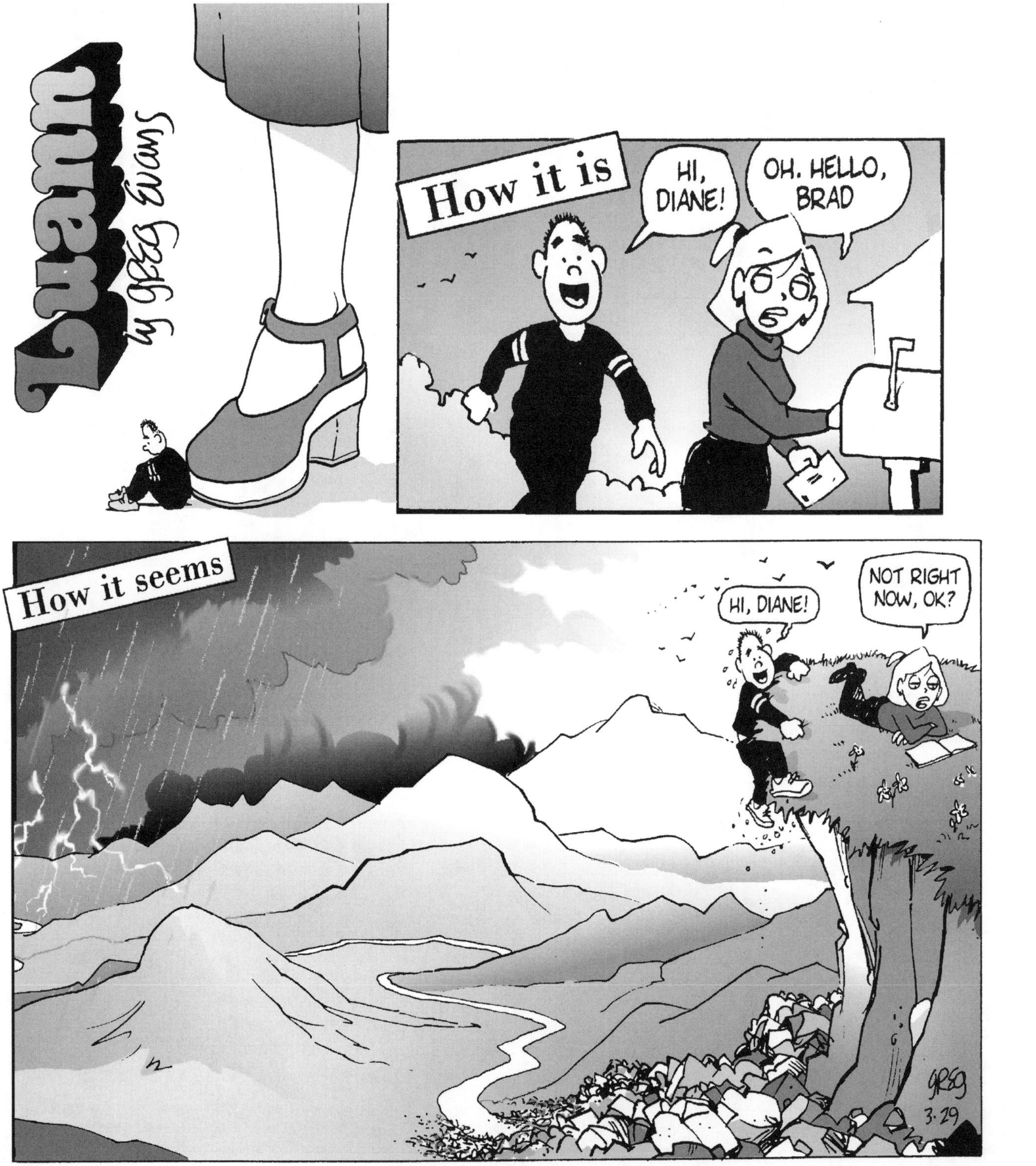
Luann
by GREG EVANS
How it is
HI, DIANE!
OH. HELLO, BRAD
How it seems
HI, DIANE!
NOT RIGHT NOW, OK?
GREG 3.29

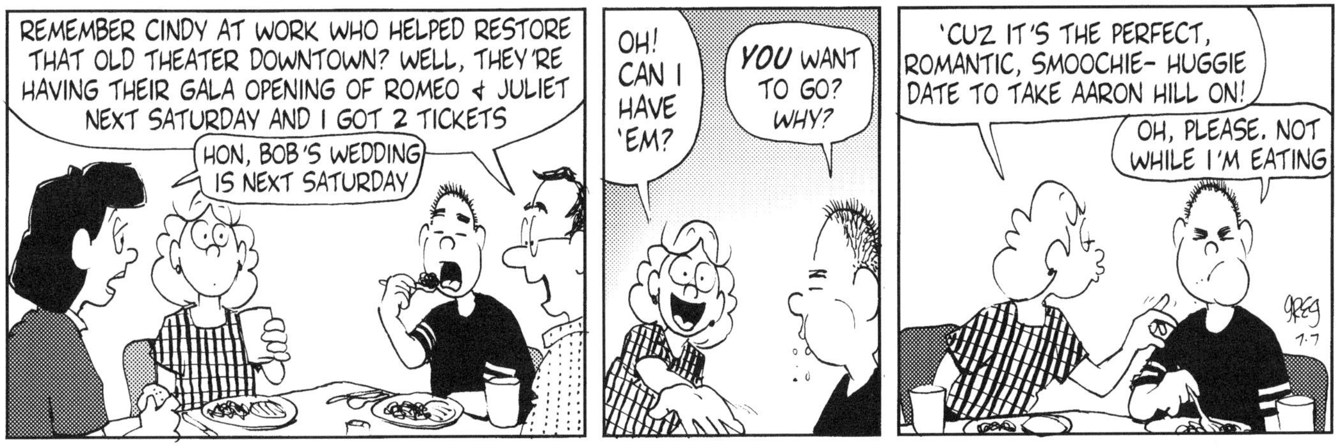
REMEMBER CINDY AT WORK WHO HELPED RESTORE THAT OLD THEATER DOWNTOWN? WELL, THEY'RE HAVING THEIR GALA OPENING OF ROMEO & JULIET NEXT SATURDAY AND I GOT 2 TICKETS
HON, BOB'S WEDDING IS NEXT SATURDAY
OH! CAN I HAVE 'EM?
YOU WANT TO GO? WHY?
'CUZ IT'S THE PERFECT, ROMANTIC, SMOOCHIE- HUGGIE DATE TO TAKE AARON HILL ON!
OH, PLEASE. NOT WHILE I'M EATING

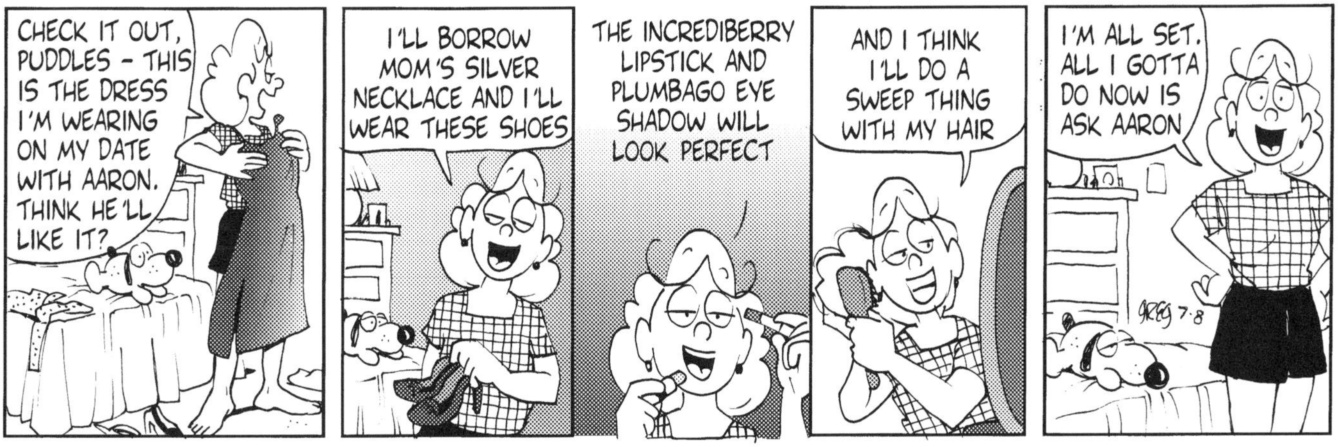
CHECK IT OUT, PUDDLES - THIS IS THE DRESS I'M WEARING ON MY DATE WITH AARON. THINK HE'LL LIKE IT?
I'LL BORROW MOM'S SILVER NECKLACE AND I'LL WEAR THESE SHOES
THE INCREDIBERRY LIPSTICK AND PLUMBAGO EYE SHADOW WILL LOOK PERFECT
AND I THINK I'LL DO A SWEEP THING WITH MY HAIR
I'M ALL SET. ALL I GOTTA DO NOW IS ASK AARON

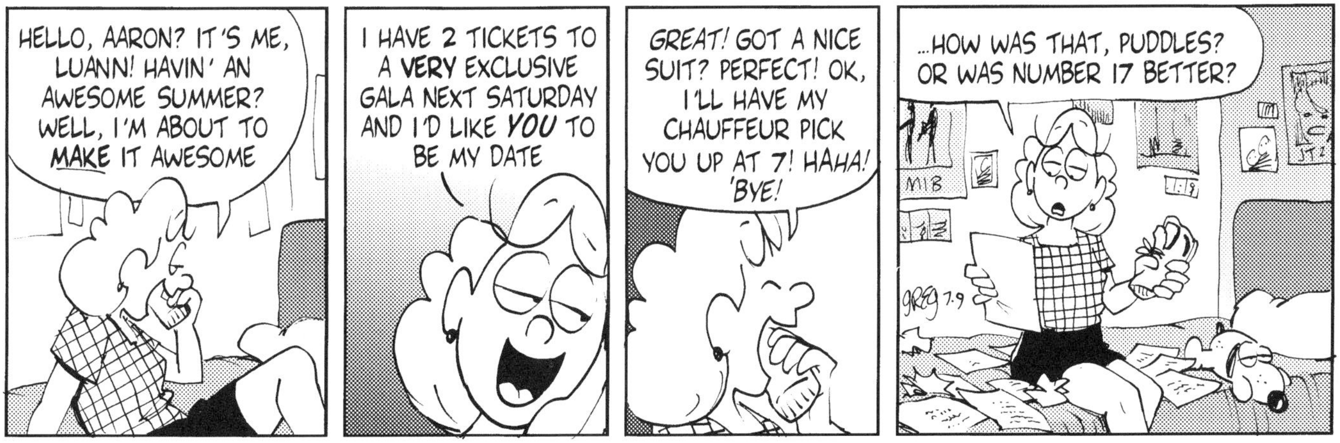
HELLO, AARON? IT'S ME, LUANN! HAVIN' AN AWESOME SUMMER? WELL, I'M ABOUT TO MAKE IT AWESOME
I HAVE 2 TICKETS TO A VERY EXCLUSIVE GALA NEXT SATURDAY AND I'D LIKE YOU TO BE MY DATE
GREAT! GOT A NICE SUIT? PERFECT! OK, I'LL HAVE MY CHAUFFEUR PICK YOU UP AT 7! HAHA! 'BYE!
...HOW WAS THAT, PUDDLES? OR WAS NUMBER 17 BETTER?

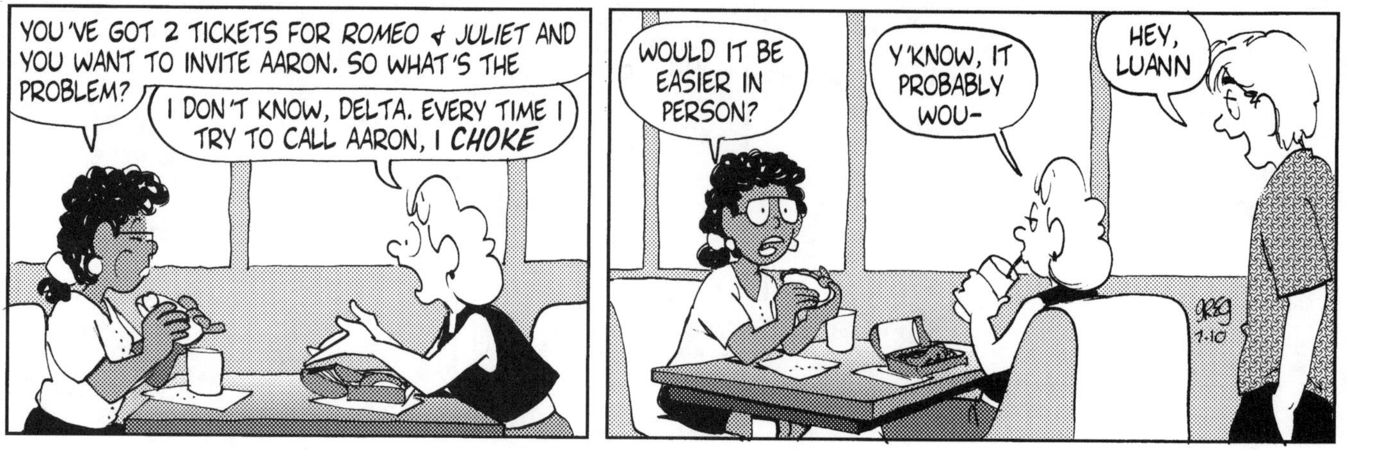
YOU'VE GOT 2 TICKETS FOR *ROMEO & JULIET* AND YOU WANT TO INVITE AARON. SO WHAT'S THE PROBLEM?
I DON'T KNOW, DELTA. EVERY TIME I TRY TO CALL AARON, I ***CHOKE***
WOULD IT BE EASIER IN PERSON?
Y'KNOW, IT PROBABLY WOU-
HEY, LUANN
GREG 7-10

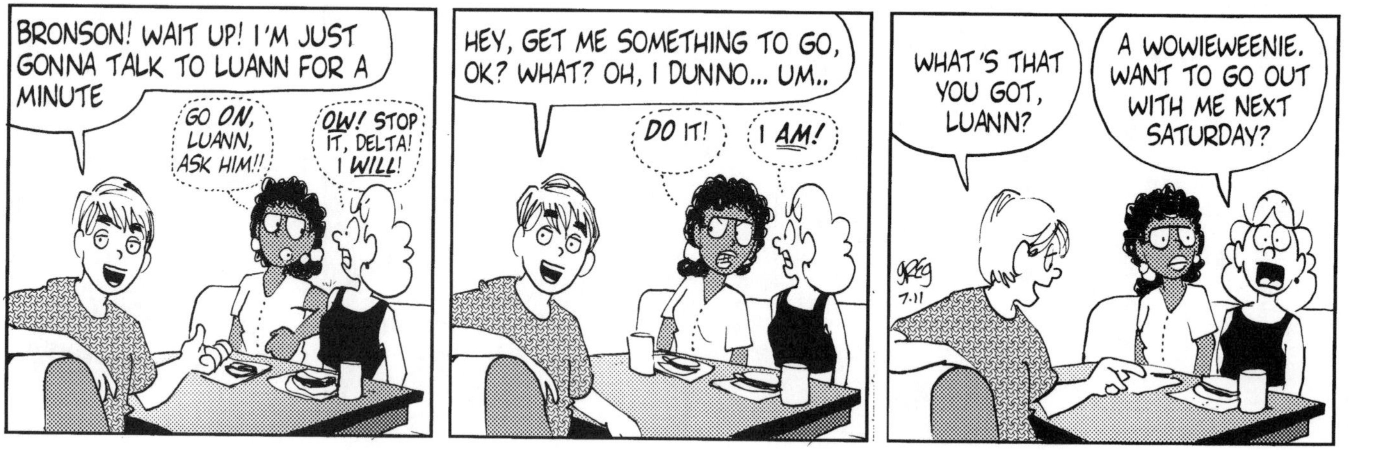
BRONSON! WAIT UP! I'M JUST GONNA TALK TO LUANN FOR A MINUTE
GO *ON*, LUANN, ASK HIM!!
OW! STOP IT, DELTA! I *WILL*!
HEY, GET ME SOMETHING TO GO, OK? WHAT? OH, I DUNNO... UM..
DO IT!
I *AM!*
WHAT'S THAT YOU GOT, LUANN?
A WOWIEWEENIE. WANT TO GO OUT WITH ME NEXT SATURDAY?
GREG 7-11

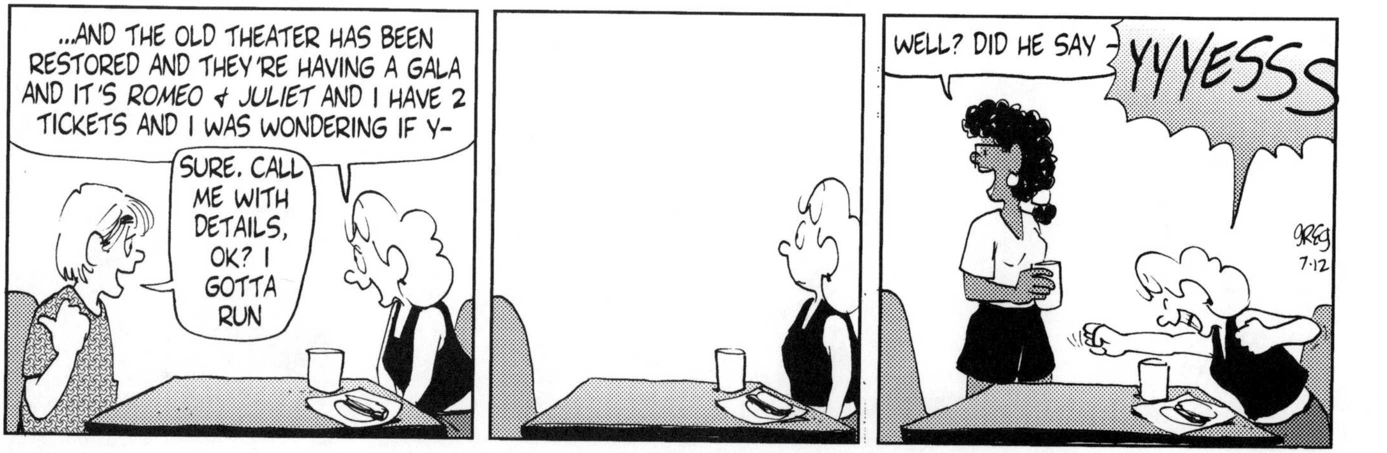
...AND THE OLD THEATER HAS BEEN RESTORED AND THEY'RE HAVING A GALA AND IT'S *ROMEO & JULIET* AND I HAVE 2 TICKETS AND I WAS WONDERING IF Y-
SURE. CALL ME WITH DETAILS, OK? I GOTTA RUN
WELL? DID HE SAY -
YYYESSS
GREG 7-12

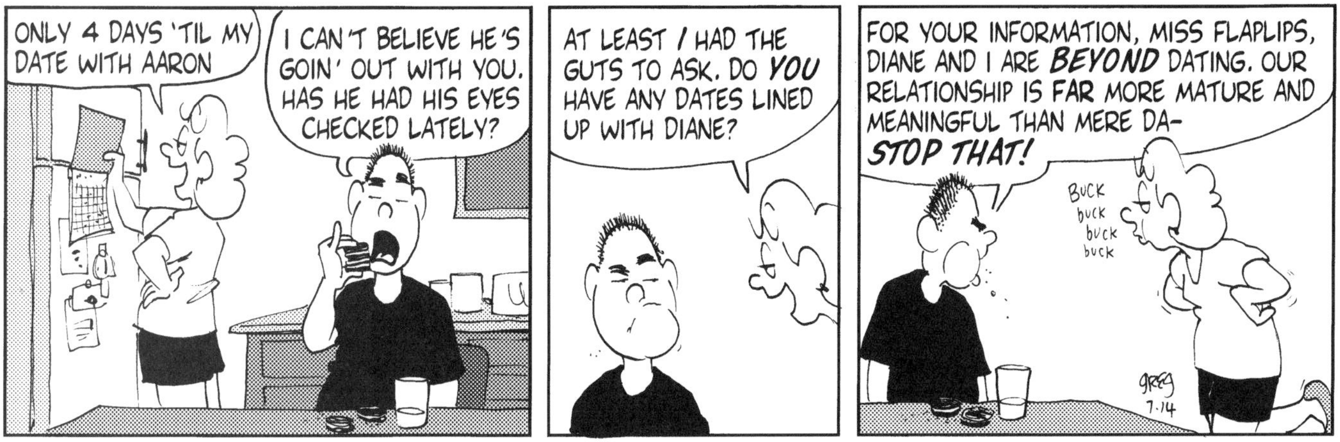
ONLY 4 DAYS 'TIL MY DATE WITH AARON
I CAN'T BELIEVE HE'S GOIN' OUT WITH YOU. HAS HE HAD HIS EYES CHECKED LATELY?
AT LEAST *I* HAD THE GUTS TO ASK. DO *YOU* HAVE ANY DATES LINED UP WITH DIANE?
FOR YOUR INFORMATION, MISS FLAPLIPS, DIANE AND I ARE *BEYOND* DATING. OUR RELATIONSHIP IS **FAR** MORE MATURE AND MEANINGFUL THAN MERE DA- **STOP THAT!**
BUCK buck buck buck
GREG 7.14

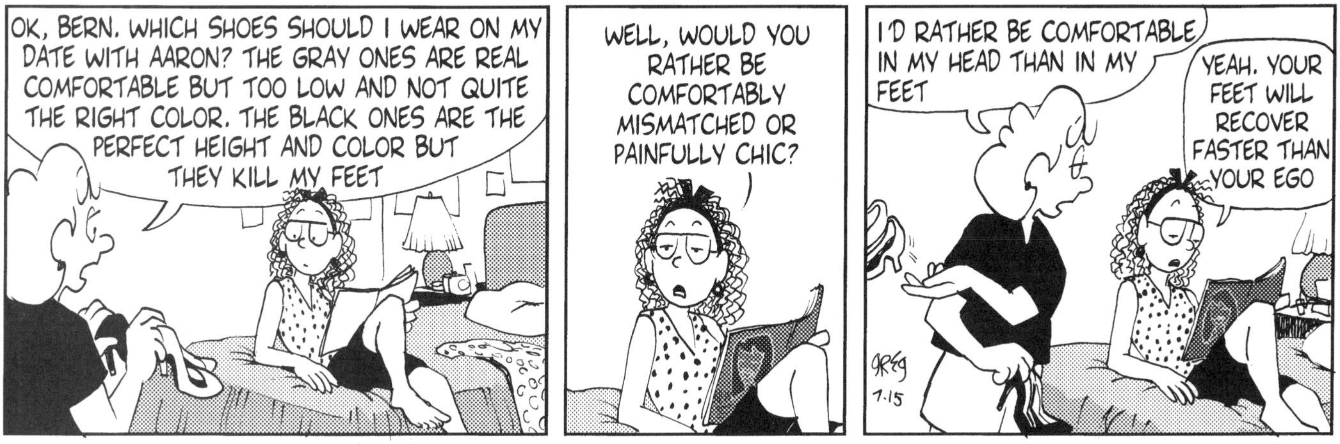
OK, BERN. WHICH SHOES SHOULD I WEAR ON MY DATE WITH AARON? THE GRAY ONES ARE REAL COMFORTABLE BUT TOO LOW AND NOT QUITE THE RIGHT COLOR. THE BLACK ONES ARE THE PERFECT HEIGHT AND COLOR BUT THEY KILL MY FEET
WELL, WOULD YOU RATHER BE COMFORTABLY MISMATCHED OR PAINFULLY CHIC?
I'D RATHER BE COMFORTABLE IN MY HEAD THAN IN MY FEET
YEAH. YOUR FEET WILL RECOVER FASTER THAN YOUR EGO
GREG 7.15

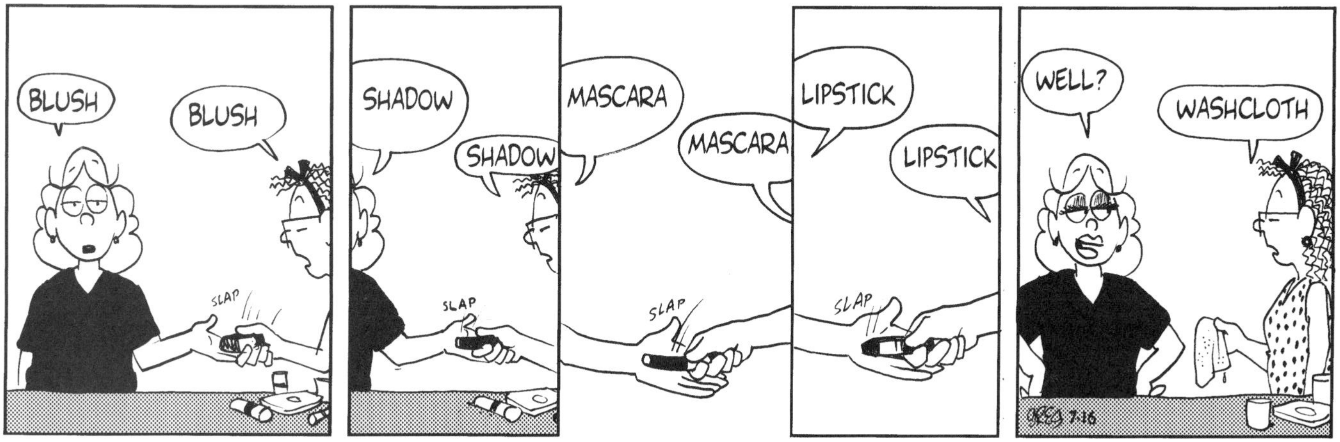
BLUSH
BLUSH
SLAP
SHADOW
SHADOW
SLAP
MASCARA
MASCARA
SLAP
LIPSTICK
LIPSTICK
SLAP
WELL?
WASHCLOTH
GREG 7.16

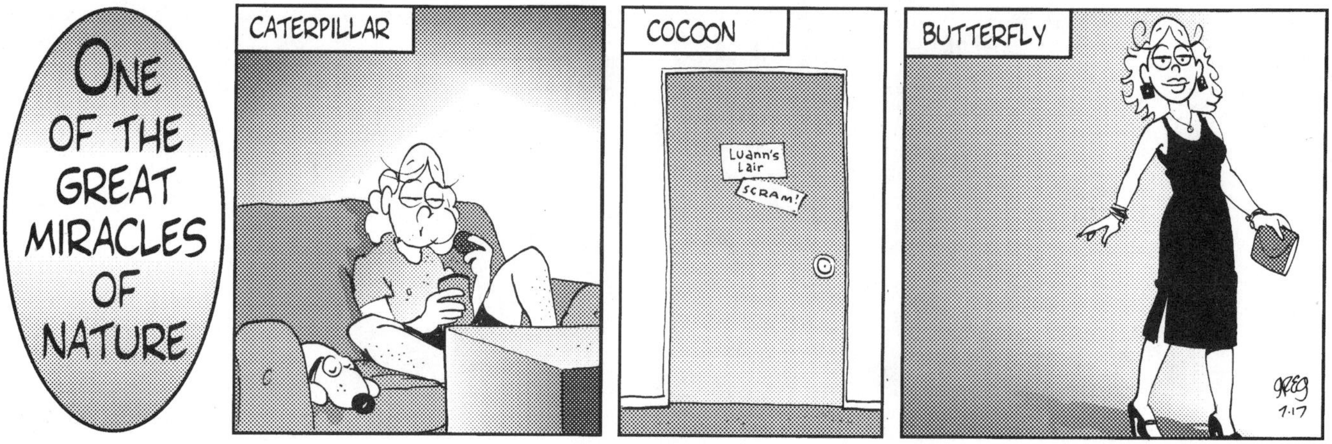
ONE OF THE GREAT MIRACLES OF NATURE
CATERPILLAR
COCOON
Luann's Lair
SCRAM!
BUTTERFLY

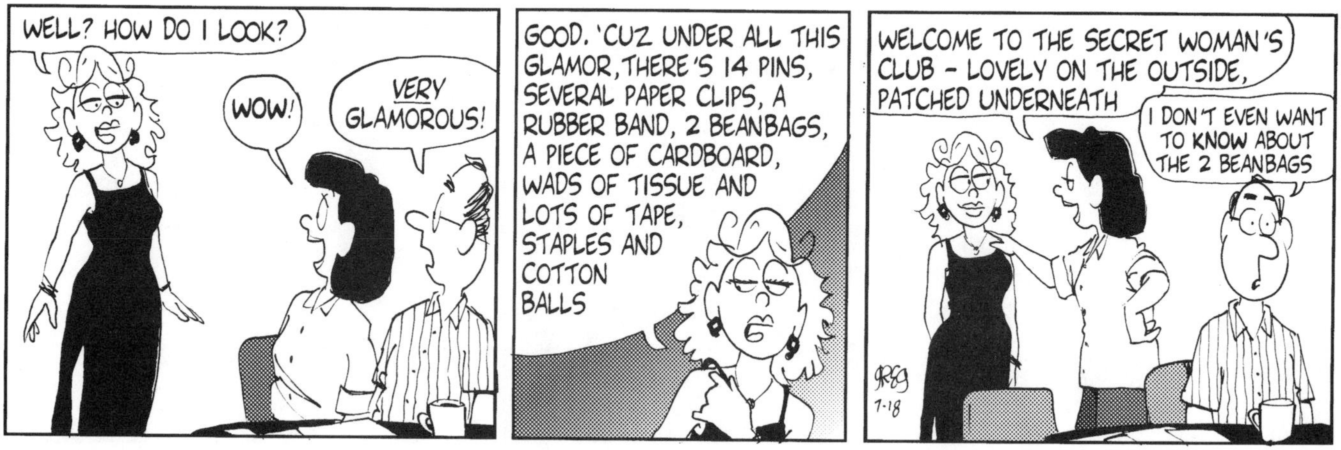
WELL? HOW DO I LOOK?
WOW!
VERY GLAMOROUS!
GOOD. 'CUZ UNDER ALL THIS GLAMOR, THERE'S 14 PINS, SEVERAL PAPER CLIPS, A RUBBER BAND, 2 BEANBAGS, A PIECE OF CARDBOARD, WADS OF TISSUE AND LOTS OF TAPE, STAPLES AND COTTON BALLS
WELCOME TO THE SECRET WOMAN'S CLUB - LOVELY ON THE OUTSIDE, PATCHED UNDERNEATH
I DON'T EVEN WANT TO KNOW ABOUT THE 2 BEANBAGS

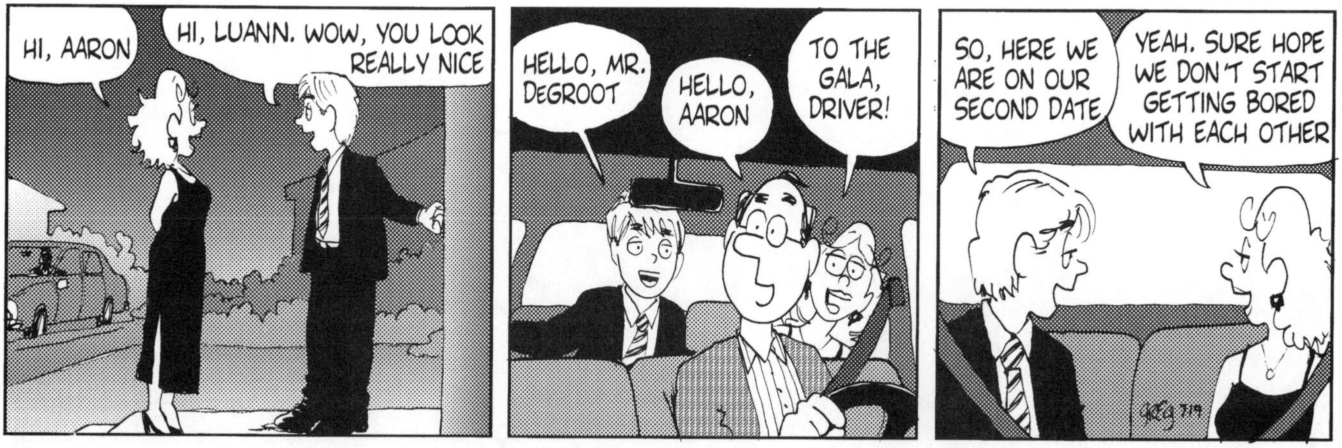
HI, AARON
HI, LUANN. WOW, YOU LOOK REALLY NICE
HELLO, MR. DEGROOT
HELLO, AARON
TO THE GALA, DRIVER!
SO, HERE WE ARE ON OUR SECOND DATE
YEAH. SURE HOPE WE DON'T START GETTING BORED WITH EACH OTHER

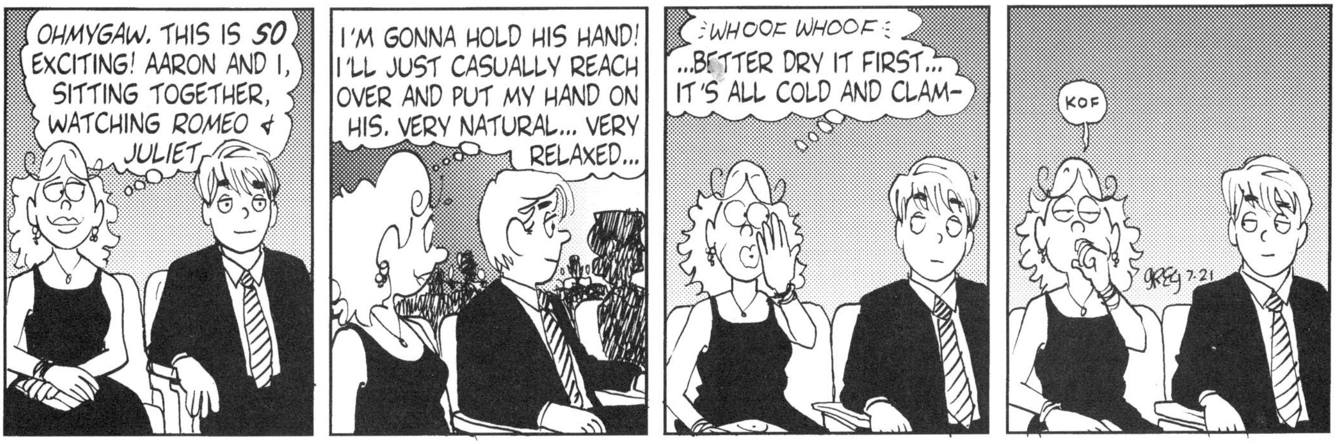
OHMYGAW. THIS IS *SO* EXCITING! AARON AND I, SITTING TOGETHER, WATCHING *ROMEO & JULIET*
I'M GONNA HOLD HIS HAND! I'LL JUST CASUALLY REACH OVER AND PUT MY HAND ON HIS. VERY NATURAL... VERY RELAXED...
WHOOF WHOOF
...BETTER DRY IT FIRST... IT'S ALL COLD AND CLAM-
KOF
GREG 7-21

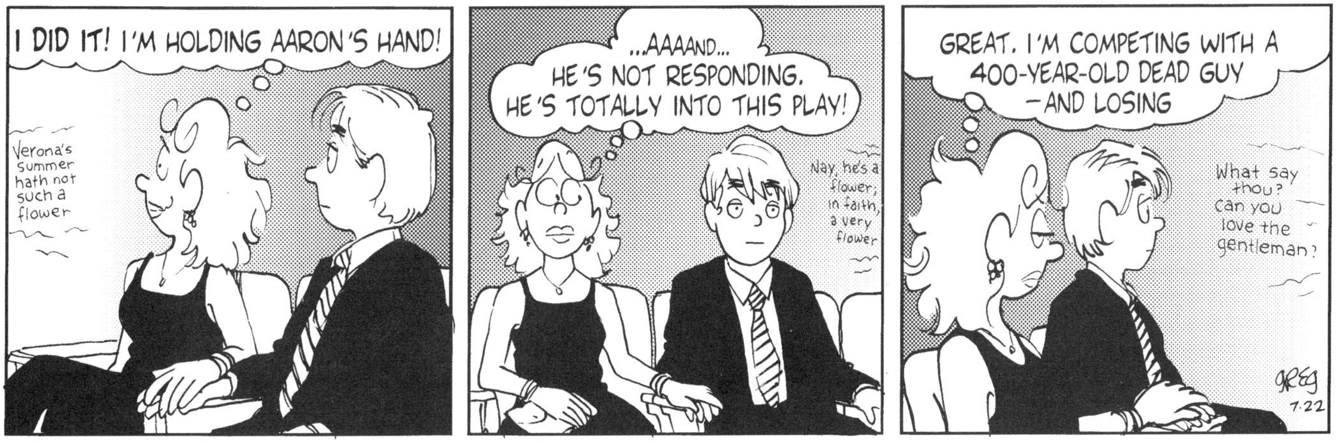
I DID IT! I'M HOLDING AARON'S HAND!
Verona's summer hath not such a flower
...AAAAND... HE'S NOT RESPONDING. HE'S TOTALLY INTO THIS PLAY!
Nay, he's a flower; in faith, a very flower
GREAT. I'M COMPETING WITH A 400-YEAR-OLD DEAD GUY —AND LOSING
What say thou? can you love the gentleman?
GREG 7-22

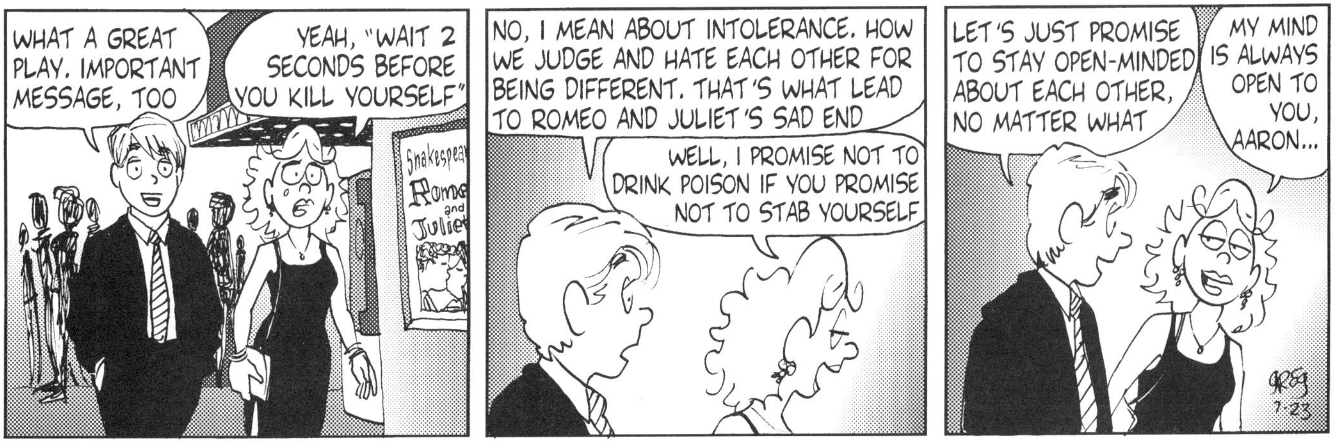
WHAT A GREAT PLAY. IMPORTANT MESSAGE, TOO
YEAH, "WAIT 2 SECONDS BEFORE YOU KILL YOURSELF"
NO, I MEAN ABOUT INTOLERANCE. HOW WE JUDGE AND HATE EACH OTHER FOR BEING DIFFERENT. THAT'S WHAT LEAD TO ROMEO AND JULIET'S SAD END
WELL, I PROMISE NOT TO DRINK POISON IF YOU PROMISE NOT TO STAB YOURSELF
LET'S JUST PROMISE TO STAY OPEN-MINDED ABOUT EACH OTHER, NO MATTER WHAT
MY MIND IS ALWAYS OPEN TO YOU, AARON...
GREG 7-23

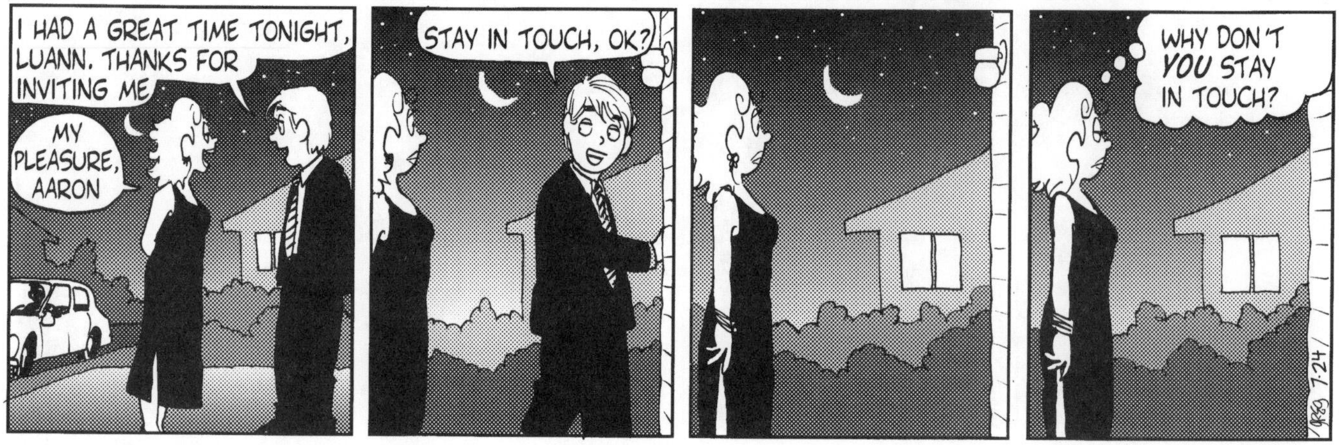
I HAD A GREAT TIME TONIGHT, LUANN. THANKS FOR INVITING ME
MY PLEASURE, AARON
STAY IN TOUCH, OK?
WHY DON'T YOU STAY IN TOUCH?
GREG 7·24

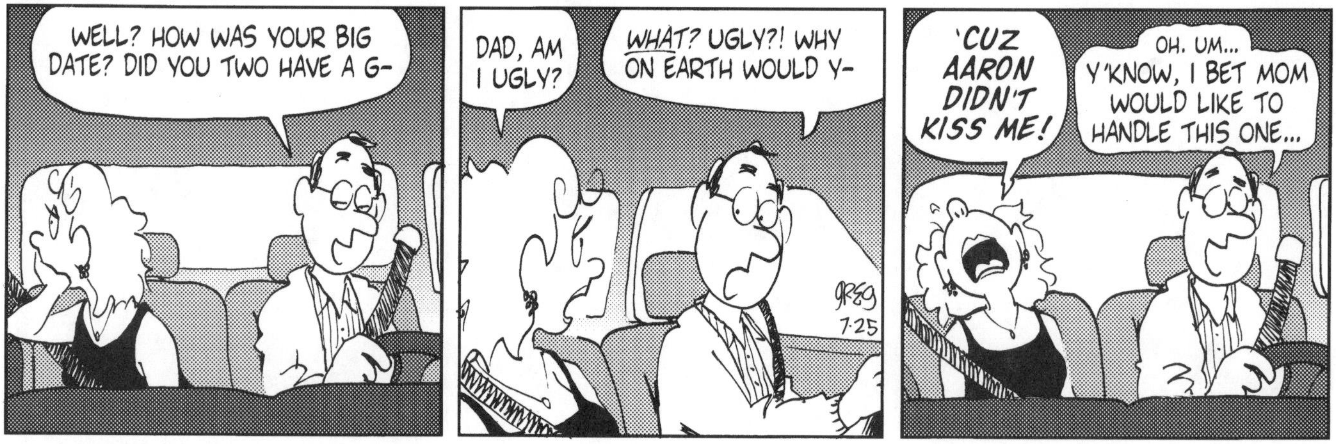
WELL? HOW WAS YOUR BIG DATE? DID YOU TWO HAVE A G-
DAD, AM I UGLY?
WHAT? UGLY?! WHY ON EARTH WOULD Y-
GREG 7·25
'CUZ AARON DIDN'T KISS ME!
OH. UM... Y'KNOW, I BET MOM WOULD LIKE TO HANDLE THIS ONE...

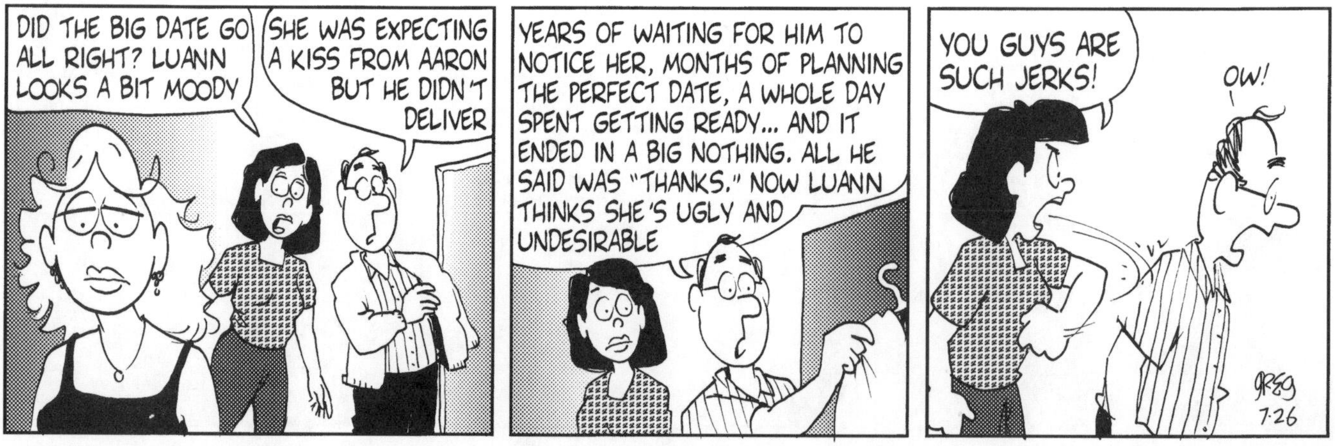
DID THE BIG DATE GO ALL RIGHT? LUANN LOOKS A BIT MOODY
SHE WAS EXPECTING A KISS FROM AARON BUT HE DIDN'T DELIVER
YEARS OF WAITING FOR HIM TO NOTICE HER, MONTHS OF PLANNING THE PERFECT DATE, A WHOLE DAY SPENT GETTING READY... AND IT ENDED IN A BIG NOTHING. ALL HE SAID WAS "THANKS." NOW LUANN THINKS SHE'S UGLY AND UNDESIRABLE
YOU GUYS ARE SUCH JERKS!
OW!
GREG 7·26

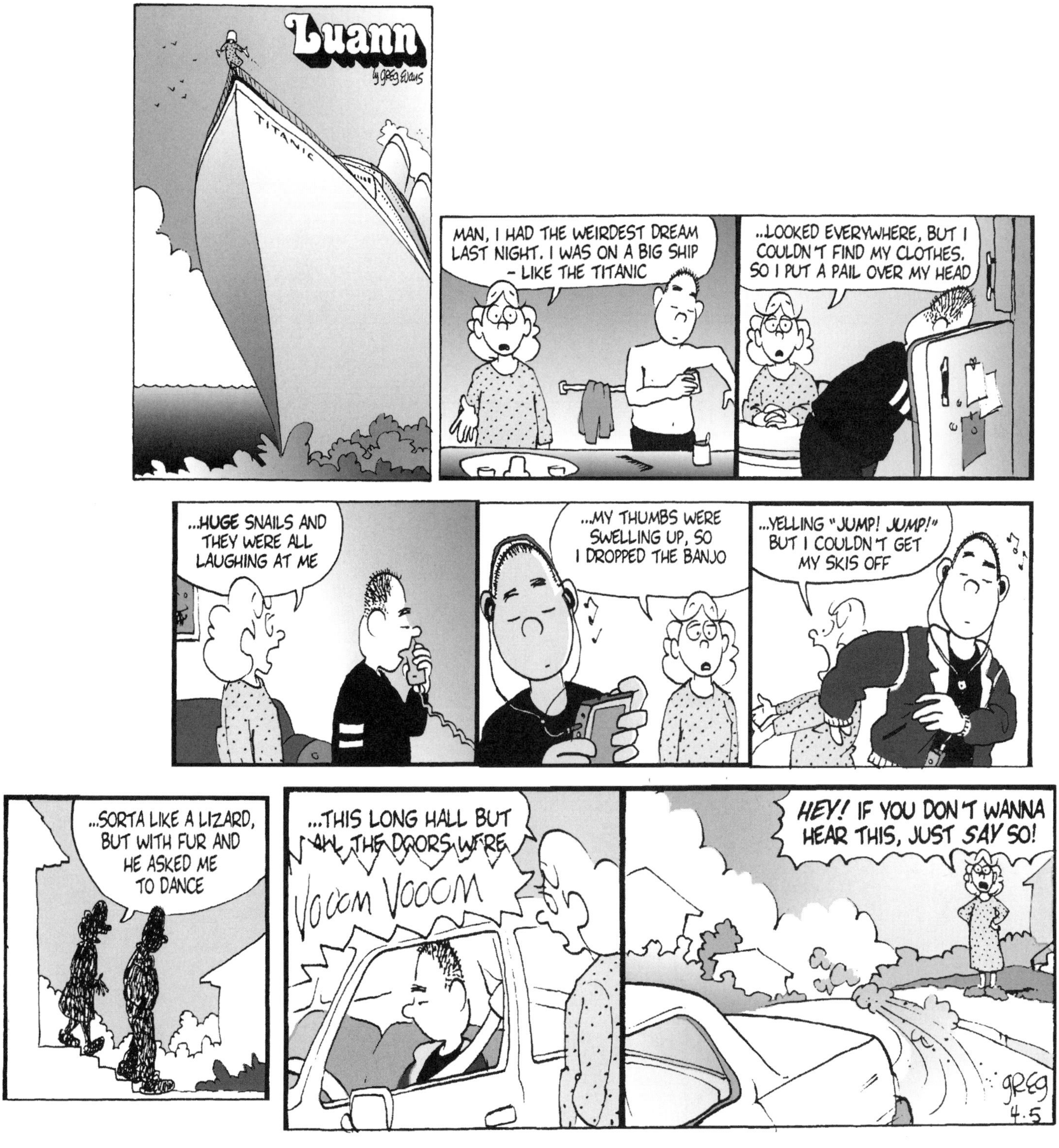
Luann
by Greg Evans
TITANIC
MAN, I HAD THE WEIRDEST DREAM LAST NIGHT. I WAS ON A BIG SHIP – LIKE THE TITANIC
...LOOKED EVERYWHERE, BUT I COULDN'T FIND MY CLOTHES. SO I PUT A PAIL OVER MY HEAD
...HUGE SNAILS AND THEY WERE ALL LAUGHING AT ME
...MY THUMBS WERE SWELLING UP, SO I DROPPED THE BANJO
...YELLING "JUMP! JUMP!" BUT I COULDN'T GET MY SKIS OFF
...SORTA LIKE A LIZARD, BUT WITH FUR AND HE ASKED ME TO DANCE
...THIS LONG HALL BUT ALL THE DOORS WERE
VOOOM VOOOM
HEY! IF YOU DON'T WANNA HEAR THIS, JUST SAY SO!
GREG 4.5

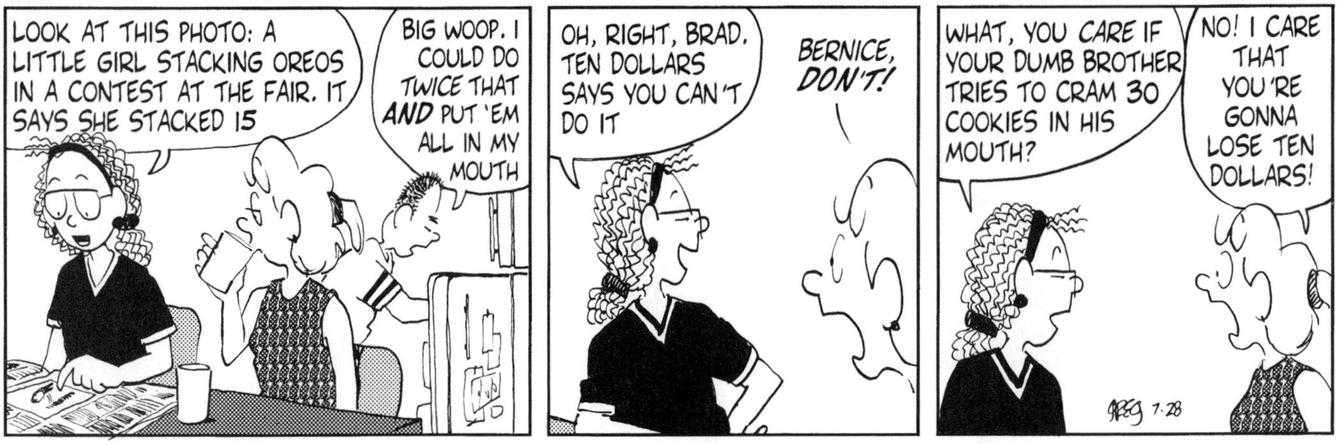
LOOK AT THIS PHOTO: A LITTLE GIRL STACKING OREOS IN A CONTEST AT THE FAIR. IT SAYS SHE STACKED 15
BIG WOOP. I COULD DO *TWICE* THAT ***AND*** PUT 'EM ALL IN MY MOUTH
OH, RIGHT, BRAD. TEN DOLLARS SAYS YOU CAN'T DO IT
*BERNICE, **DON'T!***
WHAT, YOU *CARE* IF YOUR DUMB BROTHER TRIES TO CRAM 30 COOKIES IN HIS MOUTH?
NO! I CARE THAT YOU'RE GONNA LOSE TEN DOLLARS!
GREG 7·28

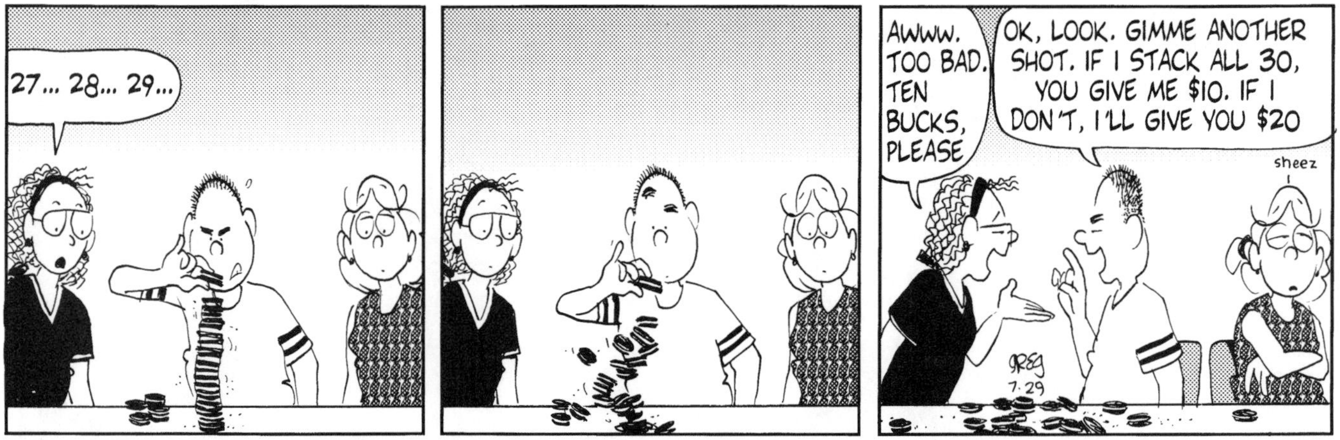
27... 28... 29...
AWWW. TOO BAD. TEN BUCKS, PLEASE
OK, LOOK. GIMME ANOTHER SHOT. IF I STACK ALL 30, YOU GIVE ME $10. IF I DON'T, I'LL GIVE YOU $20
sheez
GREG 7·29

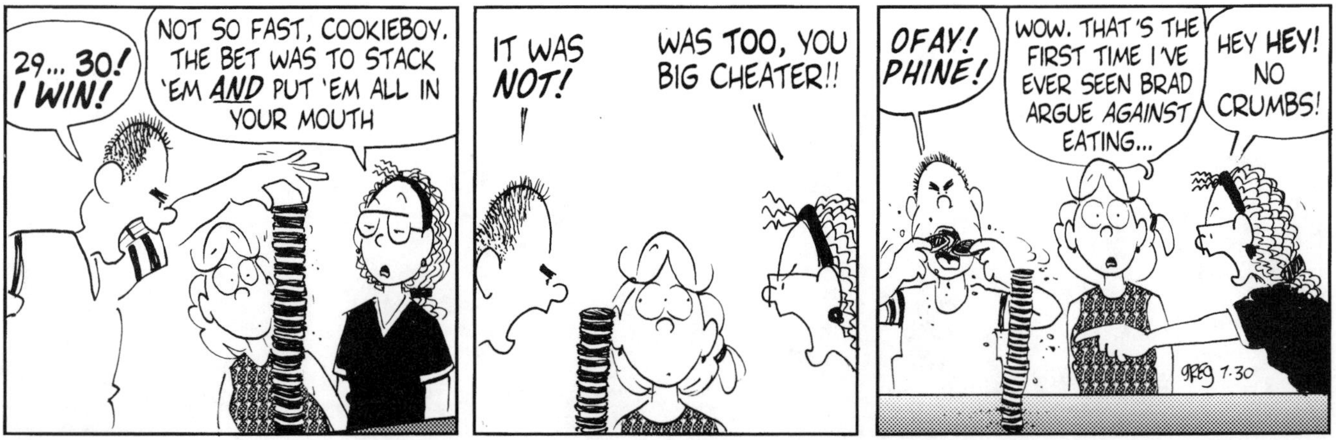
29... **30!** ***I WIN!***
NOT SO FAST, COOKIEBOY. THE BET WAS TO STACK 'EM ***AND*** PUT 'EM ALL IN YOUR MOUTH
IT WAS ***NOT!***
WAS **TOO**, YOU BIG CHEATER!!
OFAY! PHINE!
WOW. THAT'S THE FIRST TIME I'VE EVER SEEN BRAD ARGUE *AGAINST* EATING...
HEY **HEY!** NO CRUMBS!
GREG 7·30

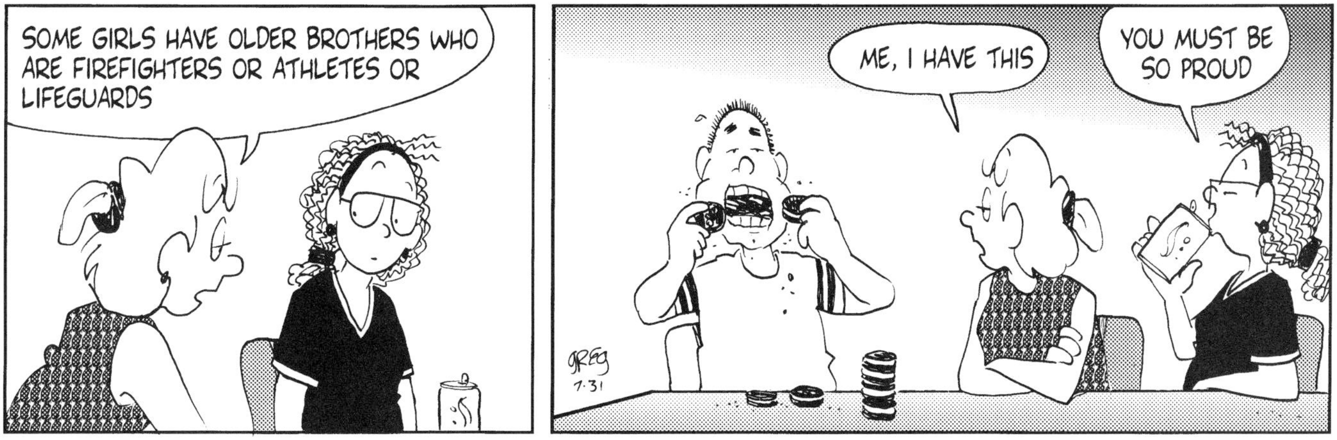
SOME GIRLS HAVE OLDER BROTHERS WHO ARE FIREFIGHTERS OR ATHLETES OR LIFEGUARDS
ME, I HAVE THIS
YOU MUST BE SO PROUD
GREG 7·31

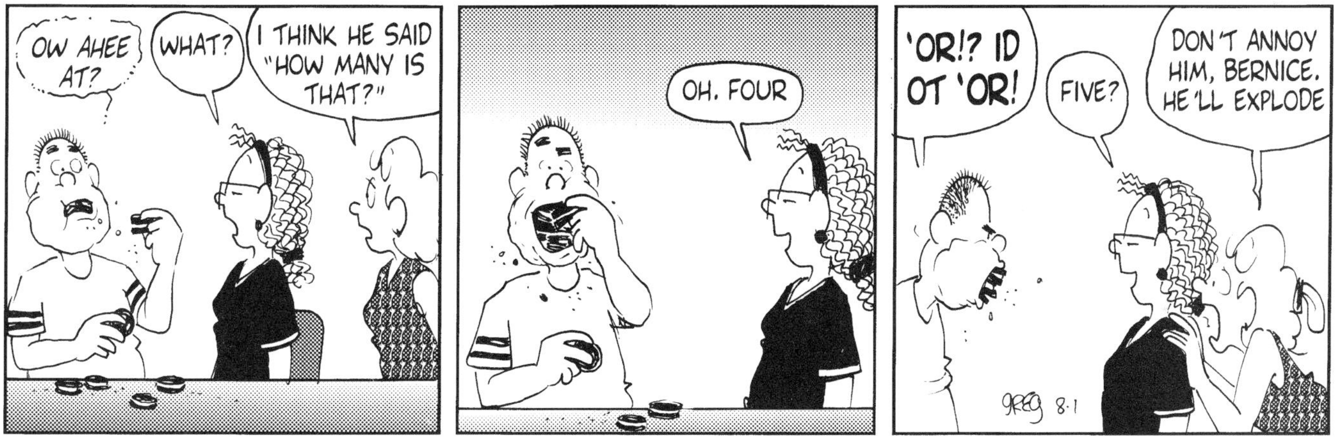
OW AHEE AT?
WHAT?
I THINK HE SAID "HOW MANY IS THAT?"
OH. FOUR
'OR!? ID OT 'OR!
FIVE?
DON'T ANNOY HIM, BERNICE. HE'LL EXPLODE
GREG 8·1

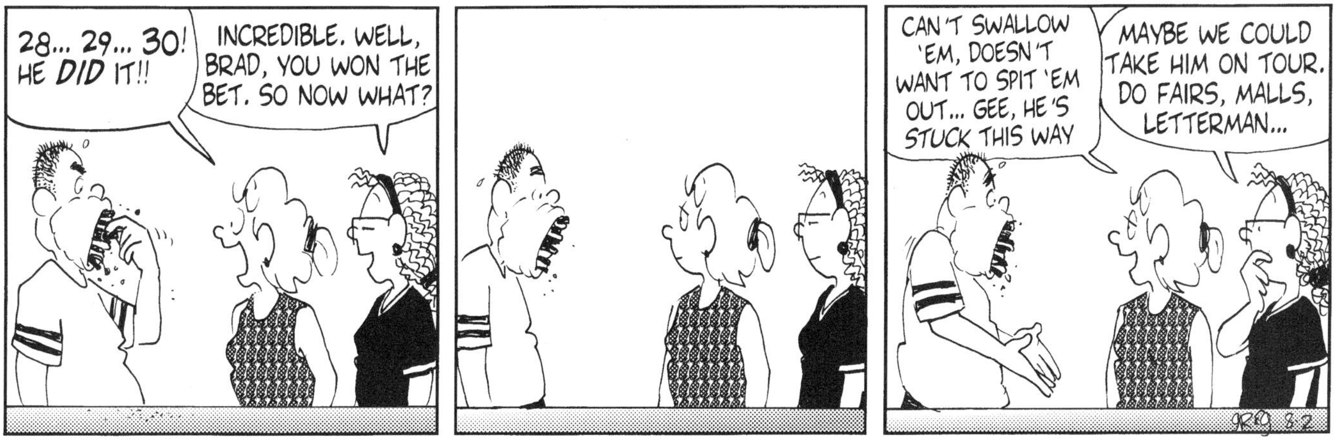
28... 29... 30! HE DID IT!!
INCREDIBLE. WELL, BRAD, YOU WON THE BET. SO NOW WHAT?
CAN'T SWALLOW 'EM, DOESN'T WANT TO SPIT 'EM OUT... GEE, HE'S STUCK THIS WAY
MAYBE WE COULD TAKE HIM ON TOUR. DO FAIRS, MALLS, LETTERMAN...
GREG 8·2

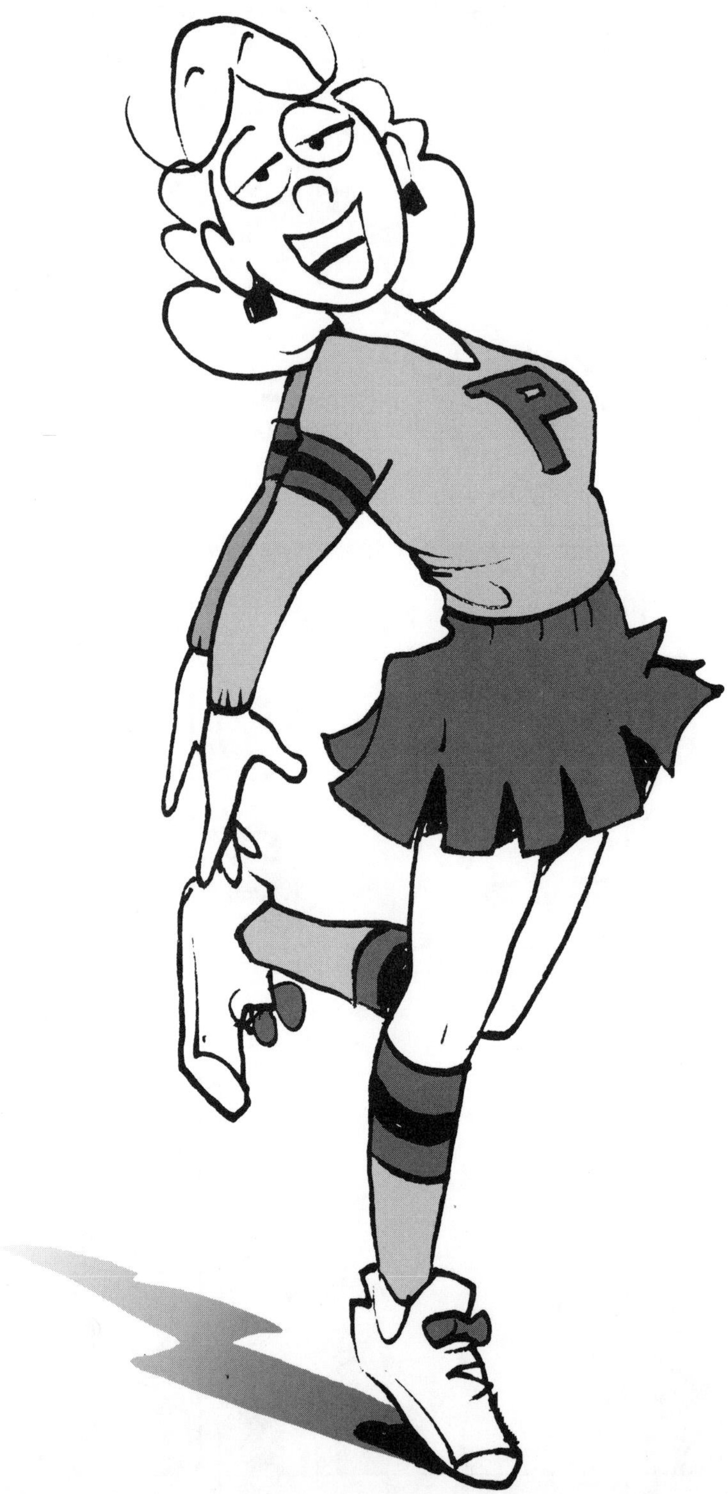
P

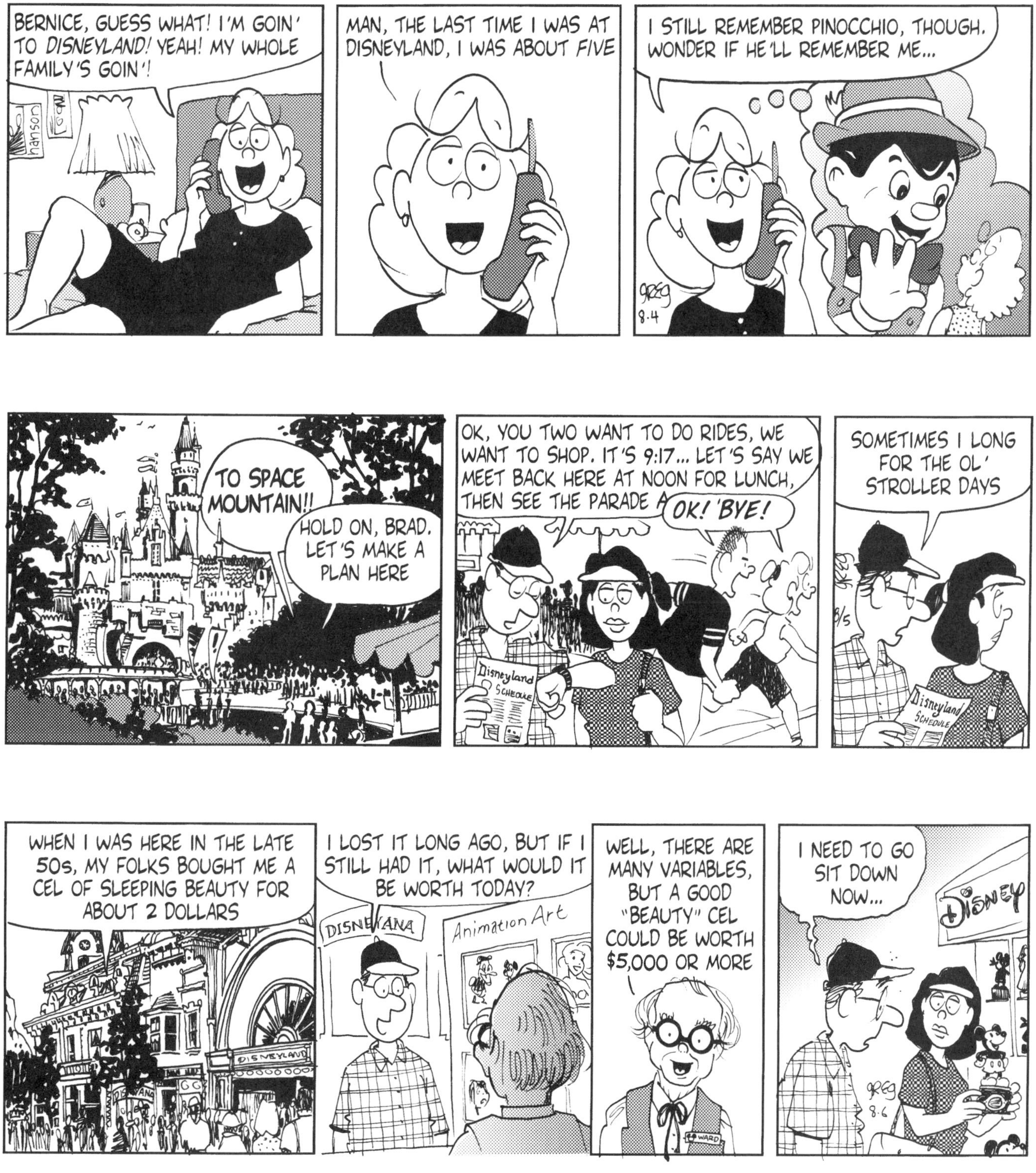
BERNICE, GUESS WHAT! I'M GOIN' TO DISNEYLAND! YEAH! MY WHOLE FAMILY'S GOIN'!
MAN, THE LAST TIME I WAS AT DISNEYLAND, I WAS ABOUT FIVE
I STILL REMEMBER PINOCCHIO, THOUGH. WONDER IF HE'LL REMEMBER ME...
GREG 8.4
TO SPACE MOUNTAIN!!
HOLD ON, BRAD. LET'S MAKE A PLAN HERE
OK, YOU TWO WANT TO DO RIDES, WE WANT TO SHOP. IT'S 9:17... LET'S SAY WE MEET BACK HERE AT NOON FOR LUNCH, THEN SEE THE PARADE A
OK! 'BYE!
Disneyland SCHEDULE
SOMETIMES I LONG FOR THE OL' STROLLER DAYS
8/5
WHEN I WAS HERE IN THE LATE 50s, MY FOLKS BOUGHT ME A CEL OF SLEEPING BEAUTY FOR ABOUT 2 DOLLARS
DISNEYLAND
I LOST IT LONG AGO, BUT IF I STILL HAD IT, WHAT WOULD IT BE WORTH TODAY?
Animation Art
WELL, THERE ARE MANY VARIABLES, BUT A GOOD "BEAUTY" CEL COULD BE WORTH $5,000 OR MORE
WARD
I NEED TO GO SIT DOWN NOW...
DISNEY
GREG 8.6

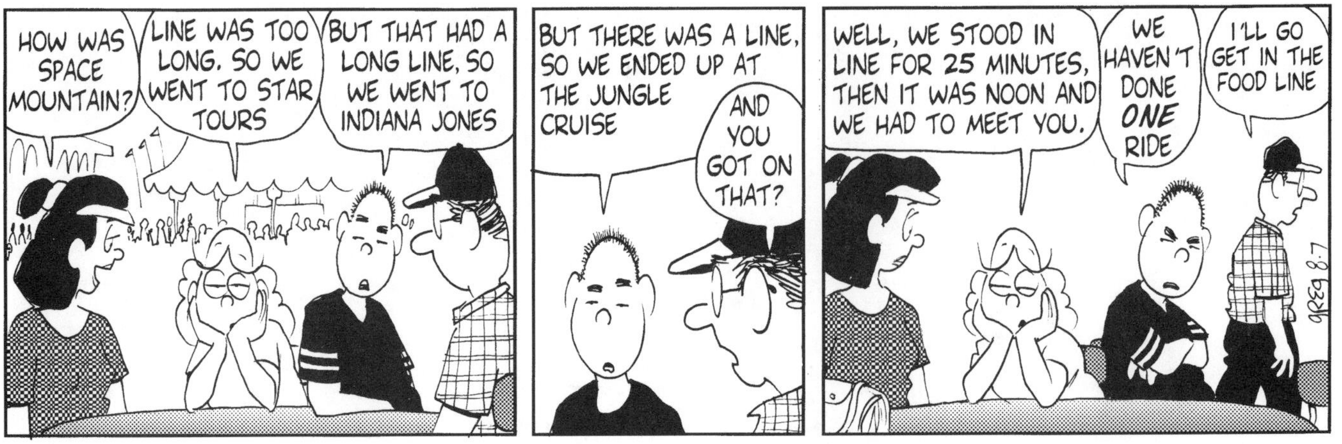
HOW WAS SPACE MOUNTAIN?
LINE WAS TOO LONG. SO WE WENT TO STAR TOURS
BUT THAT HAD A LONG LINE, SO WE WENT TO INDIANA JONES
BUT THERE WAS A LINE, SO WE ENDED UP AT THE JUNGLE CRUISE
AND YOU GOT ON THAT?
WELL, WE STOOD IN LINE FOR 25 MINUTES, THEN IT WAS NOON AND WE HAD TO MEET YOU.
WE HAVEN'T DONE ONE RIDE
I'LL GO GET IN THE FOOD LINE
GREG 8·7

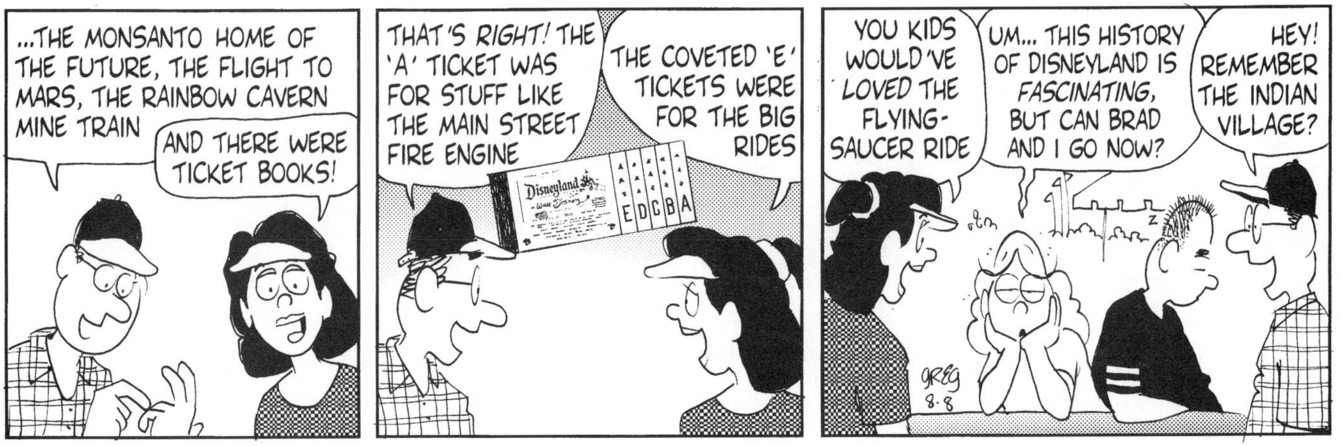
...THE MONSANTO HOME OF THE FUTURE, THE FLIGHT TO MARS, THE RAINBOW CAVERN MINE TRAIN
AND THERE WERE TICKET BOOKS!
THAT'S RIGHT! THE 'A' TICKET WAS FOR STUFF LIKE THE MAIN STREET FIRE ENGINE
THE COVETED 'E' TICKETS WERE FOR THE BIG RIDES
Disneyland
E D C B A
YOU KIDS WOULD'VE LOVED THE FLYING-SAUCER RIDE
UM... THIS HISTORY OF DISNEYLAND IS FASCINATING, BUT CAN BRAD AND I GO NOW?
HEY! REMEMBER THE INDIAN VILLAGE?
GREG 8·8

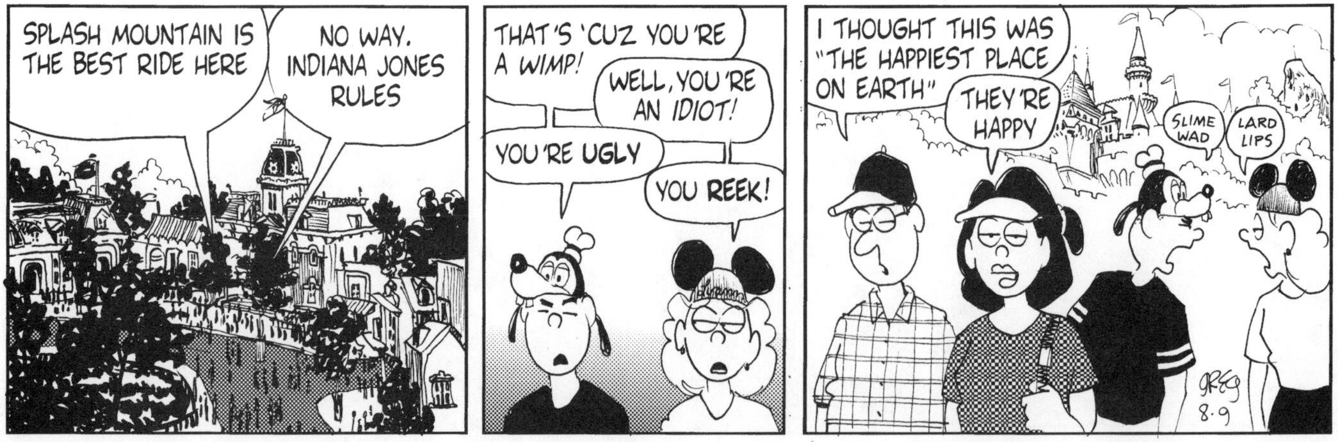
SPLASH MOUNTAIN IS THE BEST RIDE HERE
NO WAY. INDIANA JONES RULES
THAT'S 'CUZ YOU'RE A WIMP!
WELL, YOU'RE AN IDIOT!
YOU'RE UGLY
YOU REEK!
I THOUGHT THIS WAS "THE HAPPIEST PLACE ON EARTH"
THEY'RE HAPPY
SLIME WAD
LARD LIPS
GREG 8·9

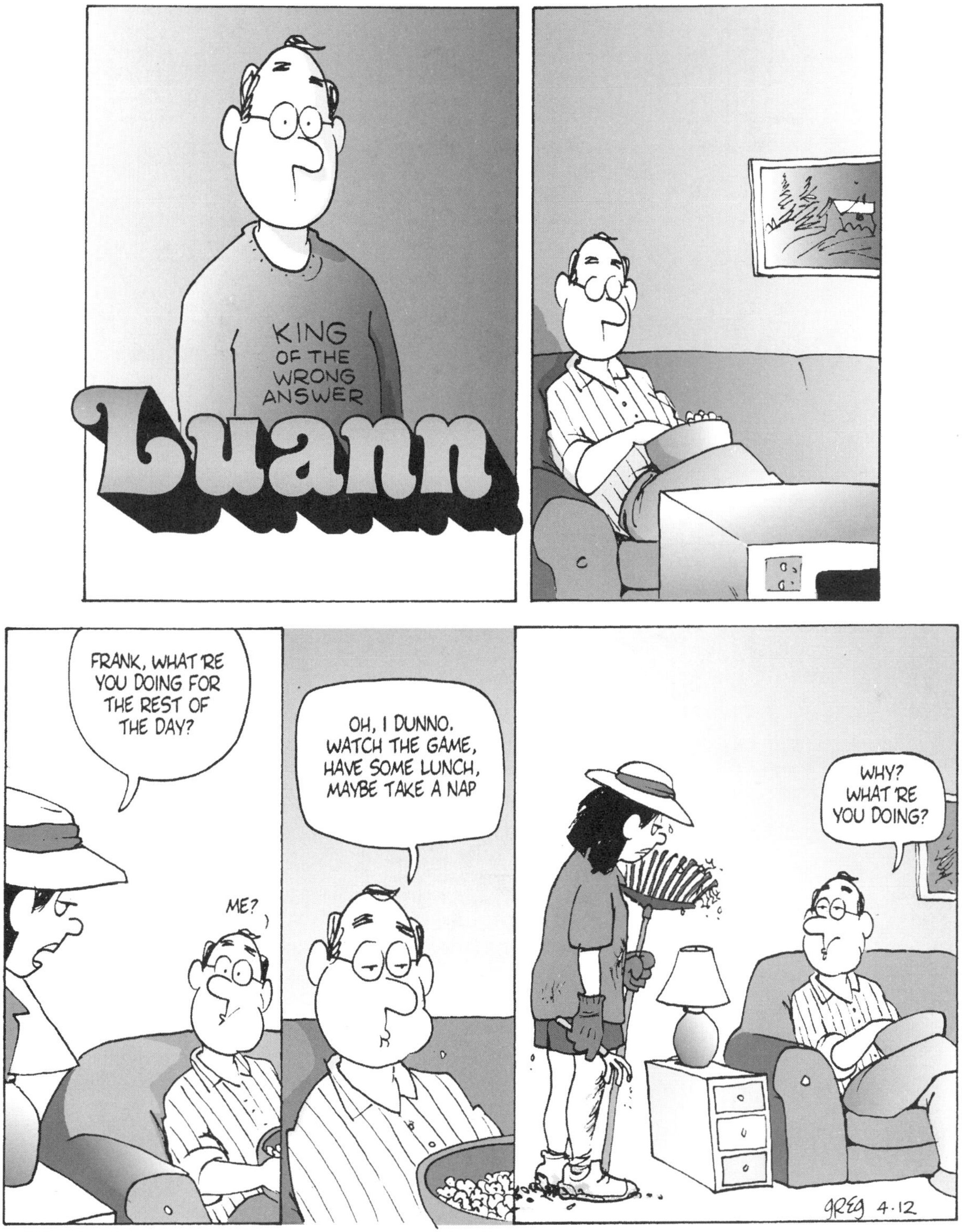
KING OF THE WRONG ANSWER
Luann
FRANK, WHAT'RE YOU DOING FOR THE REST OF THE DAY?
ME?
OH, I DUNNO. WATCH THE GAME, HAVE SOME LUNCH, MAYBE TAKE A NAP
WHY? WHAT'RE YOU DOING?
GREG 4.12

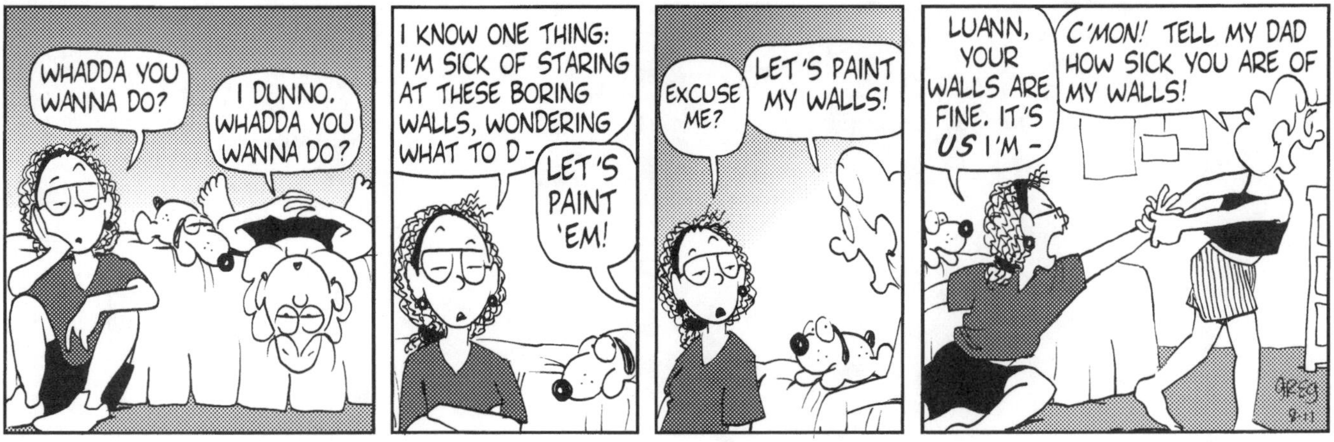
WHADDA YOU WANNA DO?
I DUNNO. WHADDA YOU WANNA DO?
I KNOW ONE THING: I'M SICK OF STARING AT THESE BORING WALLS, WONDERING WHAT TO D-
LET'S PAINT 'EM!
EXCUSE ME?
LET'S PAINT MY WALLS!
LUANN, YOUR WALLS ARE FINE. IT'S US I'M -
C'MON! TELL MY DAD HOW SICK YOU ARE OF MY WALLS!
GREG
8·11

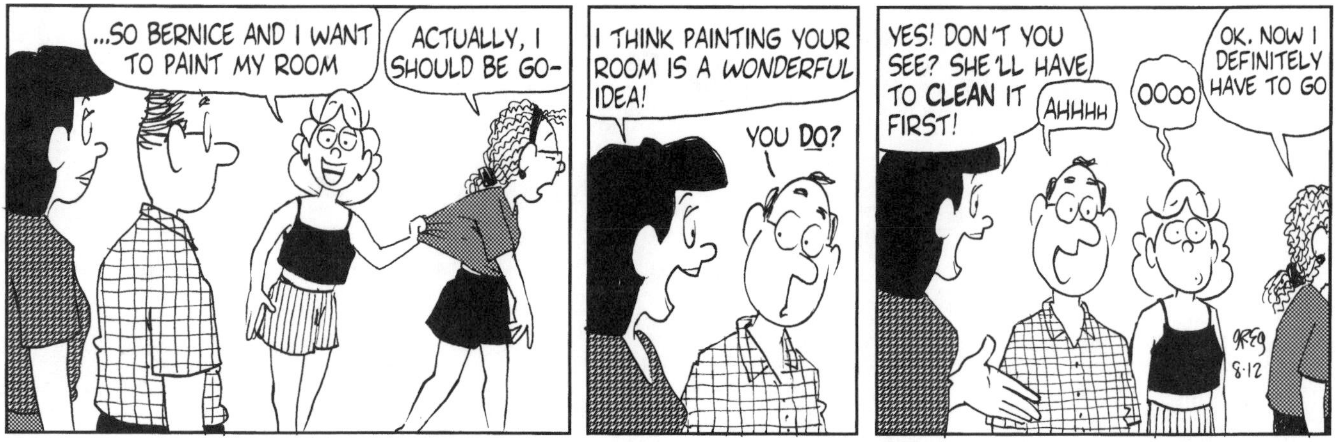
...SO BERNICE AND I WANT TO PAINT MY ROOM
ACTUALLY, I SHOULD BE GO-
I THINK PAINTING YOUR ROOM IS A WONDERFUL IDEA!
YOU DO?
YES! DON'T YOU SEE? SHE'LL HAVE TO CLEAN IT FIRST!
AHHHH
OOOO
OK. NOW I DEFINITELY HAVE TO GO
GREG
8·12

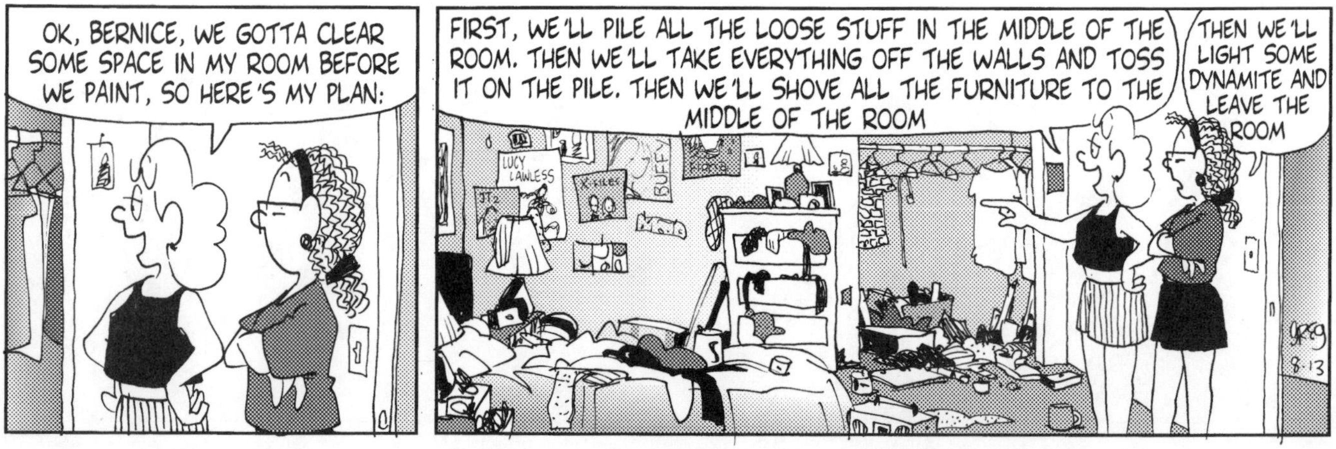
OK, BERNICE, WE GOTTA CLEAR SOME SPACE IN MY ROOM BEFORE WE PAINT, SO HERE'S MY PLAN:
FIRST, WE'LL PILE ALL THE LOOSE STUFF IN THE MIDDLE OF THE ROOM. THEN WE'LL TAKE EVERYTHING OFF THE WALLS AND TOSS IT ON THE PILE. THEN WE'LL SHOVE ALL THE FURNITURE TO THE MIDDLE OF THE ROOM
THEN WE'LL LIGHT SOME DYNAMITE AND LEAVE THE ROOM
LUCY LAWLESS
X-FILES
BUFFY
GREG
8·13

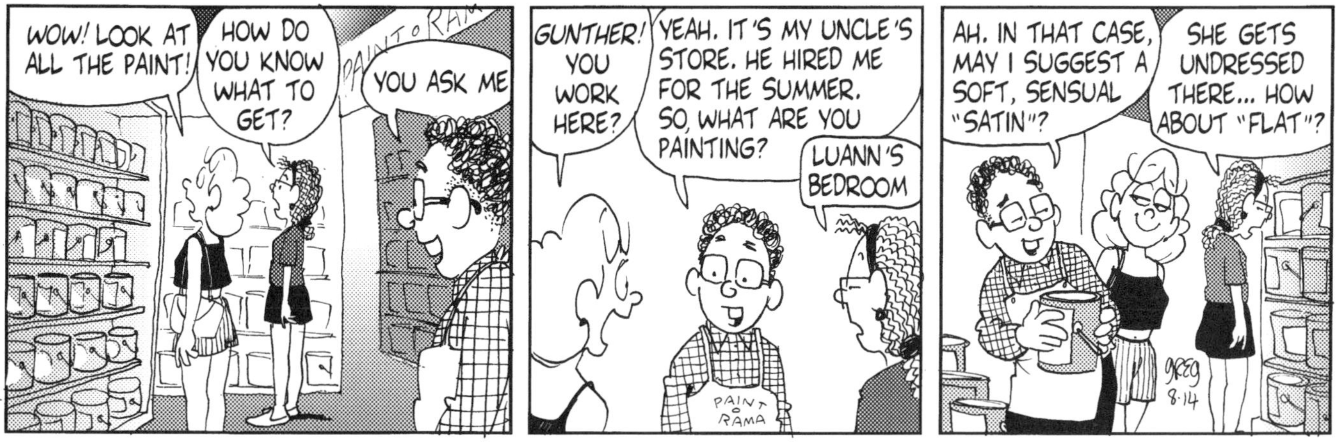
WOW! LOOK AT ALL THE PAINT!
HOW DO YOU KNOW WHAT TO GET?
YOU ASK ME
GUNTHER! YOU WORK HERE?
YEAH. IT'S MY UNCLE'S STORE. HE HIRED ME FOR THE SUMMER. SO, WHAT ARE YOU PAINTING?
LUANN'S BEDROOM
AH. IN THAT CASE, MAY I SUGGEST A SOFT, SENSUAL "SATIN"?
SHE GETS UNDRESSED THERE... HOW ABOUT "FLAT"?
GREG 8·14

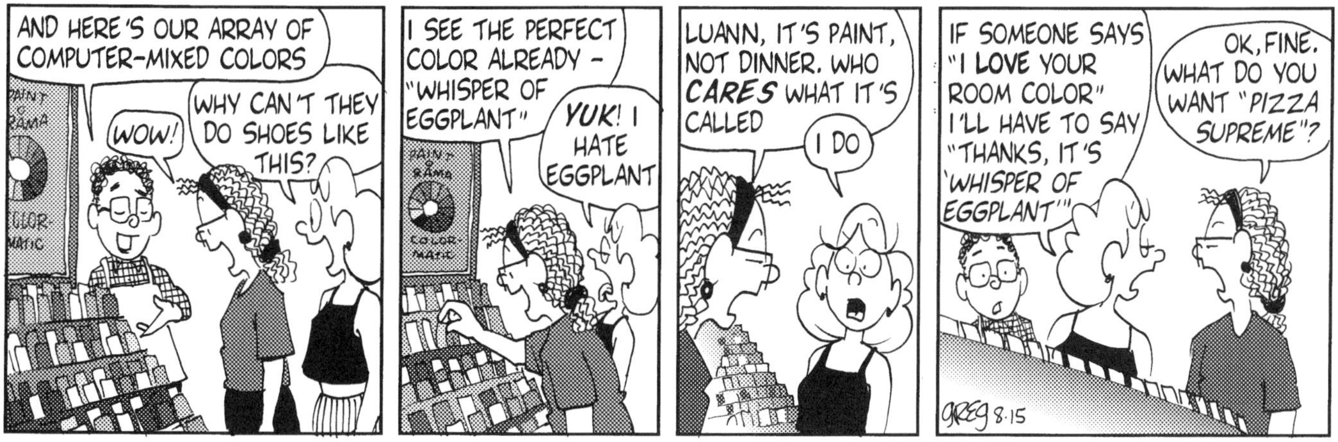
AND HERE'S OUR ARRAY OF COMPUTER-MIXED COLORS
WOW!
WHY CAN'T THEY DO SHOES LIKE THIS?
I SEE THE PERFECT COLOR ALREADY – "WHISPER OF EGGPLANT"
YUK! I HATE EGGPLANT
LUANN, IT'S PAINT, NOT DINNER. WHO CARES WHAT IT'S CALLED
I DO
IF SOMEONE SAYS "I LOVE YOUR ROOM COLOR" I'LL HAVE TO SAY "THANKS, IT'S 'WHISPER OF EGGPLANT'"
OK, FINE. WHAT DO YOU WANT "PIZZA SUPREME"?
GREG 8·15

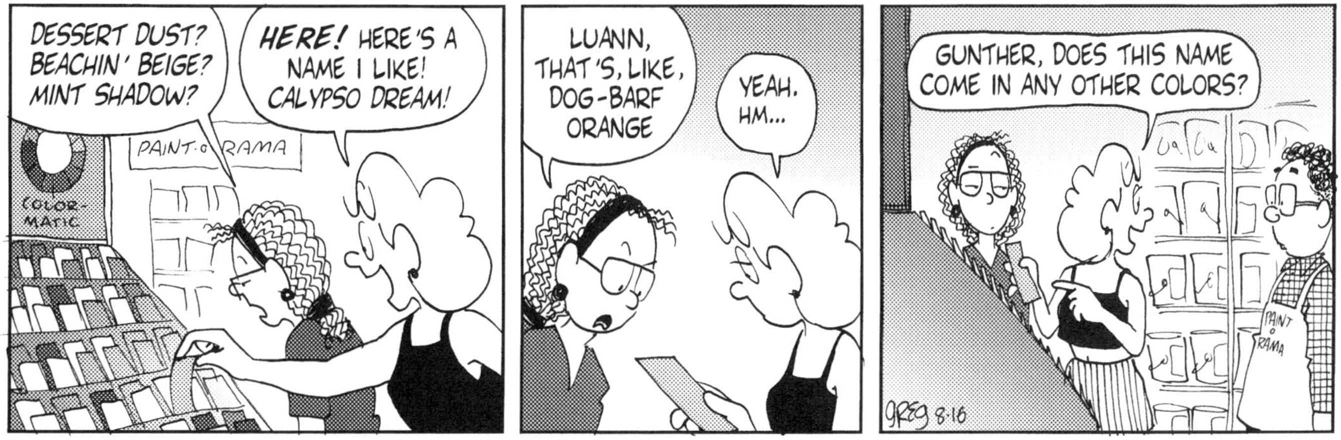
DESSERT DUST? BEACHIN' BEIGE? MINT SHADOW?
HERE! HERE'S A NAME I LIKE! CALYPSO DREAM!
LUANN, THAT'S, LIKE, DOG-BARF ORANGE
YEAH. HM...
GUNTHER, DOES THIS NAME COME IN ANY OTHER COLORS?
GREG 8·16

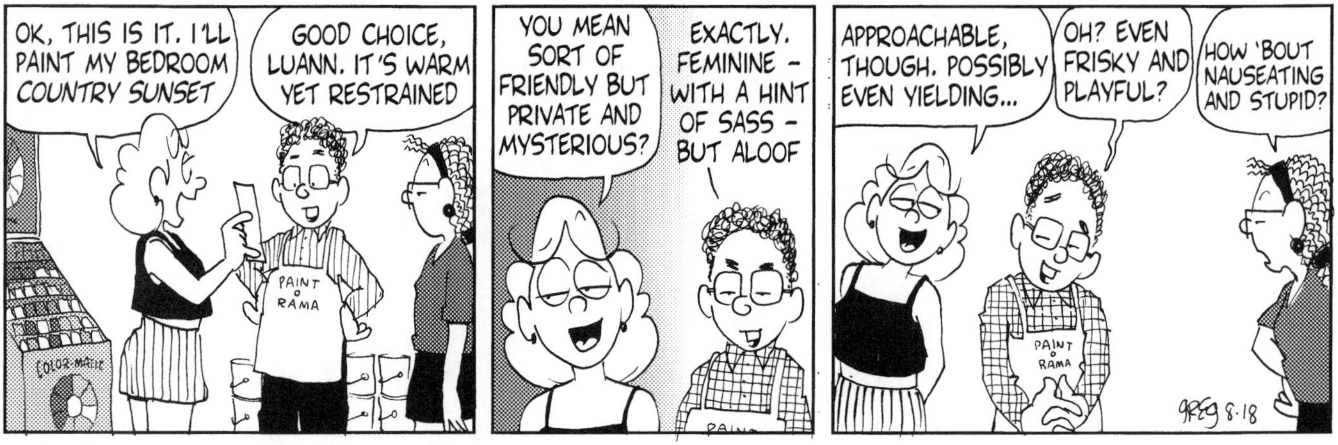
OK, THIS IS IT. I'LL PAINT MY BEDROOM COUNTRY SUNSET
GOOD CHOICE, LUANN. IT'S WARM YET RESTRAINED
PAINT O RAMA
COLOR-MATIC
YOU MEAN SORT OF FRIENDLY BUT PRIVATE AND MYSTERIOUS?
EXACTLY. FEMININE – WITH A HINT OF SASS – BUT ALOOF
APPROACHABLE, THOUGH. POSSIBLY EVEN YIELDING...
OH? EVEN FRISKY AND PLAYFUL?
HOW 'BOUT NAUSEATING AND STUPID?
PAINT O RAMA
GREG 8.18

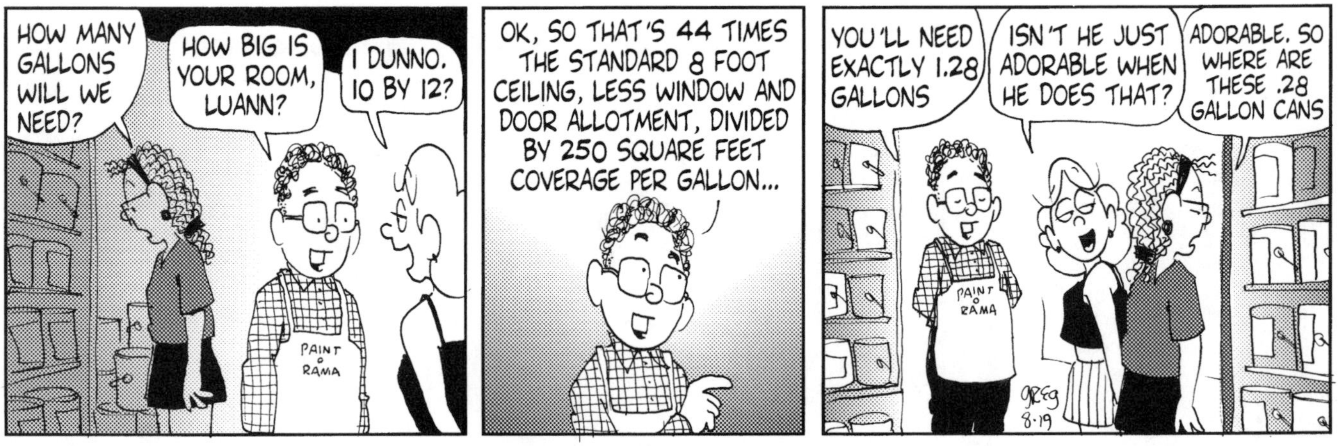
HOW MANY GALLONS WILL WE NEED?
HOW BIG IS YOUR ROOM, LUANN?
I DUNNO. 10 BY 12?
PAINT O RAMA
OK, SO THAT'S 44 TIMES THE STANDARD 8 FOOT CEILING, LESS WINDOW AND DOOR ALLOTMENT, DIVIDED BY 250 SQUARE FEET COVERAGE PER GALLON...
YOU'LL NEED EXACTLY 1.28 GALLONS
ISN'T HE JUST ADORABLE WHEN HE DOES THAT?
ADORABLE. SO WHERE ARE THESE .28 GALLON CANS
PAINT O RAMA
GREG 8.19

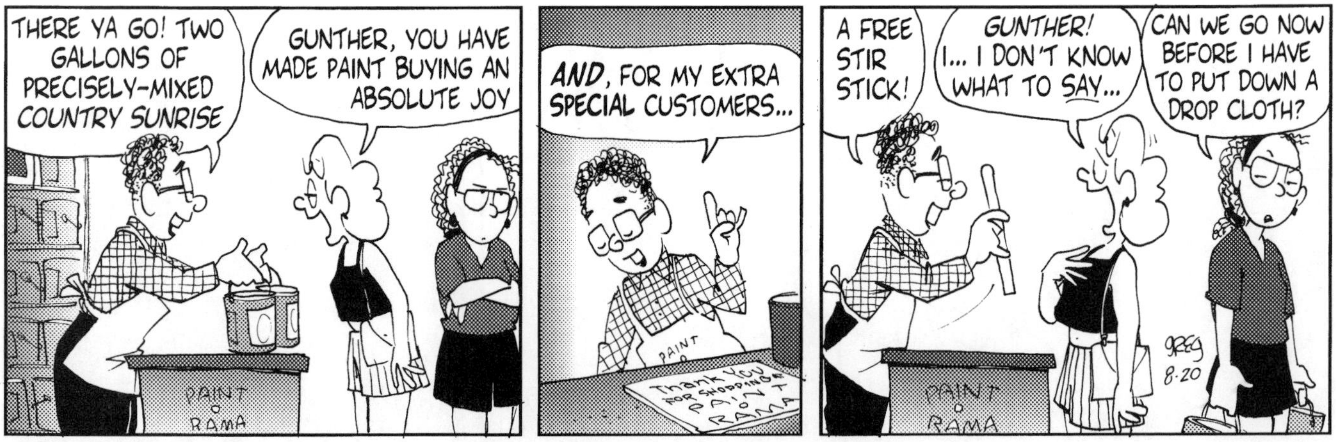
THERE YA GO! TWO GALLONS OF PRECISELY-MIXED COUNTRY SUNRISE
GUNTHER, YOU HAVE MADE PAINT BUYING AN ABSOLUTE JOY
PAINT O RAMA
AND, FOR MY EXTRA SPECIAL CUSTOMERS...
PAINT
Thank You For Shopping at PAINT O RAMA
A FREE STIR STICK!
GUNTHER! I... I DON'T KNOW WHAT TO SAY...
CAN WE GO NOW BEFORE I HAVE TO PUT DOWN A DROP CLOTH?
PAINT O RAMA
GREG 8.20

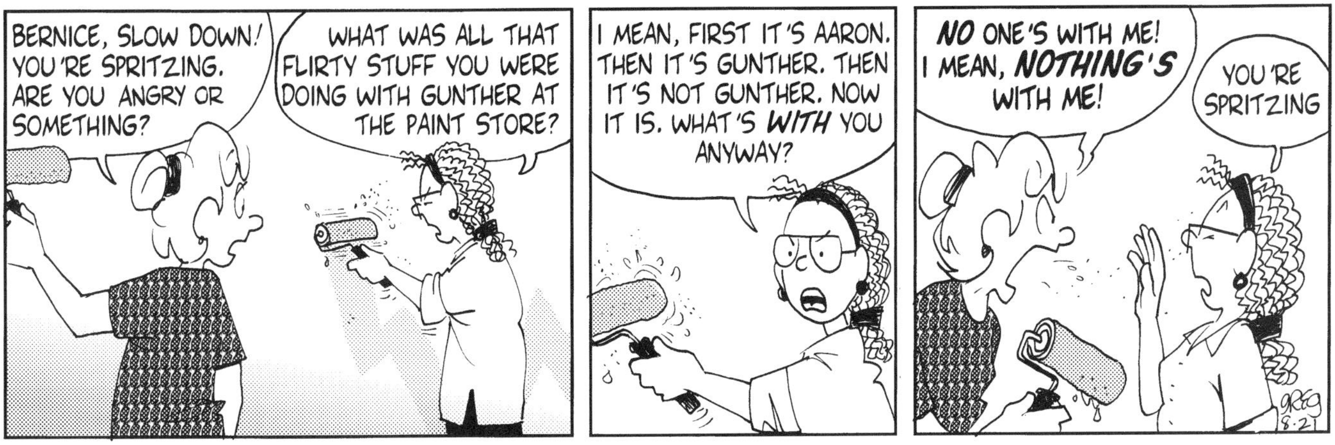
BERNICE, SLOW DOWN! YOU'RE SPRITZING. ARE YOU ANGRY OR SOMETHING?
WHAT WAS ALL THAT FLIRTY STUFF YOU WERE DOING WITH GUNTHER AT THE PAINT STORE?
I MEAN, FIRST IT'S AARON. THEN IT'S GUNTHER. THEN IT'S NOT GUNTHER. NOW IT IS. WHAT'S WITH YOU ANYWAY?
NO ONE'S WITH ME! I MEAN, NOTHING'S WITH ME!
YOU'RE SPRITZING
GREG 8·21

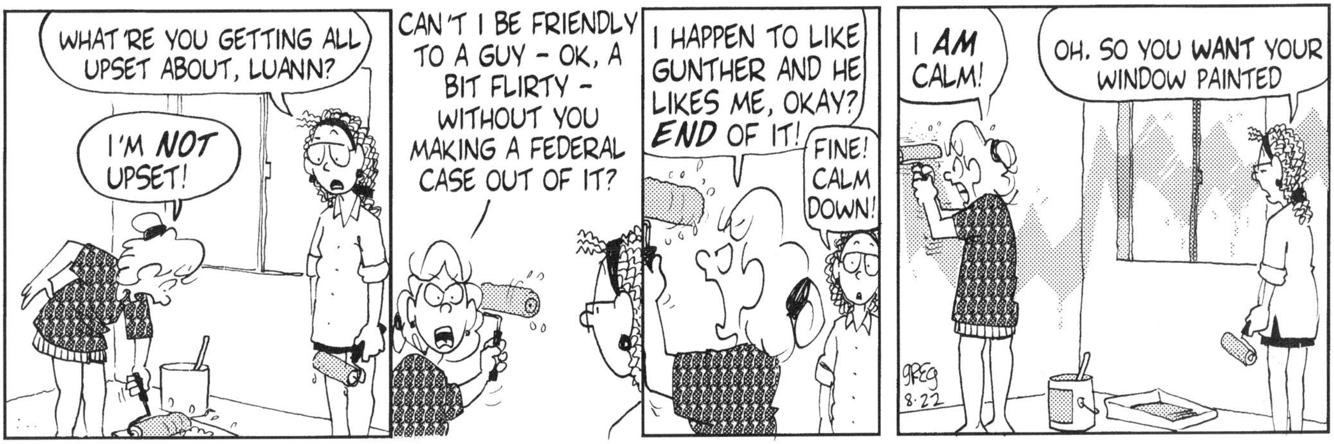
WHAT'RE YOU GETTING ALL UPSET ABOUT, LUANN?
I'M NOT UPSET!
CAN'T I BE FRIENDLY TO A GUY - OK, A BIT FLIRTY - WITHOUT YOU MAKING A FEDERAL CASE OUT OF IT?
I HAPPEN TO LIKE GUNTHER AND HE LIKES ME, OKAY? END OF IT!
FINE! CALM DOWN!
I AM CALM!
OH. SO YOU WANT YOUR WINDOW PAINTED
GREG 8·22

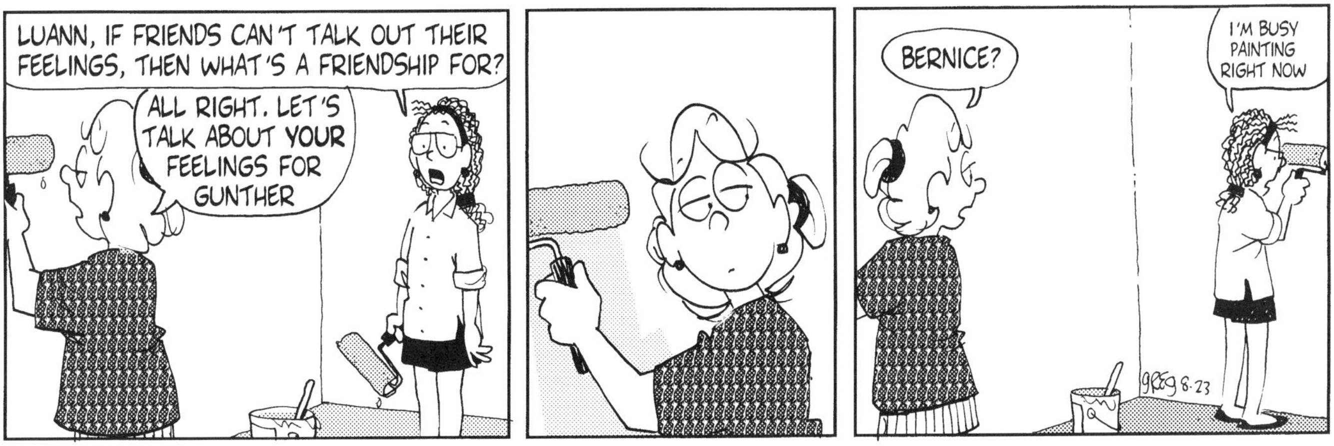
LUANN, IF FRIENDS CAN'T TALK OUT THEIR FEELINGS, THEN WHAT'S A FRIENDSHIP FOR?
ALL RIGHT. LET'S TALK ABOUT YOUR FEELINGS FOR GUNTHER
BERNICE?
I'M BUSY PAINTING RIGHT NOW
GREG 8·23

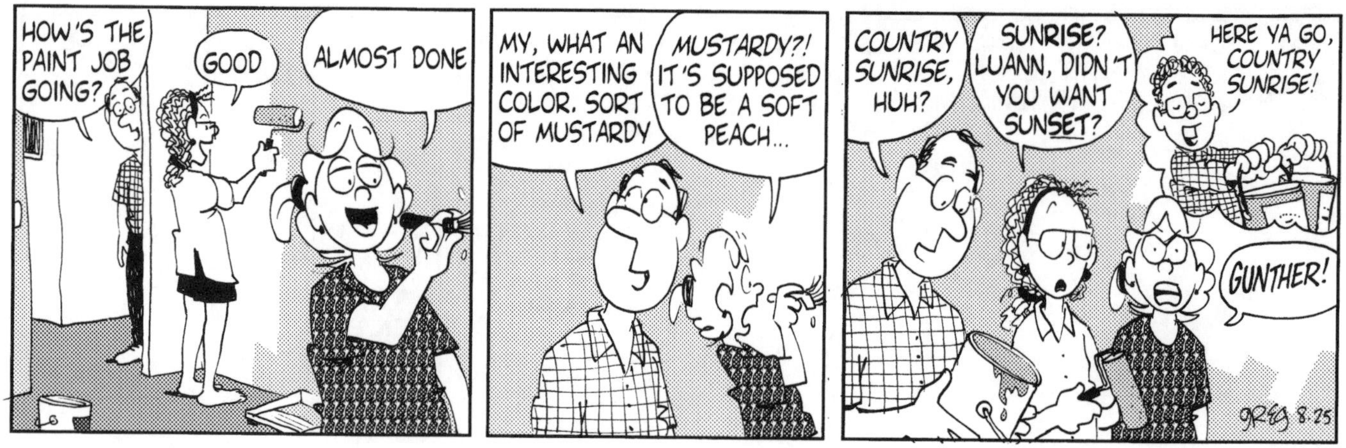
HOW'S THE PAINT JOB GOING?
GOOD
ALMOST DONE
MY, WHAT AN INTERESTING COLOR. SORT OF MUSTARDY
MUSTARDY?! IT'S SUPPOSED TO BE A SOFT PEACH...
COUNTRY SUNRISE, HUH?
SUNRISE? LUANN, DIDN'T YOU WANT SUNSET?
HERE YA GO, COUNTRY SUNRISE!
GUNTHER!
GREG 8·25

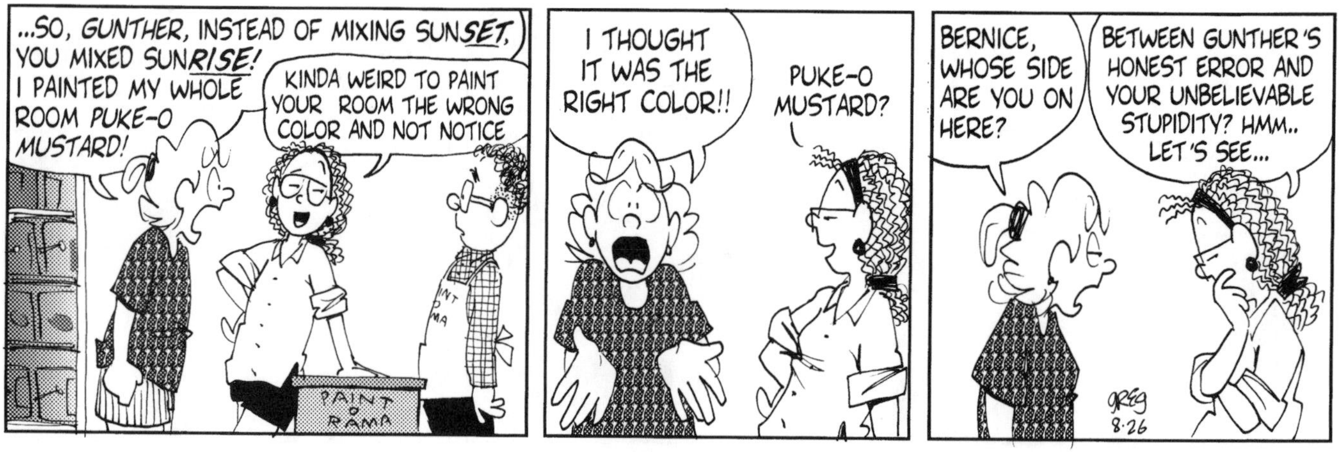
...SO, GUNTHER, INSTEAD OF MIXING SUNSET, YOU MIXED SUNRISE! I PAINTED MY WHOLE ROOM PUKE-O MUSTARD!
KINDA WEIRD TO PAINT YOUR ROOM THE WRONG COLOR AND NOT NOTICE
PAINT O RAMA
I THOUGHT IT WAS THE RIGHT COLOR!!
PUKE-O MUSTARD?
BERNICE, WHOSE SIDE ARE YOU ON HERE?
BETWEEN GUNTHER'S HONEST ERROR AND YOUR UNBELIEVABLE STUPIDITY? HMM.. LET'S SEE...
GREG 8·26

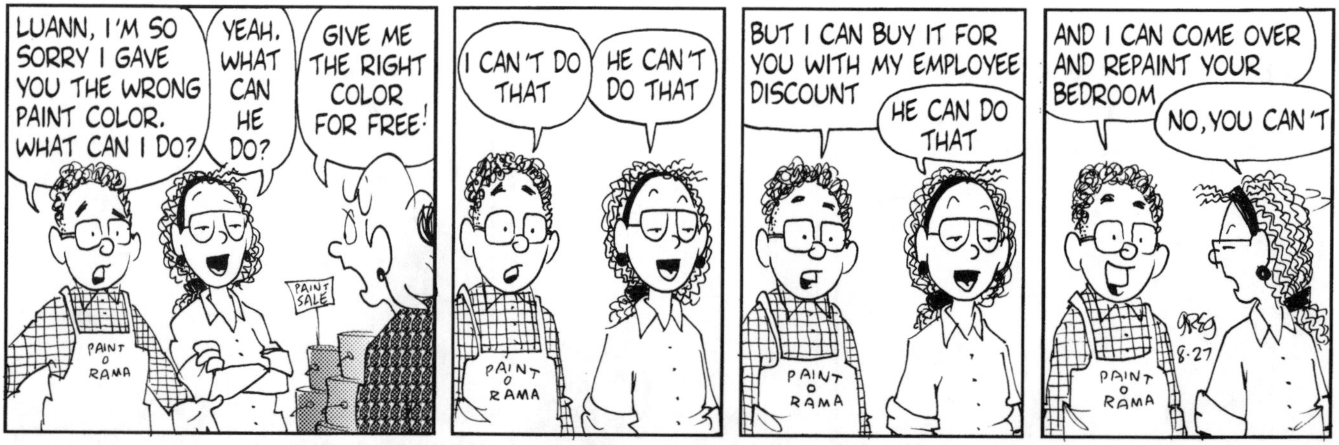
LUANN, I'M SO SORRY I GAVE YOU THE WRONG PAINT COLOR. WHAT CAN I DO?
YEAH. WHAT CAN HE DO?
GIVE ME THE RIGHT COLOR FOR FREE!
PAINT O RAMA
PAINT SALE
I CAN'T DO THAT
HE CAN'T DO THAT
BUT I CAN BUY IT FOR YOU WITH MY EMPLOYEE DISCOUNT
HE CAN DO THAT
AND I CAN COME OVER AND REPAINT YOUR BEDROOM
NO, YOU CAN'T
GREG 8·27

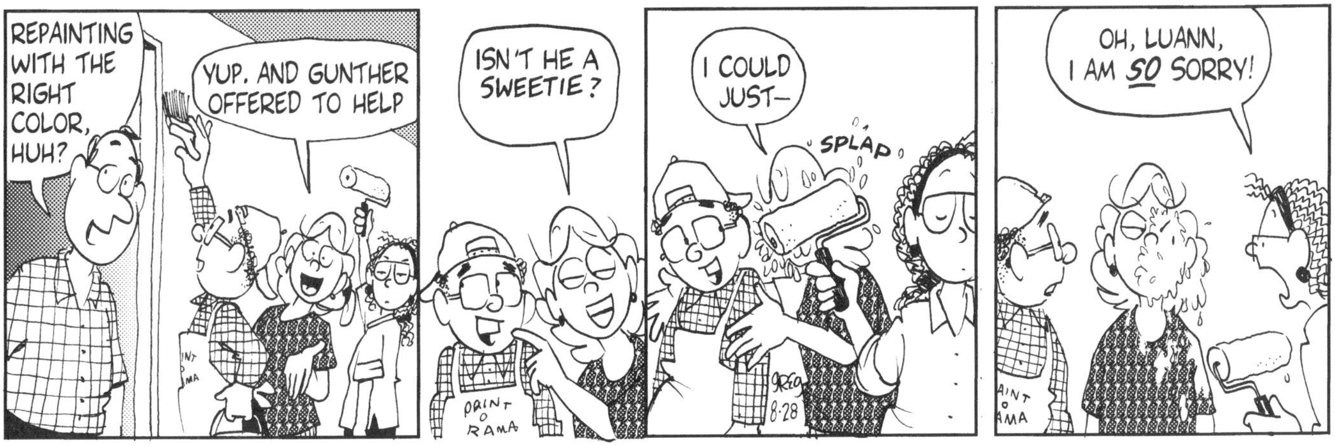
REPAINTING WITH THE RIGHT COLOR, HUH?
YUP. AND GUNTHER OFFERED TO HELP
ISN'T HE A SWEETIE?
I COULD JUST—
SPLAP
OH, LUANN, I AM SO SORRY!

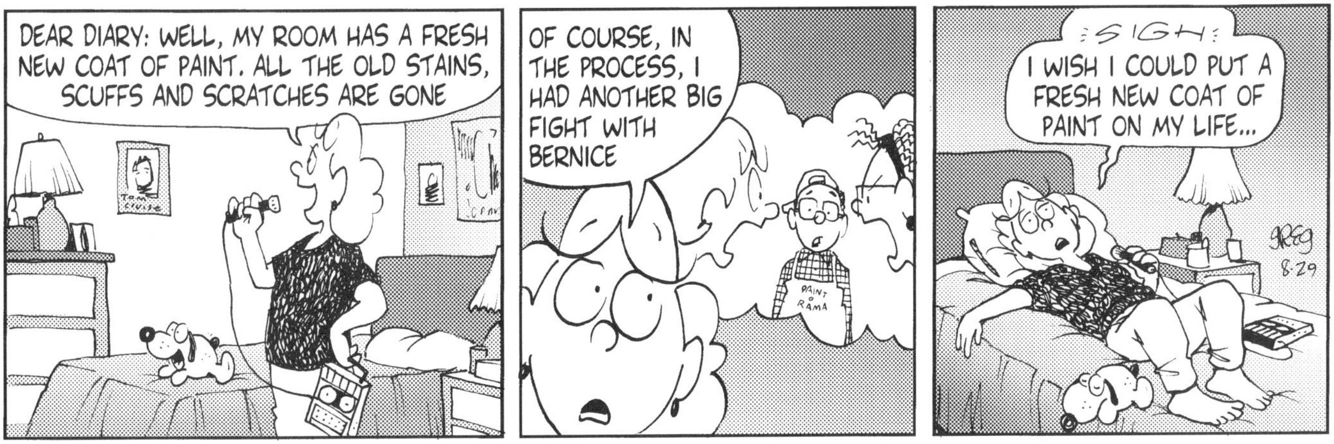
DEAR DIARY: WELL, MY ROOM HAS A FRESH NEW COAT OF PAINT. ALL THE OLD STAINS, SCUFFS AND SCRATCHES ARE GONE
OF COURSE, IN THE PROCESS, I HAD ANOTHER BIG FIGHT WITH BERNICE
SIGH
I WISH I COULD PUT A FRESH NEW COAT OF PAINT ON MY LIFE...

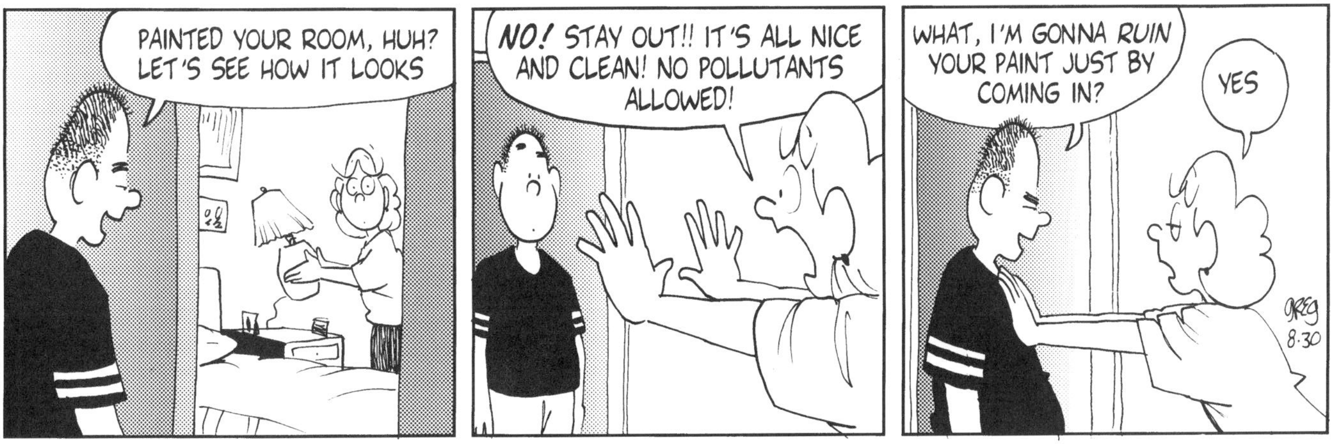
PAINTED YOUR ROOM, HUH? LET'S SEE HOW IT LOOKS
NO! STAY OUT!! IT'S ALL NICE AND CLEAN! NO POLLUTANTS ALLOWED!
WHAT, I'M GONNA RUIN YOUR PAINT JUST BY COMING IN?
YES

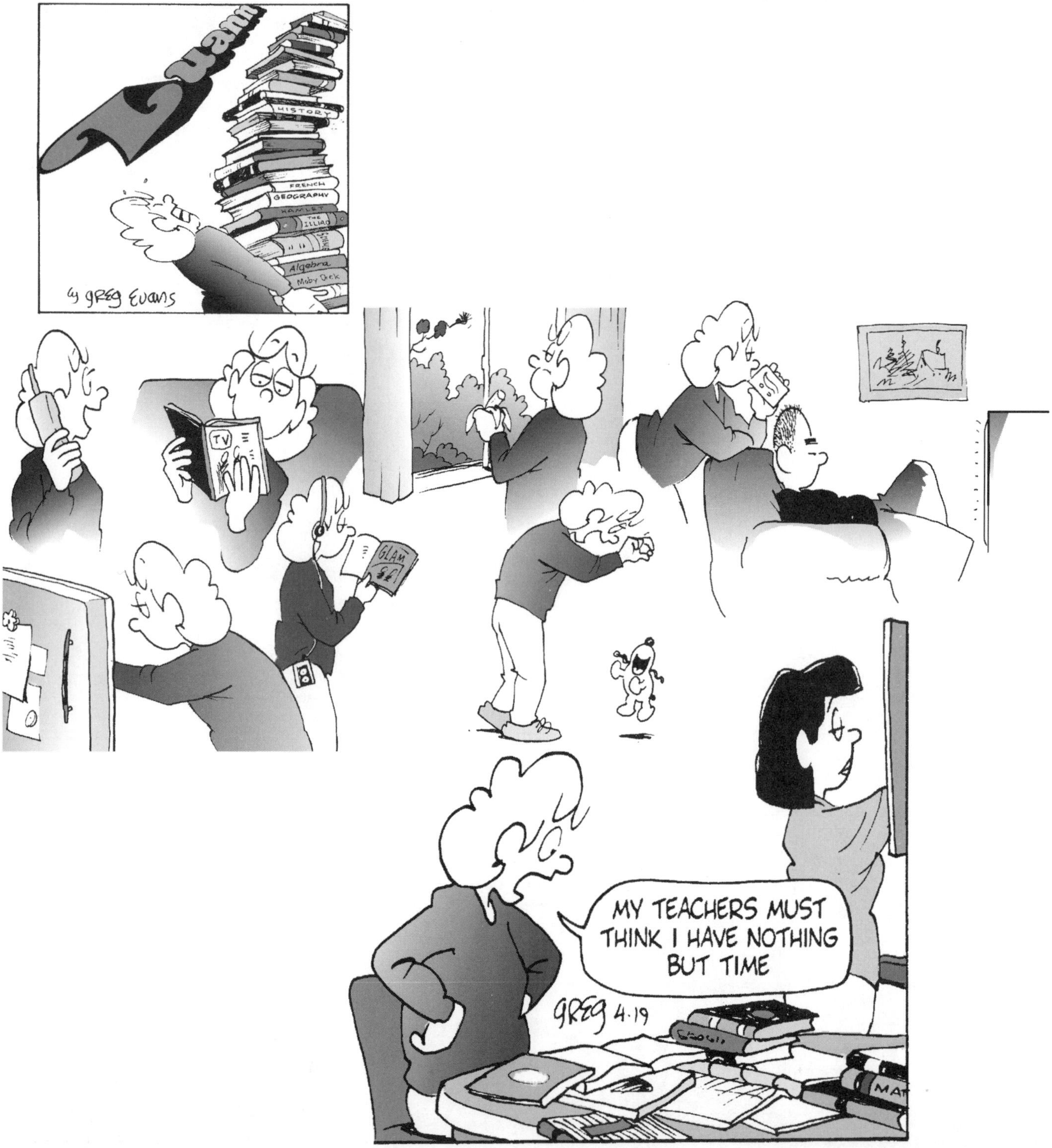
HISTORY
FRENCH
GEOGRAPHY
HAMLET
THE ILLIAD
Algebra
Moby Dick
by GREG EVANS
TV
GLAM
MY TEACHERS MUST THINK I HAVE NOTHING BUT TIME
GREG 4.19

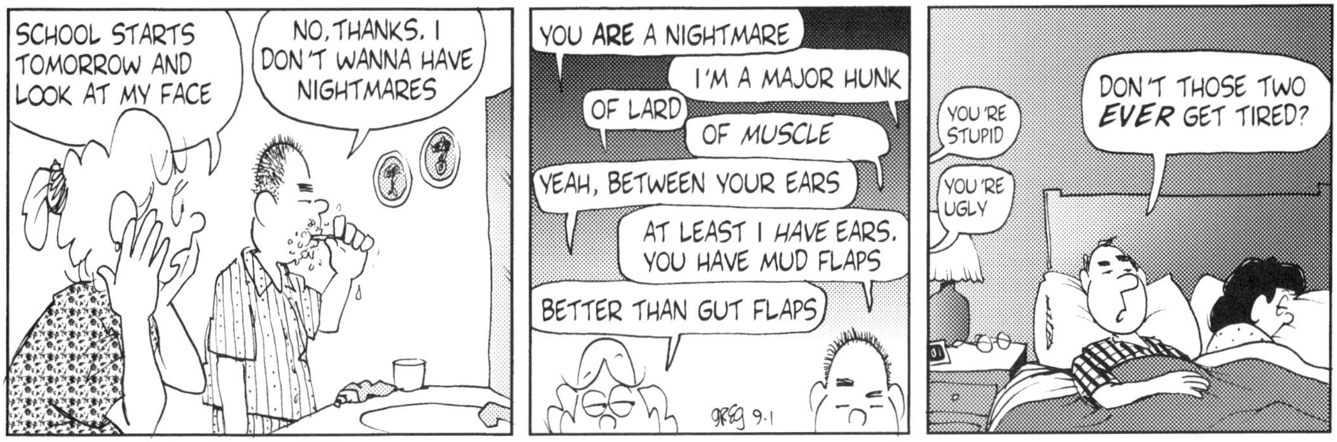
SCHOOL STARTS TOMORROW AND LOOK AT MY FACE
NO, THANKS. I DON'T WANNA HAVE NIGHTMARES
YOU **ARE** A NIGHTMARE
I'M A MAJOR HUNK
OF LARD
OF *MUSCLE*
YEAH, BETWEEN YOUR EARS
AT LEAST I *HAVE* EARS. YOU HAVE MUD FLAPS
BETTER THAN GUT FLAPS
YOU'RE STUPID
YOU'RE UGLY
DON'T THOSE TWO ***EVER*** GET TIRED?

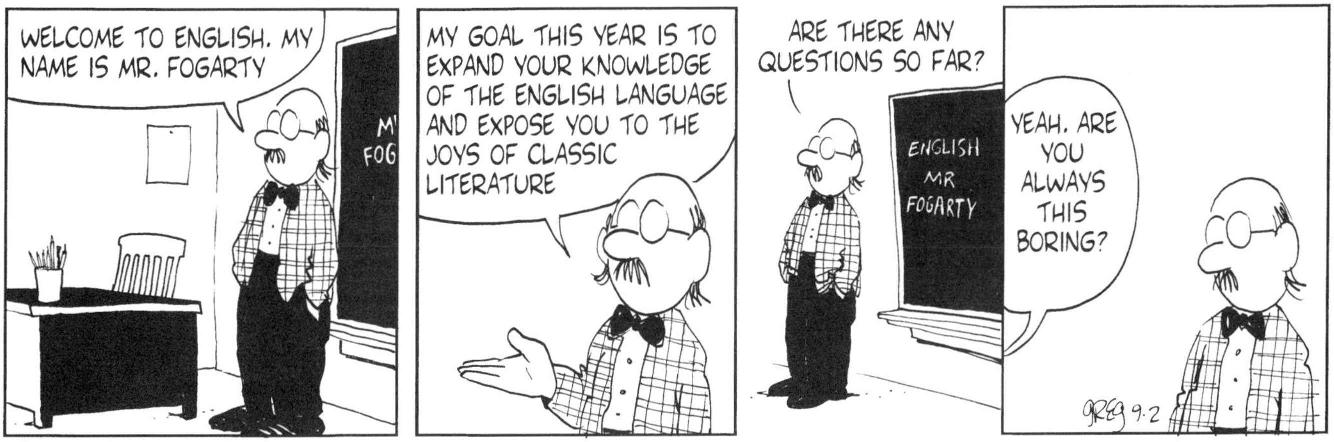
WELCOME TO ENGLISH. MY NAME IS MR. FOGARTY
MY GOAL THIS YEAR IS TO EXPAND YOUR KNOWLEDGE OF THE ENGLISH LANGUAGE AND EXPOSE YOU TO THE JOYS OF CLASSIC LITERATURE
ARE THERE ANY QUESTIONS SO FAR?
ENGLISH MR FOGARTY
YEAH. ARE YOU ALWAYS THIS BORING?

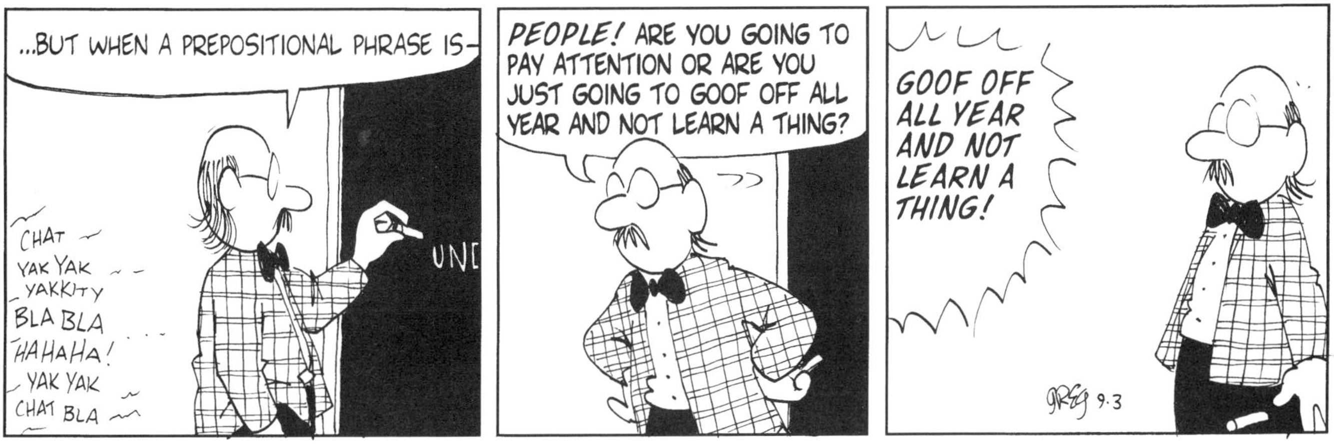
...BUT WHEN A PREPOSITIONAL PHRASE IS–
CHAT YAK YAK YAKKITY BLA BLA HAHAHA! YAK YAK CHAT BLA
UND
PEOPLE! ARE YOU GOING TO PAY ATTENTION OR ARE YOU JUST GOING TO GOOF OFF ALL YEAR AND NOT LEARN A THING?
GOOF OFF ALL YEAR AND NOT LEARN A THING!

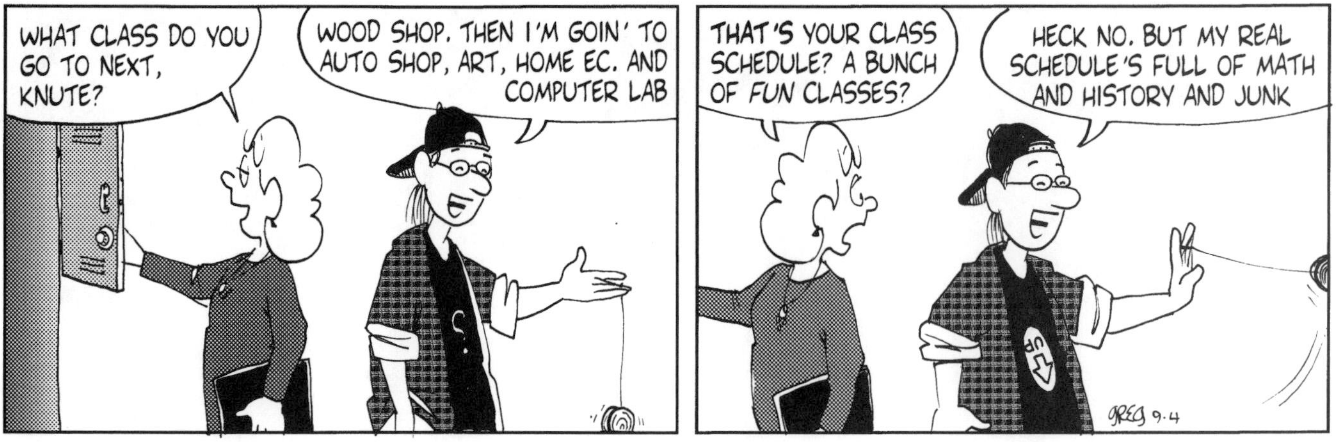
WHAT CLASS DO YOU GO TO NEXT, KNUTE?
WOOD SHOP. THEN I'M GOIN' TO AUTO SHOP, ART, HOME EC. AND COMPUTER LAB
THAT'S YOUR CLASS SCHEDULE? A BUNCH OF *FUN* CLASSES?
HECK NO. BUT MY REAL SCHEDULE'S FULL OF MATH AND HISTORY AND JUNK
GREG 9.4

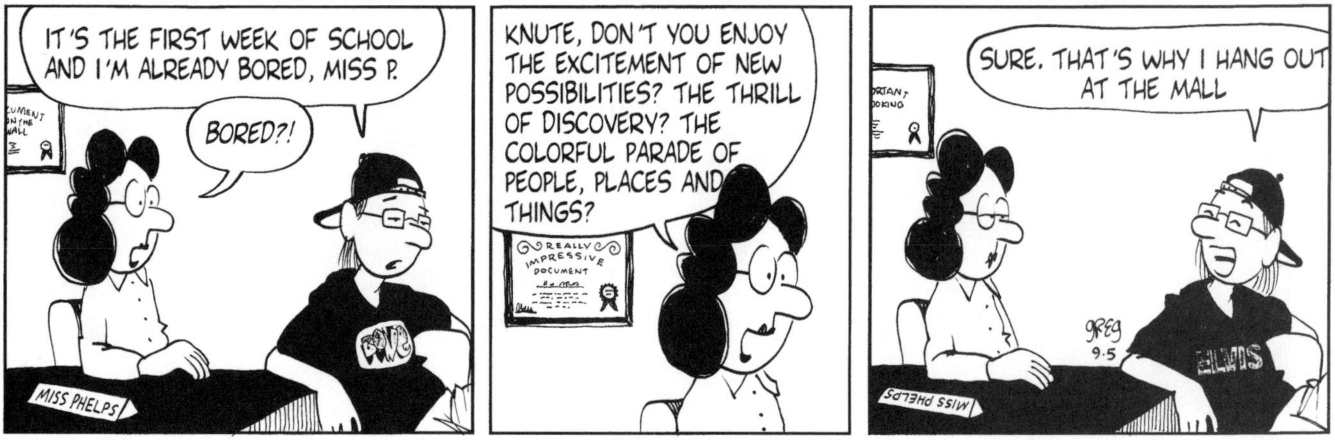
IT'S THE FIRST WEEK OF SCHOOL AND I'M ALREADY BORED, MISS P.
BORED?!
MISS PHELPS
KNUTE, DON'T YOU ENJOY THE EXCITEMENT OF NEW POSSIBILITIES? THE THRILL OF DISCOVERY? THE COLORFUL PARADE OF PEOPLE, PLACES AND THINGS?
REALLY IMPRESSIVE DOCUMENT
SURE. THAT'S WHY I HANG OUT AT THE MALL
GREG 9.5
ELVIS
MISS PHELPS

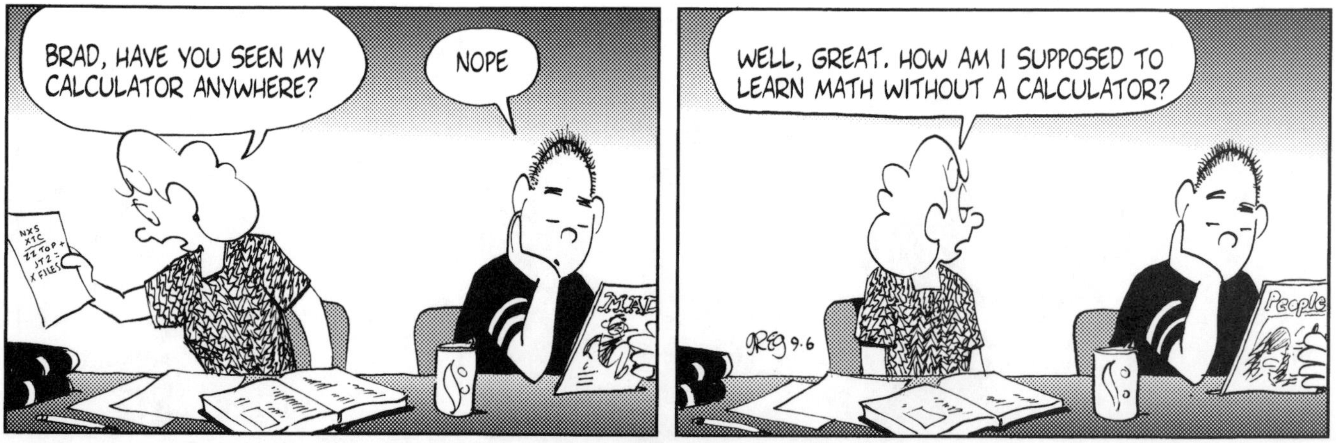
BRAD, HAVE YOU SEEN MY CALCULATOR ANYWHERE?
NOPE
MAD
WELL, GREAT. HOW AM I SUPPOSED TO LEARN MATH WITHOUT A CALCULATOR?
GREG 9.6
People

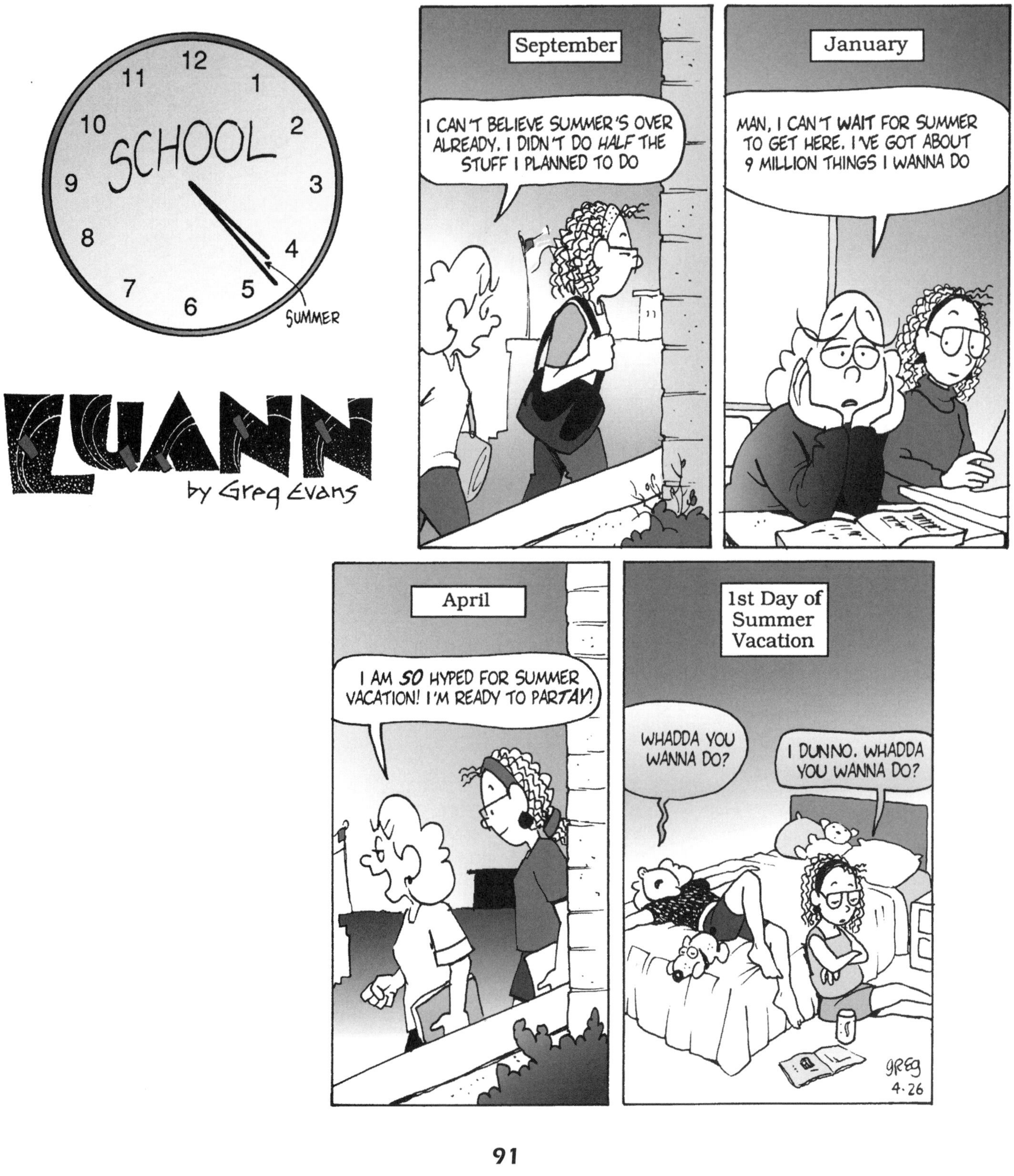
SCHOOL
SUMMER
LUANN
by Greg Evans
September
I CAN'T BELIEVE SUMMER'S OVER ALREADY. I DIDN'T DO *HALF* THE STUFF I PLANNED TO DO
January
MAN, I CAN'T **WAIT** FOR SUMMER TO GET HERE. I'VE GOT ABOUT 9 MILLION THINGS I WANNA DO
April
I AM ***SO*** HYPED FOR SUMMER VACATION! I'M READY TO PAR***TAY***!
1st Day of Summer Vacation
WHADDA YOU WANNA DO?
I DUNNO. WHADDA YOU WANNA DO?
GREG 4·26

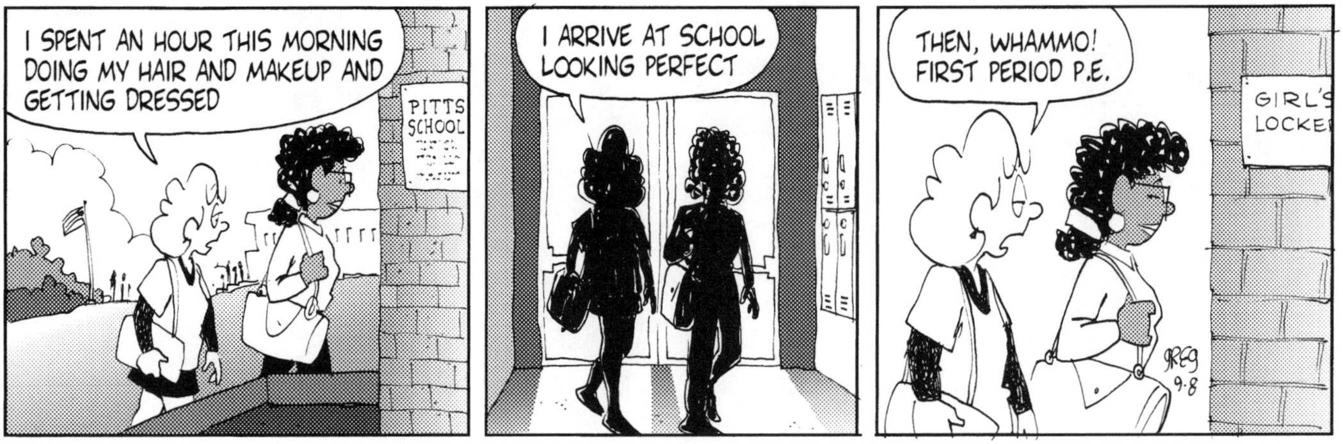
I SPENT AN HOUR THIS MORNING DOING MY HAIR AND MAKEUP AND GETTING DRESSED
PITTS SCHOOL
I ARRIVE AT SCHOOL LOOKING PERFECT
THEN, WHAMMO! FIRST PERIOD P.E.
GIRL'S LOCKE
GREG 9.8

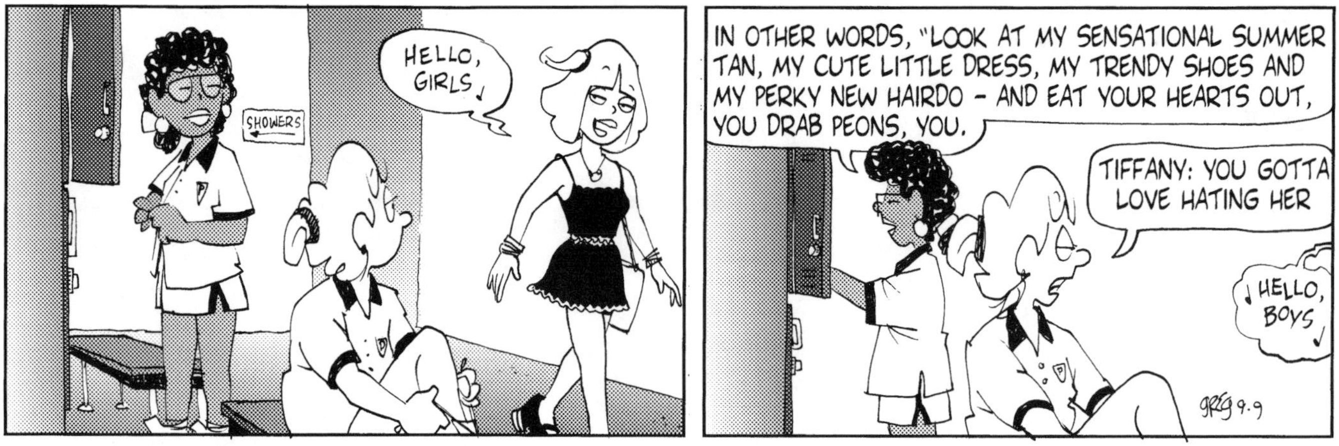
SHOWERS
HELLO, GIRLS
IN OTHER WORDS, "LOOK AT MY SENSATIONAL SUMMER TAN, MY CUTE LITTLE DRESS, MY TRENDY SHOES AND MY PERKY NEW HAIRDO - AND EAT YOUR HEARTS OUT, YOU DRAB PEONS, YOU.
TIFFANY: YOU GOTTA LOVE HATING HER
HELLO, BOYS
GREG 9.9

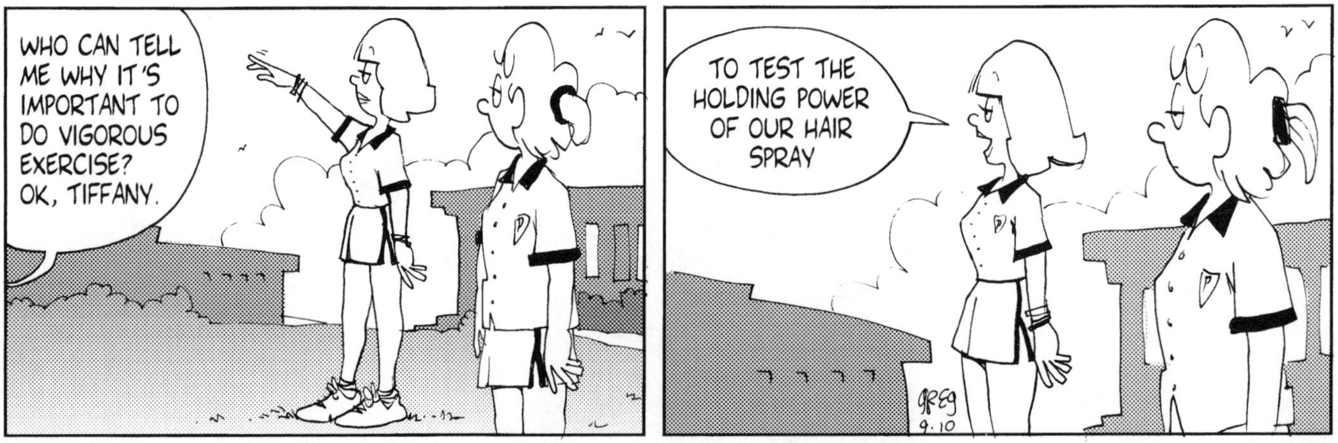
WHO CAN TELL ME WHY IT'S IMPORTANT TO DO VIGOROUS EXERCISE? OK, TIFFANY.
TO TEST THE HOLDING POWER OF OUR HAIR SPRAY
GREG 9.10

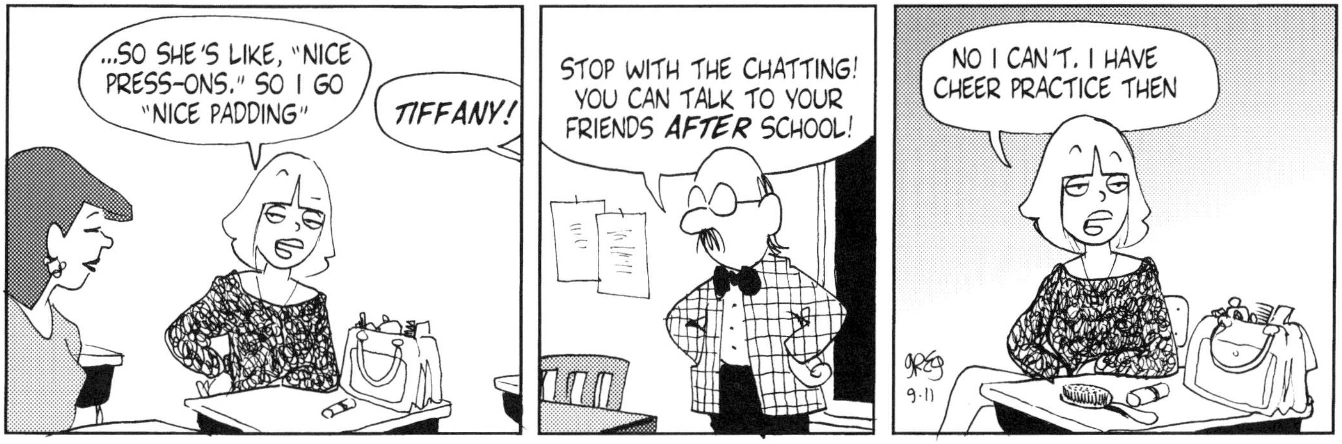
...SO SHE'S LIKE, "NICE PRESS-ONS." SO I GO "NICE PADDING"
TIFFANY!
STOP WITH THE CHATTING! YOU CAN TALK TO YOUR FRIENDS **AFTER** SCHOOL!
NO I CAN'T. I HAVE CHEER PRACTICE THEN
GREG 9-11

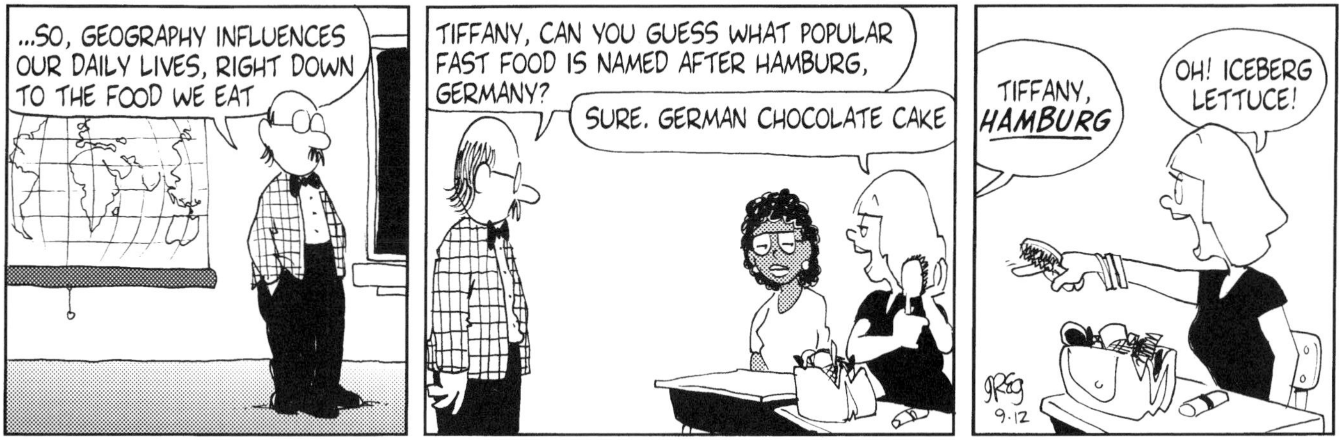
...SO, GEOGRAPHY INFLUENCES OUR DAILY LIVES, RIGHT DOWN TO THE FOOD WE EAT
TIFFANY, CAN YOU GUESS WHAT POPULAR FAST FOOD IS NAMED AFTER HAMBURG, GERMANY?
SURE. GERMAN CHOCOLATE CAKE
TIFFANY, HAMBURG
OH! ICEBERG LETTUCE!
GREG 9-12

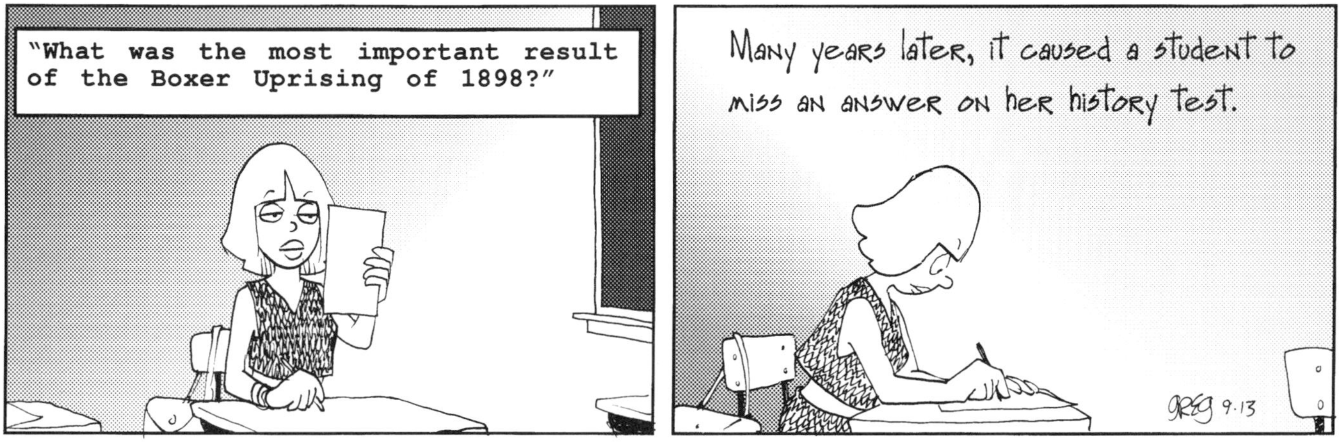
"What was the most important result of the Boxer Uprising of 1898?"
Many years later, it caused a student to miss an answer on her history test.
GREG 9-13

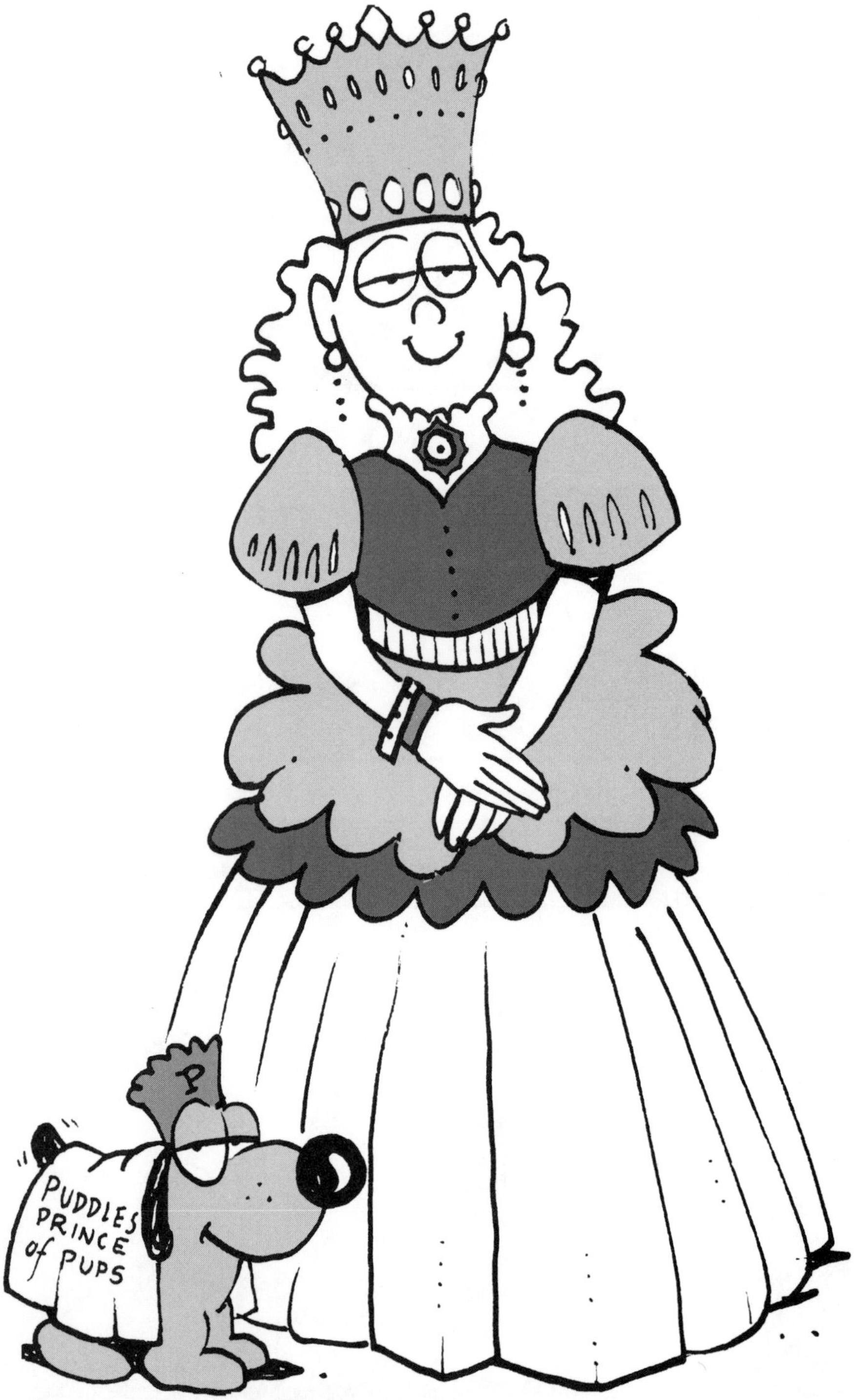
P
PUDDLES
PRINCE
of PUPS

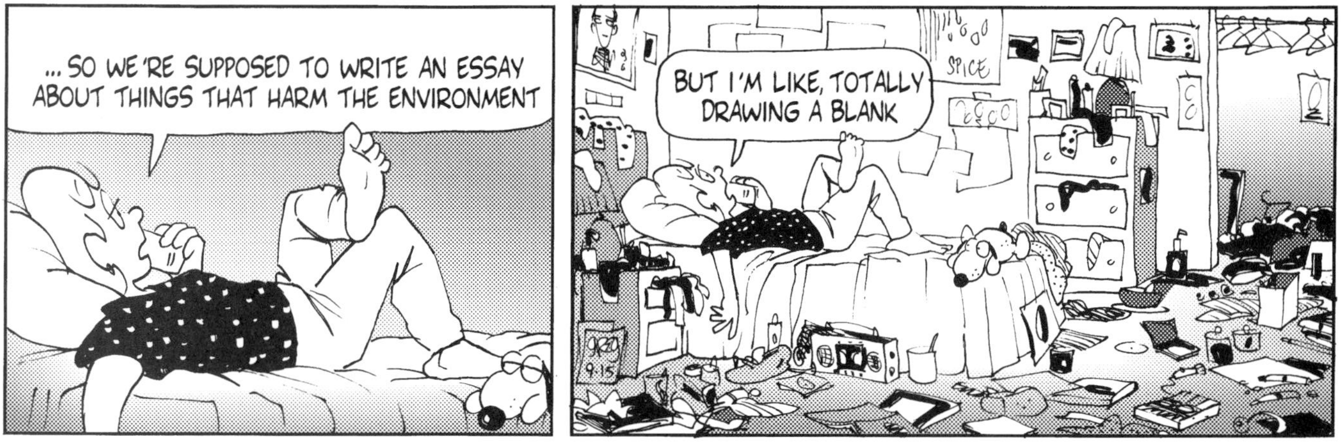
...SO WE'RE SUPPOSED TO WRITE AN ESSAY ABOUT THINGS THAT HARM THE ENVIRONMENT
BUT I'M LIKE, TOTALLY DRAWING A BLANK
SPICE

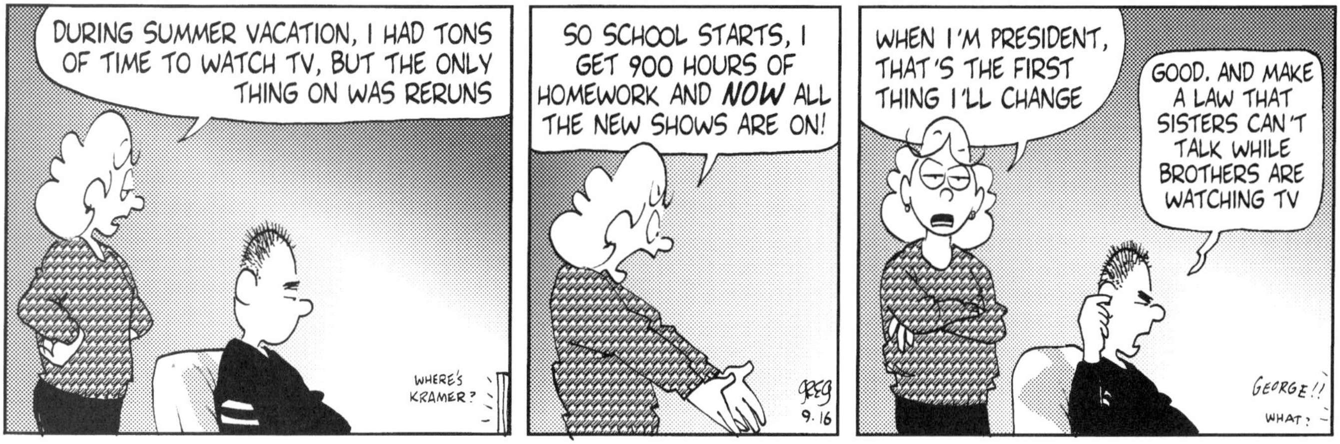
DURING SUMMER VACATION, I HAD TONS OF TIME TO WATCH TV, BUT THE ONLY THING ON WAS RERUNS
WHERE'S KRAMER?
SO SCHOOL STARTS, I GET 900 HOURS OF HOMEWORK AND NOW ALL THE NEW SHOWS ARE ON!
WHEN I'M PRESIDENT, THAT'S THE FIRST THING I'LL CHANGE
GOOD. AND MAKE A LAW THAT SISTERS CAN'T TALK WHILE BROTHERS ARE WATCHING TV
GEORGE!!
WHAT?

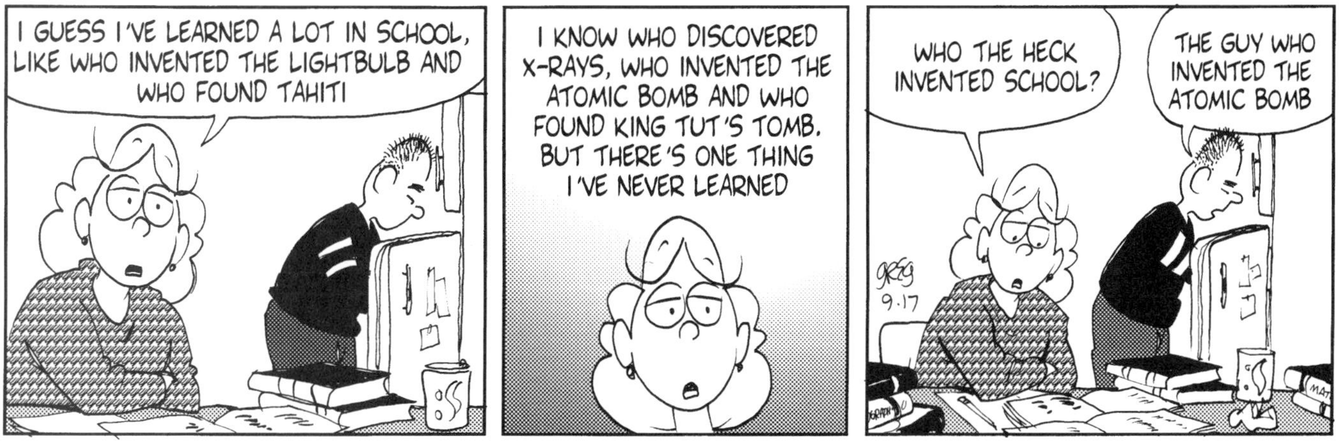
I GUESS I'VE LEARNED A LOT IN SCHOOL, LIKE WHO INVENTED THE LIGHTBULB AND WHO FOUND TAHITI
I KNOW WHO DISCOVERED X-RAYS, WHO INVENTED THE ATOMIC BOMB AND WHO FOUND KING TUT'S TOMB. BUT THERE'S ONE THING I'VE NEVER LEARNED
WHO THE HECK INVENTED SCHOOL?
THE GUY WHO INVENTED THE ATOMIC BOMB

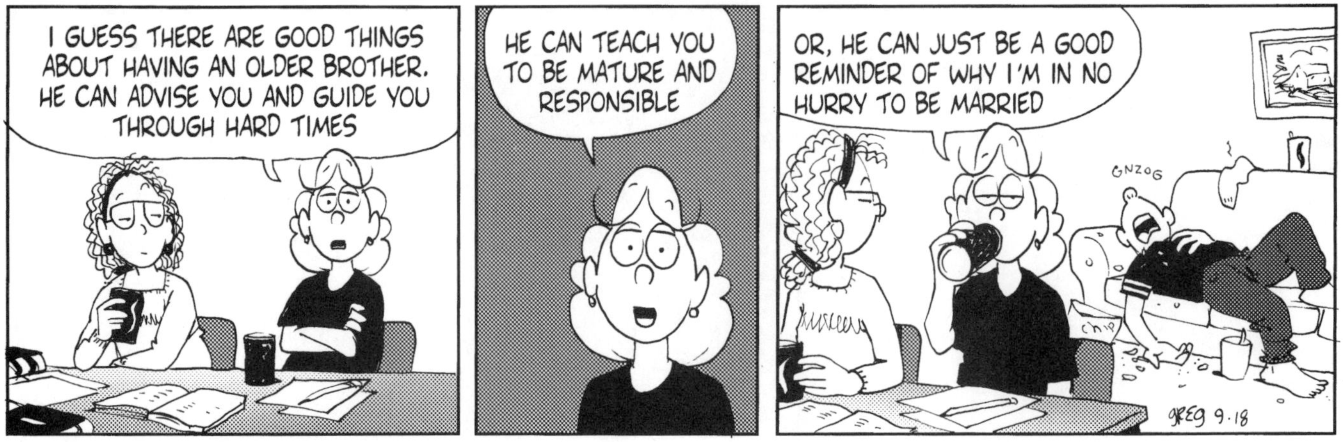
I GUESS THERE ARE GOOD THINGS ABOUT HAVING AN OLDER BROTHER. HE CAN ADVISE YOU AND GUIDE YOU THROUGH HARD TIMES
HE CAN TEACH YOU TO BE MATURE AND RESPONSIBLE
OR, HE CAN JUST BE A GOOD REMINDER OF WHY I'M IN NO HURRY TO BE MARRIED
GNZOG
GREG 9.18

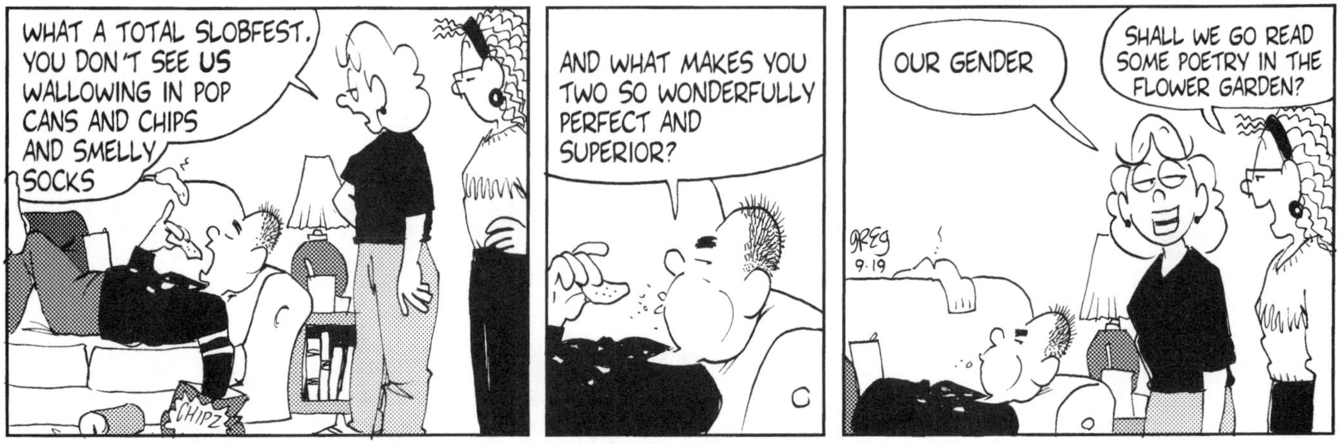
WHAT A TOTAL SLOBFEST. YOU DON'T SEE **US** WALLOWING IN POP CANS AND CHIPS AND SMELLY SOCKS
CHIPZ
AND WHAT MAKES YOU TWO SO WONDERFULLY PERFECT AND SUPERIOR?
OUR GENDER
SHALL WE GO READ SOME POETRY IN THE FLOWER GARDEN?
GREG 9.19

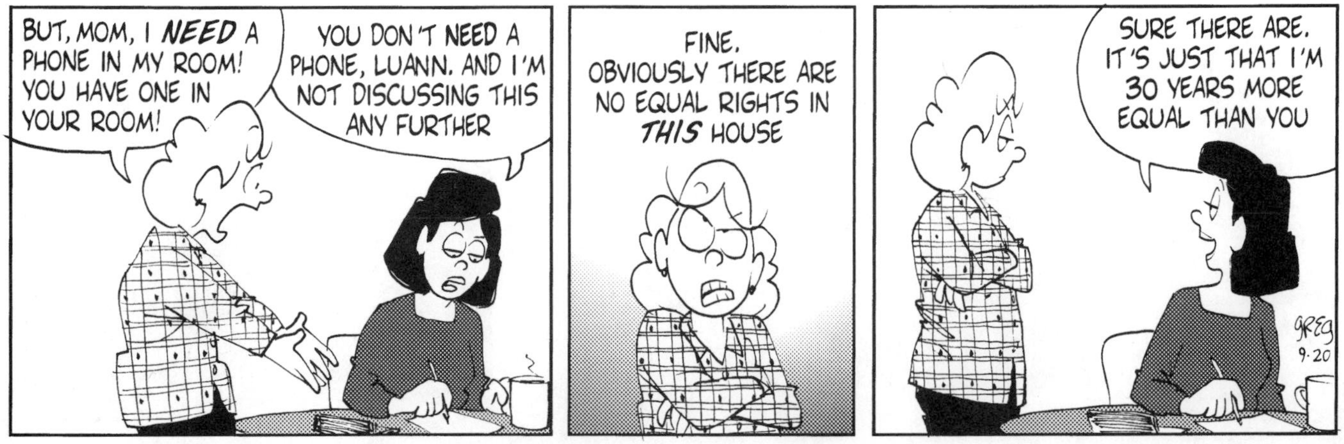
BUT, MOM, I ***NEED*** A PHONE IN MY ROOM! YOU HAVE ONE IN YOUR ROOM!
YOU DON'T NEED A PHONE, LUANN. AND I'M NOT DISCUSSING THIS ANY FURTHER
FINE. OBVIOUSLY THERE ARE NO EQUAL RIGHTS IN ***THIS*** HOUSE
SURE THERE ARE. IT'S JUST THAT I'M 30 YEARS MORE EQUAL THAN YOU
GREG 9.20

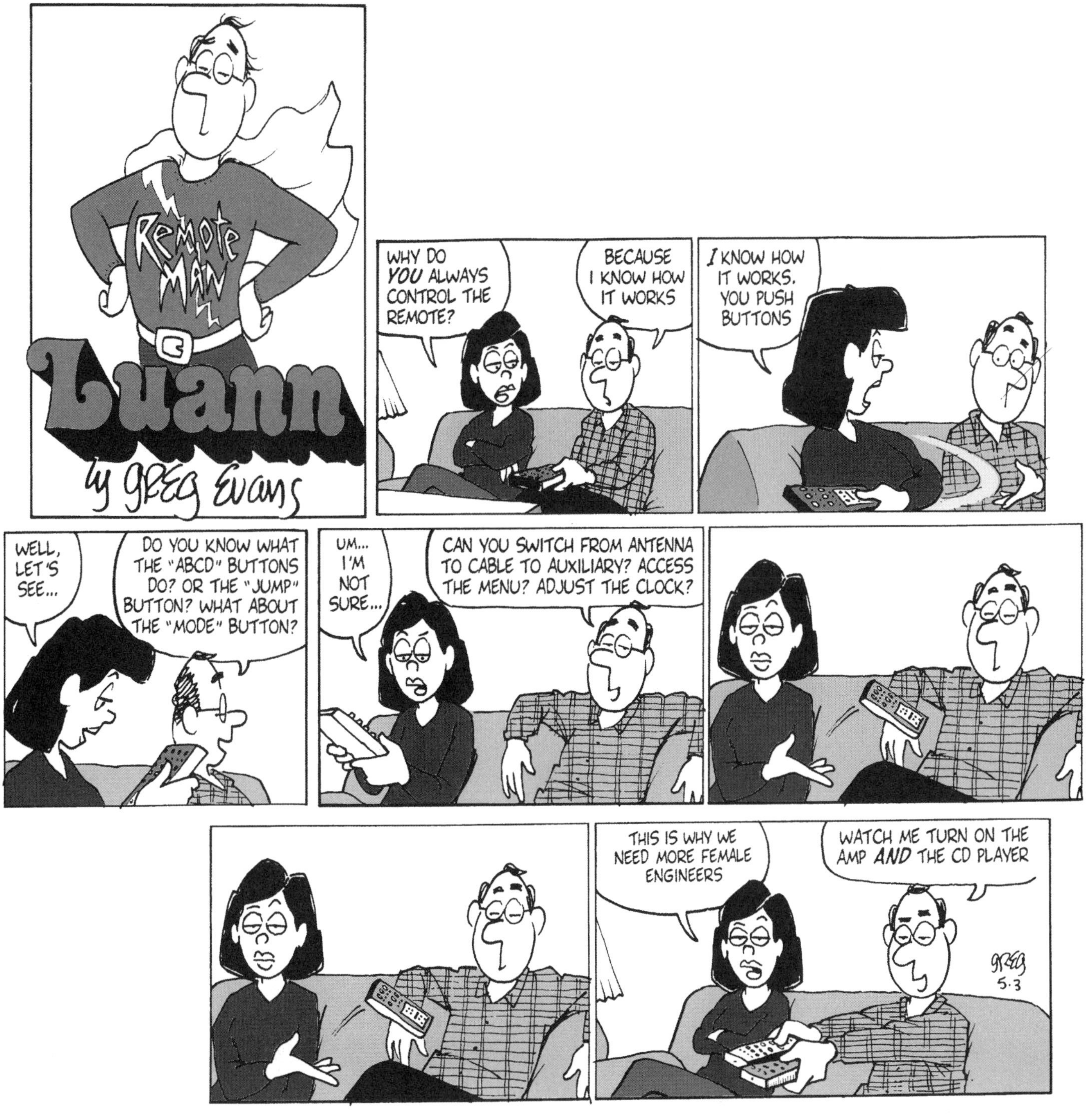
Remote Man
Luann
by GREG Evans
WHY DO YOU ALWAYS CONTROL THE REMOTE?
BECAUSE I KNOW HOW IT WORKS
I KNOW HOW IT WORKS. YOU PUSH BUTTONS
WELL, LET'S SEE...
DO YOU KNOW WHAT THE "ABCD" BUTTONS DO? OR THE "JUMP" BUTTON? WHAT ABOUT THE "MODE" BUTTON?
UM... I'M NOT SURE...
CAN YOU SWITCH FROM ANTENNA TO CABLE TO AUXILIARY? ACCESS THE MENU? ADJUST THE CLOCK?
THIS IS WHY WE NEED MORE FEMALE ENGINEERS
WATCH ME TURN ON THE AMP AND THE CD PLAYER
GREG 5·3

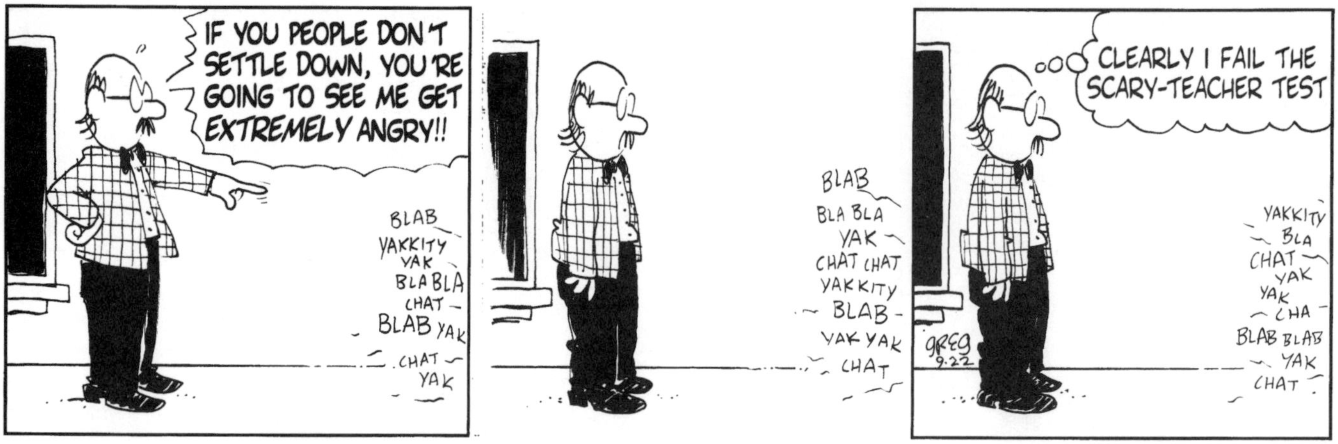
IF YOU PEOPLE DON'T SETTLE DOWN, YOU'RE GOING TO SEE ME GET *EXTREMELY* ANGRY!!
BLAB YAKKITY YAK BLA BLA CHAT BLAB YAK CHAT YAK
BLAB BLA BLA YAK CHAT CHAT YAKKITY BLAB YAK YAK CHAT
CLEARLY I FAIL THE SCARY-TEACHER TEST
YAKKITY BLA CHAT YAK YAK CHA BLAB BLAB YAK CHAT
GREG 9·22

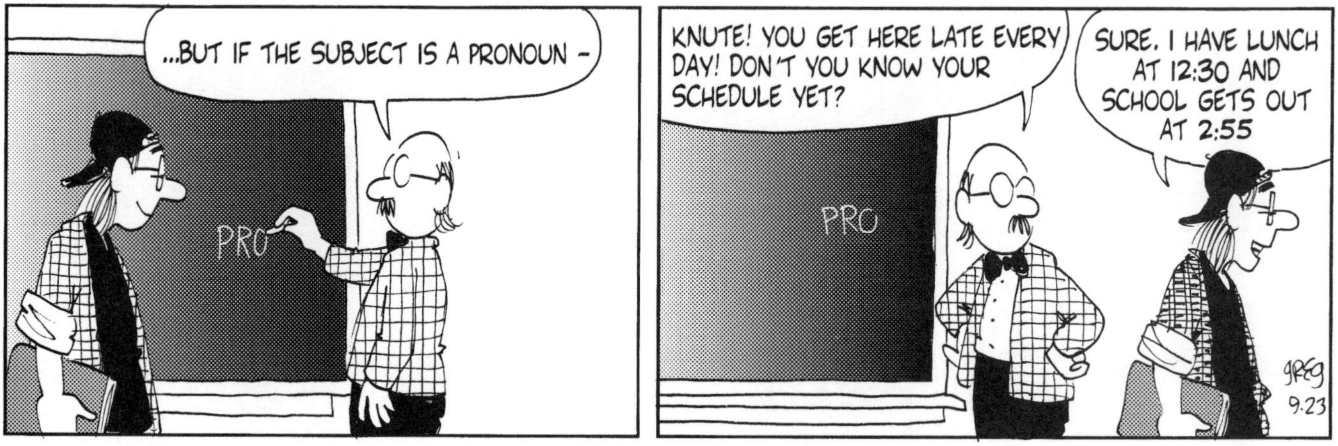
...BUT IF THE SUBJECT IS A PRONOUN –
PRO
KNUTE! YOU GET HERE LATE EVERY DAY! DON'T YOU KNOW YOUR SCHEDULE YET?
SURE. I HAVE LUNCH AT 12:30 AND SCHOOL GETS OUT AT 2:55
PRO
GREG 9·23

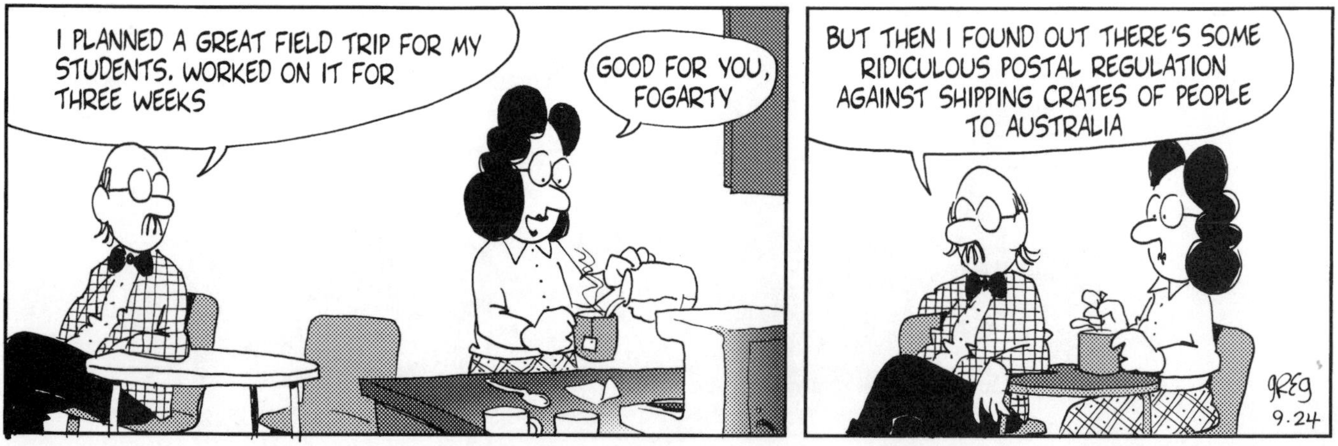
I PLANNED A GREAT FIELD TRIP FOR MY STUDENTS. WORKED ON IT FOR THREE WEEKS
GOOD FOR YOU, FOGARTY
BUT THEN I FOUND OUT THERE'S SOME RIDICULOUS POSTAL REGULATION AGAINST SHIPPING CRATES OF PEOPLE TO AUSTRALIA
GREG 9·24

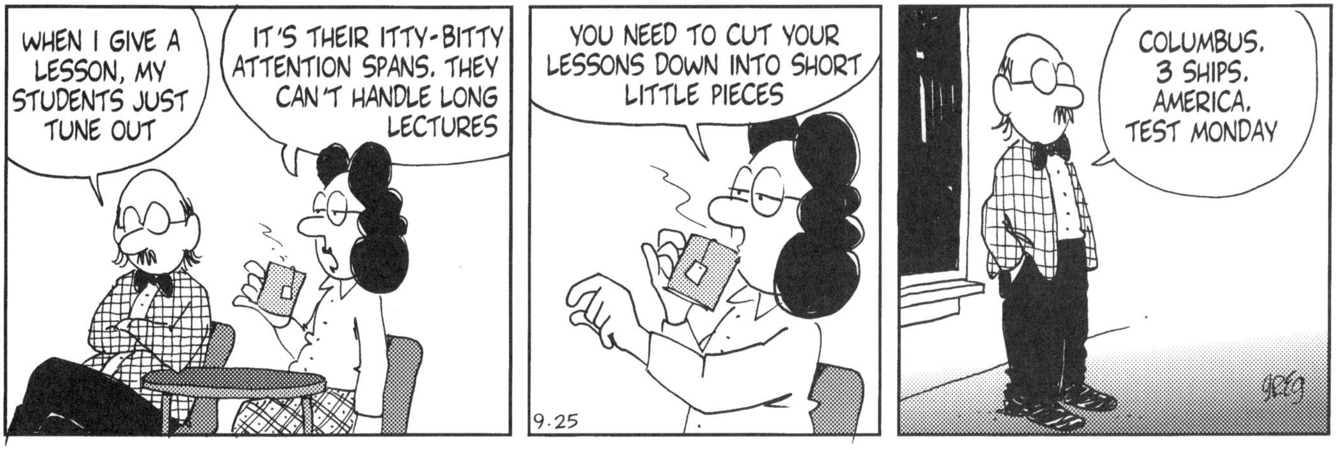
WHEN I GIVE A LESSON, MY STUDENTS JUST TUNE OUT
IT'S THEIR ITTY-BITTY ATTENTION SPANS. THEY CAN'T HANDLE LONG LECTURES
YOU NEED TO CUT YOUR LESSONS DOWN INTO SHORT LITTLE PIECES
9.25
COLUMBUS. 3 SHIPS. AMERICA. TEST MONDAY
GREG

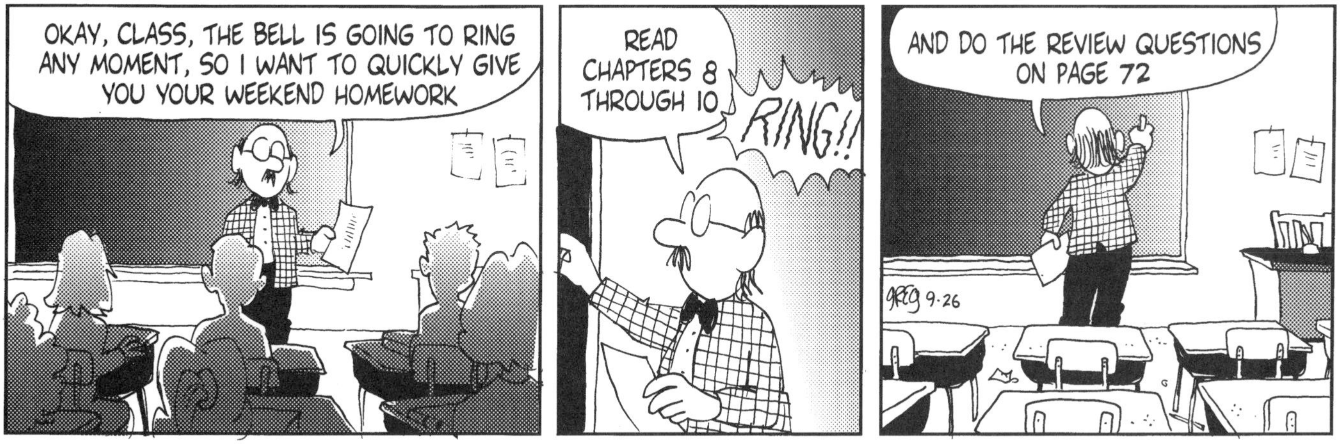
OKAY, CLASS, THE BELL IS GOING TO RING ANY MOMENT, SO I WANT TO QUICKLY GIVE YOU YOUR WEEKEND HOMEWORK
READ CHAPTERS 8 THROUGH 10
RING!!
AND DO THE REVIEW QUESTIONS ON PAGE 72
GREG 9.26

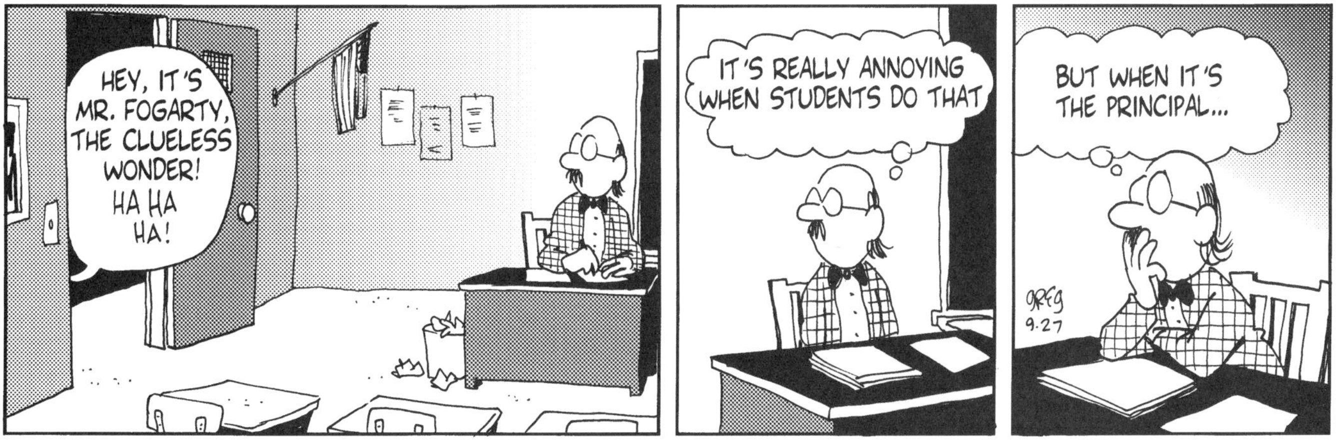
HEY, IT'S MR. FOGARTY, THE CLUELESS WONDER! HA HA HA!
IT'S REALLY ANNOYING WHEN STUDENTS DO THAT
BUT WHEN IT'S THE PRINCIPAL...
GREG 9.27

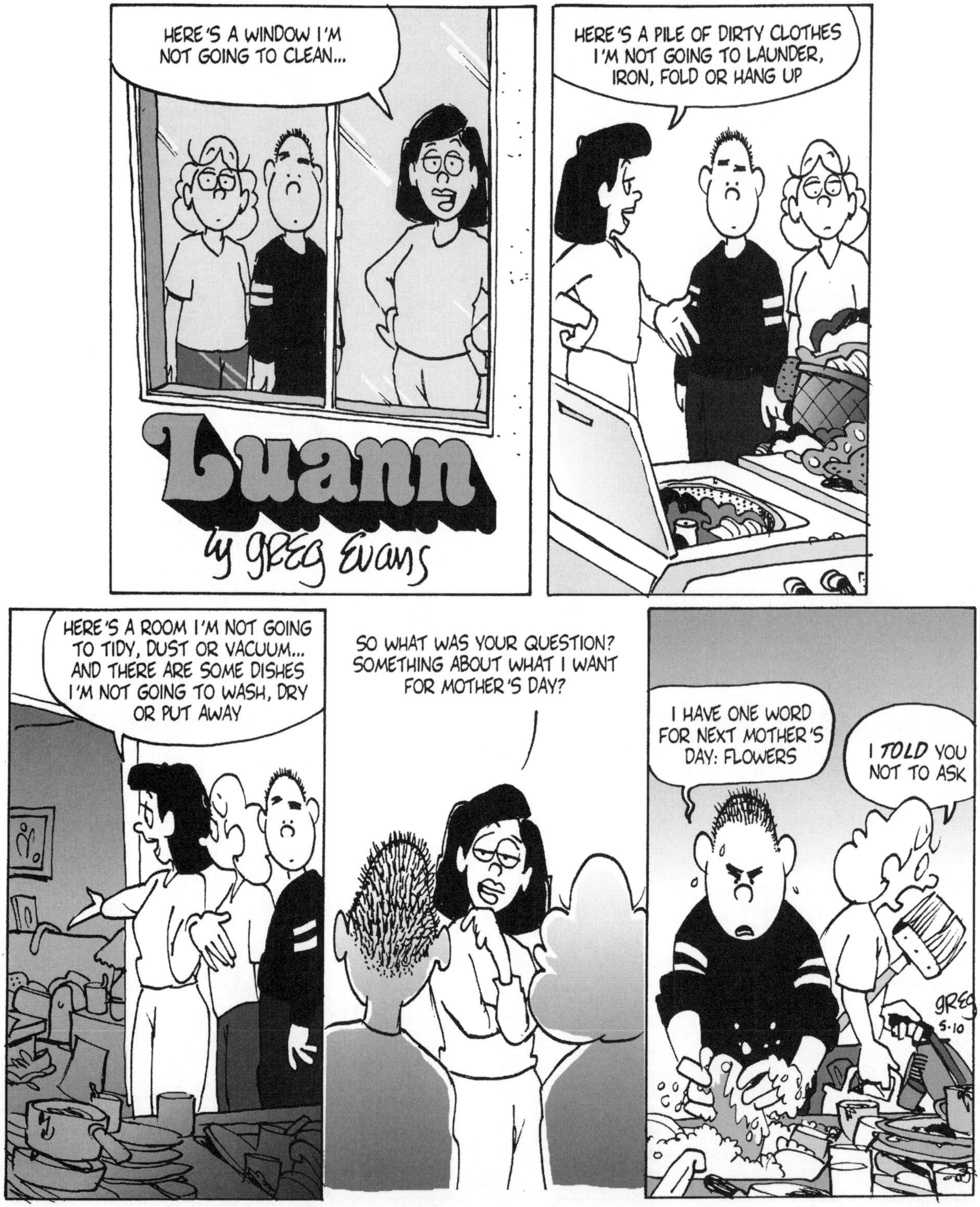
HERE'S A WINDOW I'M NOT GOING TO CLEAN...
Luann
by GREG Evans
HERE'S A PILE OF DIRTY CLOTHES I'M NOT GOING TO LAUNDER, IRON, FOLD OR HANG UP
HERE'S A ROOM I'M NOT GOING TO TIDY, DUST OR VACUUM... AND THERE ARE SOME DISHES I'M NOT GOING TO WASH, DRY OR PUT AWAY
SO WHAT WAS YOUR QUESTION? SOMETHING ABOUT WHAT I WANT FOR MOTHER'S DAY?
I HAVE ONE WORD FOR NEXT MOTHER'S DAY: FLOWERS
I TOLD YOU NOT TO ASK
GREG 5-10

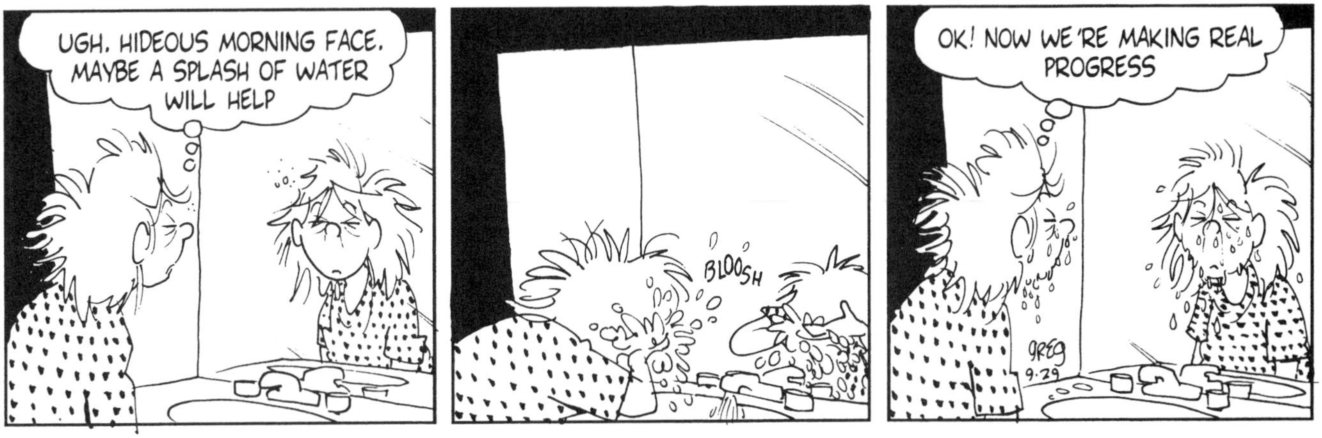
UGH. HIDEOUS MORNING FACE. MAYBE A SPLASH OF WATER WILL HELP
BLOOSH
OK! NOW WE'RE MAKING REAL PROGRESS
GREG 9·29

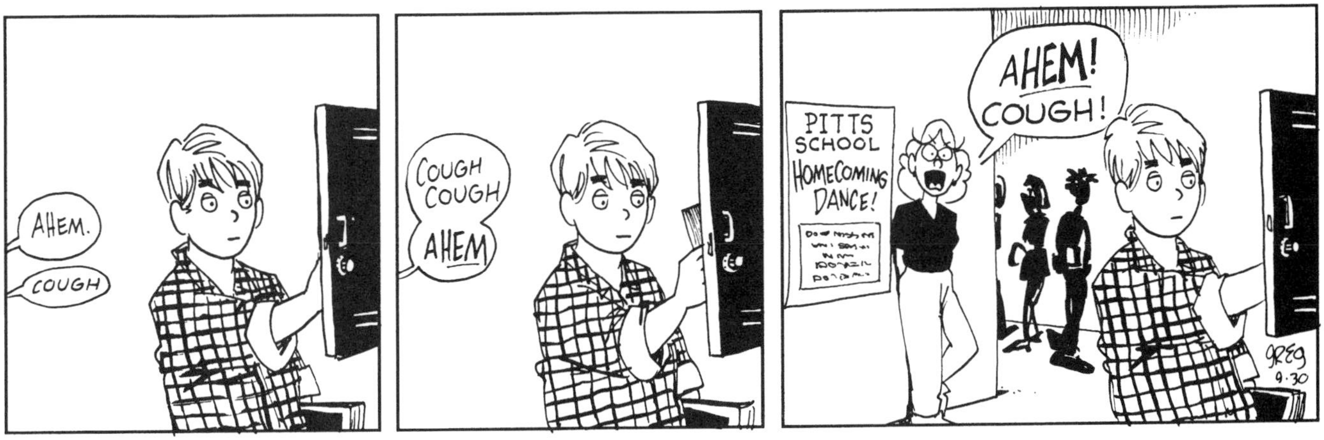
AHEM.
COUGH
COUGH COUGH
AHEM
PITTS SCHOOL HOMECOMING DANCE!
AHEM! COUGH!
GREG 9·30

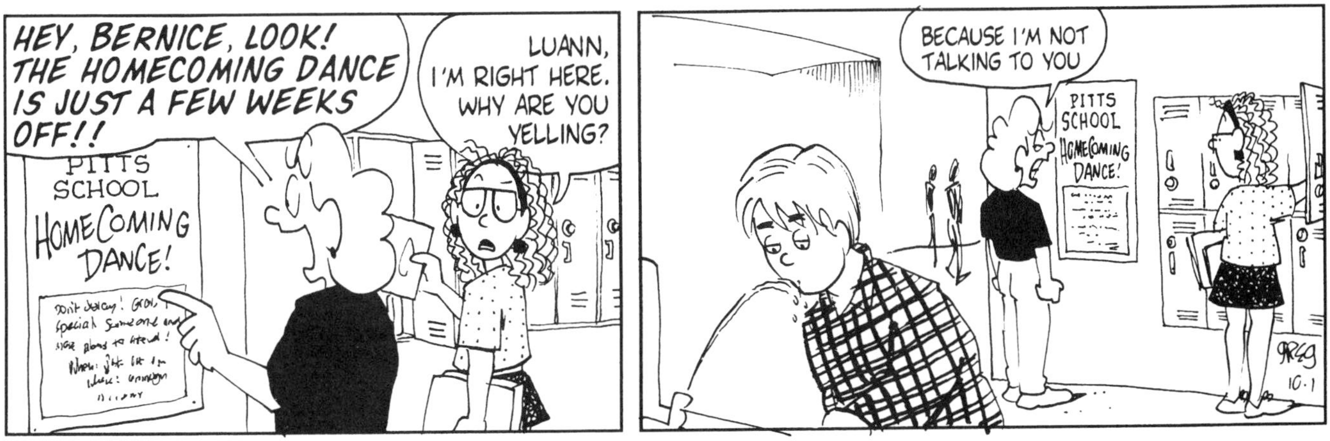
HEY, BERNICE, LOOK! THE HOMECOMING DANCE IS JUST A FEW WEEKS OFF!!
LUANN, I'M RIGHT HERE. WHY ARE YOU YELLING?
PITTS SCHOOL HOMECOMING DANCE!
BECAUSE I'M NOT TALKING TO YOU
PITTS SCHOOL HOMECOMING DANCE!
GREG 10·1

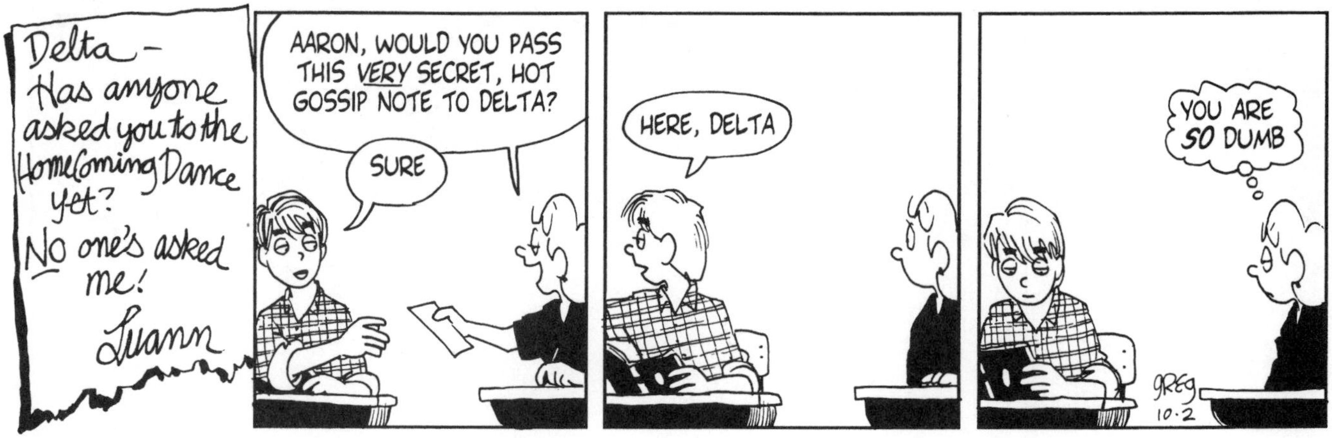
Delta - Has anyone asked you to the HomeComing Dance yet? No one's asked me! Luann
AARON, WOULD YOU PASS THIS VERY SECRET, HOT GOSSIP NOTE TO DELTA?
SURE
HERE, DELTA
YOU ARE SO DUMB
GREG 10·2

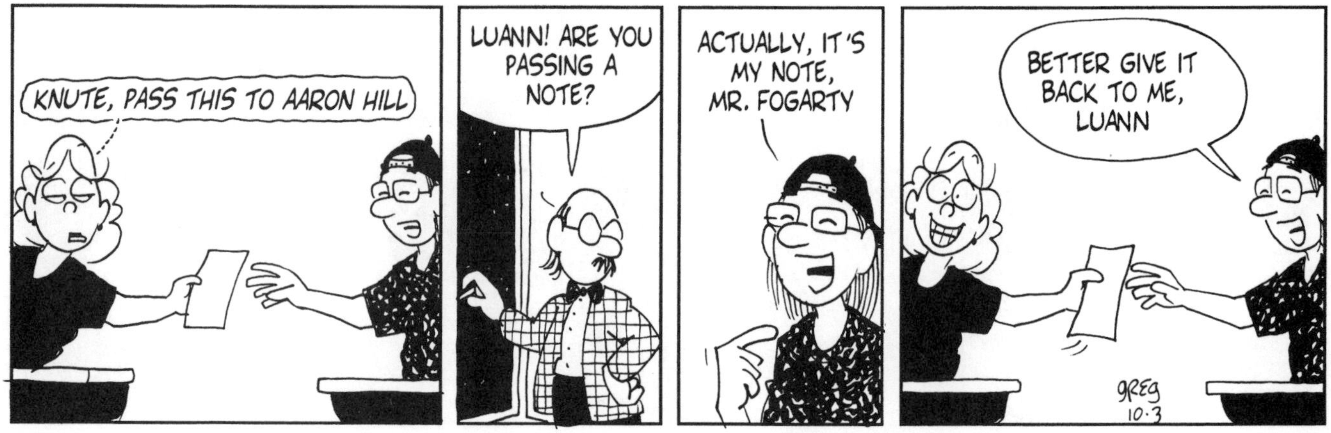
KNUTE, PASS THIS TO AARON HILL
LUANN! ARE YOU PASSING A NOTE?
ACTUALLY, IT'S MY NOTE, MR. FOGARTY
BETTER GIVE IT BACK TO ME, LUANN
GREG 10·3

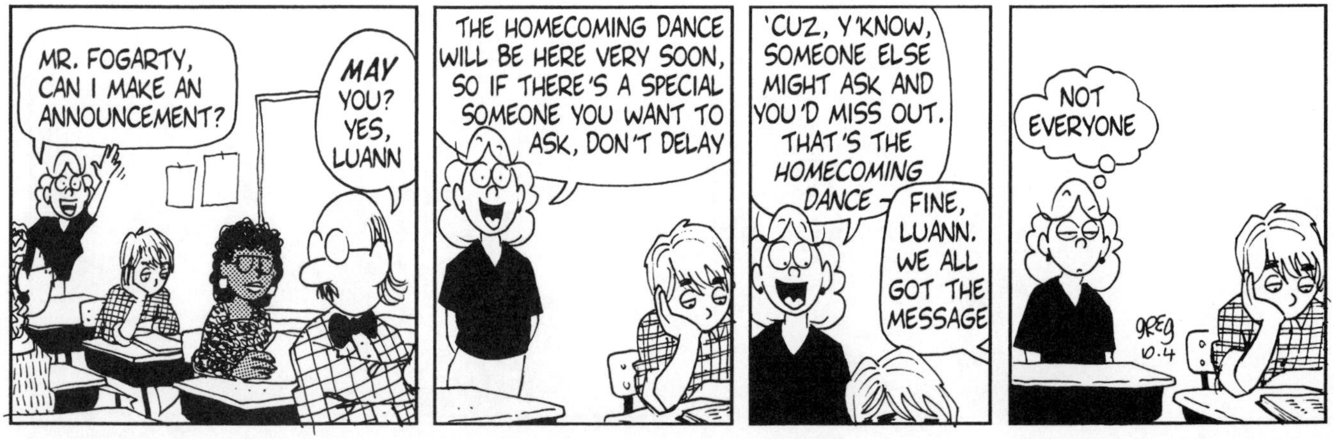
MR. FOGARTY, CAN I MAKE AN ANNOUNCEMENT?
MAY YOU? YES, LUANN
THE HOMECOMING DANCE WILL BE HERE VERY SOON, SO IF THERE'S A SPECIAL SOMEONE YOU WANT TO ASK, DON'T DELAY
'CUZ, Y'KNOW, SOMEONE ELSE MIGHT ASK AND YOU'D MISS OUT. THAT'S THE HOMECOMING DANCE -
FINE, LUANN. WE ALL GOT THE MESSAGE
NOT EVERYONE
GREG 10·4

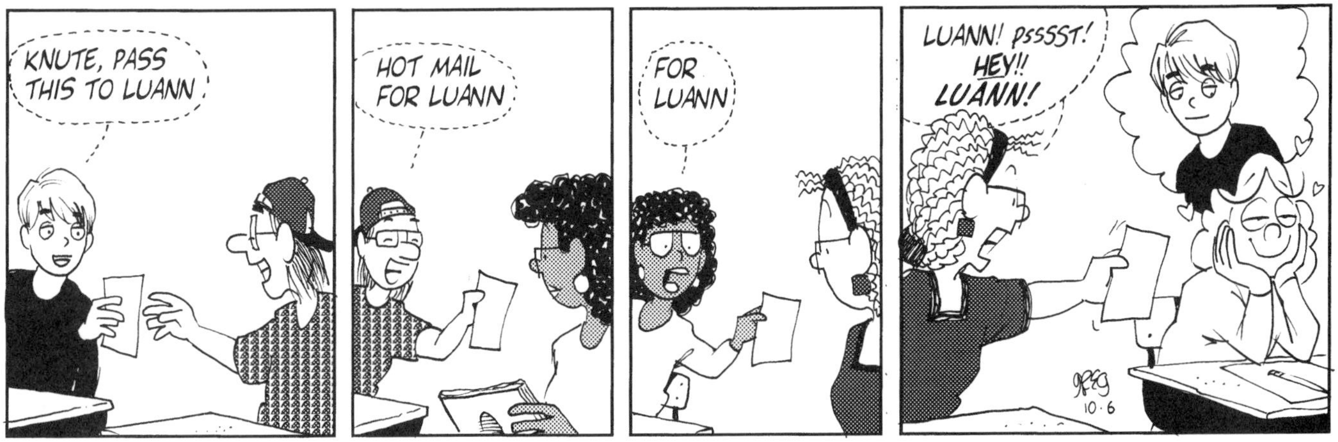
KNUTE, PASS THIS TO LUANN
HOT MAIL FOR LUANN
FOR LUANN
LUANN! PSSSST! HEY!! LUANN!

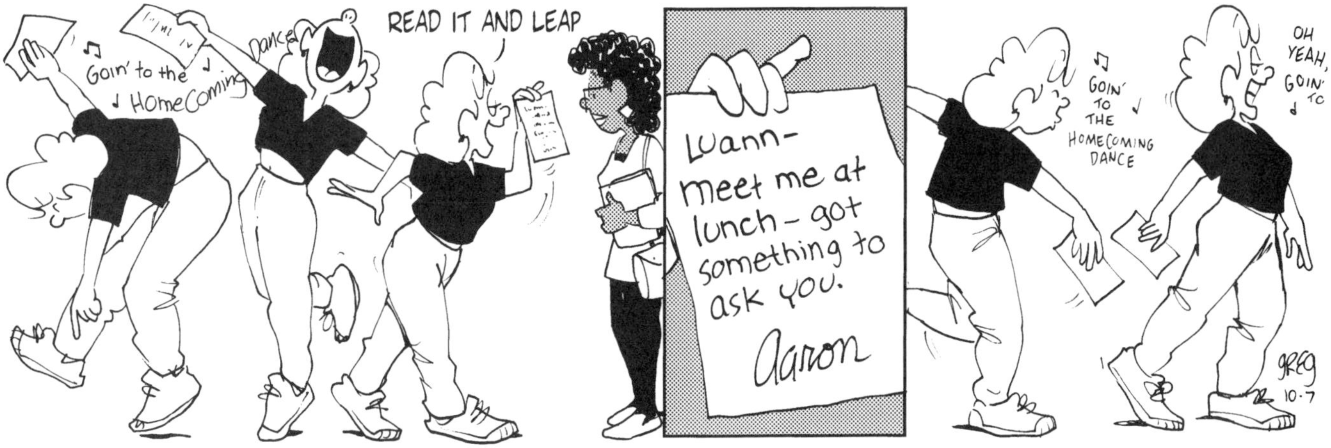
Goin' to the HomeComing Dance
READ IT AND LEAP
Luann- meet me at lunch - got something to ask you. Aaron
GOIN' TO THE HOMECOMING DANCE
OH YEAH, GOIN' TO

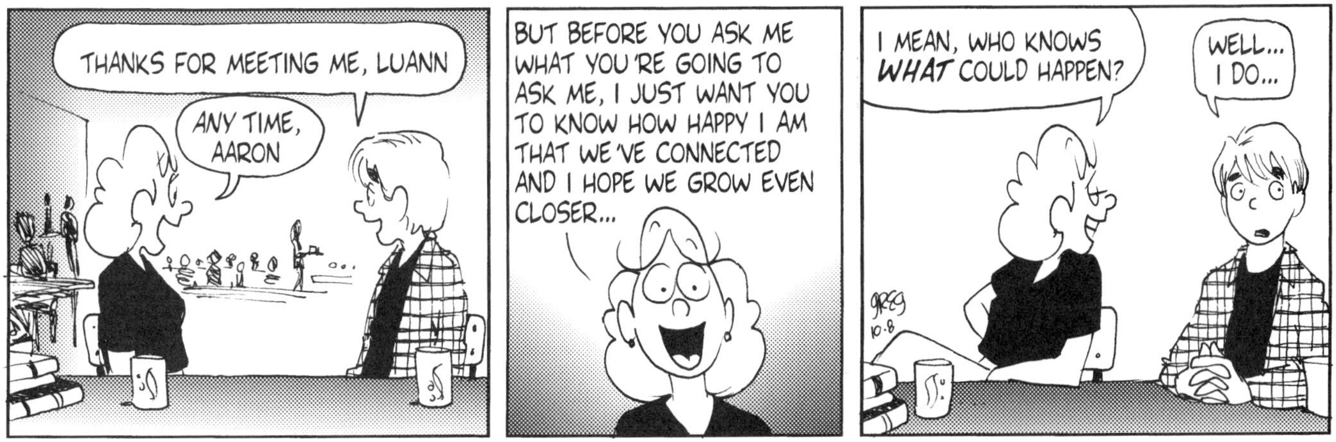
THANKS FOR MEETING ME, LUANN
ANY TIME, AARON
BUT BEFORE YOU ASK ME WHAT YOU'RE GOING TO ASK ME, I JUST WANT YOU TO KNOW HOW HAPPY I AM THAT WE'VE CONNECTED AND I HOPE WE GROW EVEN CLOSER...
I MEAN, WHO KNOWS WHAT COULD HAPPEN?
WELL... I DO...

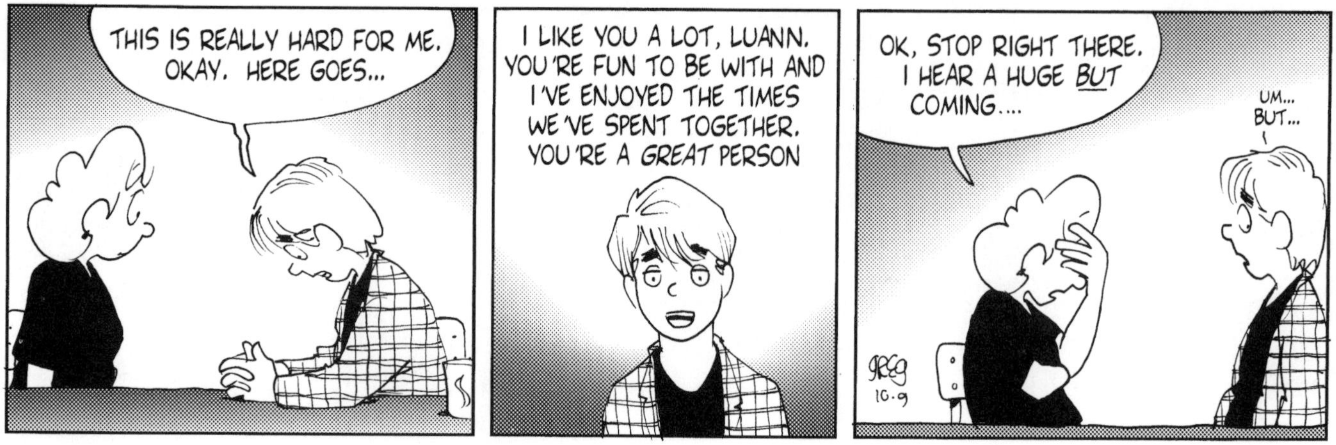

THIS IS REALLY HARD FOR ME. OKAY. HERE GOES...
I LIKE YOU A LOT, LUANN. YOU'RE FUN TO BE WITH AND I'VE ENJOYED THE TIMES WE'VE SPENT TOGETHER. YOU'RE A *GREAT* PERSON
OK, STOP RIGHT THERE. I HEAR A HUGE BUT COMING....
UM... BUT...

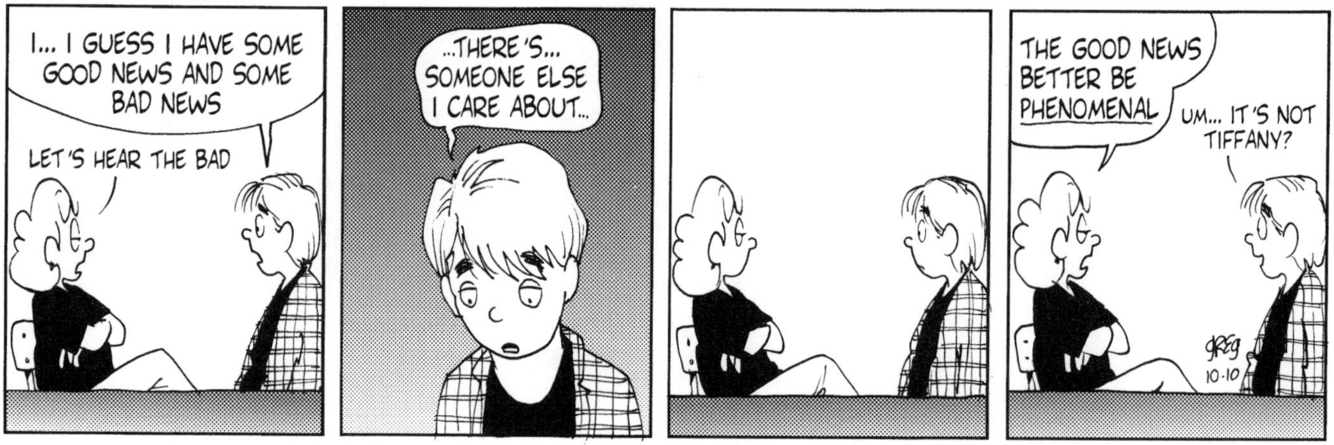

I... I GUESS I HAVE SOME GOOD NEWS AND SOME BAD NEWS
LET'S HEAR THE BAD
...THERE'S... SOMEONE ELSE I CARE ABOUT...
THE GOOD NEWS BETTER BE PHENOMENAL
UM... IT'S NOT TIFFANY?

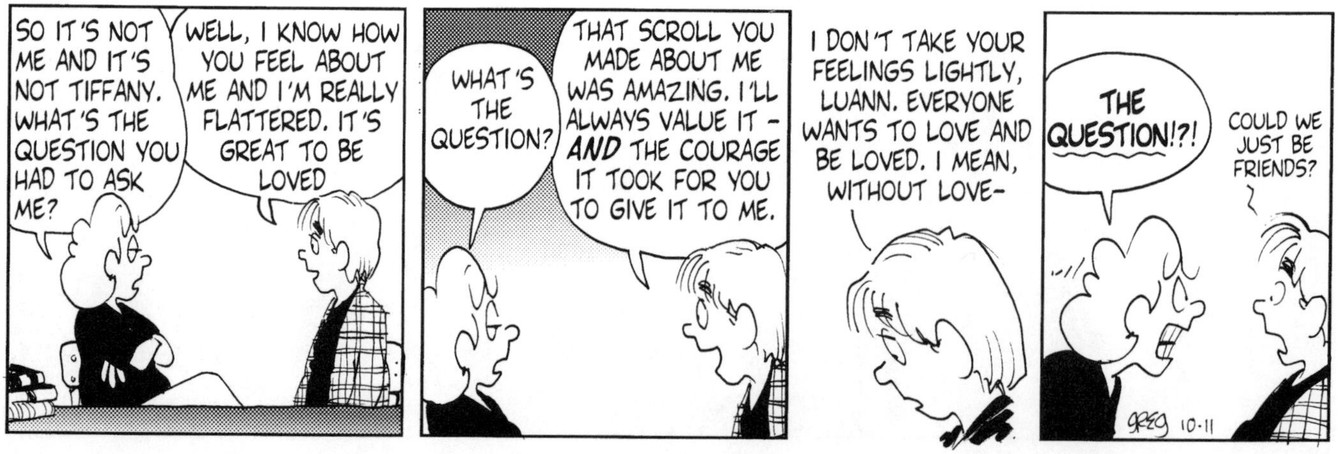

SO IT'S NOT ME AND IT'S NOT TIFFANY. WHAT'S THE QUESTION YOU HAD TO ASK ME?
WELL, I KNOW HOW YOU FEEL ABOUT ME AND I'M REALLY FLATTERED. IT'S GREAT TO BE LOVED
WHAT'S THE QUESTION?
THAT SCROLL YOU MADE ABOUT ME WAS AMAZING. I'LL ALWAYS VALUE IT - **AND** THE COURAGE IT TOOK FOR YOU TO GIVE IT TO ME.
I DON'T TAKE YOUR FEELINGS LIGHTLY, LUANN. EVERYONE WANTS TO LOVE AND BE LOVED. I MEAN, WITHOUT LOVE-
THE QUESTION!?!
COULD WE JUST BE FRIENDS?

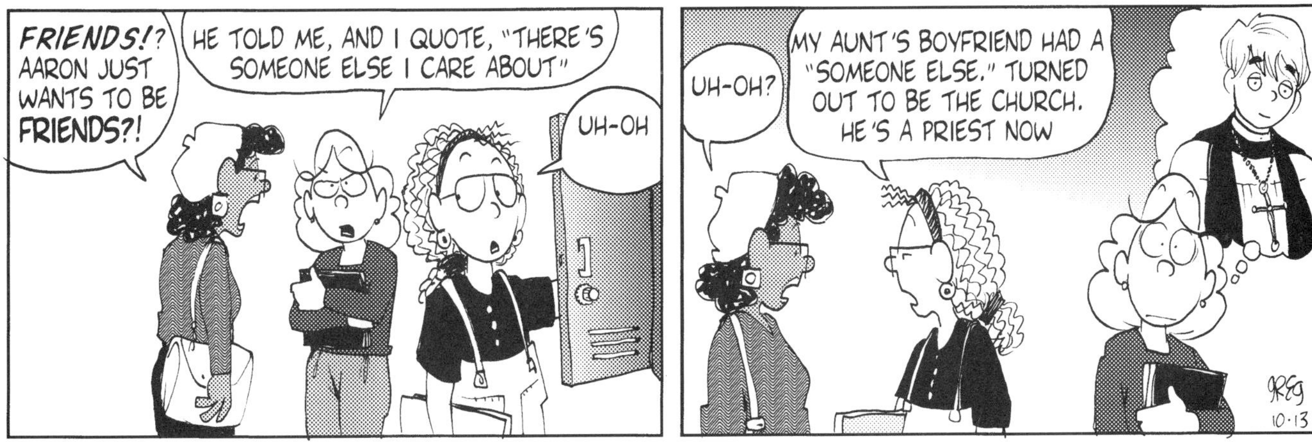
FRIENDS!? AARON JUST WANTS TO BE FRIENDS?!
HE TOLD ME, AND I QUOTE, "THERE'S SOMEONE ELSE I CARE ABOUT"
UH-OH
UH-OH?
MY AUNT'S BOYFRIEND HAD A "SOMEONE ELSE." TURNED OUT TO BE THE CHURCH. HE'S A PRIEST NOW
10.13

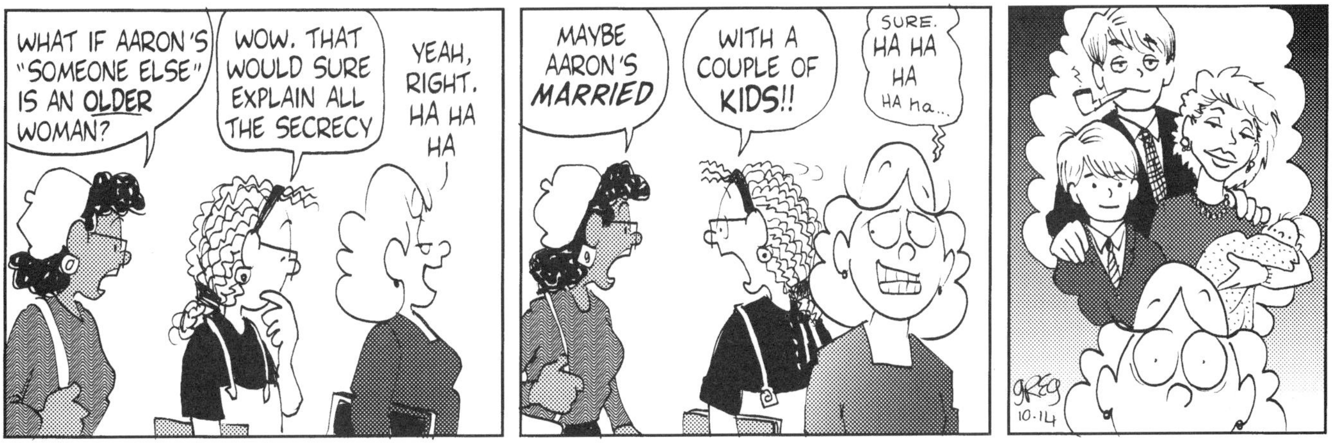
WHAT IF AARON'S "SOMEONE ELSE" IS AN OLDER WOMAN?
WOW. THAT WOULD SURE EXPLAIN ALL THE SECRECY
YEAH, RIGHT. HA HA HA
MAYBE AARON'S MARRIED
WITH A COUPLE OF KIDS!!
SURE. HA HA HA HA ha...
10.14

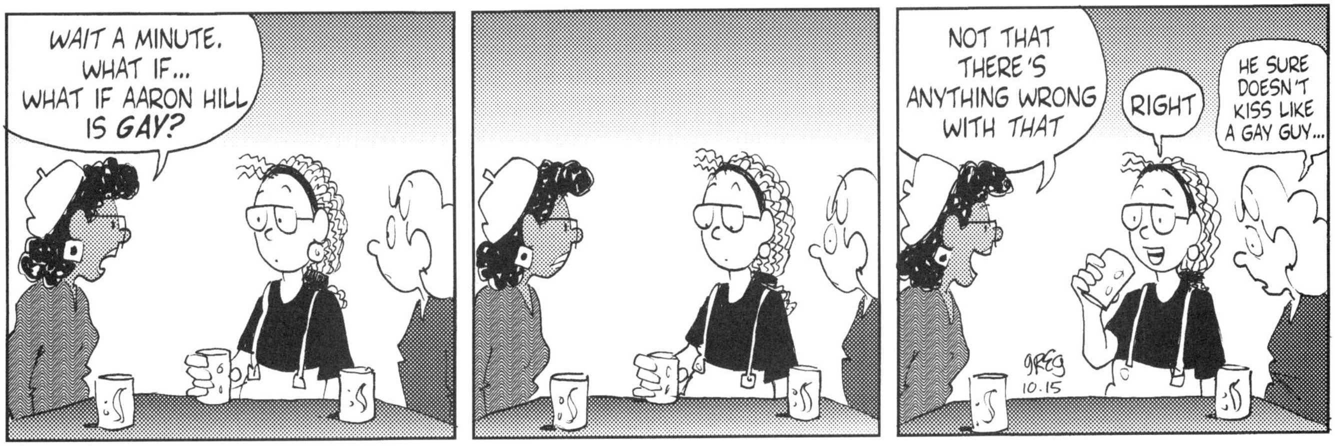
WAIT A MINUTE. WHAT IF... WHAT IF AARON HILL IS GAY?
NOT THAT THERE'S ANYTHING WRONG WITH THAT
RIGHT
HE SURE DOESN'T KISS LIKE A GAY GUY...
10.15

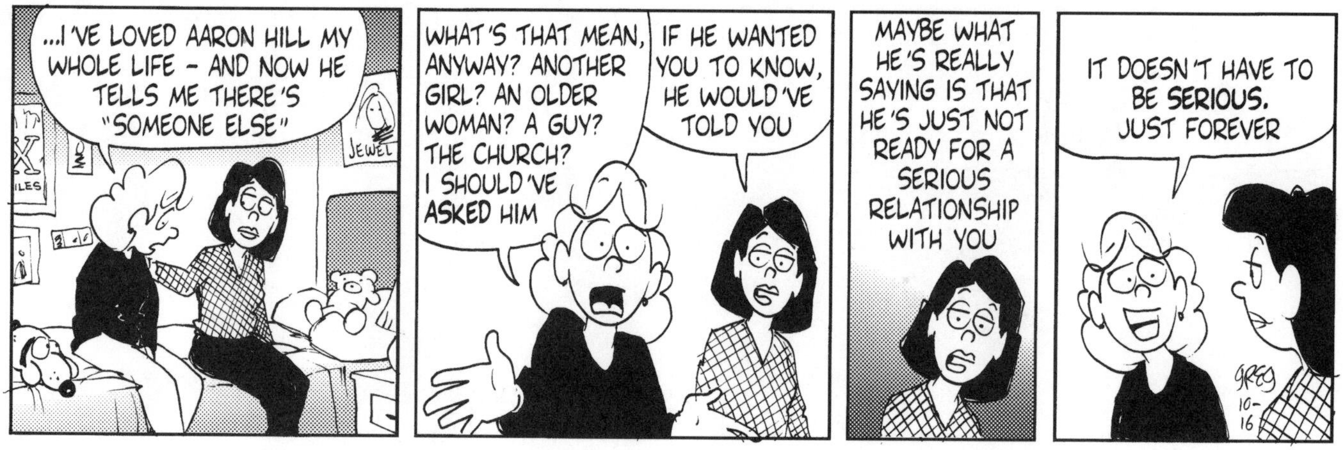
...I'VE LOVED AARON HILL MY WHOLE LIFE - AND NOW HE TELLS ME THERE'S "SOMEONE ELSE"
JEWEL
WHAT'S THAT MEAN, ANYWAY? ANOTHER GIRL? AN OLDER WOMAN? A GUY? THE CHURCH? I SHOULD'VE **ASKED** HIM
IF HE WANTED YOU TO KNOW, HE WOULD'VE TOLD YOU
MAYBE WHAT HE'S REALLY SAYING IS THAT HE'S JUST NOT READY FOR A SERIOUS RELATIONSHIP WITH YOU
IT DOESN'T HAVE TO BE **SERIOUS.** JUST FOREVER
GREG 10-16

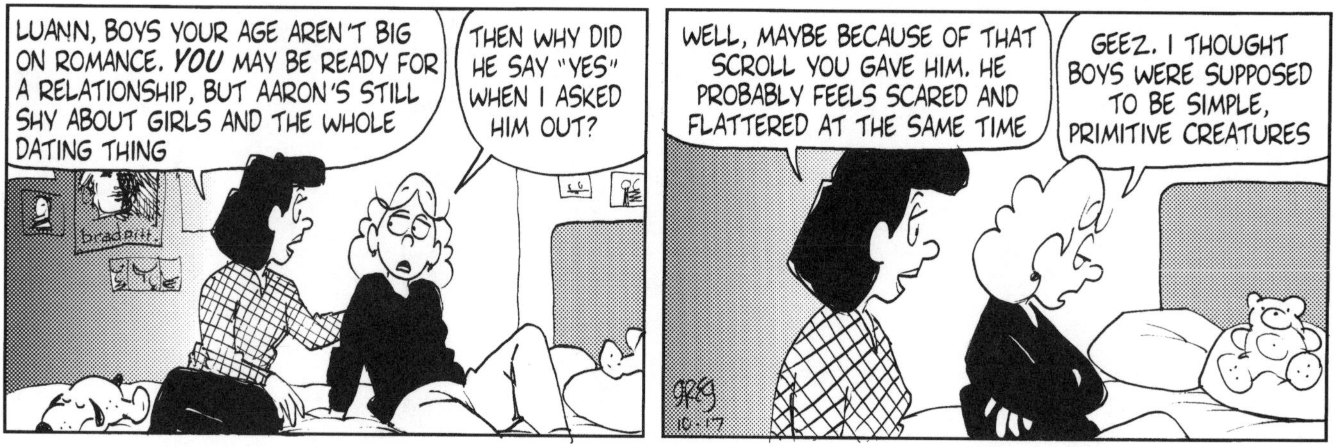
LUANN, BOYS YOUR AGE AREN'T BIG ON ROMANCE. ***YOU*** MAY BE READY FOR A RELATIONSHIP, BUT AARON'S STILL SHY ABOUT GIRLS AND THE WHOLE DATING THING
THEN WHY DID HE SAY "YES" WHEN I ASKED HIM OUT?
bradpitt
GREG 10-17
WELL, MAYBE BECAUSE OF THAT SCROLL YOU GAVE HIM. HE PROBABLY FEELS SCARED AND FLATTERED AT THE SAME TIME
GEEZ. I THOUGHT BOYS WERE SUPPOSED TO BE SIMPLE, PRIMITIVE CREATURES

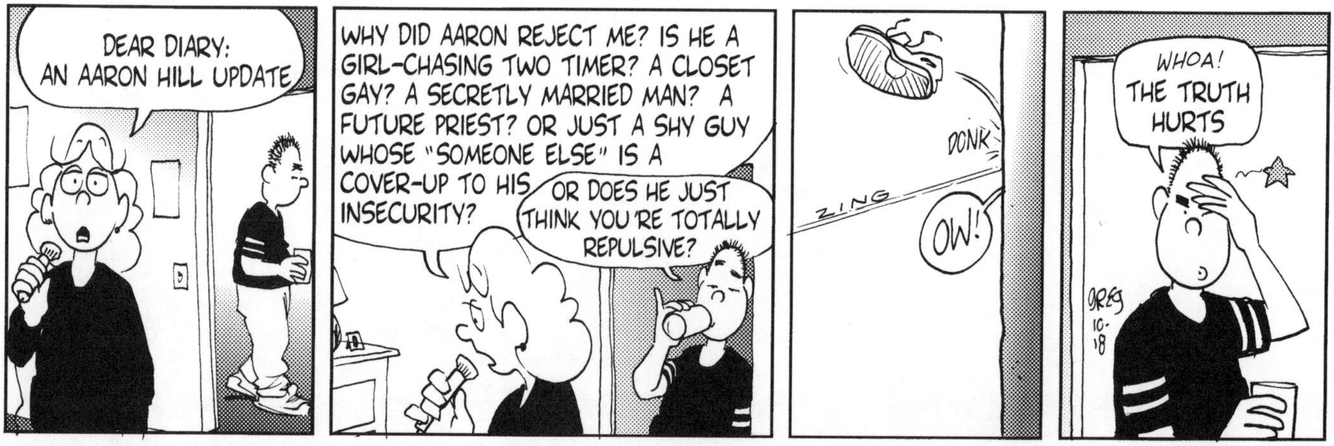
DEAR DIARY: AN AARON HILL UPDATE
WHY DID AARON REJECT ME? IS HE A GIRL-CHASING TWO TIMER? A CLOSET GAY? A SECRETLY MARRIED MAN? A FUTURE PRIEST? OR JUST A SHY GUY WHOSE "SOMEONE ELSE" IS A COVER-UP TO HIS INSECURITY?
OR DOES HE JUST THINK YOU'RE TOTALLY REPULSIVE?
DONK
ZING
OW!
WHOA! THE TRUTH HURTS
GREG 10-18

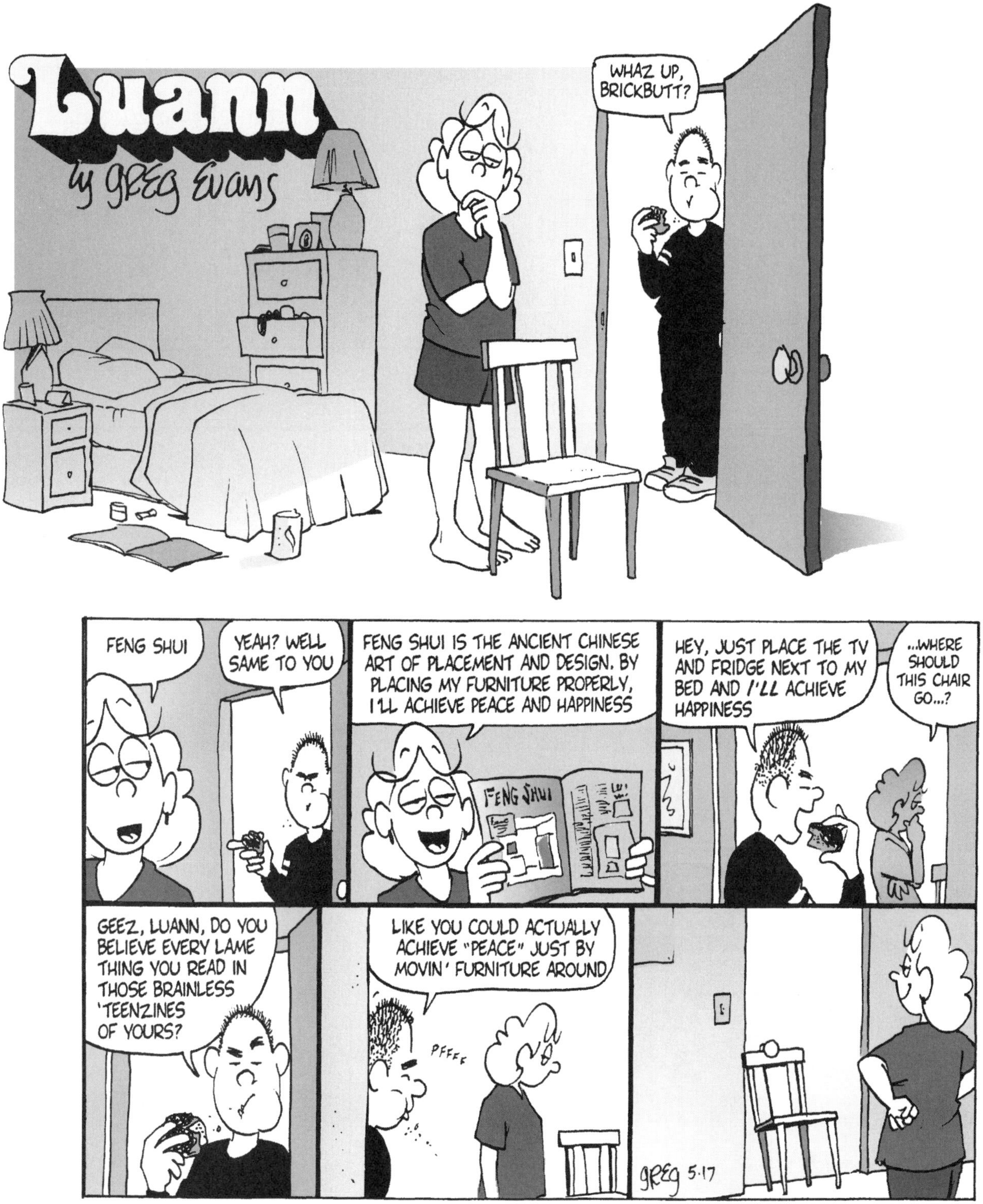
Luann
by GREG EVANS
WHAZ UP, BRICKBUTT?
FENG SHUI
YEAH? WELL SAME TO YOU
FENG SHUI IS THE ANCIENT CHINESE ART OF PLACEMENT AND DESIGN. BY PLACING MY FURNITURE PROPERLY, I'LL ACHIEVE PEACE AND HAPPINESS
FENG SHUI
HEY, JUST PLACE THE TV AND FRIDGE NEXT TO MY BED AND I'LL ACHIEVE HAPPINESS
...WHERE SHOULD THIS CHAIR GO...?
GEEZ, LUANN, DO YOU BELIEVE EVERY LAME THING YOU READ IN THOSE BRAINLESS 'TEENZINES OF YOURS?
LIKE YOU COULD ACTUALLY ACHIEVE "PEACE" JUST BY MOVIN' FURNITURE AROUND
PFFFF
GREG 5.17

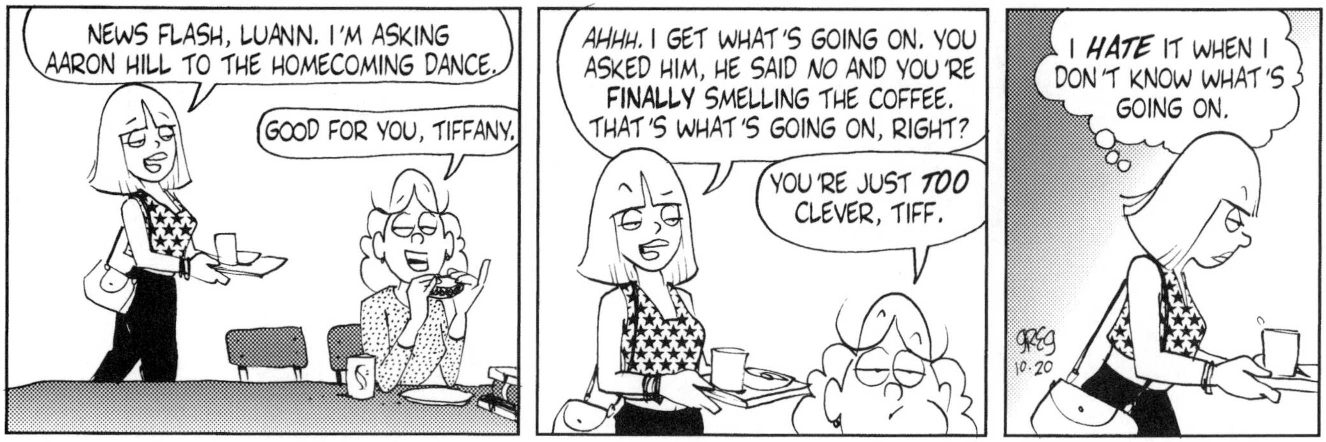
NEWS FLASH, LUANN. I'M ASKING AARON HILL TO THE HOMECOMING DANCE.
GOOD FOR YOU, TIFFANY.
AHHH. I GET WHAT'S GOING ON. YOU ASKED HIM, HE SAID NO AND YOU'RE FINALLY SMELLING THE COFFEE. THAT'S WHAT'S GOING ON, RIGHT?
YOU'RE JUST TOO CLEVER, TIFF.
I HATE IT WHEN I DON'T KNOW WHAT'S GOING ON.
GREG
10·20

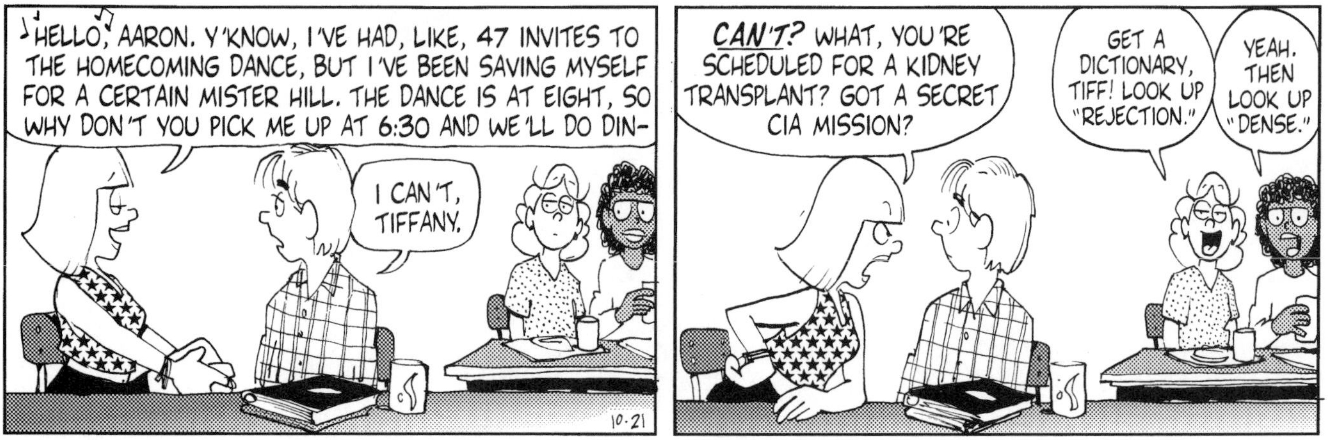
HELLO, AARON. Y'KNOW, I'VE HAD, LIKE, 47 INVITES TO THE HOMECOMING DANCE, BUT I'VE BEEN SAVING MYSELF FOR A CERTAIN MISTER HILL. THE DANCE IS AT EIGHT, SO WHY DON'T YOU PICK ME UP AT 6:30 AND WE'LL DO DIN-
I CAN'T, TIFFANY.
10·21
CAN'T? WHAT, YOU'RE SCHEDULED FOR A KIDNEY TRANSPLANT? GOT A SECRET CIA MISSION?
GET A DICTIONARY, TIFF! LOOK UP "REJECTION."
YEAH. THEN LOOK UP "DENSE."

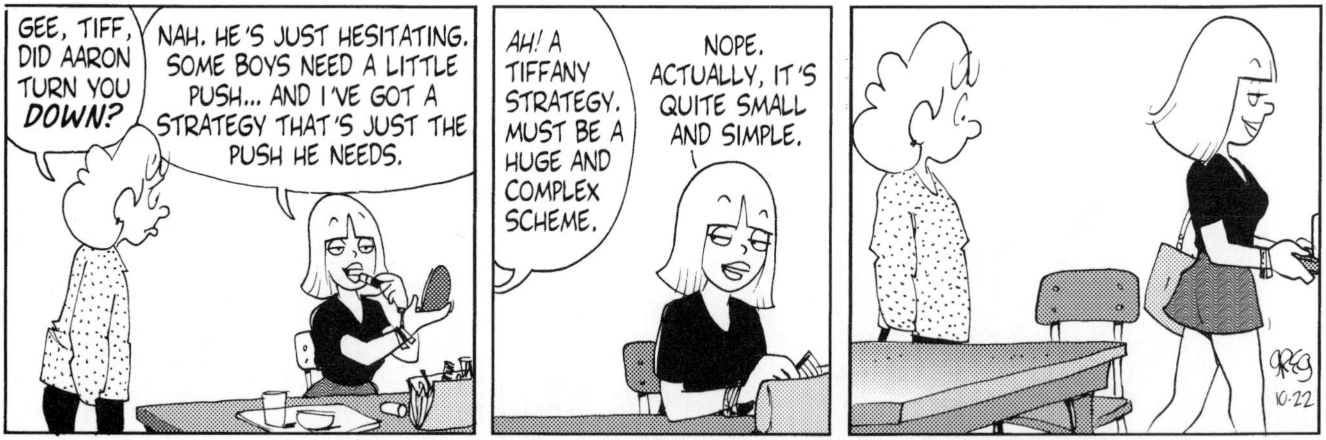
GEE, TIFF, DID AARON TURN YOU DOWN?
NAH. HE'S JUST HESITATING. SOME BOYS NEED A LITTLE PUSH... AND I'VE GOT A STRATEGY THAT'S JUST THE PUSH HE NEEDS.
AH! A TIFFANY STRATEGY. MUST BE A HUGE AND COMPLEX SCHEME.
NOPE. ACTUALLY, IT'S QUITE SMALL AND SIMPLE.
GREG
10·22

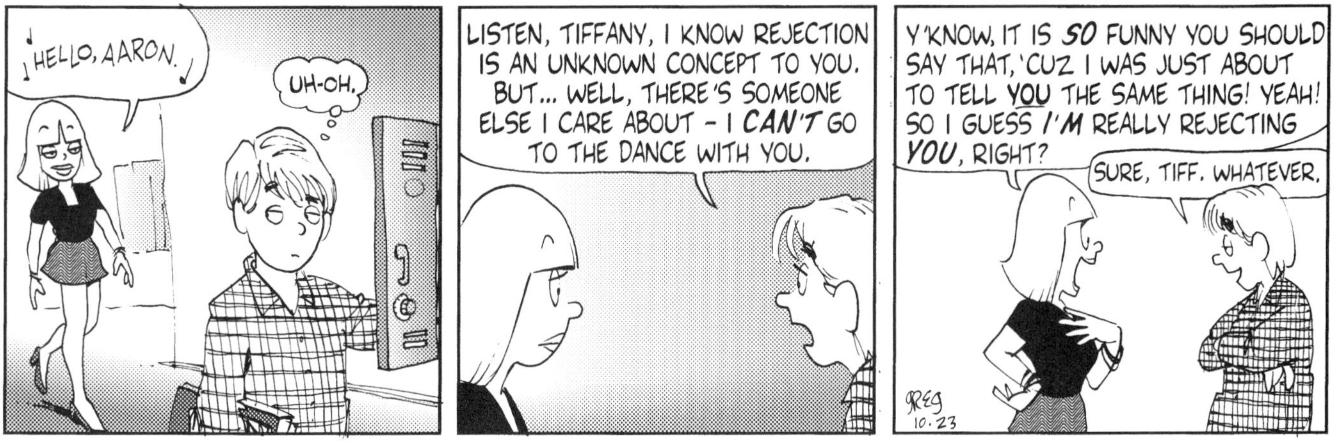
HELLO, AARON.
UH-OH.
LISTEN, TIFFANY, I KNOW REJECTION IS AN UNKNOWN CONCEPT TO YOU. BUT... WELL, THERE'S SOMEONE ELSE I CARE ABOUT – I CAN'T GO TO THE DANCE WITH YOU.
Y'KNOW, IT IS SO FUNNY YOU SHOULD SAY THAT, 'CUZ I WAS JUST ABOUT TO TELL YOU THE SAME THING! YEAH! SO I GUESS I'M REALLY REJECTING YOU, RIGHT?
SURE, TIFF. WHATEVER.
GREG 10.23

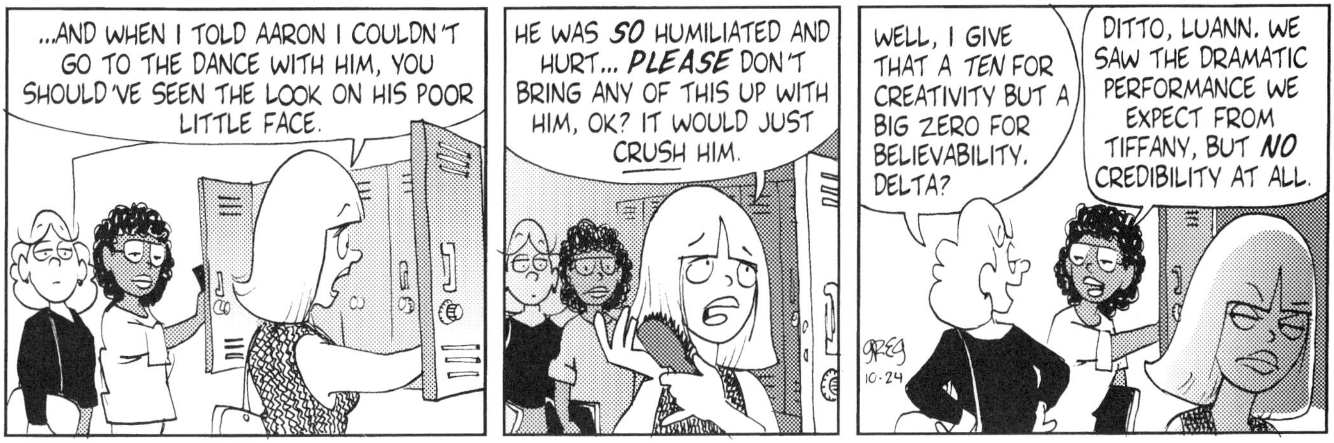
...AND WHEN I TOLD AARON I COULDN'T GO TO THE DANCE WITH HIM, YOU SHOULD'VE SEEN THE LOOK ON HIS POOR LITTLE FACE.
HE WAS SO HUMILIATED AND HURT... PLEASE DON'T BRING ANY OF THIS UP WITH HIM, OK? IT WOULD JUST CRUSH HIM.
WELL, I GIVE THAT A TEN FOR CREATIVITY BUT A BIG ZERO FOR BELIEVABILITY. DELTA?
DITTO, LUANN. WE SAW THE DRAMATIC PERFORMANCE WE EXPECT FROM TIFFANY, BUT NO CREDIBILITY AT ALL.
GREG 10.24

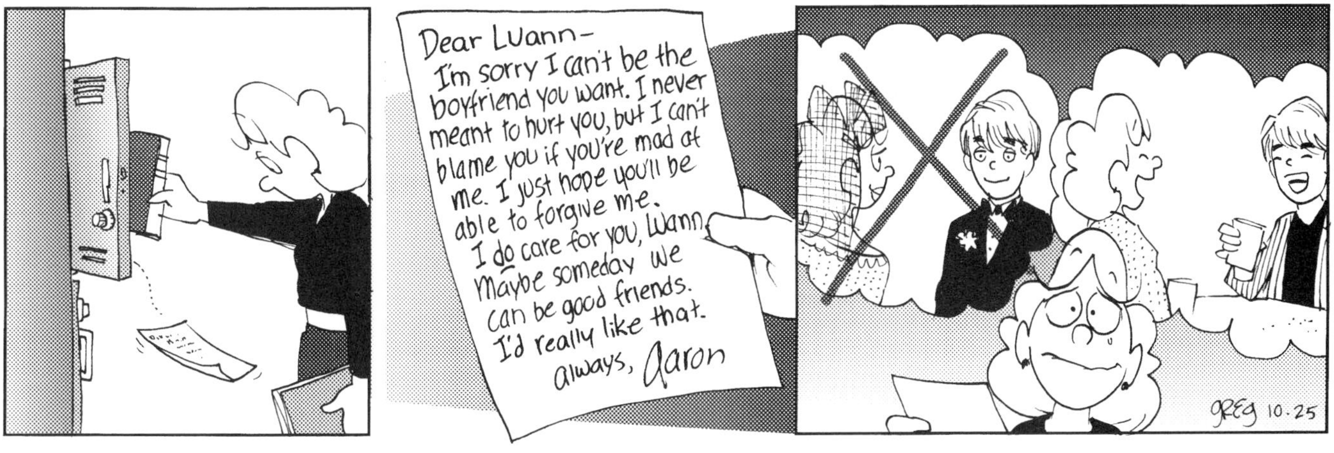
Dear Luann-
I'm sorry I can't be the boyfriend you want. I never meant to hurt you, but I can't blame you if you're mad at me. I just hope you'll be able to forgive me.
I do care for you, Luann. Maybe someday we can be good friends. I'd really like that.
always, Aaron
GREG 10.25

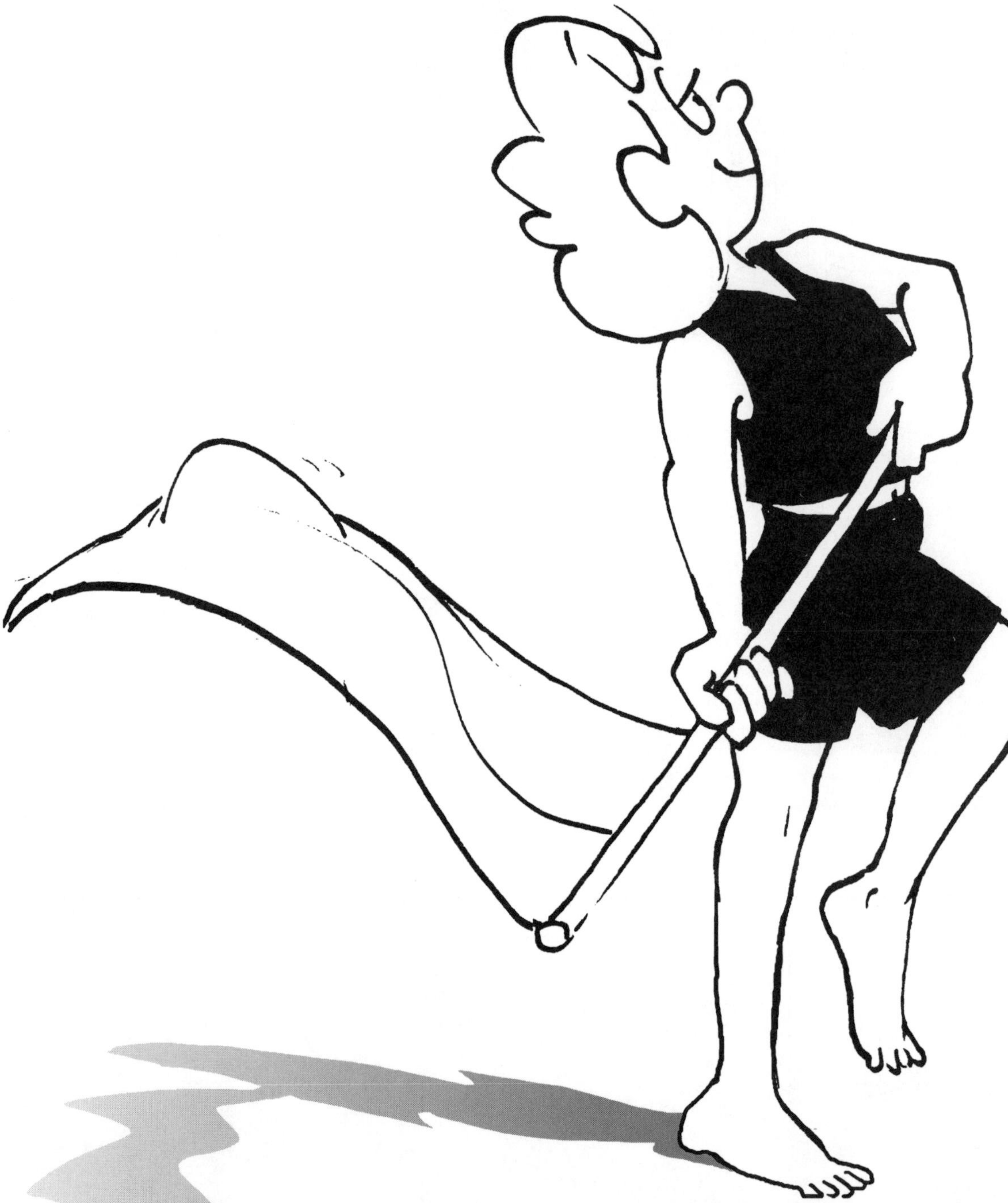

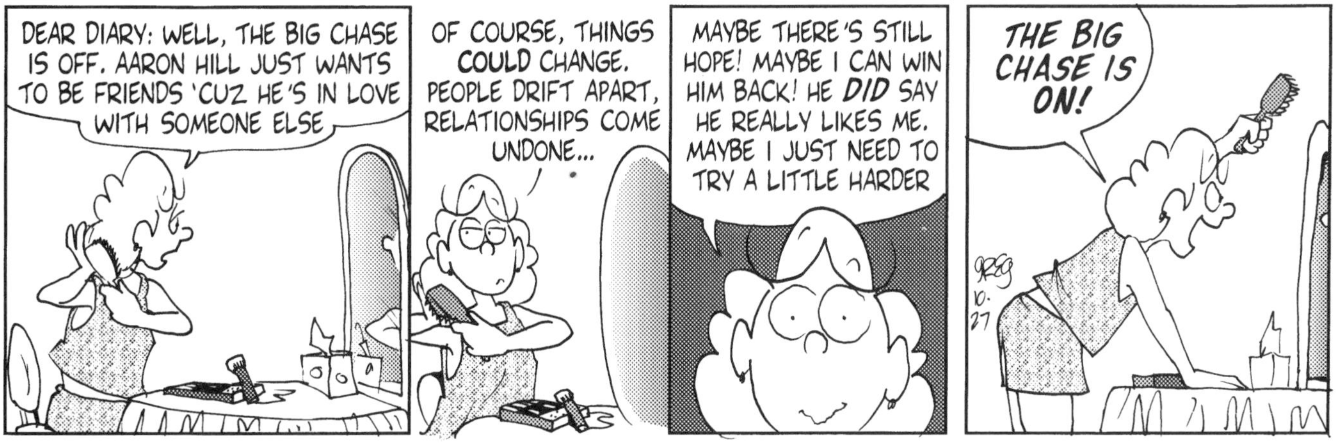
DEAR DIARY: WELL, THE BIG CHASE IS OFF. AARON HILL JUST WANTS TO BE FRIENDS 'CUZ HE'S IN LOVE WITH SOMEONE ELSE
OF COURSE, THINGS **COULD** CHANGE. PEOPLE DRIFT APART, RELATIONSHIPS COME UNDONE...
MAYBE THERE'S STILL HOPE! MAYBE I CAN WIN HIM BACK! HE ***DID*** SAY HE REALLY LIKES ME. MAYBE I JUST NEED TO TRY A LITTLE HARDER
THE BIG CHASE IS ON!
GREG 10·27

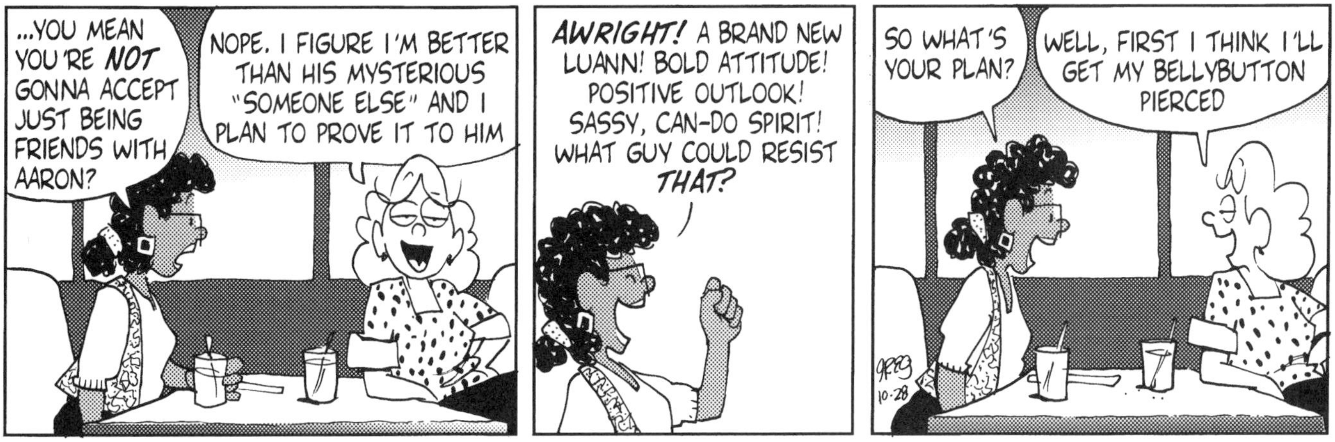
...YOU MEAN YOU'RE ***NOT*** GONNA ACCEPT JUST BEING FRIENDS WITH AARON?
NOPE. I FIGURE I'M BETTER THAN HIS MYSTERIOUS "SOMEONE ELSE" AND I PLAN TO PROVE IT TO HIM
AWRIGHT! A BRAND NEW LUANN! BOLD ATTITUDE! POSITIVE OUTLOOK! SASSY, CAN-DO SPIRIT! WHAT GUY COULD RESIST ***THAT?***
SO WHAT'S YOUR PLAN?
WELL, FIRST I THINK I'LL GET MY BELLYBUTTON PIERCED
GREG 10·28

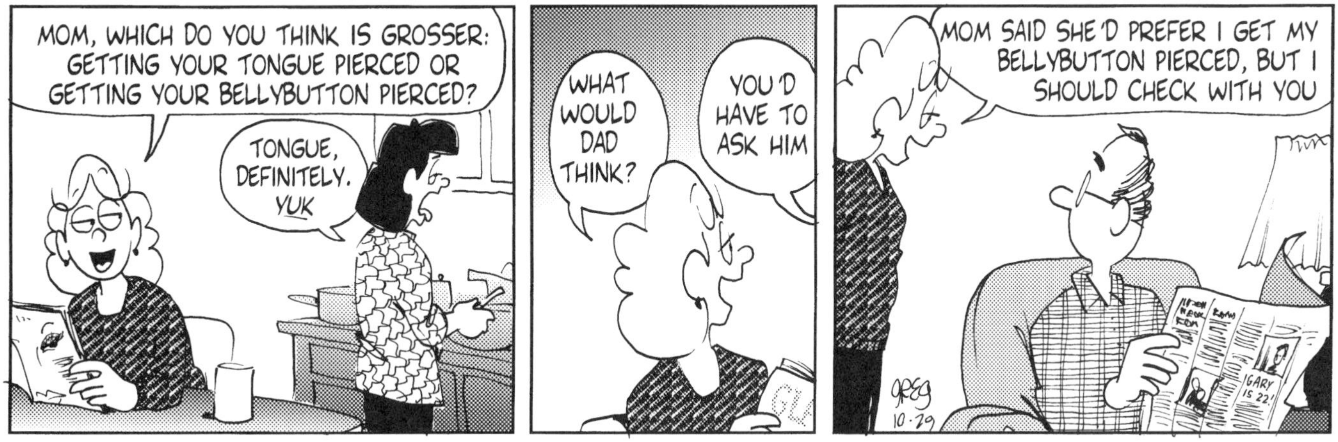
MOM, WHICH DO YOU THINK IS GROSSER: GETTING YOUR TONGUE PIERCED OR GETTING YOUR BELLYBUTTON PIERCED?
TONGUE, DEFINITELY. YUK
WHAT WOULD DAD THINK?
YOU'D HAVE TO ASK HIM
MOM SAID SHE'D PREFER I GET MY BELLYBUTTON PIERCED, BUT I SHOULD CHECK WITH YOU
GARY IS 22!
GREG 10·29

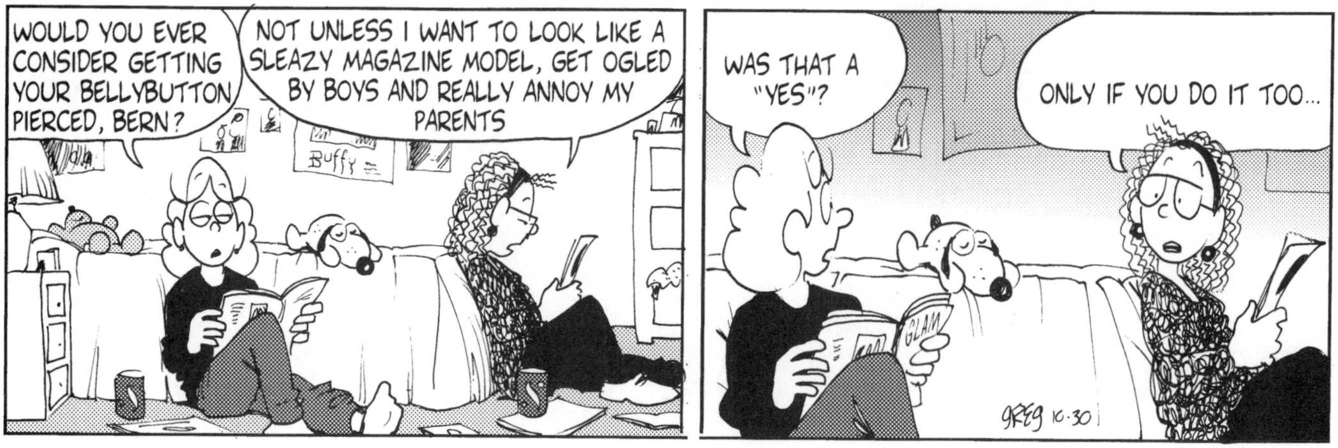
WOULD YOU EVER CONSIDER GETTING YOUR BELLYBUTTON PIERCED, BERN?
NOT UNLESS I WANT TO LOOK LIKE A SLEAZY MAGAZINE MODEL, GET OGLED BY BOYS AND REALLY ANNOY MY PARENTS
BUFFY
WAS THAT A "YES"?
ONLY IF YOU DO IT TOO...
GLAM
GREG 10·30

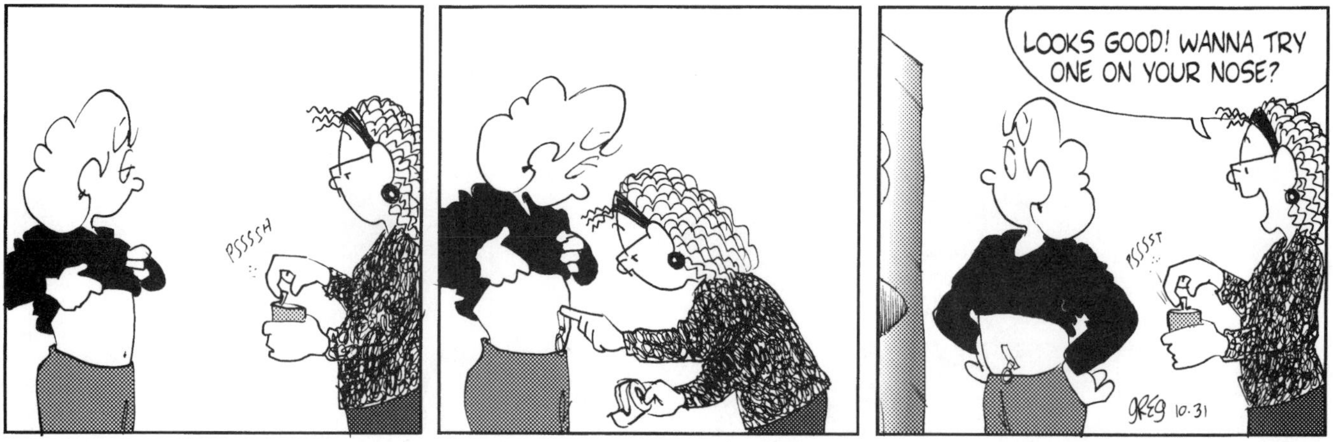
PSSSSH
LOOKS GOOD! WANNA TRY ONE ON YOUR NOSE?
PSSSST
GREG 10·31

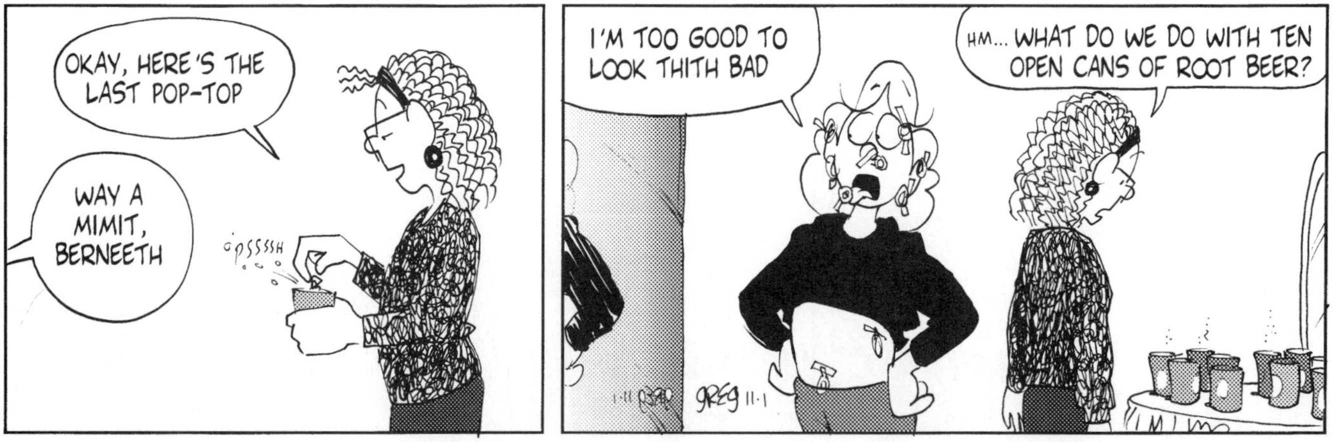
OKAY, HERE'S THE LAST POP-TOP
WAY A MIMIT, BERNEETH
PSSSSH
I'M TOO GOOD TO LOOK THITH BAD
HM... WHAT DO WE DO WITH TEN OPEN CANS OF ROOT BEER?
GREG 11·1

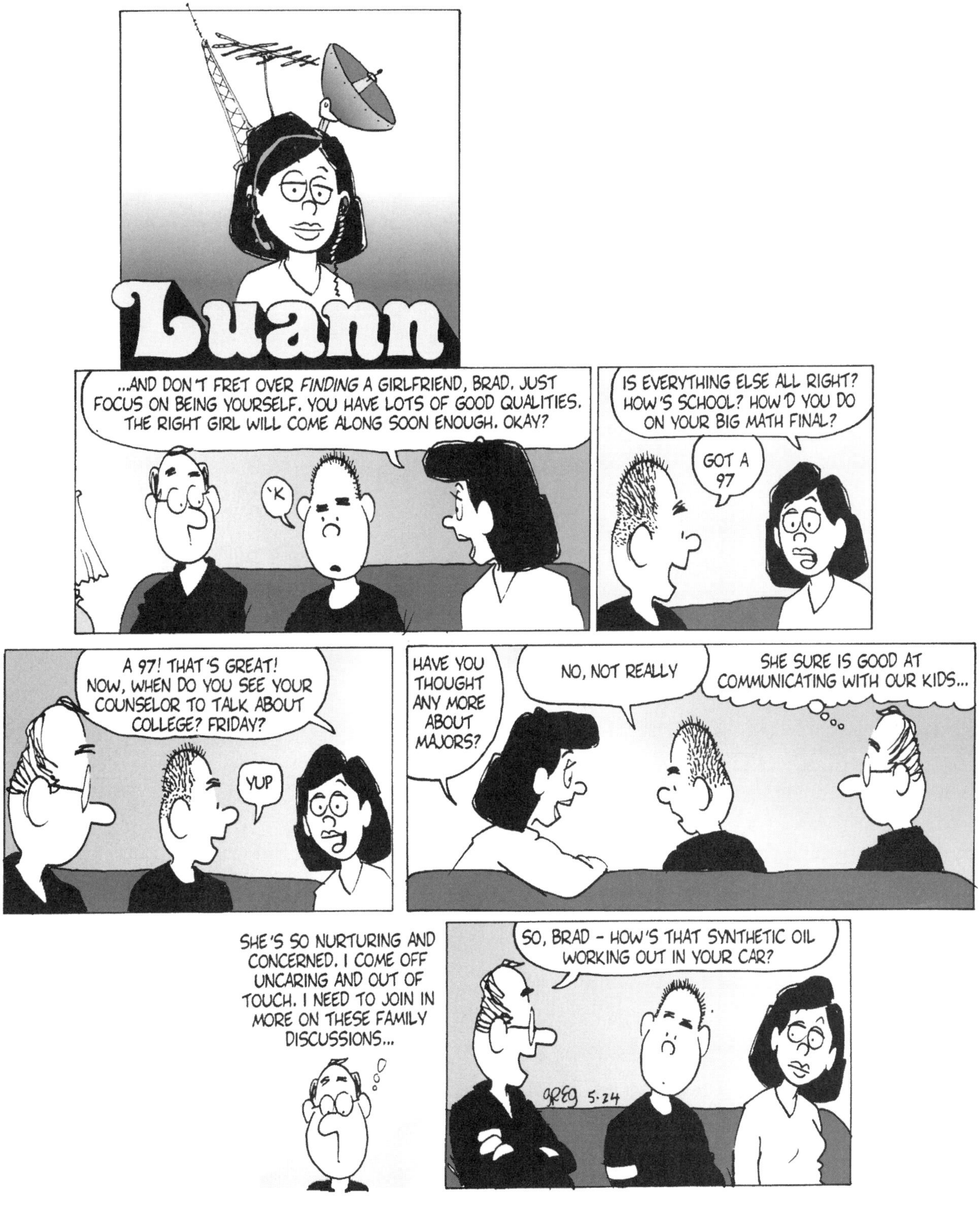
Luann
...AND DON'T FRET OVER *FINDING* A GIRLFRIEND, BRAD. JUST FOCUS ON BEING YOURSELF. YOU HAVE LOTS OF GOOD QUALITIES. THE RIGHT GIRL WILL COME ALONG SOON ENOUGH. OKAY?
'K
IS EVERYTHING ELSE ALL RIGHT? HOW'S SCHOOL? HOW'D YOU DO ON YOUR BIG MATH FINAL?
GOT A 97
A 97! THAT'S GREAT! NOW, WHEN DO YOU SEE YOUR COUNSELOR TO TALK ABOUT COLLEGE? FRIDAY?
YUP
HAVE YOU THOUGHT ANY MORE ABOUT MAJORS?
NO, NOT REALLY
SHE SURE IS GOOD AT COMMUNICATING WITH OUR KIDS...
SHE'S SO NURTURING AND CONCERNED. I COME OFF UNCARING AND OUT OF TOUCH. I NEED TO JOIN IN MORE ON THESE FAMILY DISCUSSIONS...
SO, BRAD - HOW'S THAT SYNTHETIC OIL WORKING OUT IN YOUR CAR?
GREG 5·24

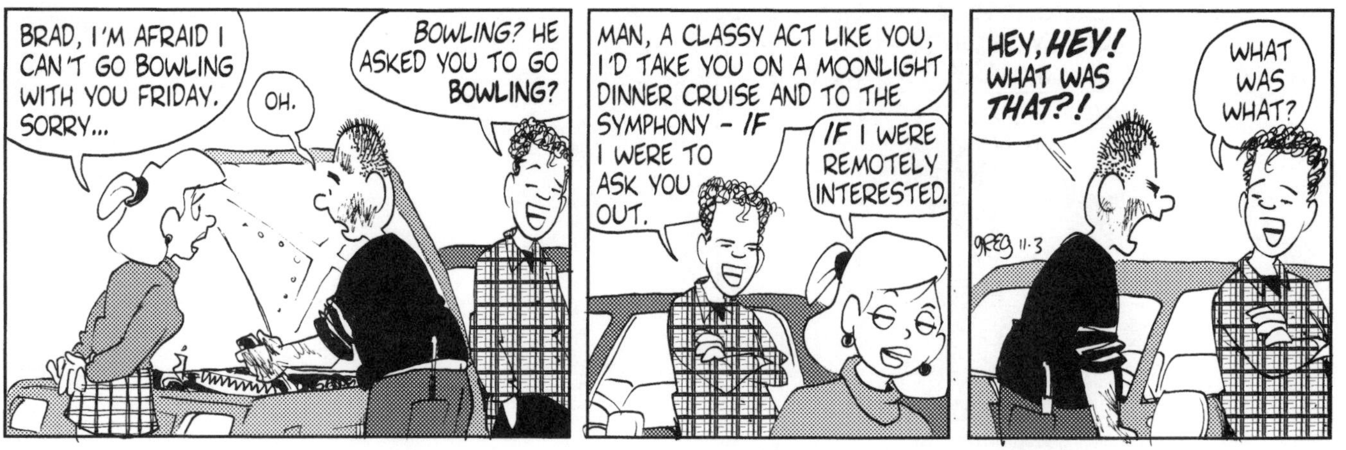
BRAD, I'M AFRAID I CAN'T GO BOWLING WITH YOU FRIDAY. SORRY...
OH.
BOWLING? HE ASKED YOU TO GO BOWLING?
MAN, A CLASSY ACT LIKE YOU, I'D TAKE YOU ON A MOONLIGHT DINNER CRUISE AND TO THE SYMPHONY - IF I WERE TO ASK YOU OUT.
IF I WERE REMOTELY INTERESTED.
HEY, HEY! WHAT WAS THAT?!
WHAT WAS WHAT?
GREG 11·3

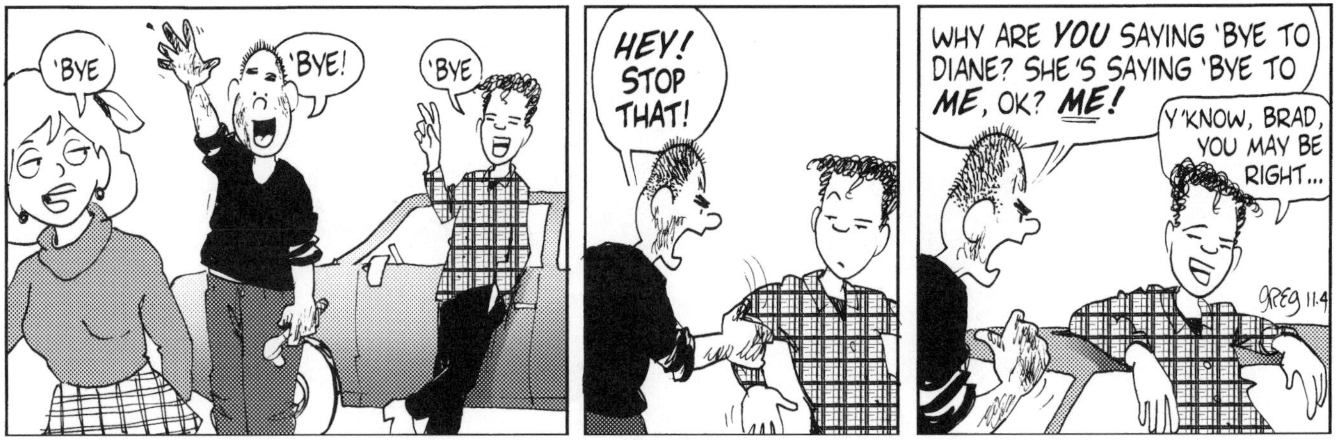
'BYE
'BYE!
'BYE
HEY! STOP THAT!
WHY ARE YOU SAYING 'BYE TO DIANE? SHE'S SAYING 'BYE TO ME, OK? ME!
Y'KNOW, BRAD, YOU MAY BE RIGHT...
GREG 11.4

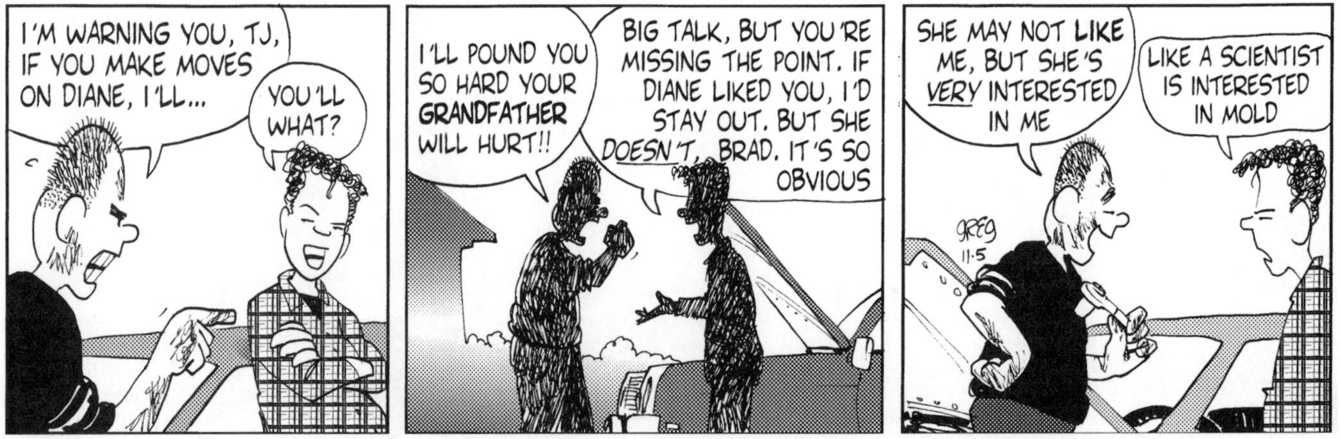
I'M WARNING YOU, TJ, IF YOU MAKE MOVES ON DIANE, I'LL...
YOU'LL WHAT?
I'LL POUND YOU SO HARD YOUR GRANDFATHER WILL HURT!!
BIG TALK, BUT YOU'RE MISSING THE POINT. IF DIANE LIKED YOU, I'D STAY OUT. BUT SHE DOESN'T, BRAD. IT'S SO OBVIOUS
SHE MAY NOT LIKE ME, BUT SHE'S VERY INTERESTED IN ME
LIKE A SCIENTIST IS INTERESTED IN MOLD
GREG 11·5

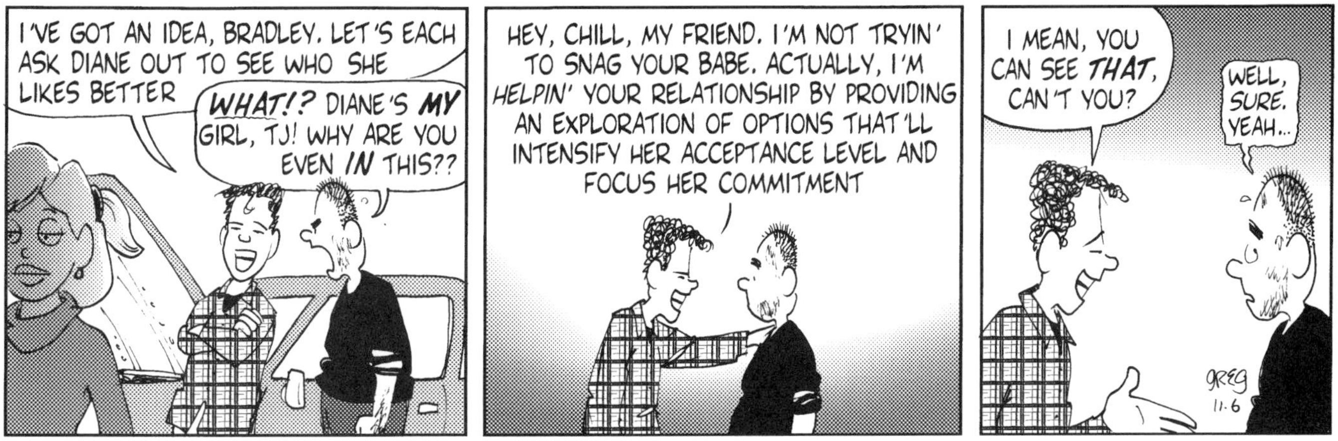
I'VE GOT AN IDEA, BRADLEY. LET'S EACH ASK DIANE OUT TO SEE WHO SHE LIKES BETTER
WHAT!? DIANE'S MY GIRL, TJ! WHY ARE YOU EVEN IN THIS??
HEY, CHILL, MY FRIEND. I'M NOT TRYIN' TO SNAG YOUR BABE. ACTUALLY, I'M HELPIN' YOUR RELATIONSHIP BY PROVIDING AN EXPLORATION OF OPTIONS THAT'LL INTENSIFY HER ACCEPTANCE LEVEL AND FOCUS HER COMMITMENT
I MEAN, YOU CAN SEE THAT, CAN'T YOU?
WELL, SURE. YEAH...
GREG 11·6

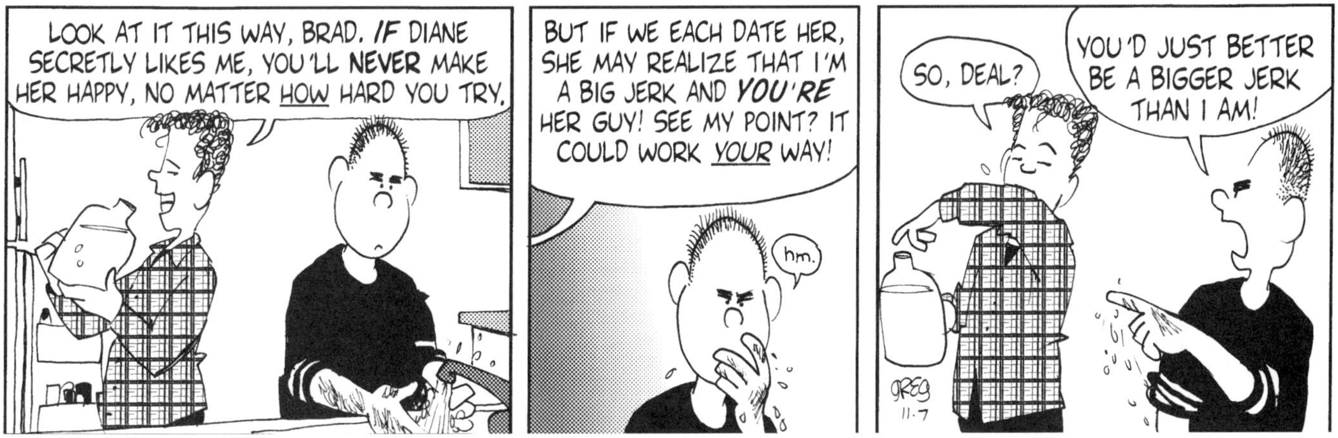
LOOK AT IT THIS WAY, BRAD. IF DIANE SECRETLY LIKES ME, YOU'LL NEVER MAKE HER HAPPY, NO MATTER HOW HARD YOU TRY.
BUT IF WE EACH DATE HER, SHE MAY REALIZE THAT I'M A BIG JERK AND YOU'RE HER GUY! SEE MY POINT? IT COULD WORK YOUR WAY!
hm.
GREG 11·7
SO, DEAL?
YOU'D JUST BETTER BE A BIGGER JERK THAN I AM!

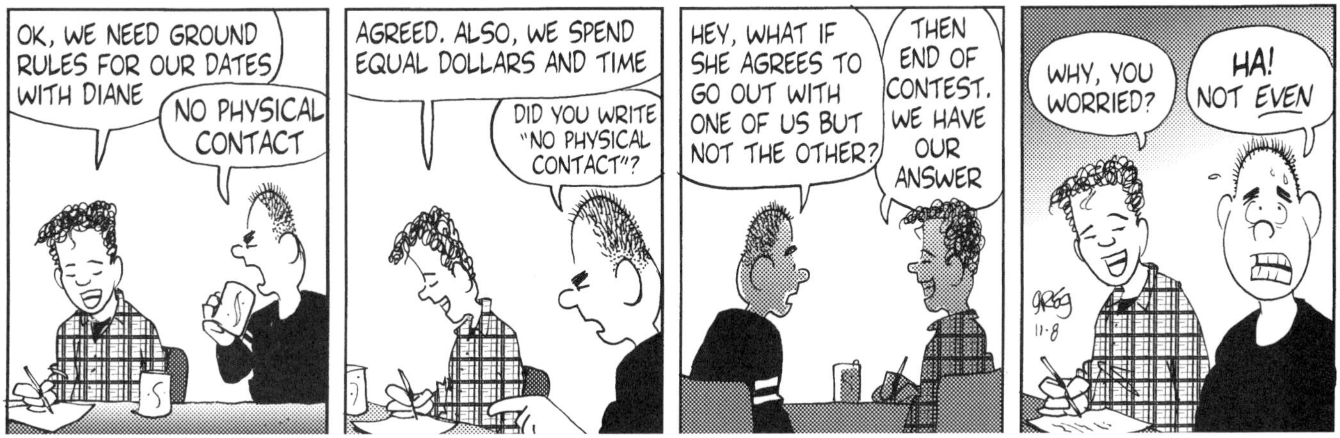
OK, WE NEED GROUND RULES FOR OUR DATES WITH DIANE
NO PHYSICAL CONTACT
AGREED. ALSO, WE SPEND EQUAL DOLLARS AND TIME
DID YOU WRITE "NO PHYSICAL CONTACT"?
HEY, WHAT IF SHE AGREES TO GO OUT WITH ONE OF US BUT NOT THE OTHER?
THEN END OF CONTEST. WE HAVE OUR ANSWER
WHY, YOU WORRIED?
HA! NOT EVEN
GREG 11·8

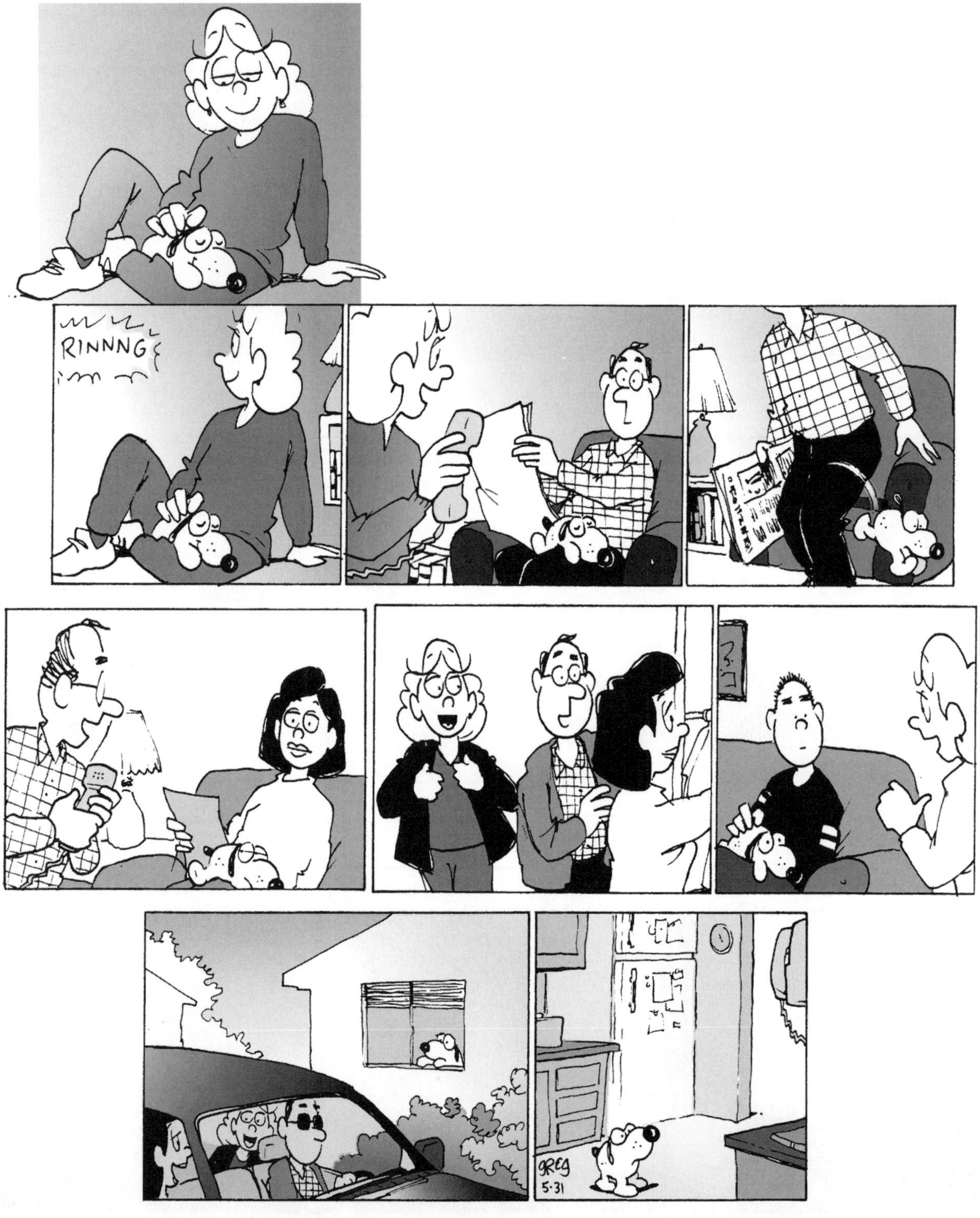
RINNNG
GREG
5·31

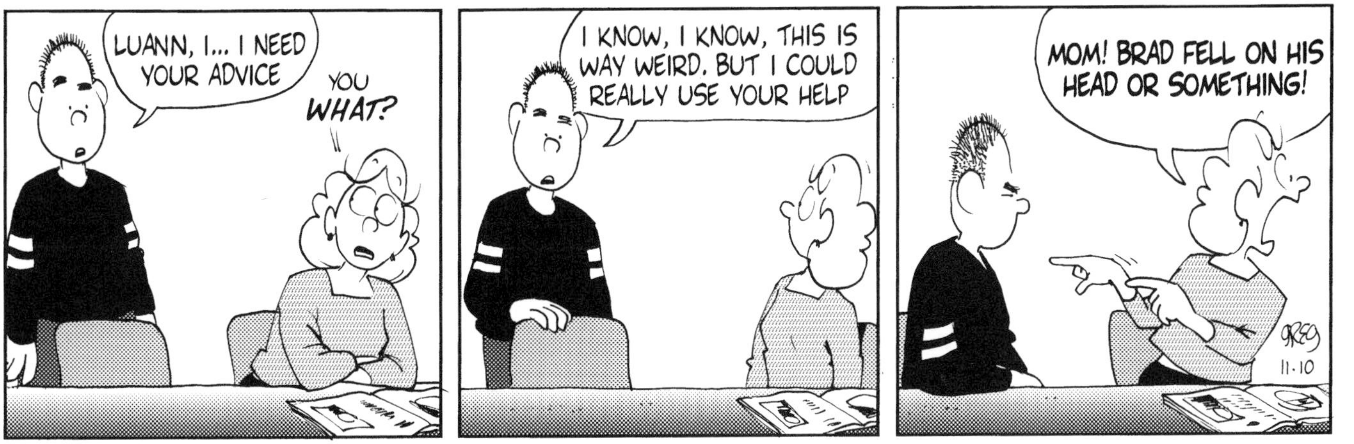
LUANN, I... I NEED YOUR ADVICE
YOU *WHAT?*
I KNOW, I KNOW, THIS IS WAY WEIRD. BUT I COULD REALLY USE YOUR HELP
MOM! BRAD FELL ON HIS HEAD OR SOMETHING!
GREG
11·10

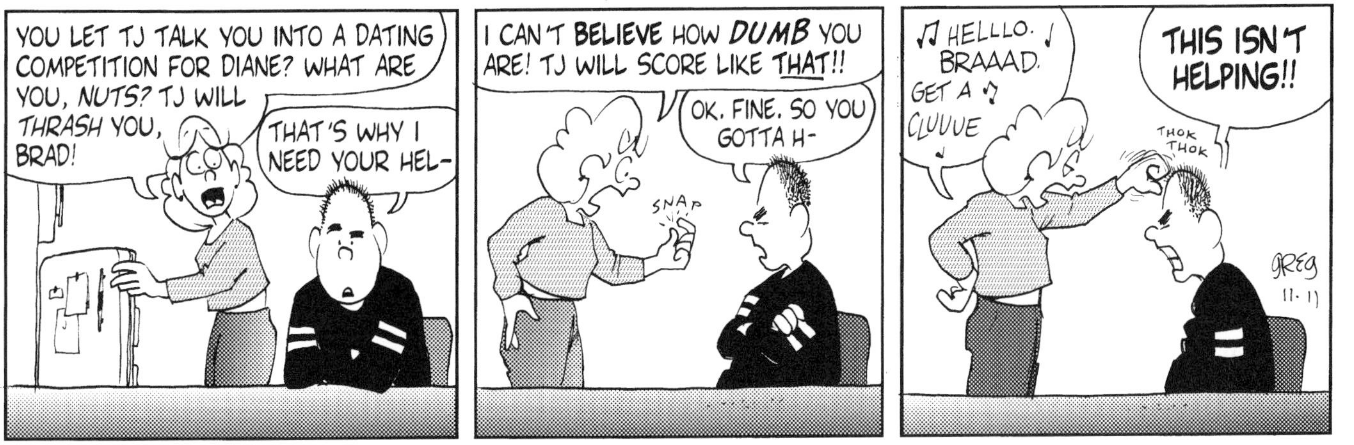
YOU LET TJ TALK YOU INTO A DATING COMPETITION FOR DIANE? WHAT ARE YOU, *NUTS?* TJ WILL *THRASH* YOU, BRAD!
THAT'S WHY I NEED YOUR HEL-
I CAN'T **BELIEVE** HOW ***DUMB*** YOU ARE! TJ WILL SCORE LIKE THAT!!
SNAP
OK. FINE. SO YOU GOTTA H-
♫ HELLLO. ♩ BRAAAD. GET A ♫ CLUUUE ♩
THOK THOK
THIS ISN'T HELPING!!
GREG
11·11

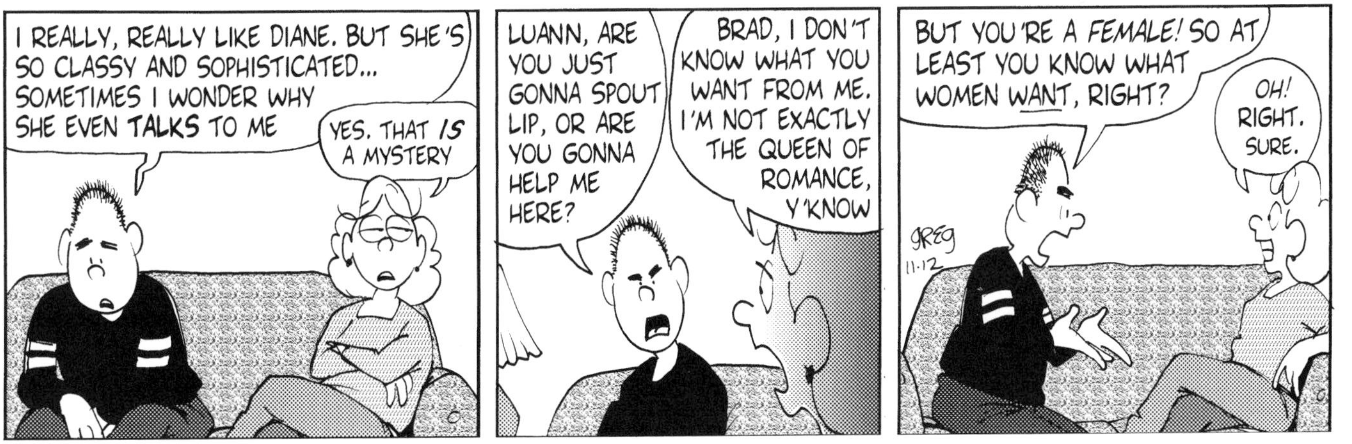
I REALLY, REALLY LIKE DIANE. BUT SHE'S SO CLASSY AND SOPHISTICATED... SOMETIMES I WONDER WHY SHE EVEN **TALKS** TO ME
YES. THAT *IS* A MYSTERY
LUANN, ARE YOU JUST GONNA SPOUT LIP, OR ARE YOU GONNA HELP ME HERE?
BRAD, I DON'T KNOW WHAT YOU WANT FROM ME. I'M NOT EXACTLY THE QUEEN OF ROMANCE, Y'KNOW
BUT YOU'RE A *FEMALE!* SO AT LEAST YOU KNOW WHAT WOMEN WANT, RIGHT?
OH! RIGHT. SURE.
GREG
11·12

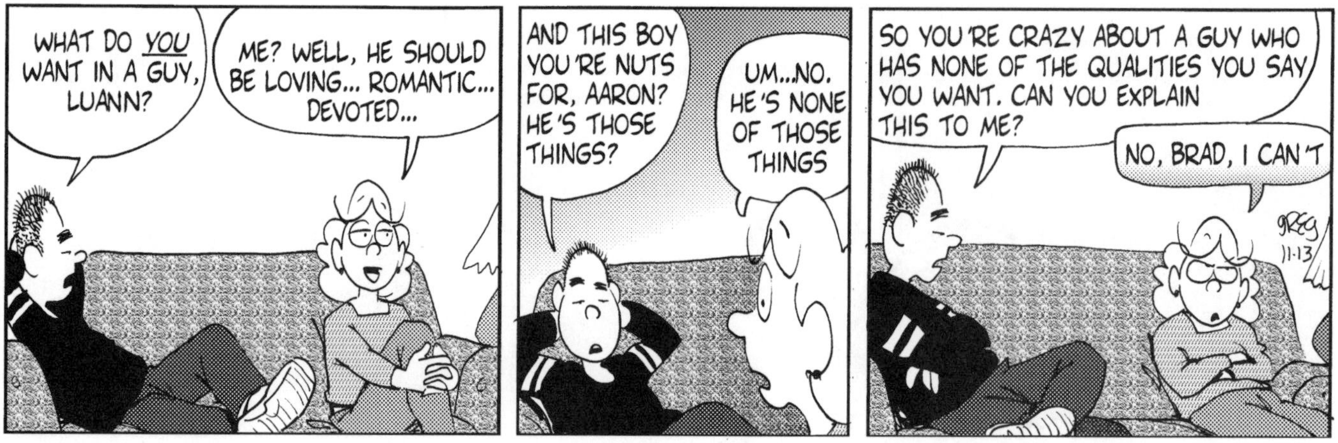
WHAT DO YOU WANT IN A GUY, LUANN?
ME? WELL, HE SHOULD BE LOVING... ROMANTIC... DEVOTED...
AND THIS BOY YOU'RE NUTS FOR, AARON? HE'S THOSE THINGS?
UM...NO. HE'S NONE OF THOSE THINGS
SO YOU'RE CRAZY ABOUT A GUY WHO HAS NONE OF THE QUALITIES YOU SAY YOU WANT. CAN YOU EXPLAIN THIS TO ME?
NO, BRAD, I CAN'T
GREG 11·13

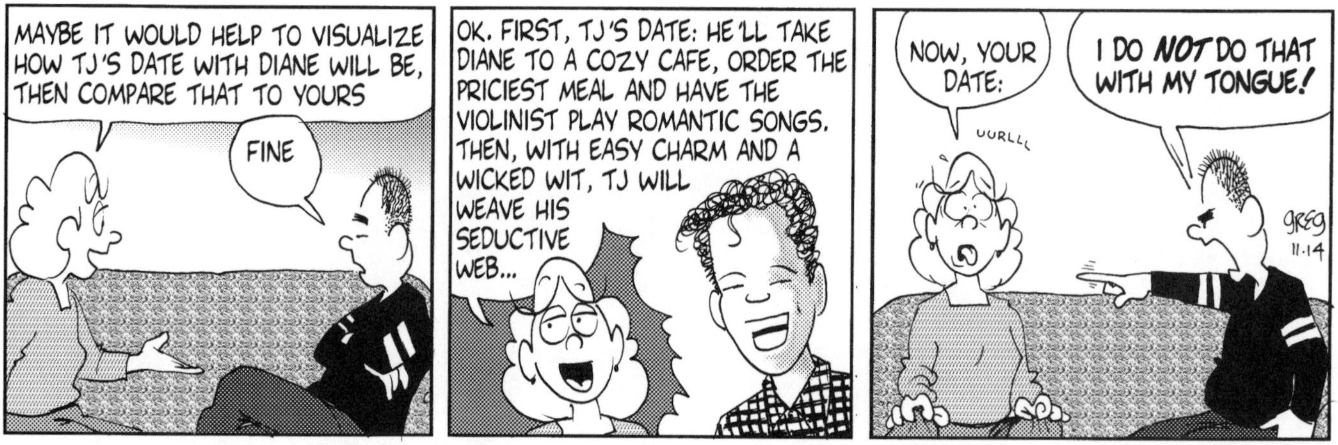
MAYBE IT WOULD HELP TO VISUALIZE HOW TJ'S DATE WITH DIANE WILL BE, THEN COMPARE THAT TO YOURS
FINE
OK. FIRST, TJ'S DATE: HE'LL TAKE DIANE TO A COZY CAFE, ORDER THE PRICIEST MEAL AND HAVE THE VIOLINIST PLAY ROMANTIC SONGS. THEN, WITH EASY CHARM AND A WICKED WIT, TJ WILL WEAVE HIS SEDUCTIVE WEB...
NOW, YOUR DATE:
UURLLL
I DO ***NOT*** DO THAT WITH MY TONGUE!
GREG 11·14

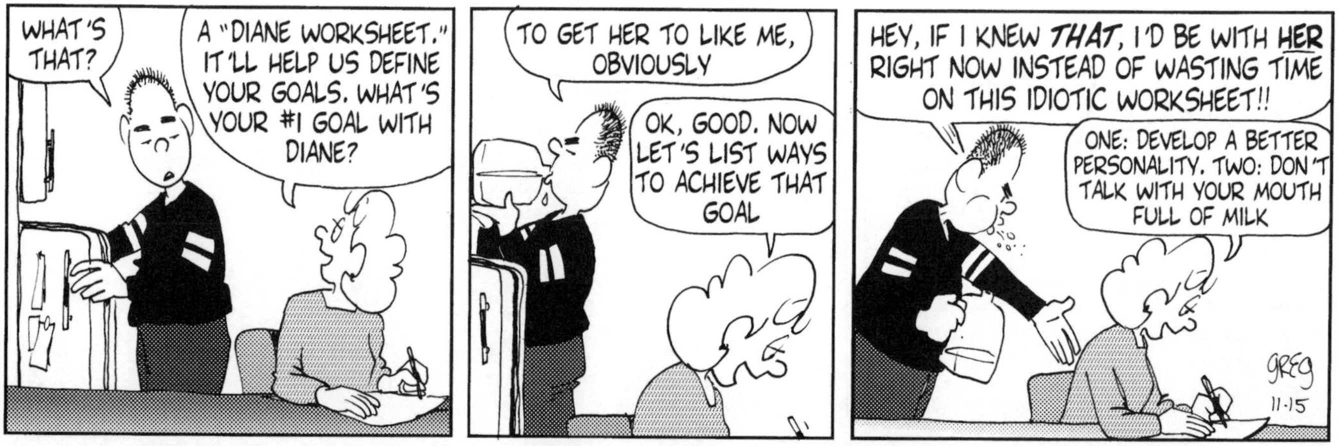
WHAT'S THAT?
A "DIANE WORKSHEET." IT'LL HELP US DEFINE YOUR GOALS. WHAT'S YOUR #1 GOAL WITH DIANE?
TO GET HER TO LIKE ME, OBVIOUSLY
OK, GOOD. NOW LET'S LIST WAYS TO ACHIEVE THAT GOAL
HEY, IF I KNEW *THAT*, I'D BE WITH HER RIGHT NOW INSTEAD OF WASTING TIME ON THIS IDIOTIC WORKSHEET!!
ONE: DEVELOP A BETTER PERSONALITY. TWO: DON'T TALK WITH YOUR MOUTH FULL OF MILK
GREG 11·15

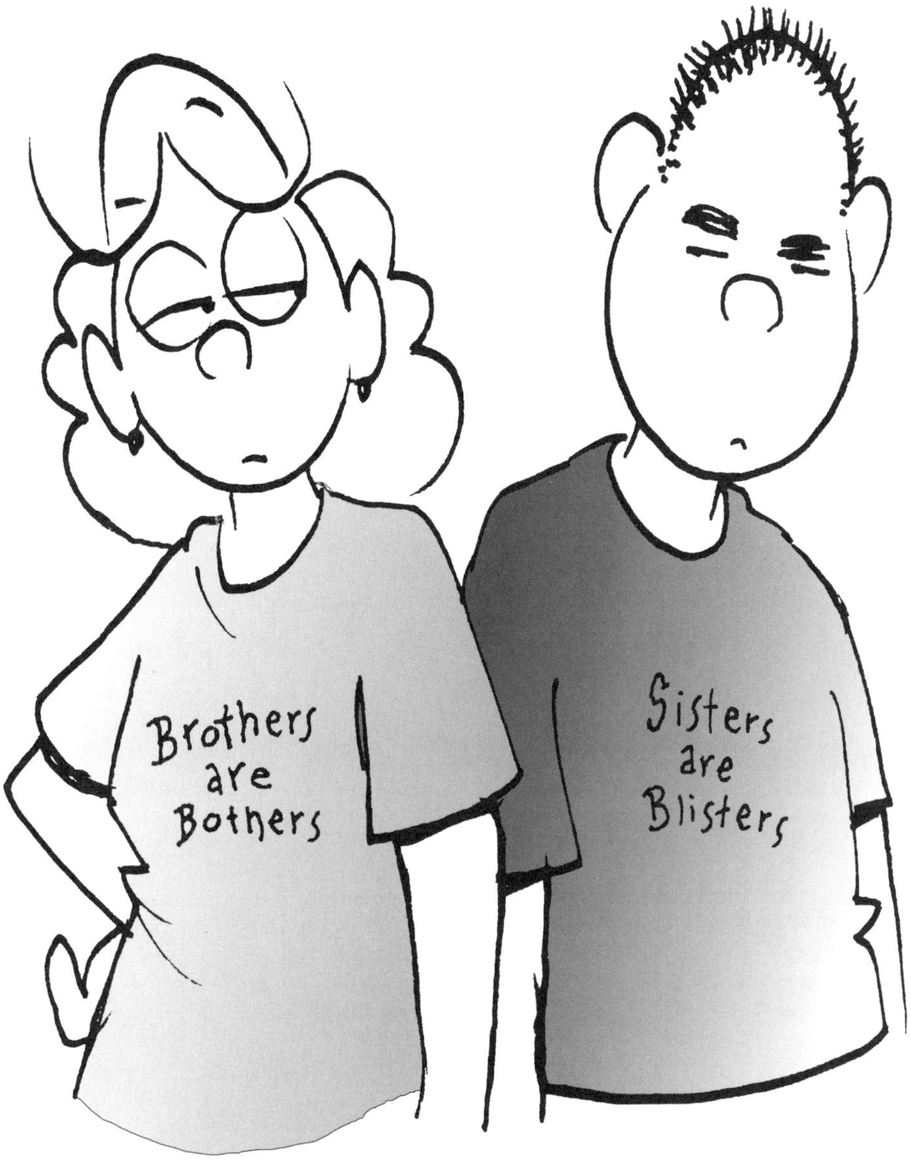
Brothers are Bothers
Sisters are Blisters

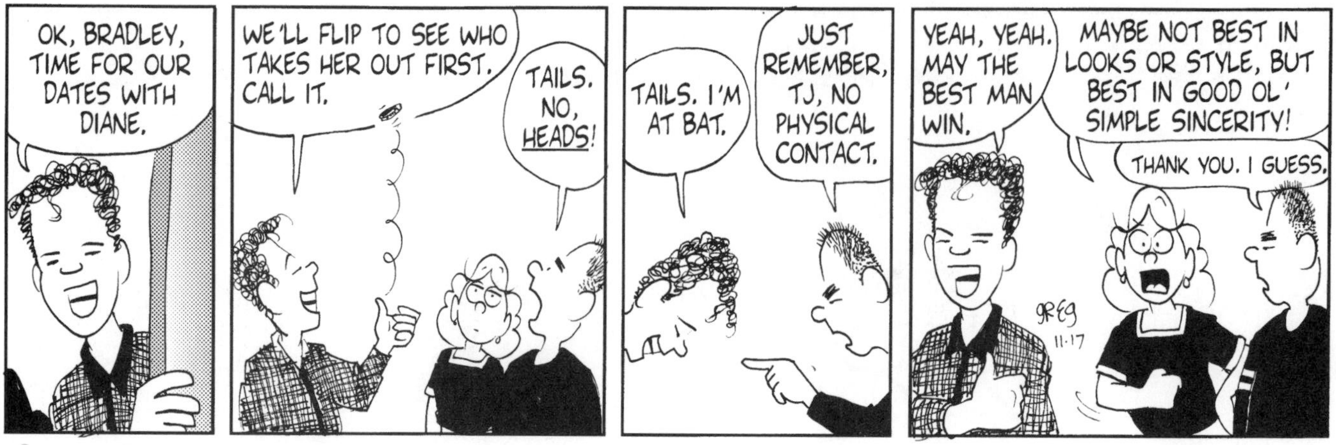
OK, BRADLEY, TIME FOR OUR DATES WITH DIANE.
WE'LL FLIP TO SEE WHO TAKES HER OUT FIRST. CALL IT.
TAILS. NO, HEADS!
TAILS. I'M AT BAT.
JUST REMEMBER, TJ, NO PHYSICAL CONTACT.
YEAH, YEAH. MAY THE BEST MAN WIN.
MAYBE NOT BEST IN LOOKS OR STYLE, BUT BEST IN GOOD OL' SIMPLE SINCERITY!
THANK YOU. I GUESS.

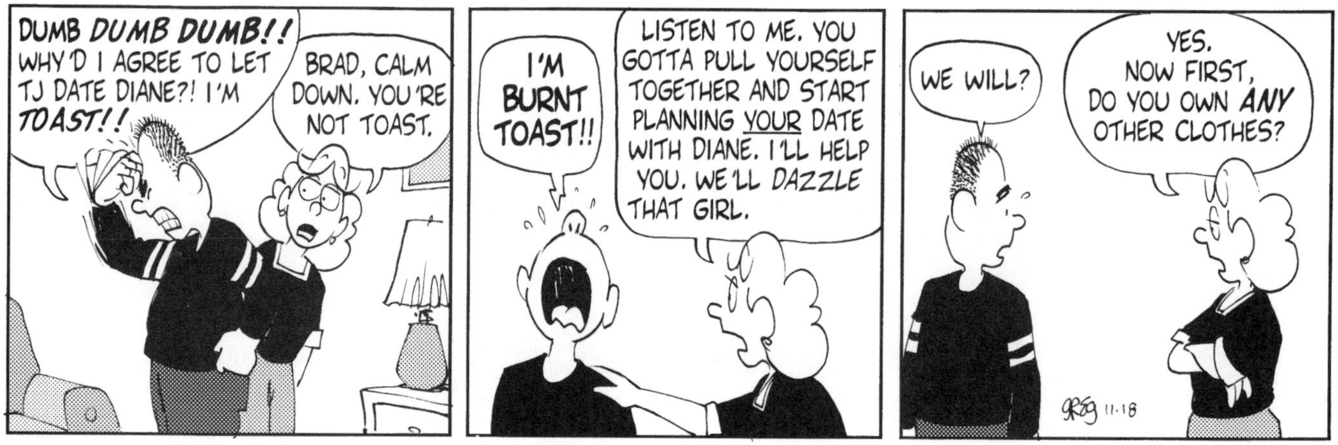
DUMB DUMB DUMB!! WHY'D I AGREE TO LET TJ DATE DIANE?! I'M TOAST!!
BRAD, CALM DOWN. YOU'RE NOT TOAST.
I'M BURNT TOAST!!
LISTEN TO ME. YOU GOTTA PULL YOURSELF TOGETHER AND START PLANNING YOUR DATE WITH DIANE. I'LL HELP YOU. WE'LL DAZZLE THAT GIRL.
WE WILL?
YES. NOW FIRST, DO YOU OWN ANY OTHER CLOTHES?

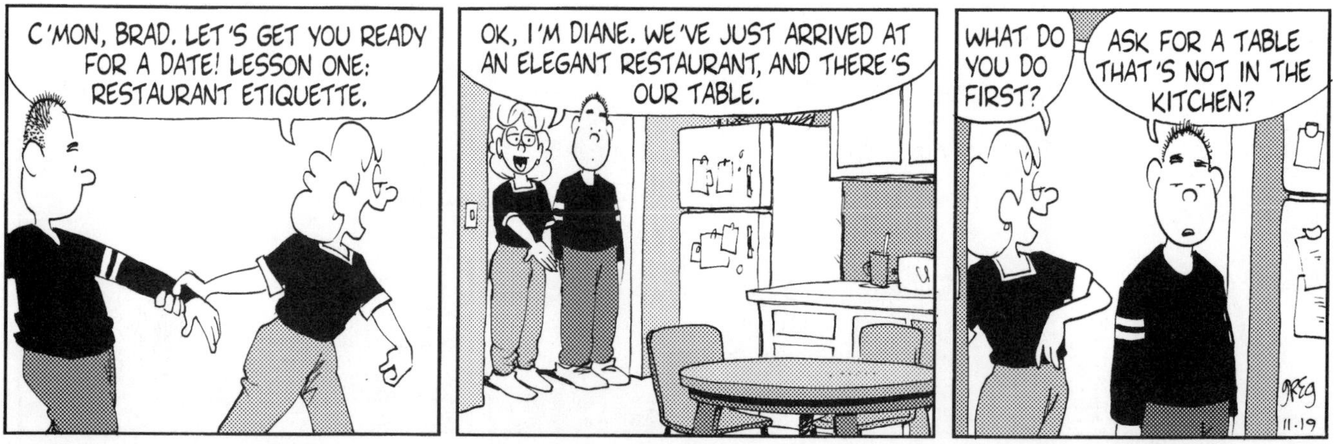
C'MON, BRAD. LET'S GET YOU READY FOR A DATE! LESSON ONE: RESTAURANT ETIQUETTE.
OK, I'M DIANE. WE'VE JUST ARRIVED AT AN ELEGANT RESTAURANT, AND THERE'S OUR TABLE.
WHAT DO YOU DO FIRST?
ASK FOR A TABLE THAT'S NOT IN THE KITCHEN?

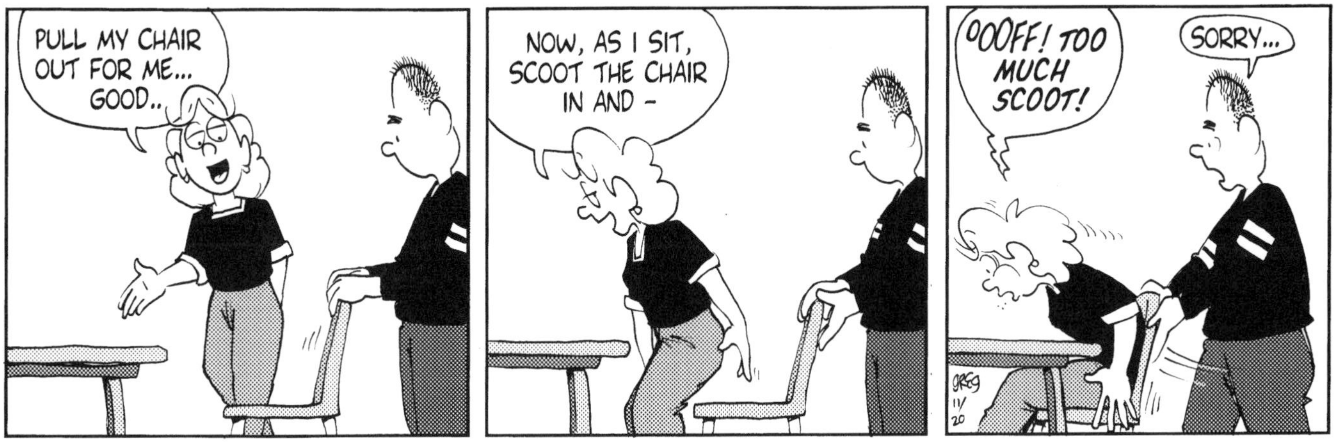
PULL MY CHAIR OUT FOR ME... GOOD..
NOW, AS I SIT, SCOOT THE CHAIR IN AND -
OOOFF! TOO MUCH SCOOT!
SORRY...
GREG 11/20

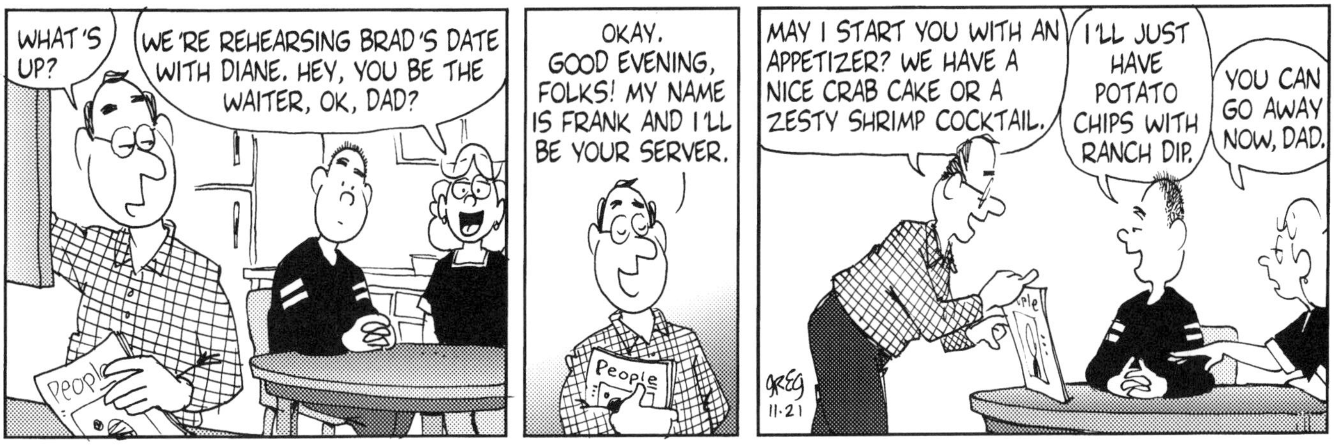
WHAT'S UP?
WE'RE REHEARSING BRAD'S DATE WITH DIANE. HEY, YOU BE THE WAITER, OK, DAD?
People
OKAY. GOOD EVENING, FOLKS! MY NAME IS FRANK AND I'LL BE YOUR SERVER.
People
MAY I START YOU WITH AN APPETIZER? WE HAVE A NICE CRAB CAKE OR A ZESTY SHRIMP COCKTAIL.
I'LL JUST HAVE POTATO CHIPS WITH RANCH DIP.
YOU CAN GO AWAY NOW, DAD.
GREG 11·21

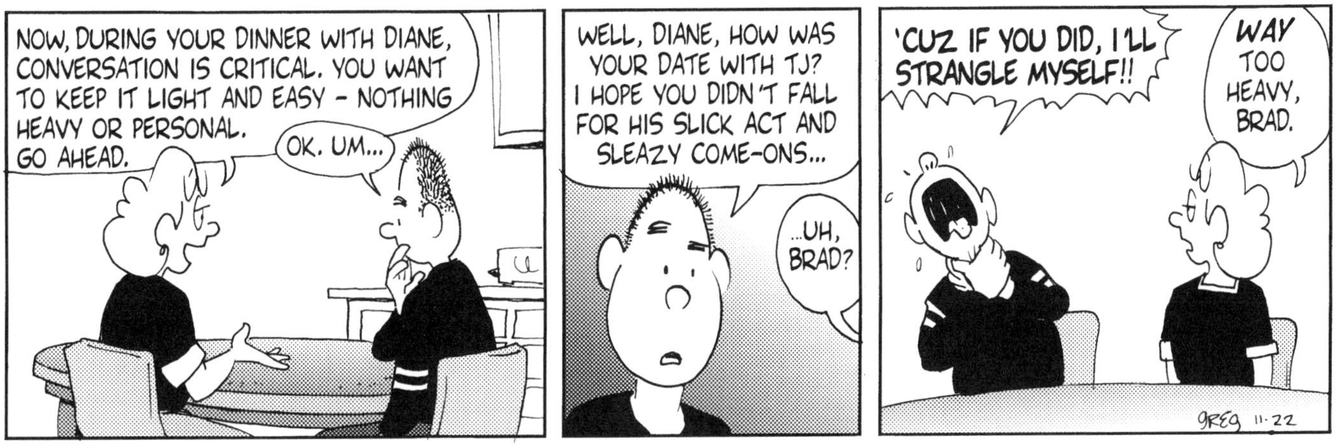
NOW, DURING YOUR DINNER WITH DIANE, CONVERSATION IS CRITICAL. YOU WANT TO KEEP IT LIGHT AND EASY - NOTHING HEAVY OR PERSONAL. GO AHEAD.
OK. UM...
WELL, DIANE, HOW WAS YOUR DATE WITH TJ? I HOPE YOU DIDN'T FALL FOR HIS SLICK ACT AND SLEAZY COME-ONS...
...UH, BRAD?
'CUZ IF YOU DID, I'LL STRANGLE MYSELF!!
WAY TOO HEAVY, BRAD.
GREG 11·22

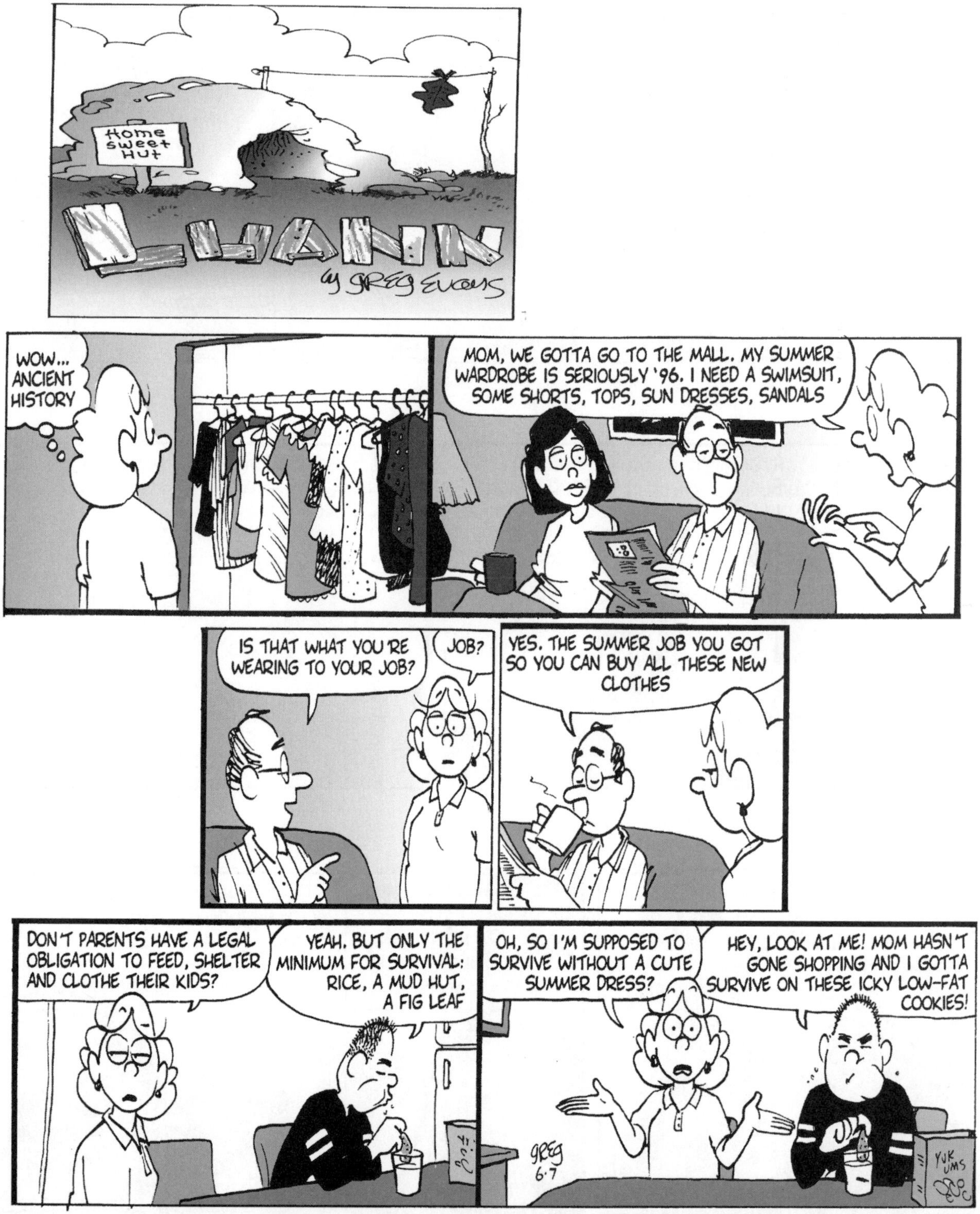
Home sweet Hut
LUANN
by GREG EVANS
WOW... ANCIENT HISTORY
MOM, WE GOTTA GO TO THE MALL. MY SUMMER WARDROBE IS SERIOUSLY '96. I NEED A SWIMSUIT, SOME SHORTS, TOPS, SUN DRESSES, SANDALS
IS THAT WHAT YOU'RE WEARING TO YOUR JOB?
JOB?
YES. THE SUMMER JOB YOU GOT SO YOU CAN BUY ALL THESE NEW CLOTHES
DON'T PARENTS HAVE A LEGAL OBLIGATION TO FEED, SHELTER AND CLOTHE THEIR KIDS?
YEAH. BUT ONLY THE MINIMUM FOR SURVIVAL: RICE, A MUD HUT, A FIG LEAF
OH, SO I'M SUPPOSED TO SURVIVE WITHOUT A CUTE SUMMER DRESS?
HEY, LOOK AT ME! MOM HASN'T GONE SHOPPING AND I GOTTA SURVIVE ON THESE ICKY LOW-FAT COOKIES!
GREG 6.7
YUK UMS

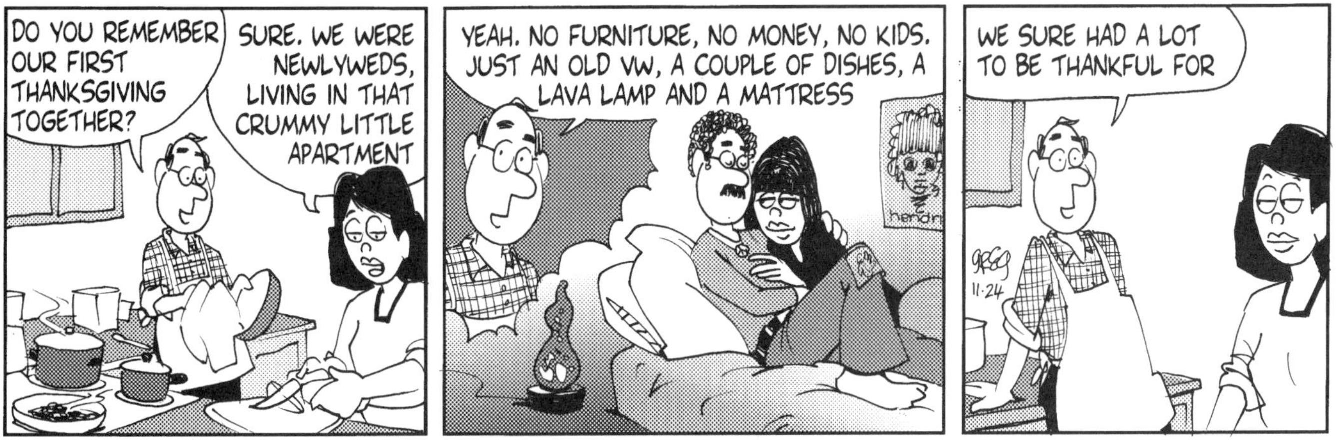
DO YOU REMEMBER OUR FIRST THANKSGIVING TOGETHER?
SURE. WE WERE NEWLYWEDS, LIVING IN THAT CRUMMY LITTLE APARTMENT
YEAH. NO FURNITURE, NO MONEY, NO KIDS. JUST AN OLD VW, A COUPLE OF DISHES, A LAVA LAMP AND A MATTRESS
WE SURE HAD A LOT TO BE THANKFUL FOR
GREG 11·24

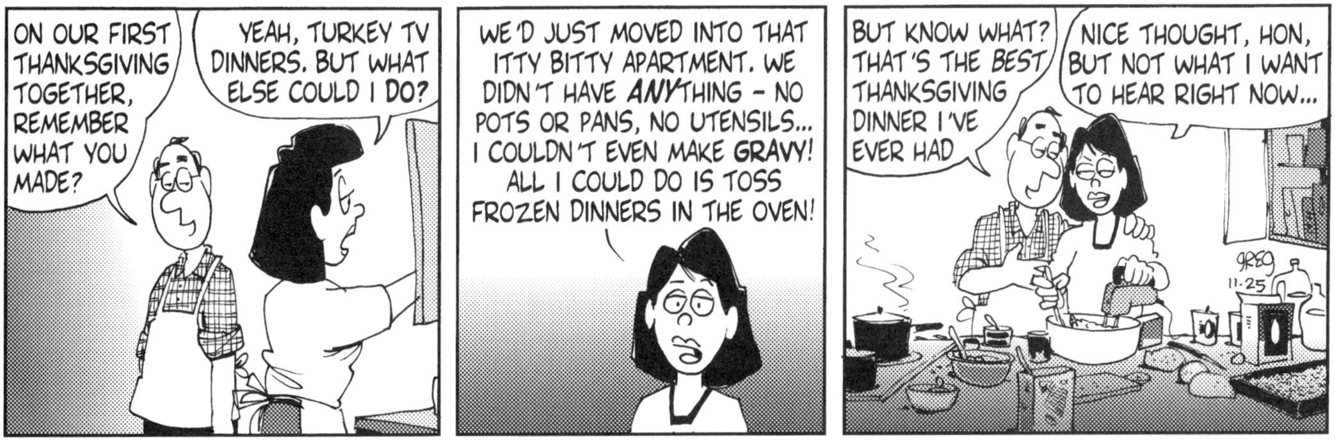
ON OUR FIRST THANKSGIVING TOGETHER, REMEMBER WHAT YOU MADE?
YEAH, TURKEY TV DINNERS. BUT WHAT ELSE COULD I DO?
WE'D JUST MOVED INTO THAT ITTY BITTY APARTMENT. WE DIDN'T HAVE *ANY*THING – NO POTS OR PANS, NO UTENSILS... I COULDN'T EVEN MAKE **GRAVY**! ALL I COULD DO IS TOSS FROZEN DINNERS IN THE OVEN!
BUT KNOW WHAT? THAT'S THE *BEST* THANKSGIVING DINNER I'VE EVER HAD
NICE THOUGHT, HON, BUT NOT WHAT I WANT TO HEAR RIGHT NOW...
GREG 11·25

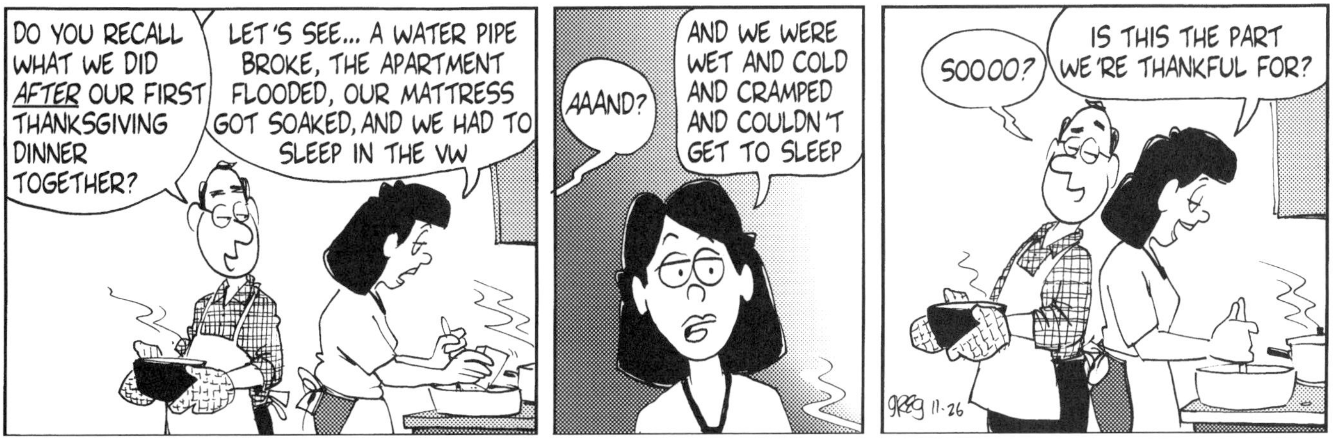
DO YOU RECALL WHAT WE DID *AFTER* OUR FIRST THANKSGIVING DINNER TOGETHER?
LET'S SEE... A WATER PIPE BROKE, THE APARTMENT FLOODED, OUR MATTRESS GOT SOAKED, AND WE HAD TO SLEEP IN THE VW
AAAND?
AND WE WERE WET AND COLD AND CRAMPED AND COULDN'T GET TO SLEEP
SOOOO?
IS THIS THE PART WE'RE THANKFUL FOR?
GREG 11·26

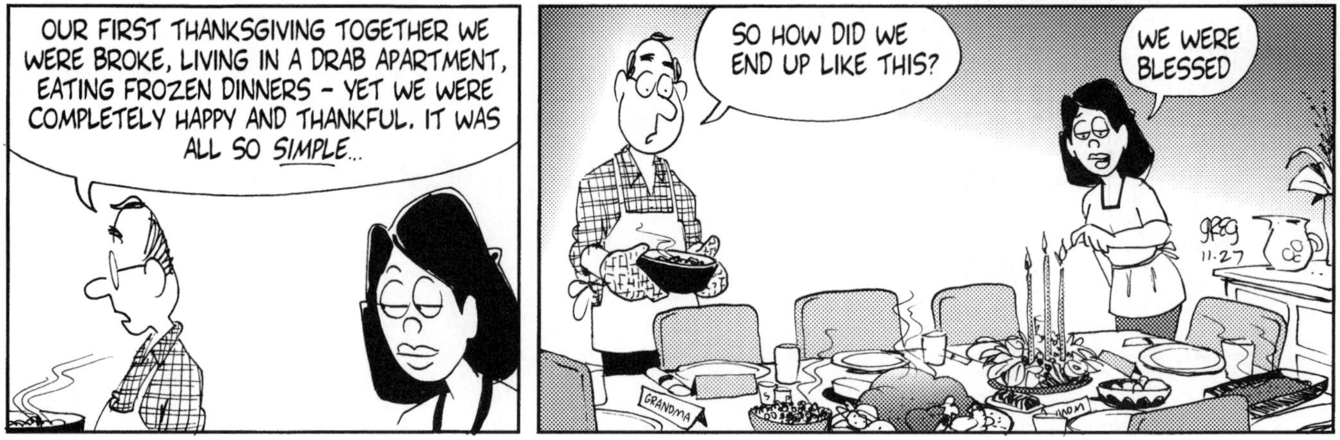
OUR FIRST THANKSGIVING TOGETHER WE WERE BROKE, LIVING IN A DRAB APARTMENT, EATING FROZEN DINNERS – YET WE WERE COMPLETELY HAPPY AND THANKFUL. IT WAS ALL SO SIMPLE...
SO HOW DID WE END UP LIKE THIS?
WE WERE BLESSED

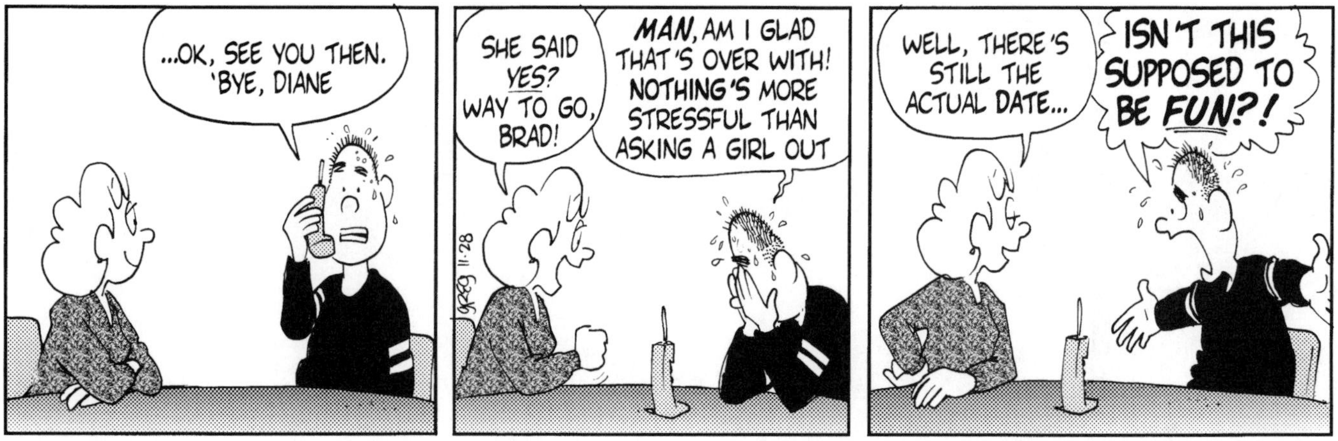
...OK, SEE YOU THEN. 'BYE, DIANE
SHE SAID YES? WAY TO GO, BRAD!
MAN, AM I GLAD THAT'S OVER WITH! NOTHING'S MORE STRESSFUL THAN ASKING A GIRL OUT
WELL, THERE'S STILL THE ACTUAL DATE...
ISN'T THIS SUPPOSED TO BE FUN?!

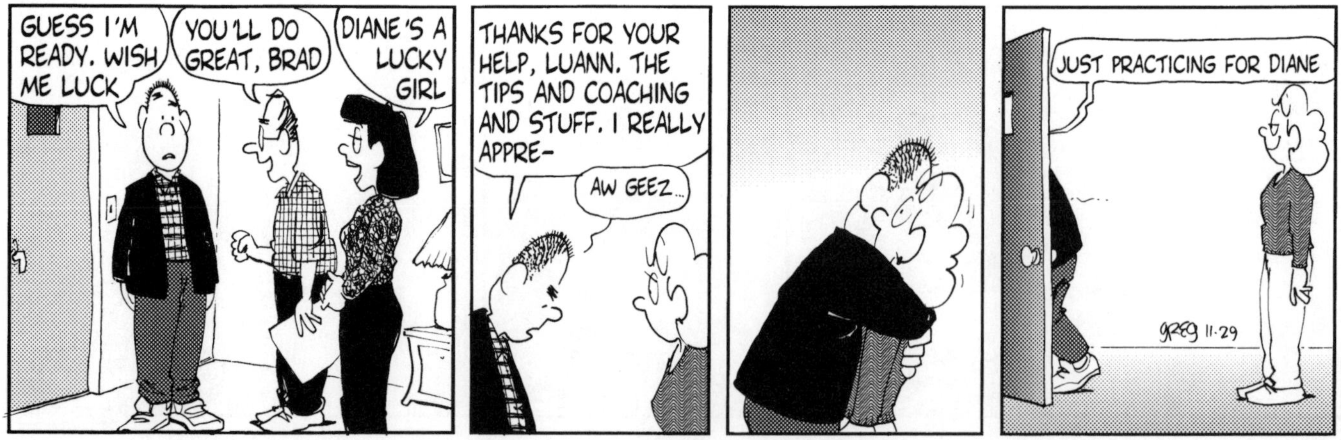
GUESS I'M READY. WISH ME LUCK
YOU'LL DO GREAT, BRAD
DIANE'S A LUCKY GIRL
THANKS FOR YOUR HELP, LUANN. THE TIPS AND COACHING AND STUFF. I REALLY APPRE-
AW GEEZ...
JUST PRACTICING FOR DIANE

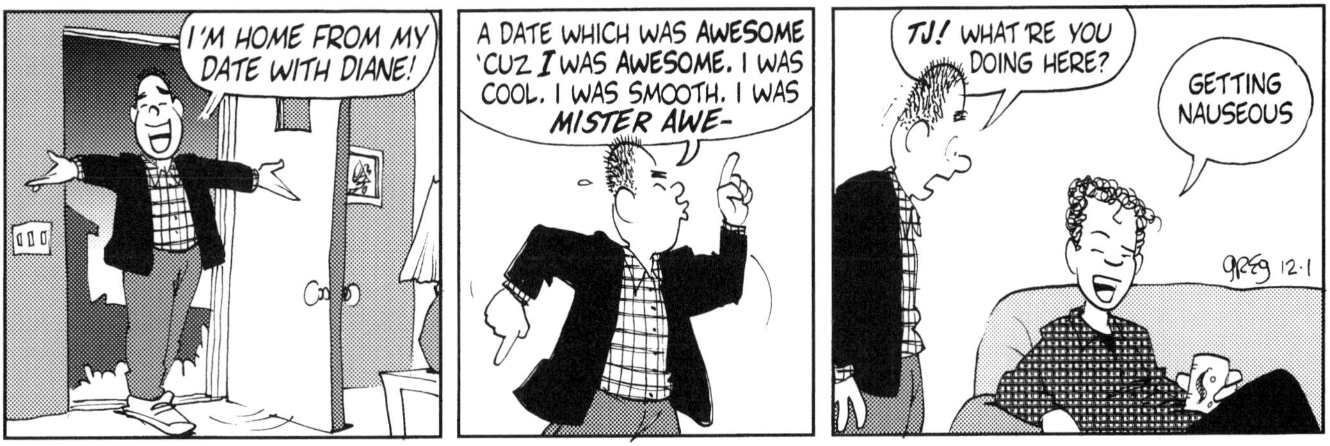
I'M HOME FROM MY DATE WITH DIANE!
A DATE WHICH WAS AWESOME 'CUZ I WAS AWESOME. I WAS COOL. I WAS SMOOTH. I WAS MISTER AWE-
TJ! WHAT'RE YOU DOING HERE?
GETTING NAUSEOUS

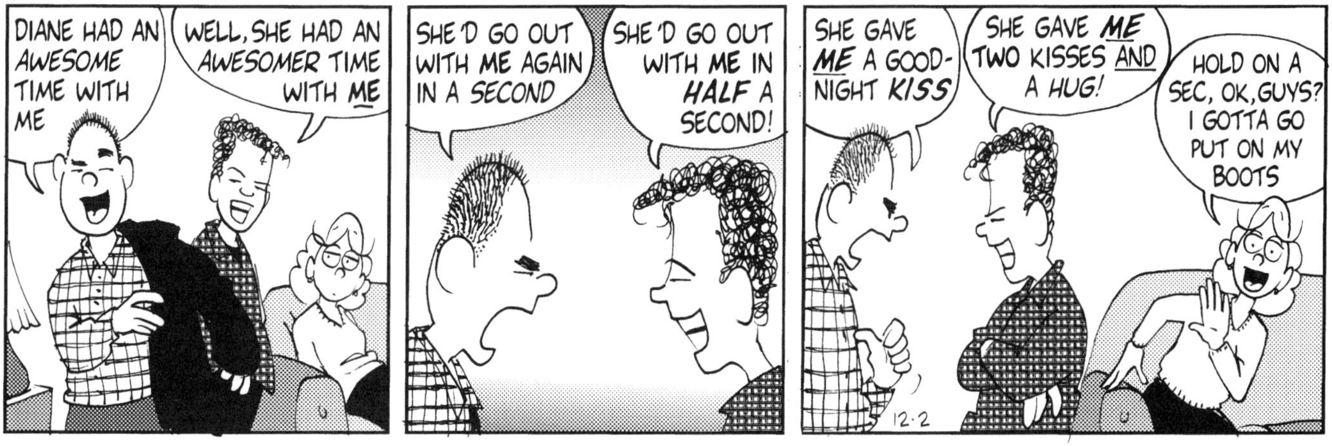
DIANE HAD AN AWESOME TIME WITH ME
WELL, SHE HAD AN AWESOMER TIME WITH ME
SHE'D GO OUT WITH ME AGAIN IN A SECOND
SHE'D GO OUT WITH ME IN HALF A SECOND!
SHE GAVE ME A GOOD-NIGHT KISS
SHE GAVE ME TWO KISSES AND A HUG!
HOLD ON A SEC, OK, GUYS? I GOTTA GO PUT ON MY BOOTS

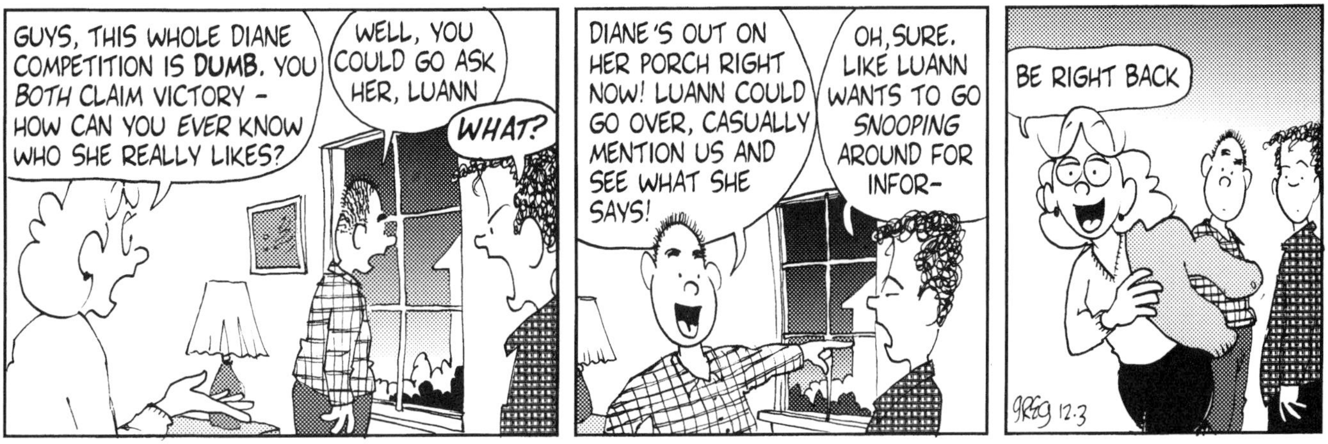
GUYS, THIS WHOLE DIANE COMPETITION IS DUMB. YOU BOTH CLAIM VICTORY - HOW CAN YOU EVER KNOW WHO SHE REALLY LIKES?
WELL, YOU COULD GO ASK HER, LUANN
WHAT?
DIANE'S OUT ON HER PORCH RIGHT NOW! LUANN COULD GO OVER, CASUALLY MENTION US AND SEE WHAT SHE SAYS!
OH, SURE. LIKE LUANN WANTS TO GO SNOOPING AROUND FOR INFOR-
BE RIGHT BACK

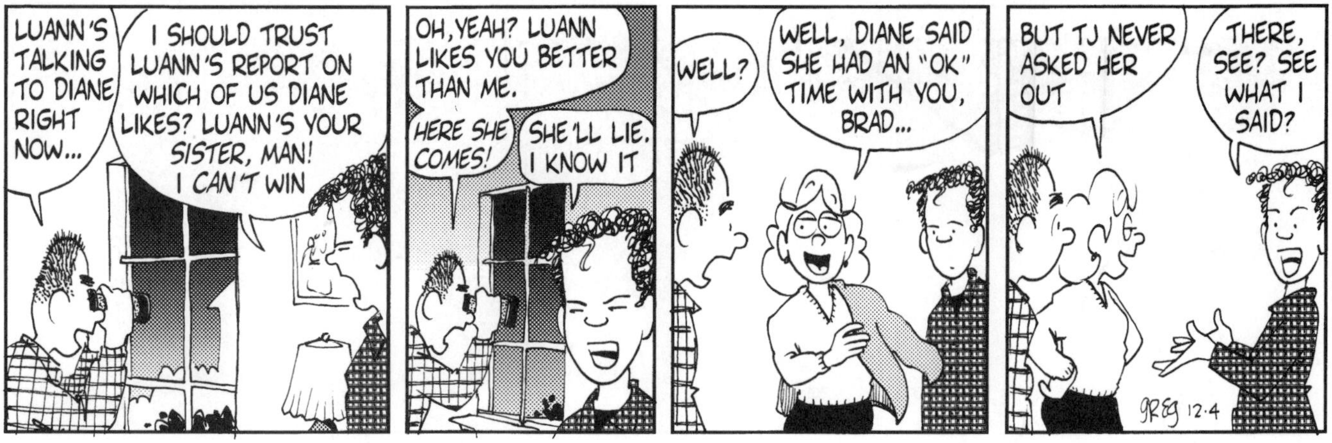
LUANN'S TALKING TO DIANE RIGHT NOW...
I SHOULD TRUST LUANN'S REPORT ON WHICH OF US DIANE LIKES? LUANN'S YOUR SISTER, MAN! I CAN'T WIN
OH, YEAH? LUANN LIKES YOU BETTER THAN ME.
HERE SHE COMES!
SHE'LL LIE. I KNOW IT
WELL?
WELL, DIANE SAID SHE HAD AN "OK" TIME WITH YOU, BRAD...
BUT TJ NEVER ASKED HER OUT
THERE, SEE? SEE WHAT I SAID?
GREG 12·4

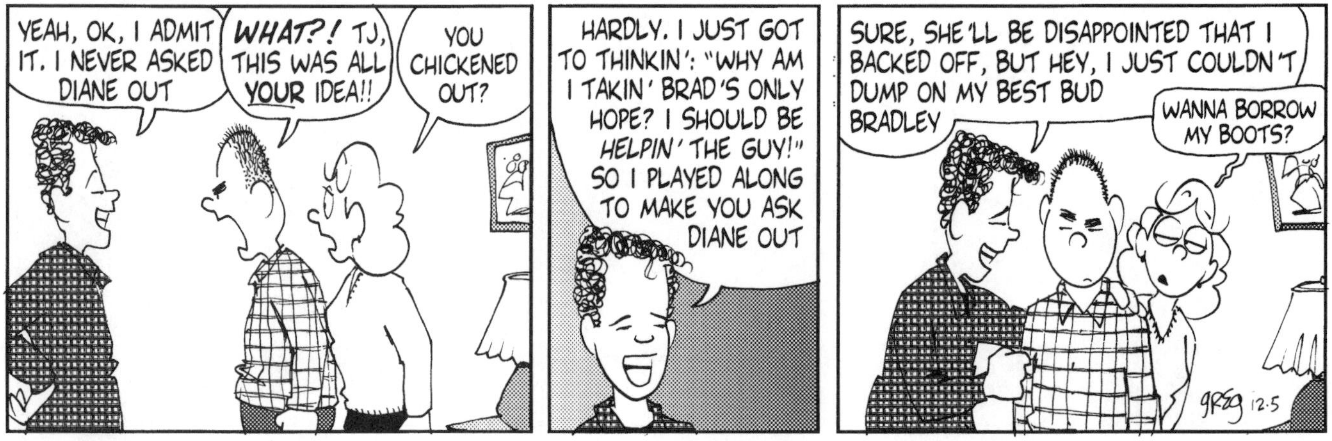
YEAH, OK, I ADMIT IT. I NEVER ASKED DIANE OUT
WHAT?! TJ, THIS WAS ALL YOUR IDEA!!
YOU CHICKENED OUT?
HARDLY. I JUST GOT TO THINKIN': "WHY AM I TAKIN' BRAD'S ONLY HOPE? I SHOULD BE HELPIN' THE GUY!" SO I PLAYED ALONG TO MAKE YOU ASK DIANE OUT
SURE, SHE'LL BE DISAPPOINTED THAT I BACKED OFF, BUT HEY, I JUST COULDN'T DUMP ON MY BEST BUD BRADLEY
WANNA BORROW MY BOOTS?
GREG 12·5

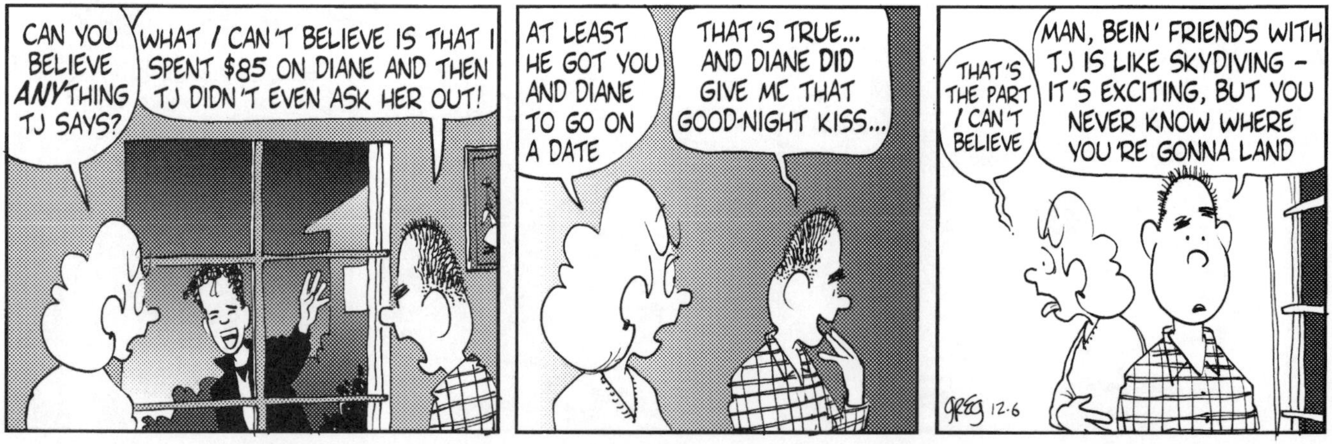
CAN YOU BELIEVE ANYTHING TJ SAYS?
WHAT I CAN'T BELIEVE IS THAT I SPENT $85 ON DIANE AND THEN TJ DIDN'T EVEN ASK HER OUT!
AT LEAST HE GOT YOU AND DIANE TO GO ON A DATE
THAT'S TRUE... AND DIANE DID GIVE ME THAT GOOD-NIGHT KISS...
THAT'S THE PART I CAN'T BELIEVE
MAN, BEIN' FRIENDS WITH TJ IS LIKE SKYDIVING – IT'S EXCITING, BUT YOU NEVER KNOW WHERE YOU'RE GONNA LAND
GREG 12·6

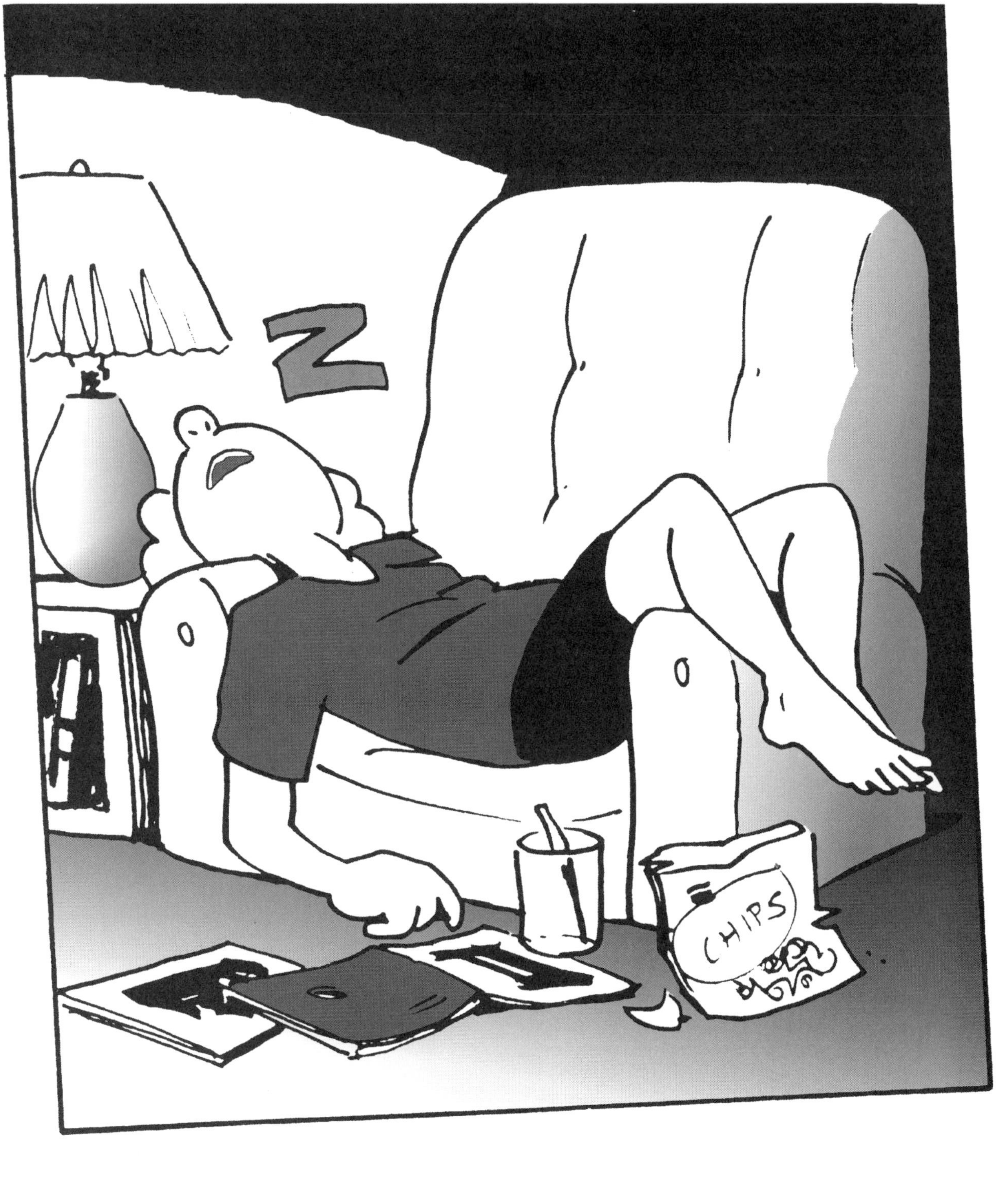
Z
CHIPS

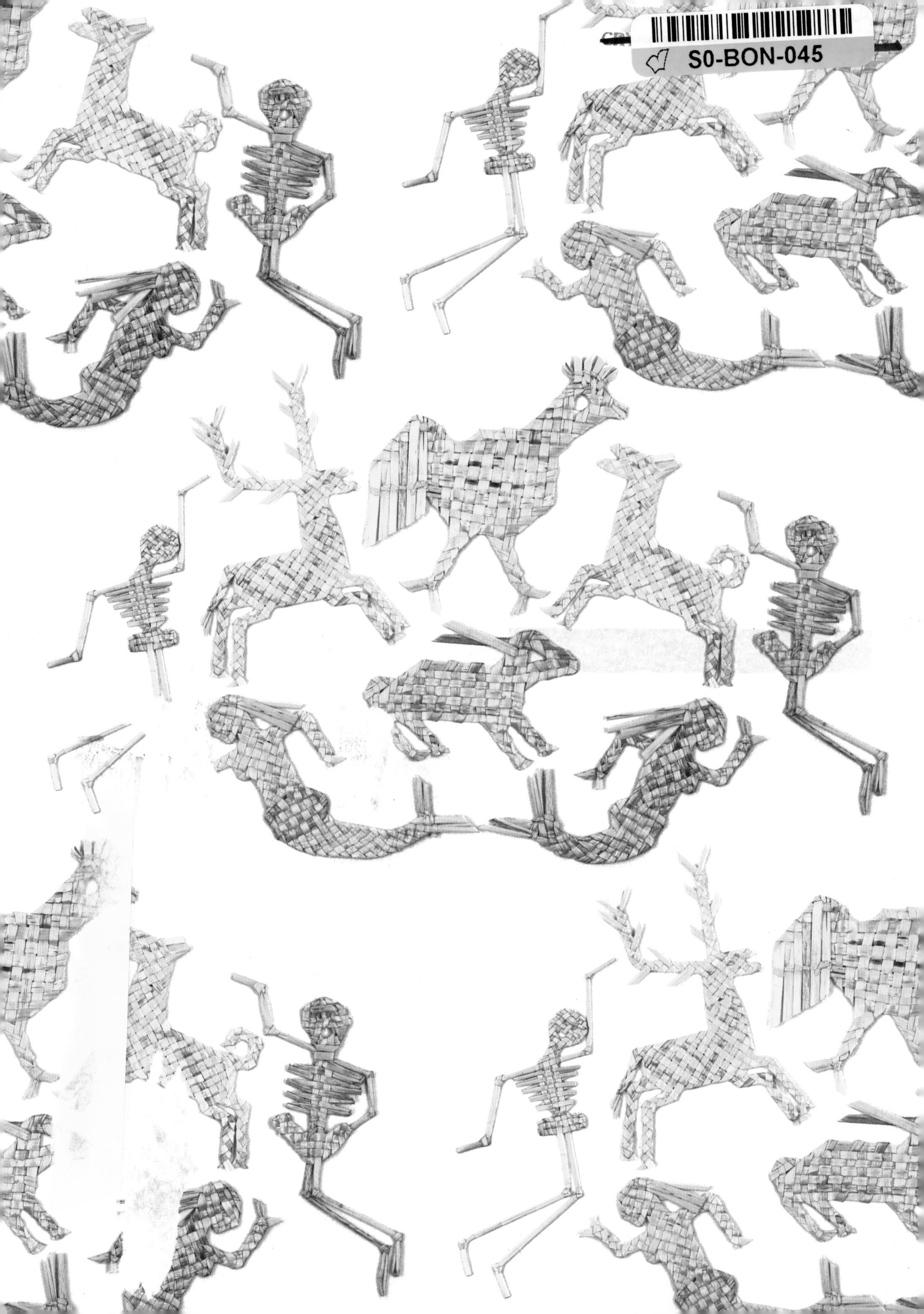